MW01094266

THE WAY OF A PILGRIM
AND OTHER CLASSICS OF
RUSSIAN SPIRITUALITY

OUR LADY OF VLADIMIR (DETAIL)
XITH-XIITH CENTURY
CATHEDRAL OF THE ASSUMPTION, MOSCOW

THE WAY OF A PILGRIM
AND OTHER CLASSICS OF
RUSSIAN SPIRITUALITY

Edited by
G. P. Fedotov

DOVER PUBLICATIONS, INC.
Mineola, New York

The following selections have been translated for inclusion in this anthology by Helen Iswolsky: *St. Theodosius, St. Sergius, St. Nilus Sorsky, The Life of Archpriest Avvakum by Himself, St. Tychon, St. Seraphim, Father Yelchaninov.* The translation of *The Way of a Pilgrim* has been done by Nina A. Toumanova.

We wish to thank Cassell & Co., Ltd., London, for their kindness in permitting us to include "My Life in Christ," by John Sergieff: from *My Life in Christ* translated by E. E. Goulaeff.

Bibliographical Note

This Dover edition, first published in 2003, is an unabridged reprint of *A Treasury of Russian Spirituality*, published by Harper Torchbooks, New York, 1965. The original edition was first published in 1950 by Sheed and Ward, London. As in the Harper edition, the main text begins on page 11; however, nothing has been left out.

Library of Congress Cataloging-in-Publication Data

Treasury of Russian spirituality.
    The way of a pilgrim and other classics of Russian spirituality / edited by G. P. Fedotov.
       p. cm.
    Originally published: A treasury of Russian spirituality. New York : Harper Torchbooks, 1965.
    Includes bibliographical references.
    ISBN 0-486-42712-9 (pbk.)
    1. Mysticism—Russia. 2. Mysticism—Russkaëĭ pravoslavnaëĭ ëĭerkov§' I. Fedotov, G. P. (Georgii Petrovich), 1886–1951. II. Title.

BV5077.R8F4 2003
248'.0947—dc21
                                        2002041769

Manufactured in the United States of America
Dover Publications, Inc., 31 East 2nd Street, Mineola, N.Y. 11501

CONTENTS

Contents

LIST OF ILLUSTRATIONS

PREFACE

THE TERM "SPIRITUALITY" IS USED IN VARIOUS SENSES. IN THE BROADEST, IT DEFINES THE LOFTIEST MORAL AND INTELLECTUal qualities of man in his relation to God and to nature, to himself and to his fellow-men. In social or cultural life, spirituality in this sense finds expression in the philosophy, art, and ethic of a nation or of a civilization. Wordsworth or Keats, for example, is highly representative of English spirituality as it is expressed in the Romantic Movement of the nineteenth century.

In its stricter, or narrower, connotation, spirituality is applied to the religious life in its innermost and deepest strata, the life with God and all spiritual experiences arising from this source. Prayer is the center, the core, of spirituality—and this is true not of mystical prayer alone. As a matter of fact, mysticism as the experience of union with God (a feature of many religions besides Christianity) is a rare phenomenon in religious life. It is true, of course, that the spiritual energies generated by this prayer of union do not remain sealed in the cell of the contemplative saint but diffuse themselves, sometimes fructifying very remote areas in the civilized world of his age. The spiritual influences exerted by St. Francis and St. Teresa are historical examples of this, and in our own day a non-Christian, Eastern mysticism, emanating from India, is seeping into an English literature lately emancipated from the Puritan tradition, with results not wholly salutary. Nevertheless the most powerful influence upon a people is exercised, not by the mystical, but by the common kind of prayer, by the attitude of the ordinary man towards God, in his prayer and in his moral life. Here also the saints, the heroically spiritual, are leaders; but chiefly such of them as stand on common ground with the men of their time; who can share more or less freely their spiritual experience with their fellow-men.

Spirituality, even in the specific religious sense, is not confined to prayer but embraces the whole world-outlook of the individual, particularly the ethical code which his religious experience inspires. In the art of the best epochs of civilization, religious spirituality is reflected; its rays, although gradually weakened, penetrate into the densest strata of social life, into political movements, popular customs, the wisdom of the common man, folk-lore. But, of course, in these exterior strata spirituality encounters the ponderous resistance of material forces and very often is distorted by them. Indeed there has never been a Christian civilization in the full meaning of the word—that is, not as an endeavor, but as a realization. It is different in the case of a natural, or pagan, religion. The outgrowth of physical environment and tribal custom, it reflects, in its very deficiencies, the impact of natural and social forces; and in that it is fully conformed to its environment, it exerts the more powerful influence. A pagan civilization always presents a more harmonious unity than does a Christian civilization. Christian society is ever the arena of a struggle for domination between Christian and pagan, or secular, forces. Yet this struggle has not as its end the annihilation of the natural forces opposed to Christian principles, for grace does not destroy nature, but transforms it. The Christian Church, coming to a newly converted people, does not efface the character of this people as a collective personality, but, after a period of sharp conflict with the forces of paganism, accepts all those elements which are reconcilable with Christian dogma and ethic. With baptism, or the influx of grace, a new national personality comes into being, different from all others and reflecting in all its Christian manifestations the pre-Christian culture. And of course, side by side with the national inheritance, purified and transformed by Christianity, live many survivals of rude paganism which, although endangering ethical practice, are yet capable of a mighty creative unfolding in the culture of a nation, particularly in her art. Thus, in both its Christian (conquering) and pagan (yielding) elements, the spiritual life of a nation is a clue to the understanding of her culture.

Russia imposed herself upon the attention of the West but
recently through her literature, music, and art — finally through
the tremendous social upheaval of the Communist Revolution.
A widespread curiosity with regard to the spiritual background
of this newly disclosed world has been awakened but scarcely
satisfied. Russia remains a great enigma to the West. There is,
for instance, no obvious link between her classical literature of
the nineteenth century and the spirit of her Revolution.

Now it is plain that neither the modern literature of Russia
nor her political and social tragedy can be understood without
a clear vision of her past. Russia had been a medieval civilization
until the time of Peter the Great (about 1700), knowing no Renaissance nor any cleavage between religious and secular culture.
And until their emancipation from serfdom (1861), the Russian
"people"—in contrast to the gentry and the "intelligentsia"—
were medieval in their religion and in their world-outlook.
Without too violent a pressure on facts, one can venture the
statement that the people leaped directly out of the Middle
Ages into the atheistic society of Communism. As for the intelligentsia, although living mainly by Western ideas and ideals,
they had never completely lost contact with the peasantry; particularly in the nineteenth century the "people" were studied
and idealized, as a basic stratum of Russian culture and a source
of Russia's moral strength. All the great classical writers (especially Dostoevsky and Tolstoy) paid a generous tribute to "pop-
ulism" and were dependent upon popular beliefs and traditions
for their own religious and moral attitudes.

The national religion of Russia, known as Eastern Orthodox,
or Greek Orthodox, continues the uninterrupted tradition of
the ancient Eastern and the Byzantine Church, the "Mother
Church" of Russia. Since the middle of the eleventh century
(1054), the Christian East has been separated from the Western, Roman Catholic Church by schism. The characteristics of
the Eastern Church in its liturgical and canonical life, even in
its dogmatic thought, have long been studied by specialists in
theology; but the core of Eastern Christianity, its spiritual life,
has just begun to be the object of scholarly investigation. Even

in Russia there are extant few special studies on this rich and engrossing matter.

In the present book there is offered to the reader, not a study, but a selection from original sources, of Russian spirituality, the first attempt at such an anthology in any language. The material is taken from the lives of saints, ascetical and mystical treatises, and spiritual autobiographies (a very rare species of literature in Russia), embracing the centuries from the eleventh to the twentieth. All the authors selected have belonged to the Russian Orthodox Church and occupy, with one exception (Avvakum), an authoritative place in the sphere of spiritual guidance. The editor has tried to prevent any personal preference from influencing his choice; the emphasis had already been placed by tradition and by present-day Russian ecclesiastical opinion.

From what is said above, it can be inferred that the material, authoritative as it is, has its limitations. The reader will not find: (1) Russian folk-lore in which Christian piety is mingled with pagan survivals; (2) the literature of the Russian sects so numerous in the last two centuries; (3) the works of secular poets and novelists reflecting modern Russian spirituality of very complex origins. For the inclusion of these three groups of sources would broaden the scope of the book to the detriment of unity and purpose. The third group—that of fiction—is moreover already partly accessible to the English and American reader in translations.

Political events, sometimes of a catastrophic nature, divide the history of Russia into clear-cut periods; and the bearing of these divisions extends even into the spiritual domain. The first historical shape of Russia, that of the Kievan period (the ninth to the thirteenth centuries), was the loose confederation of principalities under the prince of Kiev on the Dnieper River. Converted to Christianity by her prince, St. Vladimir (988), Russia received her Church hierarchy from Constantinople, and her whole religious and cultural life was molded on the Byzantine pattern. In spite of this primordial condition, Kievan Russia was in close communication with the "Latin" West, and her social and political life had more in common with Western feudalism than with the Byzantine monarchical state. The Tartar, or Mongolian, conquest (circa 1240) destroyed this flourishing culture, and for centuries thereafter the bulk of the Russian population, the northeastern, or "Great," Russians, were cut off from their southwestern brothers, the Ukranians and White Russians, who were included in the Polish and Lithuanian states. Under the Mongol yoke Great Russia preserved her religious and cultural heritage, although eventually in a rather impoverished condition. Detached from the West (though not impenetrable to Western influences), Russia was continually in touch with Byzantium and moreover exposed to the new and dangerous influences emanating from the East. Until well into the fifteenth century, Russia was a quasi-feudal conglomeration of small principalities, with even some great democratic free cities, such as Novgorod and Pscov, and her cultural atmosphere was still independent, in spite of the political oppression and financial extortion of the Tartars.

The principality of Moscow, with the support of the Church, and to some extent of the Tartars, gradually succeeded in destroying the feudal system and uniting all Russian lands and free cities under the absolute power of the Great Prince of Moscow (circa 1500). He threw off the domination of the Tartars (1480), crowned himself (1547) Tsar ("Caesar"), after the Byzantine pattern, and began the conquest of the vast territories held by the Mongolians. The rulers of the Muscovite State thus succeeded both the Mongols and the Byzantine Emperors, since the Eastern Empire had fallen to the Turks. This government was totalitarian, and very severe and exacting in its claims upon its subjects. The peasants, who for the most part had been free in the Middle Ages, were now turned into serfs, and all classes of the population were forced into the service of the state.

The fact that the cultural and technical backwardness of Muscovy was a serious handicap to her political relations with the West moved Peter the Great (d. 1725) to carry out his great reforms, which actually amounted to a cultural revolution. He Westernized Russia forcibly, relentlessly, at least so far as the *lite* and *thought* of her upper classes was concerned. In the period of the Empire (Peter was the first Russian ruler called "Emperor"), Russian political power reached its height and Russian culture its full flowering—literary, artistic, scientific. This culture was Western European in its form and ideas; yet, in the most striking and profound of its artistic creations, the spirit of the thousand-year-old past breaks through and manifests itself, a past still living in the masses of the peasants, the petty bourgeoisie, and the clergy, who were the guardians of the national tradition. In the pattern of Russian culture during the last two centuries there have been two motifs: one, the European—modern, abreast of the times; the other, ancient Muscovite, deriving from the seventeenth century, with a residue of a past still more remote. The fact that these motifs have been able, to some extent, to blend has preserved the original genius of the high Russian culture.

Yet the cultural breach between the upper classes and the people was so wide, and the social pressure upon the latter so heavy (despite the emancipation of the serfs in 1861), that the tensions arising from World War I were too great for the unsteady Empire, and the War ended for Russia in a revolutionary breakdown. The Revolution inaugurated a new period of Russian history (the fifth, according to our scheme), which, however, is not within the scope of this study: the Bolshevist Revolution, by its very intention, meant the destruction of every kind of spirituality (not only Christian), and although spiritual life did not die out in Russia, it has been unable to find any literary expression up to the present day.

The spirituality of the Russian Church, from the beginning to the present, has been shaped mainly by the Byzantine, or Greek, tradition. There have been, however, variations in the degree of the influence and in the elements of Greek piety chosen as the pattern in different periods of Russian life. Newly converted Russia received from the Bulgarian Slavs an enormous treasury of translated Greek sermons, lives of saints, and Patericons (i.e., collections of legends which had their source in

Egyptian, Syrian, and Palestinian monasticism). For a millennium John Climacus was the prevailing authority on the spiritual life. The Palestinian group of saints (Sts. Sabbas, Euthymius, and others) were the main teachers of Russian ascetics in ancient times.

In the Kievan period, the most remarkable fact is the absence of a mystical tradition in the translated, as well as the original, Russian literature. The severe asceticism of the penitential ("metanoic") Syrian type is represented in the Kievan Cave Patericon, a collection of the biographies of the outstanding fathers of the most famous Russian monastery. Yet simultaneously with the imitation of the Greek and Oriental patterns, newly converted Russia discloses in the persons of her first canonized saints, Boris and Gleb, a quite original view of the Christian way of salvation. This spiritual tendency we call "kenotic," understanding by the term the imitation of Christ in His kenosis, His self-humiliation and His voluntary, sacrificial death. When their elder brother sought to wrest their principalities from them, these two young princes chose the course of non-resistance, preferring to be murdered by him rather than to enter into fratricidal combat. In the monastic life St. Theodosius brings the virtue of humility to extreme social consequences which suggest, somewhat, the practices of St. Francis of Assisi. The most remarkable phenomenon of early Russian spirituality is the immediate impact of the Gospels upon the minds of the first Russian saints. Thus the rediscovery of the Christ of the Gospels, of the Christ in His human nature behind the Byzantine Pantocrator (the "omnipotent" or the "Divine Monarch"), which was a great feat of the twelfth century in the West, was anticipated by about a century in the spiritual life of Russia. Doubtless the use of the Slavonic language in the Bible and in the celebration of the Mass contributed to the originality of the Russian religious genius, but whatever its cause, kenoticism, in the sense of charitable humility as well as of non-resistance, or voluntary suffering, remains forever the most precious and typical, even though not always the dominant, motif of Russian Christianity.

The Russian Middle Ages, or the Mongolian period (the thirteenth to the fifteenth centuries), adopted the Kievan religious tradition but enriched it by one essential feature: the mystical life which found its way into Russia from the Greek monasteries of Mount Athos in the fourteenth and fifteenth centuries. A contemplative type of monasticism was engendered in Russia, and specific exercises were practised to create a "spiritual prayer." The Greek form of mystical prayer was grafted onto the Russian kenotic and caritative type of monastic life. The only literary spokesman of numerous silent Hesychasts in the forests of Northern Russia was St. Nilus Sorsky (fifteenth century), but the origins of this movement are traced to St. Sergius (fourteenth century), the head and the restorer of Russian monasticism after the long period of its decay which followed the terrors of the Monogolian conquest. But Sergius, if a mystic, had likewise a social and national mission; one modern writer goes so far as to call him one of the "builders of Russia."

In contradiction to what is commonly supposed concerning the Christian East, ancient Russian Christianity was always marked by strong social tendencies. But soon after the time of Sergius is the beginning of a fatal separation: St. Sergius stands at the crossroads; from his teachings, Russian monasticism took two divergent directions—the mystical and the social. The mystics of the northern forests cultivated absolute poverty, silence, and spiritual prayer, preserving a great moral independence of secular powers, which they even held it their obligation to teach and reprove. This kind of spirituality undoubtedly inspired the highest manifestations of the Russian art in icon painting, which reached its peak in the fifteenth century: this was the golden age of Russian saints and artists.

The other line of Sergius' disciples, culminating in St. Joseph Volotsky, struck a different note: they were active, practical, social; good farmers and administrators, social leaders in the surrounding countryside, political advisers of the Muscovite princes in the building of a unified, autocratic state. Their religious life was founded upon the fear of God and the meticu-

lous observance of ritual, mitigated by their esthetic appreciation of liturgical worship.

These two groups found grounds of conflict at the beginning
of the sixteenth century, when their adherents disagreed violently on the two great problems of the time: the question of
the legitimacy of monastic landowning (the mystics stood, of
course, for absolute poverty), and that of the policy to be
adopted in dealing with a new group of heretics, the Judaizers
(the mystics were opposed to capital punishment and in general to any severe persecution). The Josephites won the battle,
thanks to their close connection with the princes of Moscow.
And they made the most of their victory: the outstanding disciples of St. Nilus were themselves condemned as heretics,
and thereupon the whole mystical movement disappears from
the surface manifestations in Russian history for about two
centuries.

The age of the Muscovite tsardom (the sixteenth and seventeenth centuries), so favorable to the growth of Russia's political
power, was very unfruitful with regard to the spiritual life.
Josephitism degenerated into static ritualism with the gradual
suppression of the caritative elements in Russian traditional
piety. But in spite of the general barbarization of morality during this period, it is impossible to deny the strengthening of
social discipline, the training of the will in public service, which
shaped the "Great Russian" character as it is known through
modern Russian literature and history.

The spiritual energies latent during this age were unleashed
in the great explosion known as the Raskol (schism) in the Russian Church, which resulted from liturgical reforms introduced
by the patriarch Nicon (1652-58). The conservative national
party, the remote descendents of St. Joseph, having identified
religion with ritual, preferred to die rather than to accept the
new, corrected service books, and finally they separated themselves from the state Church, becoming the first of a long series
of sectarian movements characteristic of modern developments
in Russian religion. The original Old Ritualists, or Old Be-

lievers, stood entirely upon traditional ecclesiastical grounds, and since they represented the strongest moral force in Muscovite society, it seems justifiable to select for our consideration the leading figure of the movement, the priest Avvakum, a writer of genius, as the exponent of Muscovite spirituality.

During the period of the Empire (the eighteenth to the twentieth centuries), with the abrupt Westernizing of Russia, the Church lost its hold upon the influential strata of aristocratic society and the intelligentsia. The masses of the people, as has already been noted, lived in a Muscovite civilization, as a whole faithful to the established state church but with strong sectarian minorities. The Church itself was not a direct inheritor of the Muscovite tradition. It entered the schools of Western Theology, Catholic and Protestant, and tried to find its own, Orthodox way among these Western "extremes." Together with theological thought, some of the currents of Western spirituality penetrated into Russia; these were for the most part Protestant—such as the pietism of the eighteenth century or the mysticism of the early nineteenth. This latter was helpful in overcoming the rationalism of the Enlightenment and in introducing a fervent emotional note into the rather dry moral preaching of the Church. Yet, in spite of this and many other Western influences, the strongest current of Orthodox spirituality remained faithful to the Eastern tradition. At this time, however, it was the tradition of Christian Greece, ancient and medieval, which dominated, and not that of ancient Russia. The break with Muscovy was so complete, even in ecclesiastical education, that it was never completely healed, although the second half of the nineteenth and the present century have been marked by the gradual revival of "holy Russia."

One of the most prominent features of Peter's reform was an almost complete elimination of the Church from all fields of social and political life. In drastic alteration of conditions from those of ancient Russia, the Church was forced to give up every attempt at Christianizing, or even influencing, social life. The only role left to it (and, as a matter of fact, required of it) was that of apologist for the established order. Accepting this part, willingly or unwillingly, the Church was forced to concentrate its moral action upon the individual. And it made a virtue of necessity, regarding this religious individualism as a blessing, the special vocation of Orthodoxy. In this prejudice it was supported by many foreigners, who were in the habit of opposing the Eastern Mary to the Western Martha.

Under these conditions, ancient Russia could not be a secure guide in spiritual practice, and monastic Greece superseded her Russian daughter and pupil to a degree unprecedented in the history of the Church. This impact of Greece was received through two media: the contemporary monasticism of Mount Athos, where the Russians had—and still have—their own communities, and ancient ascetical literature, which was now collected into a large anthology called the Philocalia. The influence of this book (particularly after the publication of the second, more comprehensive, edition prepared by the Russian bishop Theophanes) grew from generation to generation. It was at its height at the Revolutionary and post-Revolutionary period. The Optina cloister, a center for the influential startzy, was the chief guardian and promoter of the Greek ascetical and mystical tradition. The mystical, or spiritual, form of prayer was revived, and Nilus Sorsky found a posthumous disciple in the person of Païsius Velichkovsky, to whose influence the monastic revival after the general decay of the eighteenth century is due. Spiritual prayer was popularized and became the practice even of a certain proportion of laymen—a fact to which the famous Way of a Pilgrim bears eloquent witness.

In the middle of the nineteenth century the evangelical and humanitarian tendencies which largely dominated Russian secular literature tempered the ascetical spirituality of the Church. The Slavophiles, a liberal national party in the Church, tried to create (or, rather, to resuscitate) a spirituality based on social ethic. But the breach between the ascetical-mystical and the evangelical elements within the Church widened, and each tendency found political expression in the period immediately preceding the Revolution. The evangelicals stood for ecclesiastical reforms and allied themselves with the liberal political groups of the nation; the mystics supported the absolutism of the tsar as a remnant of Byzantine tradition. The reformers and liberals did not succeed in developing a type of spirituality of their own deep enough to counterbalance the reactionary, or "black," influence of monasticism, and this dualism played a fatal part in the disintegration of the moral forces of pre-Revolutionary Russian society.

THE FIRST REPRESENTATIVE OF KENOTICISM

THEODOSIUS WAS THE FIRST MONAS-TIC SAINT CANONIZED
by the Russian Church. Soon after his death (1074) the task
of recording his life story was undertaken by the famous chron-
icler Nestor, a monk of his Kievan Caves cloister. Although
Nestor had at his disposal, as a pattern for his literary work,
numerous Greek lives of saints, from which he quoted abundantly, he drew still more upon the testimony of the great
abbot's acquaintances and companions. Thus his work has
always been held in high esteem by Russian historians for its
trustworthiness and its richness in factual detail.

The reader will find the events of Theodosius' life clearly related by Nestor, and his chronicle has been our one source of
information. Here we have only to emphasize the predominant
features of his spirituality. These characteristics become evident
in the earliest part of the story of his childhood, for which Nestor had no literary model. The ideal of the literal imitation of
Christ in His poverty and humiliation on earth is an apprehension of religious genius which was to mold permanently the
mentality of the Russian people. The social aspect of this "kenotic" ideal is of first importance: the love of an "uncouth garb"
and the manual labor in the fields with the serfs both represent
an abandonment of class privilege which encountered the long
and bitter opposition of the saint's mother. The intimate spiritual association of Theodosius with the person of Christ in His
life on earth and in the Sacrament is revealed in Theodosius' attempted journey to the Holy Land, "where our Lord had walked
in the flesh," and in his predilection for the task of baking the
altar-bread: the boy rejoiced in the thought of being a collabora-
tor in "creating the flesh" of Christ, Who "became poor and
humbled Himself" for our salvation.

The monastic life of Theodosius is patterned upon that of the Palestinian ascetics—Sts. Sabbas and Euthymius and St. Theodosius, after whom he is named. However severe or even unnatural Theodosius' asceticism may appear to our age, it was a mitigated, or humanized, form of mortification if gauged by the classical standards of monastic Egypt or Syria. His was a combination of community life and seclusion, of manual labor, prayer, and the exterior work of educational activities among the laity. His bodily asceticism consisted mainly in fasting and abstention from sleep. Only in the narrative of his early youth is mention made of the chains which he wore under his shirt, after the Syrian example followed in Russia. Rather exceptional, also, is the most painful of his acts of mortification: the exposure of his body to the bites of mosquitoes as a measure against temptation. In general, acute pain in mortification is avoided; no self-flagellations occur in the practice of the Christian East; the aim of mortification is rather the "drying up" of the body, the weakening of the passions.

Although Theodosius was the disciple of a senior monk, St. Anthony, his own spirituality is a departure from that of his teacher. Anthony, who had been initiated into the monastic life on Mount Athos, seems to have engaged in the more severe forms of ascetic practice and to have committed himself to absolute solitude, spending all his days in a dark cave. Theodosius found this manner of life "oppressive and narrow." His ideal was rather that of community life and service to the world. He earnestly tried to introduce and put into practice in his monastery, the Greek rule of the Studion (in Constantinople), which became the classical type in the monastic institutions of medieval Russia. The spirit of this rule, and even the form, resemble in many details the rule of St. Benedict.

The greatest danger to the social order that Theodosius sought to create in organizing his cloister was the form which his own holiness assumed. For in becoming the leader of his community he did not betray his ideal of kenotic humility, but clung to his coarse clothing and rejected all outward signs of authority. He never punished erring brethren, but would weep over an incorrigible runaway and, again and again, receive with joy a returning prodigal who could not be relied upon to remain. His harshness was directed, not towards sinners, but only towards the material goods which would tempt the brethren to vitiate their holy poverty by care for the morrow. Thus, on occasion, he destroyed precious food in order to strike at the root of worldly prudence. Discipline was never up to the mark in the Cave cloister, and the homilies of St. Theodosius give evidence of his grievous disappointment.

But the kenotic humility of the abbot was no obstacle to his influence outside the cloister walls. On the contrary, his mildness and charity gained for him the devotion of princes and boyars, and he used his authority in spiritual matters for promoting the cause of justice and charity. A true kenotic, in imitation of Christ, humbles himself before the lowly, not before the powerful. Theodosius could be terrible in his denunciation of the crimes of the rich, and to this valuable social implication of the kenotic virtues ancient Russia was faithful for centuries. This, above all, distinguishes the old Russia from both Byzantine civilization and that of modern Russia.

The great historical importance of St. Theodosius is in the fact that he provided a pattern and an ideal for all monastic life in ancient Russia. His life was a source for all subsequent Russian hagiography, and many features of his personal behavior, including his "uncouth garb," were imitated for centuries. In a certain sense, all Russian monasticism, in spite of the various and divergent tendencies in her spirituality, belongs to the wide family of St. Theodosius' disciples and their heirs.

But far exceeding the limits of the monastic life, the kenotic ideal of St. Theodosius imprinted itself upon the mentality of the whole Russian nation. In the nineteenth century it is easily discoverable in all the literature which portrays Russian folklife, and in Russian folk-lore itself. But, what is still more surprising, the great literary classics of that time also belong to this religious type. This is obvious in the cases of Tolstoy and Dostoevsky, but the influence is none the less present in the works of most of the non-religious writers, even in those of the atheistic radicals, the "narodniks" (populists). Indeed the bulk of the revolutionary intelligentsia, especially during the 1870's, in their "simple life" their coarse clothing, and their positive search for identification with the underprivileged, were unconscious imitators of St. Theodosius. But it was a kenoticism detached from God, in direct contradiction to the charitable humility which is the essence of St. Theodosius' teaching—and thus purely negative. This kenoticism, completely divorced from the spirit of supernatural love, is at the root both of Russian atheism and of Tolstoy's radical negation of culture.

All this would seem to imply that kenoticism may justly be considered the dominant motif in Russian spirituality—one might almost venture to say, the specific Russian approach to Christianity. Yet this statement is correct only in a limited sense. For, actually, kenoticism was never the exclusive, nor even the quantitatively predominant, feature of Russian religion. It has always been moderated, diluted and supplemented by other currents: ritualistic, liturgical, mystical or culturally creative, some of them deriving from foreign sources—from Byzantium or, in modern times, from the Christian West.

A LIFE OF ST. THEODOSIUS

By NESTOR

I THANK YOU, MY LORD AND MASTER JESUS CHRIST, FOR HOLD-ING ME WORTHY TO CHRONICLE THE ACHIEVEMENTS OF YOUR saints. For I first recorded the life, the slaying, and the miracles of the saints and blessed passion-bearers Boris and Gleb[1], and I am now about to undertake another writing. It is a task too great for my powers, I am not fit for it, since I am neither wise nor learned, but I have in my mind the words "If you have faith as a grain of mustard seed, you shall say to this mountain, re-move from hence thither and it shall remove." Reflecting on these words I, sinful Nestor, have girded myself with faith and hope in order to relate the life of blessed Theodosius, the former abbot of the Caves Monastery dedicated to the Holy Mother of God.[2]

Brothers, when I realized that no one had yet recorded the life of this saint, I was greatly distressed, and I asked in prayer for God's help in setting down in their proper order all the facts concerning our father and God-bearer, Theodosius, so that the monks who come after us, reading this chronicle and seeing the virtues of this man, might glorify God in His saint. May they be confirmed in their religious vocation by the knowl-edge that so holy a man has lived in this land. For these words of God may well be applied to him: "Many shall come from the east and the west and shall sit down with Abraham and Isaac and Jacob in the kingdom of heaven"; and, again: "Many that are first shall be last; and the last shall be first." Indeed, this saint of the latter day has shown himself greater than the ancient Fathers. As it was said in the *Patericon* that there would be laxness in the last generation, it is surprising that in this last generation Theodosius should be made known by Christ as a great laborer for His sake and a true pastor to his monks. For from boyhood he was distinguished for the purity and goodness of his life, and especially for the faith and understanding with which he was endowed.

Brothers, listen attentively, for this story is of great benefit to all who hear it. I implore you, my beloved, do not condemn me for my ignorance if, because I am so filled with love for the saint, I have attempted to tell everything concerning him. For, in addition to this, I feared that Our Lord's words with regard to the "wicked and slothful servant" might be applied to me. But apart from these considerations, it is not right to conceal God's miracles, especially in view of what He said to His disciples: "That which I tell you in the dark, speak ye in the light; and that which you hear in the ear, preach ye upon the housetops."

It is therefore my intention to write for the benefit and edification of my readers. May they glorify God and be rewarded by Him. But first of all I turn to God with a prayer: "My Lord Omnipotent, giver of grace, Father of our Master Jesus Christ, come to my aid. Illumine my heart for the understanding of Thy commandments and open my mouth for the proclaiming of Thy miracles and the praise of Thy saint. May Thy name be sanctified, for Thou art the only helper of those who hope in Thee. Amen."

The Childhood of Theodosius

There is a town called Vasilev, lying at a distance of fifty versts[3] from Kiev. In this town lived our saint's parents, who were enlightened Christians of exemplary piety, and here it was that blessed Theodosius was born to them. On the eighth day after his birth, according to the custom, they brought the child to God's priest in order that a name should be given him. The priest, perceiving with spiritual insight that the newborn child would devote himself to God's service from infancy, gave him the name Theodosius.[4] Then, after forty days, he baptized the child. Theodosius grew up under the tutelage of his parents. God's grace was with him, and he had the light of the Holy Ghost from his first years.

By the decree of the Prince,[5] the saint's parents soon transferred their residence to another town called Kursk—but it would be more exact to say that this was done according to the will of God, so that this town also might be enlightened by the presence of the good youth. Thus Theodosius rose for us in the East like a morning star, attracting many other stars in expectation of the Sun of Justice, Our Lord Jesus Christ, so that he might say: "Here I am, my Lord, and here are the children whom I have nourished with Thy spiritual food. Here, my Lord, are my disciples. I have brought them to Thee, having taught them to despise all earthly things and to love Thee alone, my Lord God. Here, Master, is the flock which Thou hast enlightened, whose shepherd Thou hast chosen me to be. I have led them to graze in Thy pastures. I have brought them to Thee, having kept them pure and innocent." And God will answer, "Good and faithful servant, because thou hast been faithful over a few things, I will place thee over many things." And He will say to the disciples: "Come, good flock; come, divinely enlightened sheep of the good shepherd; you who have hungered and labored for my sake shall now receive the kingdom prepared for you since the beginning of the world."

Therefore, brothers, let us also be zealous imitators of the life of St. Theodosius and the disciples he sent to God before him, for then we too shall be worthy to hear the voice of the Master saying, "Enter thou into the joy of thy Lord."

And now let us turn once more to the story of the holy youth. As he matured in body and spirit, he was drawn by the love of God to go to church daily, devoting all his attention to the sacred books. Unlike most boys, he kept aloof from children at play and was unwilling to join in their games. He wore coarse and patched garments, and when his parents tried to make him put on fresh clothing and play with other children, he would not obey, for he wanted to be identified with the poor. Moreover he begged his parents to entrust him to a teacher, so that he might be instructed in the reading of the sacred books, and they consented to this. The boy acquired knowledge rapidly, so that everyone was astonished at his wisdom and the quickness with which he learned. And how can we measure the virtues of obedience and humility which he practised, not only towards his teachers, but also towards all with whom he shared his studies?

The Struggles of His Youth

When blessed Theodosius was about thirteen years old, his father died. From that time on, he applied himself even more zealously to his undertakings. That is, he now went into the fields with his serfs, where he did the humblest work. To prevent this, his mother used to keep him indoors. She also tried to prevail upon him to put on good clothes and go out to play with boys of his own age, for she said that if he were so poorly dressed, he would expose himself and his family to disgrace. But he would not obey her, and often she beat him in her vexation. She was robust of body, and if you could not see her, but could only hear her voice, you might well have mistaken her for a man.

The devout youth, meanwhile, was meditating and searching for the means of salvation. When he heard of the Holy Land, where Our Lord had walked in the flesh, he longed to make a pilgrimage to this place. He prayed to God, saying, "My Lord Jesus, listen to my prayer, and grant that I may go to the Holy Land." After he had prayed in this manner for a long time, some pilgrims came to the city. The holy youth rejoiced when he saw them. He went out to meet them and welcomed them affectionately, asking them whence they had come and whither they were going. And when they told him that they had come from the Holy Land and that, God permitting, they intended to return there, he begged to be taken with them. They promised to take him, and Theodosius returned home rejoicing. When the pilgrims had decided to set out on their journey, they informed the boy of their intention, and rising in the night, he left his home secretly, taking nothing with him except the poor clothes he had on. It was in this manner that he set out to join the pilgrims.

But God, in his mercy, would not permit the one whom He had predestined in his mother's womb to be the shepherd of the divinely enlightened sheep to leave this land; for, when the shepherd had departed, the pastures that God had blessed would lie desolate, overgrown with thorns and haunted by wolves which would scatter the flock. After three days the mother learned that he had gone with the pilgrims, and taking her other son (who was younger than Theodosius) with her, she set out to overtake him. After a long pursuit, they caught up with him. Carried away by fury, she seized him by the hair, flung him to the ground, and trampled on him. Then, having rebuked the pilgrims, she returned home, leading the saint bound like a criminal. So greatly incensed was she, that when they had entered the house she beat her son until she was exhausted. Then she flung him into a room, shackled him, and locked the door. The holy youth suffered all this joyfully, giving thanks to God in prayer.

After two days his mother returned, unfastened him, and placed food before him. But her anger was still unsatisfied, so she put chains on his feet and ordered him to go about the house in them, and she watched him, so that he might not run away from her again. He wore these chains for some time, but at last his mother relented. She began to beg him not to run away again, saying that she loved him more than all her other children and could not live without him. And when he had promised that he would not leave her, she removed the chains from his feet, telling him that he might now do as he pleased.

Blessed Theodosius returned to his former practice and visited the church daily. When he saw that often Mass could not be celebrated because there was no altar bread,[6] he was greatly distressed and resolved humbly that he would devote himself to this work. And he kept his resolution. He began to bake altar bread and sell it; some of the money thus earned, he gave to the poor, and some he kept in order to buy more wheat, which he would grind with his own hands. And in this manner his work of baking the loaves continued. Now this was according to God's will, so that the church might be provided with pure altar bread made by the hands of a chaste and innocent youth. He carried on the work for two years or more.

Boys of his own age, inspired by the enemy, ridiculed him for performing such a task. But the saint suffered all this joyfully and without complaint.

Now the enemy, who hates all that is good, seeing the humility of the God-enlightened youth triumphing over him, knew no peace; in the attempt to divert the boy from his task, he persuaded the mother that she must prevent Theodosius from pursuing his activities. The mother, who could not bear to have her son the object of ridicule, said to him gently, "I beg of you, my son, give up this work. You are bringing disgrace upon your family; indeed it is not right for a young man to be engaged in such work." Good Theodosius replied humbly: "Listen to me. Our Lord Jesus Christ became poor and humbled Himself, offering Himself as an example, so that we should humble ourselves in His name. He suffered insults, was spat upon and beaten, for our salvation; how just it is, then, that we should suffer in order to gain Christ. As to my work, listen to me. When Jesus Christ sat with His disciples at the Last Supper, He took bread, and having blessed it, broke it, and gave it to His disciples, saying, 'Take ye, and eat. This is My body.' If Our Lord called bread His body, should I not rejoice that God lets me share in the making of His body?"

When she heard this, his mother marvelled at the boy's wisdom, and from that day forth she let him alone.

He was so humble of heart and so submissive towards everyone, that the governor of the city, observing the boy's virtues, was greatly attracted to him and engaged him to serve in his own house. He gave him fine clothes to wear, and for a few days the saint wore them, looking as if he were heavily burdened; then he divested himself and, giving the new clothing to beggars, went about in the old. On seeing this, the governor gave him other garments finer than the first. These likewise Theodosius gave away. And this happened several times. The governor then held the boy in even greater esteem, marvelling at his humility. After that blessed Theodosius went to a blacksmith and ordered iron chains with which he girded his loins, and went about wearing them. The tightly bound chains bit into his flesh, but he was at peace, as if he suffered no bodily pain.[7]

After some time Theodosius heard the words of the holy Gospel "He that loveth father or mother more than Me, is not worthy of Me." And again "Come to Me, all you that labor, and are burdened, and I will refresh you." And so, filled with devotion and with the love of Our Lord, the God-inspired youth cast about for the best way of escaping from his mother and finding a place where he might enter the religious life.

Now it was the will of God that his mother should go to the country at this time for a long visit. The saint rejoiced, prayed, and stole out of his home, taking with him nothing but the clothes he had on and enough food to sustain him. He went in the direction of Kiev, for he had heard that there were many monasteries in that city. Since he did not know the way, he asked God to send him fellow-travellers to guide him. It was the will of God that a company of merchants should be travelling along that road with their wagons heavily laden. Learning that they too were going to Kiev, the saint thanked God and followed them at a distance, unobserved. When they halted for the night, the saint also paused for rest. Still they did not notice him; God alone watched over him. After travelling in this manner for three weeks he reached the city of Kiev, where he went from one monastery to another begging the monks to admit him.[8] But, seeing before them a simple youth, poorly dressed, they were unwilling to accept him. This happened in accordance with the divine will, in order that Theodosius might finally be conducted to the place to which God had called him from his very childhood.

Hearing that blessed Anthony was living in a cave outside Kiev, Theodosius went eagerly to the hermit's dwelling.[9] When he saw Anthony, he wept and fell on his knees before him, begging for permission to remain in that place. The great Anthony replied, "My child, look about, and you shall see that this cave is dark and narrow. You are young and, I should think, unable to suffer such hardships." Venerable Anthony said this, not only because he wished to try the youth, but also because he prophetically foresaw that Theodosius would build a large cloister in place of this narrow cave and gather around him a great number of monks. The God-inspired Theodosius answered, with humble sincerity, "You know, most venerable father, that the all-seeing God has brought me to you because He desires my salvation. I will therefore obey you in all things." Then blessed Anthony said to him, "My child, glory be to God, Who has given you strength for such a vocation. This is the place; remain here with me." Theodosius fell once more onto his knees, and Anthony blessed him and ordered the great Nicon, who was an experienced monk and an ordained priest, to bestow the tonsure upon the youth. Nicon led Theodosius away, gave him the tonsure, and invested him with the monastic robe.

From that day on, our father Theodosius submitted himself completely to God and to venerable Anthony. He mortified his body, keeping vigils, singing the praises of God throughout the night in order to hold off the weight of sleep. He also observed abstinence from food with the help of manual work, recalling the words of the psalm "I humbled my soul through fasting, and mortified my body through labor and penance." Venerable Anthony and the great Nicon were astonished at his humility and obedience, thinking that such great virtue was remarkable in one so young.

Meanwhile Theodosius' mother, having searched for him in vain in her own city and its vicinity, was weeping bitterly and beating her breast as if he were dead. A proclamation was issued offering a reward to anyone who should see the youth and let his mother know his whereabouts without delay. And so it was that some travellers from Kiev told the woman that four years earlier they had seen the boy in their city, and that he had then expressed the wish to receive the holy tonsure in a monastery. When she heard this, the mother hastened to Kiev, not minding the long journey, so intent was she upon finding her son. She inquired for Theodosius at all the monasteries, and at last she was told that he was living in the cave of venerable Anthony. So she went to the hermitage and introduced herself cleverly by asking to see the staretz.[10] "Tell the abbot that I beg him to come out and speak to me," she said, "for I have travelled a long distance to see him, to pay my respects to his holiness, and to receive his blessing."

When he was informed of her presence, Anthony emerged from the cave to speak to her, and she knelt before him. Then, as they sat down, she began to talk to him, touching upon a variety of matters. Finally she disclosed the true purpose of her visit. "I beg of you, father," she said, "tell me where my son is. For I am greatly distressed at not knowing whether he is alive." The staretz, who was a simple man, quite unaware of her mischievous intentions, said to her. "Your son is here. Do not grieve, for he is alive." And she asked, "How is it, then, that I do not see him? I have come a long way but to set eyes on my son and then to return home." The staretz answered, "If you wish to see him, retire for the present, and I shall try to persuade him; for as yet he wishes to see no one. Return tomorrow and you shall see your son." The woman obeyed and went away, hoping to see Theodosius on the following day.

Venerable Anthony gave blessed Theodosius a full account of the occurrence, and the youth was greatly perturbed by the knowledge that he could no longer hide from his mother. The next day the woman returned, and the staretz tried to persuade her son to go out and see her, but he would not. Then the staretz said to her, "I have urged him to see you, but he is unwilling to do so." Thereupon the woman cried angrily, "The staretz has done me an injustice! He has taken my son away from me and hidden him in his cave. Bring him forth, staretz, so that I can look upon him. For I cannot live if I do not see him once more. I will put an end to my life with my own hands at this door." At this Anthony was exceedingly distressed. Returning to the cave, he implored blessed Theodosius to go to his mother.

In order not to disobey the staretz, Theodosius did so. When she saw her son and observed his worn appearance (for his labors and abstinence had produced a great change in his face), she burst into tears and embraced him. Then, somewhat appeased, she seated herself and began to remonstrate with God's servant in the following words: "My son, come home," she said, "and you shall be free to do all that is necessary for your salvation. Do not stay away from me any longer. When I am dead and you have buried me, you may return to this cave if you wish, but as long as I live, I cannot bear to be separated from you." The holy youth replied: "If you wish to see me every day, go to the city and take the holy tonsure in some women's convent; then you may come here to see me, and yet you will be gaining the salvation of your soul. Unless you do this, I say in earnest that you shall never see my face again!"

With these and many other words, the youth tried from day to day to prevail over his mother's determination, but she would not listen to him. After she had left him, the saint would go into the cave and pray fervently for his mother's salvation, asking that her heart might be inclined to obedience. God heard the prayer of His saint, and one day the woman returned and said to her son: "My child, I am ready to do as you have commanded; I shall not go back to my own city, but, if God is willing, I shall enter a women's convent, and, taking the tonsure, I shall spend the rest of my days there. Your teaching has brought me to the realization of the emptiness of this passing world."

When he heard this, the saint rejoiced in spirit and went to inform the great Anthony. The staretz praised God, Who had moved the woman's heart to repentance. He went out to speak to her and instructed her concerning many things for the good of her soul. Moreover, he put her case before the prince's wife and she was permitted to enter the women's convent of St. Nicholas. Here she took the tonsure and the habit, and after having lived many years in the true monastic spirit, she passed away peacefully.

Such is the life of our blessed father Theodosius from his childhood until the day when he entered the cave. His mother related all this to one of the brethren, Theodore by name, who was the cellarer of our father Theodosius. I heard this account from Theodore's own lips, and set it down, in order that all who read may remember his deeds.

Theodosius' Life as a Monk

From that time on, great numbers of people came to the Caves to receive the father's blessing; by the grace of God, some became monks. Then the great Nicon and another monk, who had belonged to the monastery of Saint Minas[11] and had been a boyar before entering religion, left the Caves with one accord, in order to live apart from the community.

The great Nicon settled on the peninsula of Tmutarakan,[12] where, in a pleasant place near the city, he founded a monastery; this community increased by the grace of God, living after the pattern of the Caves monastery. Euphrem the Eunuch also left the Caves; he went to Constantinople and retired there to a monastery, where he lived until the time when he was called back and appointed bishop of Pereyaslavl.

Blessed Theodosius was ordained to the priesthood according to the wish of blessed Anthony, and each day he celebrated the divine service with the deepest humility. He was simple, of a gentle and quiet disposition, but full of spiritual wisdom and a pure love for all his brethren. The latter had now reached the number of fifteen.

As for blessed Anthony, who was accustomed to living alone and wished to be undisturbed, he retired to one of the Caves' cells and appointed blessed Barlaam in his place. Later on, Anthony moved to another hill and dug himself a cave which he was never to leave, and in which his venerable body rests even to this day.

Blessed Barlaam built a small church consecrated to Our Lady over the Caves and ordered the brethren to assemble there for prayer. From that time on, the monastery could be seen by people in the surrounding countryside, whereas formerly they had scarcely known of the brethren living in the caves.

I shall now tell of the primitive life of these monks. God alone can measure the suffering they endured because of the narrow space to which they were confined in the caves; human lips cannot describe it. They lived on rye bread and water. On Sundays and Saturdays they partook of a little boiled grain; sometimes, however, even such fare as this would be lacking, and they were satisfied with a small portion of cooked vegetables. They worked with their hands, weaving cowls and headgear for the brethren and plying other manual trades.

They sold the products of their labor in the town in order to purchase grain, and this was equally divided among the brethren. At night, each monk would grind his share of flour for the baking of loaves. In the early morning, they would sing Matins, then work in the vegetable garden. Afterwards, returning once more to church to praise God, they would sing the Hours and offer holy Mass; then they would eat a small portion of bread, and each brother would return to his occupation. Thus they lived and labored in the spirit of charity.

Our father Theodosius surpassed all the other monks in wisdom and obedience, and he undertook greater labors than the others, for he was strong and healthy in body. He would assist his brethren in carrying water and fire-wood from the nearby forest. At night, while the other monks took their rest, he would remain wakeful, praising God. Moreover, the saint would grind all the grain which had been divided among the monks, and would leave the flour in its proper places. Sometimes at night, mosquitoes and gad-flies would swarm to the mouth of the cave; then Theodosius would go forth, and, stripping himself to the waist, sit in the open, spinning wool and singing the psalms of David.[13] His body would be covered with blood drawn by the mosquitoes and flies which devoured it, but our father would sit there quietly until Matins. He entered the church before all the others, and never left his place, singing the divine praises with an untroubled mind. He was also the last to leave the church. Because of all these things, he was revered by the brethren, who loved him as a father, marvelling at his humility and obedience.

After some time, blessed Barlaam was ordered by the prince to leave the cave and was appointed abbot of the Monastery of Saint Demetrius the Martyr. The brethren living in the cave gathered together and informed blessed Anthony that they had named Theodosius abbot of the community. Even in the post of authority, our father Theodosius did not alter his rule or his humble way of life, for he kept in mind the words of our Lord: "Whosoever will be the greater among you, let him be your minister." And so he humbled himself, and was the least of all, serving everyone and offering himself as an example. He was still the first to rise for work or for holy Mass. From that time on, the community grew and prospered, thanks to the prayers of the saint, for it has been said: "The just shall flourish like the palm tree: he shall grow up like the cedar of Libanus."

As the number of the brothers increased, the community flourished in virtues, prayers and devout customs, so that many noblemen came to seek the brethren's blessing and bring them small offerings. In spite of this, our venerable father Theodosius, who was an earthly angel and a heavenly man,[14] was well aware that their dwelling was poor and crowded, and that the church was too small to contain the brethren. Nevertheless he was without anxiety. Each day he would comfort the monks, instructing them to disregard their bodily needs and reminding them of the words of our Lord: "Be not solicitous therefore, saying, What shall we eat: or what shall we drink?" The saint himself kept these words in his mind, and God gave generously all that was required. Finding a clear space near the Caves, which he saw to be suitable for a building, Theodosius was enabled by the Grace of God to undertake the construction of a monastery. First, with the help of God, he built a church consecrated to our Holy and Most Glorious Lady. He encircled the church with a fence, and built a number of cells around it, and in the year 1062 he took his brethren to live in the new monastery. From that time on, the community prospered, and was widely known as the Caves Monastery.

After some time, Theodosius sent one of the brothers to Constantinople to visit Ephrem the Eunuch with the request that the Rule of the Studion Monastery should be copied and sent to Kiev. Ephrem complied with our venerable father's wishes. When he had received the Studite Rule, Theodosius ordered that it should be read to the assembled brethren, and from that time on the monastery was governed according to this rule, which is observed there even to this day.

All those who came to our father Theodosius with the intention of becoming monks were accepted by him, rich and poor, without distinction. He rejected no one, but received all kindly, for he remembered the ordeal which he had undergone in his youth, when he had left his own town and gone from one monastery to another but was admitted by none. Indeed, he well knew the suffering caused to a man who wishes to enter the réligious life and is rejected, and that is why he admitted all gladly. However, he did not give the tonsure at once, but told the postulant to wear his ordinary attire until he had become accustomed to the life of the community. Then he would invest him with the monastic robe and test him in various services. Finally, he would give him the tonsure and the mantle. When the monk had been proved as to the purity of his life, he would be allowed to take the holy schema.[15]

Every year during Lent, holy Theodosius would retire to the caves in which, after his death, his venerated body was to rest. He would remain secluded in this cave until the Friday of Passion Week, when he would return to the brethren at Vespers. Standing at the door of the church, he would speak words of instruction and encouragement, saying that he was unworthy of them since they had far surpassed him in fasting and mortification.

Like St. Anthony before him, our blessed father suffered the frequent and savage attacks of evil spirits, which even inflicted wounds on his body.[16] But God, Who had manifested Himself to Anthony in the course of such trials, infused into Theodosius the strength to conquer these adversaries. We cannot but marvel at the saint's fortitude. He was alone in the darkness of the cave; yet he had no fear of the hordes of demons which he could not see, but remained resolute and courageous, standing erect and calling our Lord Jesus Christ to his aid. And thanks to the power of Christ, he triumphed over the devils, so that they no longer dared come near him, but only sought to delude him at a distance.

When Theodosius rested after evening prayers, he would never lie down, but would seat himself on a chair, and when he had dozed for a while, he would rise to his feet again for night prayers and genuflections. One evening, when our father was resting, a great tumult arose in the caves, caused by a horde of demons. It sounded as if some of them were driving round in a carriage, while others played on tambourines and flutes; all together they made a hubbub that shook the caves to their very foundations. But father Theodosius remained untroubled and unafraid. He arose, made the sign of the cross and began to chant the psalms of David, and at once the noise subsided. But when his prayer was ended, and he had sat down, the voices of innumerable demons were heard once more. Again the saint rose to his feet and began to chant the psalms, and he continued until the demons were silenced. The evil spirits pursued him in this manner for many days and nights, hindering him from sleep, until at last, by the grace of Christ, he had conquered them and could exercise authority over them. From that day on they dared not come near the place where he was praying. However, they made mischief in the bakery where the brethren made their bread, scattering the flour, upsetting the yeast which had been prepared for the loaves, and carrying off many other attacks. When the head-baker informed Theodosius of these occurrences, the saint, confident that he had received from God power over these unclean spirits, locked himself in the bakery one night and remained closeted there, praying until morning. The devils never returned to the bakery, nor did they trouble the bakers further.

At night the great Theodosius was wont to make the round of the monks' cells, so that he might learn how each of the brethren spent his time.[17] When he could hear a monk praying in his cell, he would pause on his way to praise God. But if he should overhear two or three monks gathered together and engaged in conversation, he would tap on the door, and having thus apprised the brethren of his visit, he would withdraw. In the morning, he would call the culprits to his cell. Yet he would be in no haste to rebuke them; instead he would speak indirectly and in parables, waiting to see whether they were filled with divine fervor. If a brother's heart were light and ardent with the love of God, he would quickly bow his head and acknowledge his sin, asking his abbot's forgiveness. But if his heart were burdened with the devices of the Devil, he would listen without confusion to the abbot's admonitions, considering that they had reference to some other monk and holding himself blameless. Then the saint would rebuke him, and having imposed a penance, would let him go. Thus he taught them all to pray attentively, not to converse after evening service, not to go from one cell to another, but to remain each in his own cell. There the brother was to pray according to his ability and to occupy himself with manual work while chanting the psalms of David.

The saintly teacher himself accomplished what he taught to others. And they absorbed his words like earth thirsting for moisture and offered the fruits of their industry to God.

You could see these monks living like angels on earth. The monastery was like a heaven in which the good works of our father Theodosius shone more brightly than the sun. This was manifested in a supernatural manner to the abbot of the nearby monastery of St. Michael the Archangel. One night this religious, Sophronius by name, was returning to his own monastery. It was dark, but Sophronius saw a light diffused over our blessed father's monastery. This light was seen by many other witnesses, who often told of it.

The prince[18] and his boyars, hearing of the devout life of this community, visited blessed Theodosius, confessed their sins to him, and received great spiritual benefit. Thereupon they offered Theodosius part of their riches for the building of the church and for the accommodations of the monks, and even gave up some of their estates. Pious Prince Isiaslav in particular, who at that time sat on his father's throne, was deeply attached to the holy man and often sent for him; or else, he would himself visit the saint and return provided with spiritual food. From that time on, God granted the monastery an abundance of all good things through the prayers of His saint.

Our father Theodosius forbade the gate-keeper to open the gates to anyone after the noonday meal; no one might enter the monastery until Vespers, for during the afternoon the brethren rested before the night and morning prayers. One day at noon pious Prince Isiaslav came to the monastery with only a few attendants (for when he visited the saint, he was in the habit of dismissing his boyars and going to the monastery with but five or six servants to attend him). On this occasion, having reached the Caves, he dismounted (for he never rode into the monastery yard), and walking up to the gates, ordered the keeper to open them. The keeper replied that the great father had forbidden him to do so before Vespers. The pious prince said to him: "It is I, and to me alone you may open the gates." The keeper, not knowing that it was the prince who stood before him, answered: "I have already told you of our abbot's instructions: if the prince himself were to come here, I might not open the gates. If you wish, you may wait here a little, until Vespers." Then the visitor spoke again: "I am the prince, will you not open the gates for me?" The keeper looked out and recognized the prince; nevertheless he would not open the gates himself, but hurried to make Isiaslav's presence known to the saint.

The prince stood by the gates and waited patiently. Now in this experience he was like the senior Apostle, Peter; for when the latter, freed from prison by the angel, reached the house where the disciples were assembled and knocked at the door, the servant who peeped out and saw him was so filled with joy that she did not open the door, but ran first to inform the others. And this gate-keeper did the same thing.

The saint went to the gate, and seeing the prince, bowed to him. The prince said: "Father, what is this rule of which the keeper has told me, that forbids even the prince to enter?" The saint answered: "This rule, my good Lord, has been made in order that the brethren shall not leave the monastery at noontime, but shall take the proper rest before the evening prayers. But your devotion to the home of our Lady is good and salutary, and we are well pleased with your coming here."

They entered the church, and when they had prayed, they sat down. The devout prince drank in the honeyed words which flowed from the lips of our reverend father Theodosius and returned home greatly comforted, praising God.

From that day on, the prince's love for Theodosius was even greater, for he looked upon him as one like the saints of old; and he did all that our father Theodosius commanded.

Upon the death of Rostislav, Prince of Tmutarakan, the citizens prevailed on Nicon to go to Prince Sviatoslav[19] and asked him to let his son take the succession of Rostislav's throne. On his way Nicon visited St. Theodosius; when they met, they fell at each other's feet; then, having embraced each other, they wept, for there had been no meeting between them for many years. St. Theodosius asked Nicon to remain with him as long as he lived. The great Nicon answered: "I must first go for a little while to my monastery, in order to settle my affairs; then I shall return without delay." He kept his promise, gave all his possessions to the saint and was gladly subject to him.

Having related all that concerns these two, I shall now speak only of blessed Theodosius and of his good works. He was like a lamp enlightening all the monks. He shone by his humility, his obedience, his labors, all that he did. Each day he devoted himself to manual labor. He often worked in the bakery, side by side with the bakers; with a joyful spirit he would mix the dough and place the loaves in the oven—for, as we have said, he was strong and healthy in body. He would advise, encourage, and comfort anyone who was suffering, and was himself tireless in his undertakings.

One day, it being the eve of Our Lady's Feast, there was no water, and the above-mentioned Theodore, who was at that time cellarer (it was he who told me many things concerning Theodosius), informed the abbot that there was no one to fetch the water from the well. The saint rose at once and undertook the task. One of the brethren, observing this, hurried to inform the other monks, and they came running to assist their abbot. On another occasion, when no wood had been chopped for the kitchen, Theodore the cellarer went to blessed Theodosius and said to him, "Order some of these brothers who are idle to get wood ready for the fire." The saint answered, "I am idle, so I will do it." He told the brethren to go into the refectory, and he himself took a hatchet and started to chop wood. When dinner was over, the brethren leaving the refectory saw their venerable abbot still at work. Then each of them took a hatchet, and they chopped a quantity of wood that sufficed for many days. These are examples of our blessed spiritual father Theodosius' zeal.

He was animated by real humility and great gentleness; in everything he imitated Christ, our true God, Who said: "He that will be first among you shall be your servant." Contemplating Christ's humility, he humbled himself, putting himself in the lowest place as an example to the others. He was the first to begin his work; he entered the church before the rest of the community and was the last to leave it. Often, when the great Nicon was busy binding books, the saint would sit at his side and spin the thread needed for Nicon's work. No one ever saw him lying down or bathing. He wore a hair-shirt on his naked body, and over it a coat of coarse material, only to hide the hair-shirt. Because of his attire, many foolish persons ridiculed him, and the saint accepted this ridicule joyfully, having always in mind the divine words in which he found comfort: "Blessed are ye when they shall revile you, and persecute you, and speak all that is evil against you, untruly, for my sake; be glad and rejoice, for your reward is very great in heaven." Meditating on this, the saint suffered mockery and provocation patiently.

One day the great Theodosius visited pious Isiaslav on some matter of business. The prince lived at a great distance from the city. Theodosius remained with him until evening and Isiaslav ordered that the saint should be driven home in his coach, so that our father would be able to take some rest. During the journey the coachman, observing his poor clothes, decided that he must be a beggar, so he said to him: "Look here, monk, you are free every day to do as you please, while I must spend my life in toil. Let me lie down in the coach, and you ride the horse." The saint humbly stepped out and mounted the horse, and the coachman lay down in the coach. Theodosius rode on his way, rejoicing and praising God. When sleep overcame him, he would dismount and go on foot. And when he was weary with walking, he would mount the horse once more. When the sun rose, and the noblemen were on the way to the prince's palace, they recognized the saint from a distance, and they dismounted and bowed to him. The venerable monk then said to the coachman: "My child, it is light. Mount your horse." When the youth saw everyone bowing to the saint, he was filled with dismay and confusion. He rose to his feet and mounted the horse, and Theodosius re-entered the coach. All the boyars whom they met on their way paid their respects to our father, and the coachman's consternation increased. And great indeed was his terror when they arrived at the monastery and all the brethren hastened to greet Theodosius, bowing to the ground. "Who can this man be," the youth wondered, "who is worthy of such a reception?" Theodosius took the coachman by the hand and led him to the refectory and ordered that he should be given as much food and drink as he wished. Then he paid him money and let him go. Venerable Theodosius said nothing of what had occurred on their way, but the coachman himself related all this to the brethren.[20]

Our father Theodosius taught the brethren not to be vain about anything but to be humble monks; to regard themselves as of the least importance, not to be proud but to practise obedience towards everyone. "When walking," he said to them, "fold your arms across your breast. When you pass one another, bow humbly, as is proper for a monk. Do not wander from cell to cell, but each of you, pray in your own cell." Thus, and in many other words, he instructed the brethren. If he were informed that a monk was troubled by diabolical illusions, he would call him and test him in every fashion; he would exhort the monk firmly to resist the assaults of the devil, not to yield or weaken, or leave his place in the monastery, but to guard himself with prayer and fasting and appeal more frequently to God for help. He told the brethren that he himself had suffered these attacks in the beginning: "One day," he related, "as I was chanting the ordinary psalms, a black dog suddenly appeared before me and prevented me from making my genuflection. The dog remained for a long time before me, hindering me from prayer, and I was about to strike him when suddenly he vanished. Then I was seized with fear and trembling, so that I should have fled from that place had not God come to my assistance. When I had recollected myself, I began to pray diligently, with many genuflections. All fear left me, and from that time on such apparitions held no terrors for me." He told them many other things to fortify them against evil spirits. And when he let them return to their cells, they went away rejoicing and praising God for having given them such a good master.

The following events were described to me by a brother named Hilarion: "The evil spirits," he said, "played many wicked tricks on me. If I lay down on my couch, a multitude of devils would immediately appear, seize me by the hair, and drag and push me about. And others would pound the wall until it shook, saying: 'Let us crush him under this wall.' And they did this every night." Unable to endure these attacks any longer, Hilarion further related, he had gone to father Theodosius and described the occurrences to him, asking to be moved to another cell. The saint remonstrated with him in this manner: "No, brother, do not leave your cell, for then the devils would boast that they had defeated you and gained a victory; after this, they will persecute you even more, for they have acquired power over you. Pray to God diligently in your cell; when He sees your patience, He will grant you the victory over your enemies, so that they will not dare even to come near you." Hilarion said to Theodosius: "I beseech you, father, I cannot live in that cell any longer, with such a crowd of devils inhabiting it." Then the saint made the sign of the cross on him and said: "Go, and stay in your cell; from now on, the evil spirits shall harass you no longer; you shall see no more of them." Hilarion trusted in the blessed father's words; he bowed before him, then returned to his cell. That night he lay down and slept peacefully. The devils thereafter dared not go near that place. Repulsed by the prayers of our father Theodosius, they departed hastily.

Here is another story told me by Hilarion. He was an able copyist of books, and every night he would write in the cell of our father Theodosius, while the saint recited psalms in his gentle voice and occupied himself with weaving or some other task. One evening, as they were working thus side by side, the steward entered and said: "I have no money to purchase food and other necessities for the brethren tomorrow." The saint answered: "It is evening, and tomorrow is still far away. Therefore, have patience and pray: will not God take pity on us and provide for our needs in the way He thinks best?" When he heard this, the steward withdrew. The saint retired and prayed, as he was in the habit of doing, then resumed his task. The steward returned, repeating what he had said before. The saint replied: "I told you, go and pray; tomorrow you shall go to the town and purchase all that the brethren need on credit; later, with the help of God, we shall repay our debt, since God has said: 'Be not solicitous for tomorrow.' He will not abandon us."

As the steward went out, there entered a young man in shining armor. He bowed before our father, placed a gold coin on the table, and vanished without uttering a word. The saint picked up the gold coin and, with tears in his eyes, recited a mental prayer. Then he summoned the gate-keeper and asked him whether he had seen anyone enter the monastery that night. The gate-keeper swore that he had locked the gates before sunset and had not opened them since, so that no one could have entered. Then the saint called the steward, and placing the gold coin in his hand, said to him: "Brother Anastasius, now you shall complain no longer of having no money to buy food for the brethren. And tomorrow God will again provide for us." The steward bowed before our father, who went on to say: "Never despair, but be firm in your faith. Entrust your burden to God; He will provide for our needs. And since such is His pleasure, prepare a feast for our brethren." After this God generously sent Theodosius all that was needed for his blessed flock.

Venerable Theodosius prayed every night to obtain all these things, depriving himself of sleep, weeping and making genuflections. The monks had many intimations of this. For example, when it was time to wake him, the brethren would come to ask for his blessing, and on one occasion a certain monk stole up and stood at his door. He heard our father praying and weeping unrestrainedly and beating his head on the ground. The monk withdrew. Later he returned. This time the saint heard him approach, so he interrupted his prayers and pretended to be asleep. And when the monk knocked at his door, saying. "Give me your blessing, father," venerable Theodosius was silent until the call had been repeated three times. Only then, as if he were just awakening, did he answer, "May our Lord Jesus Christ bless you." And this, according to the brethren's testimony, occurred every night.

In the monastery lived a monk named Damian who was a priest. He zealously imitated the life and the humility of our blessed father. There were many witnesses to his holiness and obedience. One day, having fallen seriously ill, he was on the brink of death, and he began to pray: "My Lord Jesus Christ, allow me to share the glory of Thy saints, and to be a member of Thy kingdom. And do not separate me, I beseech Thee, my Lord, from my father and master, venerable Theodosius. Let me remain at his side in the world prepared for the just." He was praying in this manner when blessed Theodosius suddenly appeared, standing at his bedside. He leaned on Damian's breast, embraced him affectionately, and said: "My son, I have been sent to inform you that your prayer will be answered. You shall be with the saints in the kingdom of our heavenly Lord. When our Lord Jesus Christ orders me to be transferred from this world and to come to you, we shall not be separated, but shall remain together in the next world." When he had said this,

the saint vanished from Damian's sight. Now the priest knew
that this had been a vision, for he had not seen Theodosius
enter through the door, and he had become invisible right where
he stood.

Then Damian sent the brother who was caring for him to
fetch Theodosius. When our father entered, Damian asked
happily, "Father, shall it be as you promised just now, when
you appeared to me?" The saint replied that he did not know
of what promise Damian was speaking. Then the priest told
him what he had seen and heard. The God-inspired Theodosius, smiling gently and weeping a little, said: "My son, it
shall be as was promised by the angel who appeared to you in
my image. As for me, how could such a sinner share in the
glory prepared for the just?" But Damian rejoiced in the
saint's promise. When the brethren gathered around his bed, he
took leave of them all, and gave up his soul peacefully when
the angels came to bear it away. Then the saint ordered that
the bell should be tolled for all the other brethren to assemble,
so that Damian's body might be buried with proper respect in
the monks' cemetery.

When the brethren increased in number and many postu-
lants came to join them, Theodosius was compelled to enlarge
the monastery, building many other cells. With the assistance
of his monks, he fenced in the monastery court with his own
hands. But one dark night before the fence was completed,
robbers entered the premises. They did not approach the cells,
but hastened to the church in the belief that it contained many
precious articles. From within came the sound of singing, and
the robbers, thinking that the brethren were chanting Vespers,
withdrew. When they had waited for a time in the woods, they
said to each other that the prayers must by this time be ended,
so they returned to the church. Once more they heard the sound
of chanting; they also saw a strange light in the church and
could smell the odor of incense. Now it was angels that were
singing, but the robbers thought that the monks were chanting
the midnight service, and they withdrew once more, with the
firm intention of breaking into the church and plundering it

as soon as the service should be over. They approached the church many times in this manner, and each time they heard the singing.

When the hour of Matins came, and the sexton began to summon the monks to prayer, the robbers hid in the wood, saying to each other: "What shall we do? We must have been hearing ghosts. But when all the brethren have gathered in the church, we shall break in, lock the doors, murder the monks and take away their riches." Now this plan was inspired by the enemy, who desired the death of the holy flock; but his design miscarried, and he himself suffered defeat through God's intervention and the prayers of blessed Theodosius.

As the venerable flock gathered about their blessed teacher Theodosius in the church began to chant the holy morning psalms, the cruel robbers, pausing only for a moment, bore down upon the church like a pack of wild beasts. But just at that moment a miraculous event took place. The church rose into the air, out of reach of the attackers. Those who were assembled in the church with the saint were unaware of this, but the robbers fled in panic, vowing that never again would they harm anyone. Their leader went to Theodosius in repentance and described the occurrence to him. The saint thanked God for His protection of the monastery and for the opportunity He had given the thieves to save their souls.

When the boyars visited the monastery, the saint, after having given them spiritual instruction, would offer them a meal from the Caves' victuals, such as boiled grain, bread, and fish. Pious Prince Isiaslav himself often shared these meals. One day when he was in high spirits, the prince said to the saint: "Father, you know that my house is full of all kinds of worldly riches; but I have never eaten better food than this. Often my servants prepare a variety of expensive foods, but their dishes are not so palatable as these. Tell me, father, I beg of you, why is your food so delicious?" Our God-inspired Theodosius, wishing to incline the prince's heart to the love of God, answered: "My good Lord, I shall tell you the reason if you want to know it.

When the brethren of the Caves are about to cook food or bake bread, one of them first of all asks for the abbot's blessing. Then he bows three times before the holy altar and lights a candle from the altar-lamp, and with this he kindles the fire in the oven. When a monk fills the kettle with water, he says to the senior-brother: 'Father, give me your blessing,' and the senior-brother answers: 'May God bless you, brother.' And so it is with everything that is done in the community. Now take your servants. They quarrel among themselves while they are preparing the food. They complain and lie about each other, and often the stewards beat them. Therefore their work is done in a sinful manner." When he heard this, pious Prince Isiaslav exclaimed: "Indeed, father, it is as you say!"

Our venerable father Theodosius, truly filled with the Holy Ghost, multiplied the talents which God had given him. He drew great numbers of monks to this once desolate land and made his monastery famous; yet he was never willing to put away reserves, for he felt that it was better to be fortified by faith and hope in God than to put one's trust in property. When he visited the cells of the brethren and found food or clothing in a greater quantity than was allowed by the rule, he would cast these into the fire as the devil's portion acquired through disobedience. He would say to the brothers: "It is wrong for us, who are monks and have renounced the world, to collect property in our cells. How can a monk offer God a pure prayer if he has hidden possessions? Are you deaf to the words of Our Lord: 'For where thy treasure is, there is thy heart also' and 'Thou fool, this night do they require thy soul of thee: and whose shall those things be which thou hast provided'? Therefore, brothers, let us be satisfied with such clothes and food as we receive from the cellarer according to the rule; let us keep nothing in our cell, so that we may pray to God with our whole heart and mind."

In this way Theodosius taught his brothers, giving them many other instructions with tears and in great humility. He never gave way to anger, but was gentle and merciful and charitable towards everyone. If one of the holy flock weakened in his faith and left the monastery, the saint would be deeply grieved and would pray for the return of the lost sheep. And when the brother returned, the saint would joyfully teach him how to resist the wiles of the enemy—not to let him come near but to stand firmly. He said that only a cowardly soul allows itself to be weakened by these contemptible devices. And when he had instructed and comforted the returning brother, Theodosius would send him back to his cell in peace.

A certain brother in the community often left the Caves, and each time he returned, the saint received him, saying that God would not allow him to die outside the monastery. Theodosius prayed with tears for this brother, begging God to be patient with him. One day the vagrant monk returned for still another time and asked our blessed father to take him in. And Theodosius, who was full of true charity, welcomed the brother as he had done on previous occasions. Then the monk brought the few possessions he had and laid them before the venerable father. Theodosius said to him: "If you would become a perfect monk, consider these objects as the fruit of disobedience and throw them into the fire." The monk, who had ardent faith, did as he was told. Thus his property was burned, and from that time on he stayed in the Caves and died there peacefully, according to our father's prediction. Such was the love which the saint bore his flock; he cared for them as the good shepherd tends his sheep, comforted them, instructed and nourished them spiritually, directing them towards divine wisdom and thus guiding them to the kingdom of heaven.

So intense was our father Theodosius' charity that if he saw a beggar or a miserable and poorly dressed person, he would weep with compassion as he gave him alms. He built a church dedicated to St. Stephen, with a courtyard on the monastery grounds, and here he gathered together the beggars, the blind, the lame and the sick. He fed them from the monastery kitchen and gave them a tenth of all he had. Moreover, each Saturday, he would send a cartload of bread to the prisoners in jail.

At one time a feud was inspired by the evil one between three princes who were brothers. The two younger rose against their

elder brother, pious Isiaslav, and drove him out of the capital.[21]
When the brothers entered the city, they sent for blessed father
Theodosius, asking him to dine with them and to take part in
their iniquitous council. Theodosius, who had heard of the
unjust treatment accorded to Isiaslav, was inspired by the Holy
Ghost to answer in the words of Scripture: "I shall not go to
the feast of Jezebel or taste the fruit of murder and injustice."
Adding many other words of reproach to his reply, the saint sent
the messenger back to the princes. They listened to his message
without any expression of anger, for they considered our venerable father to be a man of God. Nevertheless they refused
to be influenced by him and continued to persecute their
brother; Sviatoslav, Prince of Chernigov, ascended the throne
of his brother Isiaslav, while the other, Vsevolod, returned to
his own princedom of Pereyaslavl. Then our father Theodosius,
inspired by the Holy Ghost, began to rebuke Sviatoslav for
having usurped his brother's throne and driven him out of his
kingdom. Sometimes the saint would reproach Sviatoslav by
letter and sometimes by word of mouth, addressing himself
to the noblemen who visited the Caves and telling them to
repeat his words to Sviatoslav. Eventually he wrote him a long
letter, charging him in the following words: "Your brother's
blood cries out to God against you, as that of Abel against
Cain." He cited the acts of the persecutors and fratricides of
antiquity and quoted many parables reflecting the prince's
behavior.

When he read this Sviatoslav was enraged. Roaring like a
lion, he flung the letter on the ground. The rumor then arose
that the saint would be condemned to exile, and the brethren,
greatly alarmed, implored our father to desist from his accusations. Many boyars came to the monastery, warning Theodosius
of the prince's wrath and begging him to offer no further resistance. They said: "The prince intends to send you into exile."
Blessed Theodosius answered: "Brothers, I am filled with joy;
for indeed, nothing could be better for me in this life. What
have I to fear? the loss of riches or property? separation from
country or children? We have brought nothing of the sort into

this world. We were born naked, and we must leave this world naked. Therefore, I am prepared for exile and death." From that time on, he began to charge Sviatoslav even more boldly with the hatred he bore his brother, for he earnestly desired exile. Though the prince was very much provoked against the saint, he nevertheless dared not do him any injury, for he was aware that Theodosius was a highly respected and just man, and he even envied his brother for having so great a religious in his realm. (This was admitted by the prince himself, and later repeated by the monk Paul, former abbot of a nearby monastery.) Our blessed father Theodosius, influenced at last by the solicitations of his brethren and the boyars, and himself convinced that his words were having no effect on the new ruler, ceased to rebuke him, deciding that it would be better to plead with him to bring his brother back. After a few days the prince learned, to his joy, that Theodosius was no longer implacably opposed to him. Since he had for long desired to take counsel with Theodosius concerning spiritual matters, he now sent a messenger asking the saint whether he might visit the Caves. As soon as Theodosius had given his permission, the prince went joyfully to the monastery, accompanied by his boyars.

The great Theodosius, according to his custom, went forth from the church followed by his brethren to meet the prince, and bowed before him in due courtesy. The prince greeted the saint and said to him: "Father, I have not dared to visit you before, for I feared that in your anger you would refuse me admittance." The saint answered: "Good prince, what effect can our anger have upon your power? It is our duty to rebuke you and to say whatever has a bearing upon the salvation of your soul, and it is your duty to listen." After this they entered the church, and having prayed, were seated. The saint began to speak, quoting the holy Scriptures and instructing the prince as to the love which he should have for his brother. But Sviatoslav put all the blame on Isiaslav, and he was therefore reluctant to make peace with him. After a prolonged conversation, the prince returned to his home, thanking God for giving him the opportunity of speaking with such a man. From that time on he often visited the saint to listen to his words, which were sweeter than honey. The great Theodosius also visited Sviatoslav frequently and reminded him of God's justice and of the love he owed his brother.

One day Theodosius entered Sviatoslav's palace and found many musicians assembled, as was the custom, to entertain the prince. Some of them were playing on the lute, others on the organ and other instruments. The saint seated himself at Sviatoslav's side, his eyes fixed on the ground. Then, raising his head, he said to the prince: "Will this be your lot in the next world?" The prince, moved by these words, wept a little and ordered the musicians to stop playing. From that day on, each time the saint entered while they were playing, Sviatoslav told them to be still.[22]

Often, when informed of our father's arrival, the prince would go eagerly to meet him at the door, and they would enter the palace side by side. One day, when he was in high spirits, Sviatoslav said to Theodosius: "If I were told that my own father had risen from the dead, truly I should not rejoice as much as I do when you visit me. Nor should I be as much afraid of him as I am of your holiness." The saint answered: "If you are as much afraid of me as you say, then fulfill my wish. Put your brother back on the throne that his good father gave him." The prince, having no answer for this, said nothing. The enemy had filled him with such resentment towards his brother that he would not even hear of him. But venerable Theodosius prayed night and day for the pious Isiaslav. He gave instructions that his name should be mentioned in the litanies as prince of Kiev and the senior of the brothers: but as for Sviatoslav, he forbade his name to be remembered in the monastery. Only later, owing to the brethren's entreaties, did he permit Sviatoslav's name to be restored in the prayers of the church, and then it might be mentioned only after that of Isiaslav.

Observing this feud between the princes, the great Nicon retired with two other monks to the aforementioned peninsula, where he founded a monastery. Although blessed Theodosius urged him not to leave, but to abide with him as long as he lived, Nicon would not be persuaded.

Many people found fault with Theodosius, but he accepted their reproaches joyfully; often he suffered rebukes and vexations from his own disciples, but he prayed to God for all. Moreover, he was not disturbed when ignorant folk ridiculed him because of his poor clothes, but rejoiced and praised God. Because of his dress, many people failed to recognize him as the abbot but rather mistook him for one of the cooks. One day, as he was on his way to the workers who were building the church, he met a poor widow who had been ill-treated by a judge. She said: "Monk, where is your abbot?" Theodosius answered: "What do you want of him? He is a sinner." The woman said: "I do not know whether he is a sinner, but I do know that he has rescued many people from sorrow and misery. Therefore, I too have come to look for him, so that he may help me." The saint, when he learned of her plight, took pity on her and said: "Woman, return to your home. When I see the abbot, I shall tell him about you, and he will help you." And when the woman had obediently departed, the saint went to the judge, spoke in her defense and saved her from the injustice which was impending.

Theodosius often intervened with the judges and the princes, and he alleviated many a misfortune, because no one dared to disobey him, his justice and holiness were so well known. He was respected, not because of fine clothes or rich estates, but for his radiant life and purity of spirit, and for his teachings, fired with the inspiration of the Holy Ghost. To him the goat-skin and the hair-shirt were more precious than a king's purple robe, and he was proud to wear them.

Death of Theodosius

When Theodosius had reached the end of his life, he learned beforehand from God the day he would go to rest (for death is repose for the just). He ordered all the brothers who were working in the fields, or were absent for some other reason, to be called back to the Caves. When they were gathered together, he instructed the bailiffs, the stewards and the servants to fulfill their tasks with industry and fear of God, in obedience and charity. Weeping, he gave instructions to them all concerning their salvation and the way of life that was pleasing to God— fasting, attendance in church and reverent behavior on its premises, brotherly love and obedience. He told them to love and obey not only their seniors, but also their equals. When he had said these things, he let them go.

After that his illness became more acute, and a burning fever drained all strength from his limbs. He lay down on his couch and said: "Thy will be done. Whatever God wills shall be done to me. But I pray Thee, O my Lord, have mercy on my soul, that it may not encounter the malice of Thy enemies, but that Thy angels may receive it and lead it through the trials of the darkness after death towards the light of Thy mercy." After this he was silent.

There was great sorrowing among the brethren. For three days, he could not speak or even raise his eyes; and many believed he was dead, although there were faint indications that his soul was still within him. But on the third day he raised himself, and when all the brethren had gathered, he said to them: "My brothers and fathers, I know that my time is drawing to an end, for it was revealed to me by God during my Lenten retreat in the cave. As for you, consult with each other, whom you wish me to appoint abbot as my successor." When they heard this, the brethren were once more plunged into grief. Withdrawing from his presence, they held a consultation and nominated Stephen, the choirmaster, as their future abbot. The next day blessed Theodosius called the brethren to his bedside and asked them: "What have you decided, my children? Whom do you think worthy of being your abbot?" The brethren told him Stephen,[23] and our father blessed him and ordered him to be abbot. And he told all the brethren to obey Stephen and dismissed them. But before he let them go, he foretold the day of his death, saying: "On Saturday, as the sun rises, my soul will be separated from my body." Then calling back Stephen alone to his bedside, he advised him with regard to the care of the flock. Stephen stayed by the saint and nursed him, for our father was now severely ill.

On Saturday at dawn, the saint sent for all the brethren and embraced each of them in turn. They wept and groaned at the thought that they were to be separated from such a pastor and teacher. The saint said to them: "My beloved children and brethren, I embrace you because I am leaving you to go to our Lord Jesus Christ. Here is the abbot you have chosen. Obey him as your spiritual father; fear him and fulfill all his commissions. God, who has created all things by His will and in His wisdom, will bless you and protect you against the enemy's devices and all misfortune, and will preserve your faith in all its firmness, unity and love until your last breath. Moreover, He will grant you the grace to work for Him without sinning and to form one spirit of love and obedience. Be perfect, as your Father in heaven is perfect. May God be with you. I entreat you all to bury me in the clothes which I am now wearing and to lay me in the cave where I spent the days of Lent. Do not wash my miserable body. Let no one see me; you alone bury me in the place I have chosen."

And as the brethren wept, he spoke again, to comfort them: "I promise you, brothers and fathers, that though I am leaving you in body, my spirit shall always be with you. Those of you who die in the monastery or at some other place where they are sent by the abbot, I shall answer for before God, even if they sin. But as for a man who leaves the Caves of his own free will, I shall have no concern with him. You know my daring before God. If you see all the goods of this monastery multiplied, you will know that I am close to our divine Lord. And if you see poverty and decrease of good, you will know that I am far from God and dare not ask Him for anything."[24]

After these words Theodosius sent all the brethren away, not allowing a single one to remain with him. But one of the brethren who had been his servant made a chink in the door and looked through it. The saint had risen and was kneeling, his face pressed to the floor, praying with tears for God's mercy upon his soul and calling all the saints to his aid, in particular our Blessed Lady. He appealed through her to our Lord Jesus Christ on behalf of his flock and his monastery. Then he went back to his couch, and when he had rested for a while, he raised his eyes, and with a radiant face spoke in a strange voice: "Blessed be God! If it is so, I need have no more fear, but may leave this world joyfully."

He said this, apparently having had a vision. Then, having straightened his habit, stretched out his limbs and crossed his hands on his breast, he gave up his holy soul to God and was united with the holy fathers.

Our blessed father Theodosius died in 6582 (1074) on Saturday, the third day of May, as he had predicted.

FROM ST. THEODOSIUS' SERMON

TO HIS MONKS

ENTITLED "ON PATIENCE AND LOVE"

Beloved, what did we bring into this world, or what have we to take out of it? Did we not leave the world and worldly things according to the commandment of Christ, Who said, "Every one of you that doth not renounce all that he possesseth, cannot be my disciple"; and again, "If anyone love me, he will keep my word"? Love of God is expressed not in words but in actions. For He said: "He that hath my commandments and keepeth them, I will love him, and will manifest myself to him. A new commandment I give unto you, that you love one another, as I have loved you." And "In this," He said, "is my Father glorified; that you bring forth very much fruit, and become my disciples."

Is it not of itself astonishing, beloved, that God can be glorified by works of ours—and what love He pours out upon us, wretches that we are: "As the Father hath loved me, I also have loved you. . . . Greater love than this no man hath, that a man lay down his life for his friends"; and, "You are my friends." What then should we, miserable men, be like? Does not our heart burn, hearing these words? . . . What good did we do to Him, that he has chosen us and rescued us from this transient life? For have not we all gone astray and became useless in His work, following our lusts? Yet He did not despise us in such an evil condition; he did not abhor our nature, but having taken the form of a slave, became like us. And all this He did that we may be saved. . . .

ST. SERGIUS

THE FIRST HERMIT AND MYSTIC

SERGIUS IS UNDOUBTEDLY THE MOST POPULAR AND BELOVED OF THE SAINTS OF Russia and is considered her patron. He became the patron of the principality of Moscow in the fifteenth century, when it began to conquer and unite under its rule the whole of Great Russia, and the extension of his cult soon after his death (1392), is partially explained by the services which he had rendered as a counsellor and adviser (and not in spiritual matters alone) to the Russian princes and as the faithful supporter of Moscow's princely line.

St. Sergius' spirituality gives the most perfect expression to the Russian kenotic ideal, but in him is found a mystical deepening of the spirituality for which St. Theodosius had established the pattern. St. Sergius was one of the most prominent exponents of a new form of Russian monasticism. All the cloisters of the pre-Mongolian era of which there is a record were situated in towns, or in the outskirts of towns, and were in close relation with the world for which they provided spiritual and cultural centers. The Tartar invasion (1237-40) laid waste to most of the old communities and produced great disorders in the religious and moral life of Russian society. Only in the fourteenth century did the nation begin gradually to recover from the spiritual inertia resulting from the continual devastations of the invaders, but now the leaders of the great monastic revival were hermits, who had taken refuge in the virgin forests of northern Russia, where they lived a life of prayer and contemplation. At first there were the huts and chapels of solitary men of prayer, but disciples soon gathered about, and eventually communities which throve economically and spiritually arose in the wilderness. Nevertheless the new spirit of silence and contemplation did not die out but penetrated deeper into the wilderness as sanctuaries more remote from society were sought by contemplatives desiring to live in solitude.

For St. Sergius years of solitary prayer in which he underwent severe spiritual conflicts with the forces of evil and the temptations of the flesh preceded the founding of the famous monastery of the Holy Trinity. The career of Sergius as monk and abbot has many features in common with that of Theodosius, and in some respects is closely parallel to it. Like that of St. Theodosius his asceticism emphasizes labor, self-deprivation, and patience rather than painful corporal penances. There is the coarse and patched clothing, the lack of exterior authority, and the self-humiliation in the presence of subordinates and persons of humble condition. Sergius seems even to have surpassed his spiritual ancestor in the practice of kenotic humility, judging by several incidents recorded of him. First there is his manual labor; he cultivates the soil of the wilderness, works as a carpenter, building first cells and then the chapel, and at the height of his national fame he is still employed in tending the kitchen garden. Although of noble origin, he is not to be distinguished from a peasant in his life as a religious. His meekness likewise is even more astonishing than that of the Kievan saint: he, the abbot, is engaged by one of his monks to build a cell and is recompensed for his services by a few mildewed loaves. And when he encounters disobedience on the part of his own brother, he leaves the monastery for a period of four years rather than enforce his authority. Like Theodosius he receives a rule for the cenobitical life from Greece and tries to establish it in the monastery, but he is even less capable than Theodosius of preserving order through severe discipline.

Yet in his interior life, in the quality of his prayer, Sergius belongs to another epoch than does Theodosius; he is the first Russian saint in whom mysticism is observed. That he was a mystic is a matter of inference: his biographer, Epiphanius, famous among his contemporaries for the elegance of his style, evidences no knowledge or understanding of this kind of prayer, which had but lately shown itself in Russia, but the visions of the saint which he describes are of a mystical character. Sergius is the earliest saint in Russian hagiography to be favored by heavenly visions in his contemplation; such graces were likewise conferred on a few of his disciples belonging to the same contemplative school. The best known is the vision of Our Lady; others are those of light and fire, often in connection with the Holy Eucharist: Sergius is assisted in the celebration of the Mass by an angel, and fire descends into the chalice after the consecration. Fire also darts forth from his hands when he blesses one of his disciples, the mystic Isaac.

St. Sergius dedicated his monastery to the Holy Trinity—a rather unusual dedication at that time; he was himself believed to have been dedicated to the Holy Trinity before his birth. Considering the primitive stage which theological thought had reached in medieval Russia, this was in the nature of mystical revelation. He was moreover contemporary with the exponents of the great movement of Greek mysticism known as Hesychasm. Intercourse between Moscow and Constantinople was not then infrequent: Sergius himself received a letter from the Patriarch; one of his disciples had been at Mount Athos for a time, and some of the manuscripts in the latter's handwriting, which include ascetical and mystical treatises by writers of the Hesychast school (Simeon the New Theologian, Gregory of Sinai, and others), are preserved. All these factors, added to the characteristic love of solitude and the celestial visions, make it extremely probable that Sergius practised mystical prayer.

But Sergius' mysticism did not cause him to decline the responsibility of service to the world. In the best tradition of Theodosius he comforted, healed, protected the oppressed. He found nothing abhorrent in political activity, but whereas Theodosius had found it necessary only to insist upon justice in political relations, the demands upon a churchman in Sergius' day entailed other and more dangerous functions. In Theodosius' time the state had been strong enough to defend itself from aggression by secular arms, but Sergius saw Russia prostrate under a foreign yoke. A national movement of resistance under the leadership of Moscow now arose, and Sergius had to give his blessing to Prince Demetrius of Moscow for open military resistance. The first Russian victory over the Tartars (in the battle of Kulikovo, 1380) raised Sergius to the eminence of a national hero, a builder of Muscovy. This was not the only instance of his intervention in the political sphere; sometimes he took part in diplomatic parleys, reconciling enemies, or even threatening the recalcitrant with the ecclesiastical interdict. In this capacity he acted, most probably, in obedience to the great statesman Metropolitan Alexis of Moscow, who was for several decades a regent in the government of the state.

Modern historians may well differ in their evaluation of the political function which these churchmen exercised: the greatness of the future Muscovite state was its fruit. In the days of St. Sergius that close union of Church and State in Russia, which is one of the chief characteristics of Russia's subsequent life as a nation, had its origin. In its development this ecclesiastical policy stands in drastic contradiction to the kenotic ideals of ancient times. St. Sergius, yielding to new historical forces, could see only the blessings attendant upon a strong union of Church and State, not the potentiality for evil likewise inherent in such a government.

THE LIFE, ACTS AND MIRACLES
OF OUR REVERED AND HOLY
FATHER ABBOT SERGIUS

By EPIPHANIUS THE WISE[1]

O UR HOLY FATHER SERGIUS WAS BORN[2] OF NOBLE, ORTHODOX, DEVOUT PARENTS. HIS FATHER WAS NAMED CYRIL AND HIS mother Mary. They found favour with God; they were honourable in the sight of God and man, and abounded in those virtues which are well-pleasing unto God.

Cyril had three sons, Stephen, Bartholomew and Peter, whom he brought up in strict piety and purity. Stephen and Peter quickly learnt to read and write, but the second boy did not so easily learn to write, and worked slowly and inattentively; his master taught him with care but the boy could not put his mind to his studies, nor understand, nor do the same as his companions who were studying with him. As a result he suffered from the many reproaches of his parents, and still more from the punishments of his teacher and the ridicule of his companions. The boy often prayed to God in secret and with many tears: "O Lord, give me understanding of this learning. Teach me, Lord, enlighten and instruct me." His reverence for God prompted him to pray that he might receive knowledge from God and not from men.

One day his father sent him to seek for a lost foal. On his way he met a monk, a venerable elder, a stranger, a priest, with the appearance of an angel. This stranger was standing beneath an oak tree, praying devoutly and with much shedding of tears. The boy, seeing him, humbly made a low obeisance, and awaited the end of his prayers.

The venerable monk, when he had ended his oraisons, glanced at the boy and, conscious that he beheld the chosen vessel of the Holy Spirit, he called him to his side, blessed him, bestowed on him a kiss in the name of Christ, and asked: "What art seeking, or what dost thou want, child?"

The boy answered, "My soul desires above all things to understand the holy scriptures. I have to study reading and writing and I am sorely vexed that I cannot learn these things. Will you, holy father, pray to God for me, that He will give me understanding of book-learning?"

The monk raised his hands and his eyes towards heaven, sighed, prayed to God, then said, "Amen."

Taking out from his satchel, as it were some treasure, with three fingers, he handed to the boy what appeared to be a little bit of white wheaten bread of the Holy Sacrament, saying to him, "Take this in thy mouth, child, and eat; this is given thee as a sign of God's grace and for the understanding of holy scriptures. Though the gift appears but small the taste thereof is very sweet."

The boy opened his mouth and ate, tasting a sweetness as of honey, wherefore he said, "Is it not written, How sweet are Thy Words to my palate, more than honey to my lips, and my soul doth cherish them exceedingly?"

The monk answered and said, "If thou believest, child, more than this will be revealed to thee; and do not vex thyself about reading and writing; thou wilt find that from this day forth the Lord will give thee learning above that of thy brothers and others of thine own age."

Having thus informed him of divine favour, the monk prepared to proceed on his way. But the boy flung himself, with his face to the ground, at the feet of the monk,[3] and besought him to come and visit his parents, saying, "My parents dearly love persons such as you are, father."

The monk, astonished at his faith, accompanied him to his parents' house. At the sight of the stranger Cyril and Mary came out to meet him, and bowed low before him. The monk blessed them, and they offered him food but, before accepting any food, the monk went into the chapel, taking with him the boy whose consecration had been signified even before birth,[4] and began a recitation of the Canonical Hours, telling the boy to read the Psalms.

The boy said, "I do not know them, father."

The monk replied, "I told thee that from to-day the Lord would give thee knowledge in reading and writing; read the Word of God nothing doubting."

Whereupon, to the astonishment of all present, the boy, receiving the monk's blessing, began to recite in excellent rhythm; and from that hour he could read. His parents and brothers praised God, and after accompanying the monk to the house placed food before him. Having eaten, and bestowed a blessing on the parents, the monk was anxious to proceed on his way. But the parents pleaded, "Reverend father, hurry not away, but stay and comfort us and calm our fears. Our humble son, whom you bless and praise, is to us an object of marvel. While he was yet in his mother's womb three times he uttered a cry in church during holy Mass. Wherefore we fear and doubt of what is to be, and what he is to do."

The holy monk, after considering and becoming aware of that which was to be, exclaimed, "O blessed pair, O worthy couple, giving birth to such a child! Why do you fear where there is no place for fear? Rather rejoice and be glad for the boy will be great before God and man, thanks to his life of godliness."

Having thus spoken the monk left, pronouncing a dark saying that their son would serve the Holy Trinity and would lead many to an understanding of the divine precepts. They accompanied him to the doorway of their house, when he became of a sudden invisible. Perplexed, they wondered if he had been an angel, sent to give the boy knowledge of reading. After the departure of the monk, it became evident that the boy could read any book, and was altogether changed; he was submissive in all things to his parents, striving to fulfill their wishes, and never disobedient. Applying himself solely to glorifying God, and rejoicing therein, he attended assiduously in God's church being present daily at Matins, at the Mass, at Vespers. He studied holy scripts, and at all times, in every way, he disciplined his body and preserved himself in purity of body and soul.

Cyril, devout servant of God, led the life of a wealthy and renowned boyar, in the province of Rostov, but in later years he was reduced to poverty. He, like others, suffered from the invasions of Tartar hordes into Russia, from the skirmishes of troops, the frequent demands for tribute, and from repeated bad harvests, in conjunction with the period of violence and disorder which followed the great Tartar war. When the principality of Rostov fell into the hands of the Grand-Duke Ivan Danilovich of Moscow, distress prevailed in the town of Rostov, and not least among the princes and boyars. They were deprived of power, of their properties, of honours and rank, of all of which Moscow became the possessor. By order of the Grand-Duke they left Rostov, and a certain noble, Vassili Kotchev, with another called Mina, were sent from Moscow to Rostov as voyevodes.[5] On arrival in the town of Rostov these two governors imposed a levy on the town and on the inhabitants. A severe persecution followed, and many of the remaining inhabitants of Rostov were constrained to surrender their estates to the Muscovites, in exchange for which they received wounds and humiliations, and went forth empty-handed and as veriest beggars. In brief, Rostov was subjected to every possible humiliation, even to the hanging, head downwards, of their Governor, Averki, one of the chief boyars of Rostov. Seeing and hearing of all this, terror spread among the people, not only in the town of Rostov but in all the surrounding country. Cyril, God's devout servant, avoided further misfortune by escaping from his native town. He assembled his entire household and family and with them removed from Rostov to Radonezh[6], where he settled near the church dedicated to the Birth of Christ, which is still standing to this day.

Cyril's two sons, Stephen and Peter, married, but his second son, Bartholomew, would not contemplate marriage, being desirous of becoming a monk. He often expressed this wish to his father, but his parents said to him, "My son, wait a little and bear with us; we are old, poor and sick, and we have no one to look after us, for both your brothers are married." The won-

drous youth gladly promised to care for them to the end of their
days, and from henceforth strove for his parents' well-being,
until they entered the monastic life and went one to a monastery and the other to a convent. They lived but a few years,
and passed away to God. Blessed Bartholomew laid his parents
in their graves, mourned for them forty days, then returned to
his house. Calling his younger brother Peter, he bestowed his
share of his father's inheritance on him, retaining nothing for
himself. The wife of his elder brother, Stephen, died also, leaving two sons, Clement and Ivan. Stephen soon renounced the
world and became a monk in the Holy Mother of God monastery at Khotkov.

Blessed Bartholomew now came to him, and begged him to
accompany him in the search for some desert place. Stephen
assented, and he and the saint together explored many parts of
the forest till, finally, they came to a waste space in the middle
of the forest, near a stream. After inspecting the place they
obeyed the voice of God and were satisfied. Having prayed, they
set about chopping wood and carrying it. First they built themselves a hut, and then constructed a small chapel. When the
chapel was finished and the time had come to dedicate it,
blessed Bartholomew said to Stephen, "Now, my lord and
eldest brother by birth and by blood, tell me, in honour of
whose feast shall this chapel be, and to which saint shall we
dedicate it?"

Stephen answered, "Why do you ask me, and why put me to
the test? You were chosen of God while you were yet in your
mother's womb, and He gave a sign concerning you before ever
you were born, that the child would be a disciple of the Blessed
Trinity, and not he alone would have devout faith, for he would
lead many others and teach them to believe in the Holy Trinity.
It behoves you, therefore, to dedicate a chapel above all others
to the Blessed Trinity."

The favoured youth gave a deep sigh and said, "To tell the
truth, my lord and brother, I asked you because I felt I must,
although I wanted and thought likewise as you do, and desired
with my whole soul to erect and dedicate this chapel to the

Blessed Trinity, but out of humility I inquired of you." And he went forthwith to obtain the blessing of the ruling prelate for its consecration. From the town came the priest sent by Theognost, Metropolitan of Kiev and all Russia, and the chapel was consecrated and dedicated to the Holy Trinity in the reign of the Grand-Duke Simeon Ivanovich[7]; we believe in the beginning of his reign. The chapel being now built and dedicated, Stephen did not long remain in the wilderness with his brother. He realized soon all the labours in this desert place, the hardships, the all-pervading need and want, and that there were no means of satisfying hunger and thirst, nor any other necessity. As yet no one came to the saint, nor brought him anything for, at this time, nowhere around was there any village, nor house, nor people; neither was there road or pathway, but everywhere on all sides was forest and waste land. Stephen, seeing this, was troubled, and he decided to leave the wilderness, and with it his own brother the saintly desert-lover and desert-dweller. He went from thence to Moscow, and when he reached this city he settled in the monastery of the Epiphany, found himself a cell and dwelt in it exercising himself in virtue. Hard labour was to him a joy, and he passed his time in ascetic practices in his cell, disciplining himself by fasting and prayer, refraining from all indulgence, even from drinking beer. Alexis, the future Metropolitan, who at this time had not been raised to the rank of bishop, was living in the monastery, leading a quiet monastic life. Stephen and he spent much time together in spiritual exercises, and they sang in the choir side by side. The Grand-Duke Simeon came to hear of Stephen and the godly life he led, and commanded the Metropolitan Theognost to ordain him priest and, later, to appoint him abbot of the monastery. Aware of his great virtues the Grand-Duke also appointed him as his confessor.

Our saint, Sergius, had not taken monastic vows at this time for, as yet, he had not enough experience of monasteries, and of all that is required of a monk. After a while, however, he invited a spiritual elder, who held the dignity of priest and abbot, named Metrophan[8], to come and visit him in his solitude. In great humility he entreated him, "Father, may the love of God be with us, and give me the tonsure of a monk. From childhood have I loved God and set my heart on Him these many years, but my parents' needs withheld me. Now, my lord and father, I am free from all bonds, and I thirst, as the hart thirsteth for the springs of living water."

The abbot forthwith went into the chapel with him, and gave him the tonsure on the 7th day of October on the feast day of the blessed martyrs Sergius and Bacchus. And Sergius was the name he received as monk. In those days it was the custom to give to the newly-tonsured monk the name of the saint whose feast day it happened to be. Our saint was twenty-three years old when he joined the order of monks. Blessed Sergius, the newly-tonsured monk, partook of the Holy Sacrament and received grace and the gift of the Holy Spirit. From one whose witness is true and sure we are told that when Sergius partook of the Holy Sacrament the chapel was filled with a sweet odour; and not only in the chapel, but all around was the same fragrant smell. The saint remained in the chapel seven days, touching no food other than one consecrated loaf given him by the abbot, refusing all else and giving himself up to fasting and prayer, having on his lips the Psalms of David.

When Metrophan bade farewell St. Sergius in all humility he said to him, "Give me your blessing and pray regarding my solitude; and instruct one living alone in the wilderness how to pray to the Lord God; how to remain unharmed; how to wrestle with the enemy and with his own temptations to pride, for I am but a novice and a newly-tonsured monk."

The abbot was astonished and almost afraid. He replied, "You ask of me concerning that which you know no less well than we do, O noble father." After discoursing with him for a while on spiritual matters, and commending him to God, Metrophan went away leaving St. Sergius alone to silence and the wilderness.

Who can recount his labours? Who can number the trials he endured living alone in the wilderness?

Under different forms and from time to time the devil

wrestled with the saint, but the demons beset St. Sergius in vain; no matter what visions they evoked, they failed to overcome the firm and fearless spirit of the ascetic. At one moment it was Satan who laid his snares, at another incursions of wild beasts took place, for many were the wild animals inhabiting this wilderness. Some of these remained at a distance, others came near the saint, surrounded him and even sniffed him. In particular a bear used to come to the holy man. Seeing the animal did not come to harm him, but in order to get some food, the saint brought a small slice of bread from his hut, and placed it on a log or stump, so the bear learnt to come for the meal thus prepared for him, and having eaten it went away again. If there was no bread, and the bear did not find his usual slice, he would wait about for a long while and look around on all sides, rather like some money-lender waiting to receive payment of his debt. At this time Sergius had no variety of foods in the wilderness, only bread and water from the spring, and a great scarcity of these. Often bread was not to be found, then both he and the bear went hungry. Sometimes, although there was but one single slice of bread, the saint gave it to the bear, being unwilling to disappoint him of his food.

He diligently read the Holy Scriptures to obtain a knowledge of all virtue; in his secret meditations training his mind in a longing for eternal bliss. Most wonderful of all, none knew the measure of his ascetic and godly life spent in solitude. God, the Beholder of all hidden things, alone saw it.

Whether he lived two years or more in the wilderness alone, we do not know; God knows only. The Lord, seeing his very great faith and patience, took compassion on him and, desirous of relieving his solitary labours, put into the hearts of certain god-fearing monks to visit him.

The saint inquired of them, "Are you able to endure the hardships of this place, hunger and thirst, and every kind of want?"

They replied, "Yes, revered father, we are willing with God's help and with your prayers."

Holy Sergius, seeing their faith and zeal, marvelled, and said, "My brethren, I desired to dwell alone in the wilderness and, furthermore, to die in this place. If it be God's will that there shall be a monastery in this place, and that many brethren will be gathered here, then may God's holy will be done. I welcome you with joy, but let each one of you build himself a cell. Furthermore, let it be known unto you, if you come to dwell in the wilderness, the beginning of righteousness is the fear of the Lord."

To increase his own fear of the Lord he spent day and night in the study of God's word. Moreover, young in years, strong and healthy in body, he could do the work of two men or more. The devil now strove to wound him with the darts of concupiscence. The saint, aware of these enemy attacks, disciplined his body and exercised his soul, mastering it with fasting, and thus was he protected by the grace of God. Although not yet raised to the office of priesthood, dwelling in company with the brethren, he was present daily with them in church for the reciting of the offices, Nocturnes, Matins, the Hours and Vespers. For the Mass a priest, who was an abbot, came from one of the villages. At first Sergius did not wish to be raised to the priesthood and especially he did not want to become an abbot; this was by reason of his extreme humility. He constantly remarked that the beginning and root of all evil lay in pride of rank, and ambition to be an abbot. The monks were but few in number, about a dozen. They constructed themselves cells, not very large ones, within the enclosure, and put up gates at the entrance. Sergius built four cells with his own hands, and performed other monastic duties at the request of the brethren; he carried logs from the forest on his shoulders, chopped them up, and carried them into the cells. The monastery, indeed, came to be a wonderful place to look upon. The forest was not far distant from it as now it is, the shade and the murmur of trees hung above the cells; around the church was a space of trunks and stumps, here many kinds of vegetables were sown.

But to return to the exploits of Saint Sergius. He flayed the grain and ground it in the mill, baked the bread and cooked the food, cut out shoes and clothing and stitched them; he drew water from the spring flowing near by, and carried it in two pails on his shoulders, and put water in each cell. He spent the night in prayer, without sleep, feeding only on bread and water, and that in small quantities; and never spent an idle hour.

Within the space of a year the abbot who had given the tonsure to St. Sergius fell ill and, after a short while, he passed out of this life. Then God put it into the hearts of the brethren to go to blessed Sergius, and to say to him, "Father, we cannot continue without an abbot. We desire you to be our abbot, and the guide of our souls and bodies."

The saint sighed from the bottom of his heart, and replied, "I have had no thought of becoming abbot, for my soul longs to finish its course here as an ordinary monk." The brethren urged him again and again to be their abbot; finally, overcome by his compassionate love, but groaning inwardly, he said, "Fathers and brethren, I will say no more against it, and will submit to the will of God; He sees into our hearts and souls. We will go into the town, to the bishop."

Alexis, the Metropolitan of all Russia, was living at this time in Constantinople, and he had nominated Bishop Athanasius Volynski in his stead in the town of Pereyaslavl. Our blessed Sergius went, therefore, to the bishop, taking with him two elders; and entering into his presence made a low obeisance. Athanasius rejoiced exceedingly at seeing him, and kissed him in the name of Christ. He had heard tell of the saint and of his beginning of good deeds, and he spoke to him of the workings of the Spirit. Our blessed father Sergius begged the bishop to give them an abbot, and a guide of their souls.

The venerable Athanasius replied, "Thyself, son and brother, God called in thy mother's womb. It is thou who wilt be father and abbot of thy brethren." Blessed Sergius refused, insisting on his unworthiness, but Athanasius said to him, "Beloved, thou hast acquired all virtue save obedience."

Blessed Sergius, bowing low, replied, "May God's will be done. Praise be the Lord forever and forever." They all answered, "Amen."

Without delay the holy bishop, Athanasius, led blessed

Sergius to the church, and ordained him subdeacon and then deacon. The following morning the saint was raised to the dignity of priesthood, and was told to say the holy liturgy and to offer the Bloodless Sacrifice. Later, taking him apart, the bishop spoke to him of the teachings of the apostles and of the holy fathers, for the edification and guidance of souls. After bestowing on him a kiss in the name of Christ, he sent him forth, in very deed an abbot, pastor and guardian, and physician of his spiritual brethren. He had not taken upon himself the rank of abbot, he received the leadership from God; he had not sought it, nor striven for it; he did not obtain it by payment, as do others who have pride of rank, chasing hither and thither, plotting and snatching power from one another. God Himself led His chosen disciple and exalted him to the dignity of abbot.

Our revered father and abbot Sergius returned to his monastery, to the abode dedicated to the Holy Trinity, and the brethren, coming out to meet him, bowed low to the ground before him. He blessed them, and said, "Brethren, pray for me. I am altogether ignorant, and I have received a talent from the Highest, and I shall have to render an account of it, and of the flock committed to me."

There were twelve brethren when he first became abbot, and he was the thirteenth. And this number remained, neither increasing nor diminishing, until Simon, the archimandrite of Smolensk, arrived among them. From that time onwards their numbers constantly increased. This wondrous man, Simon, was chief archimandrite, excellent, eminent, abounding in virtue. Having heard of our revered father Sergius' way of life he laid aside honours, left the goodly city of Smolensk, and arrived at the monastery where, greeting our revered father Sergius with the greatest humility, he entreated him to allow him to live under him and his rules in all submission and obedience: and he offered the estate he owned as a gift to the abbot for the benefit of the monastery. Blessed Sergius welcomed him with great joy. Simon lived many years, submissive and obedient, abounding in virtue, and died in advanced old age.

Stephen, the saint's brother, came with his younger son,

Ivan, from Moscow and, presenting him to Abbot Sergius, asked him to give him the tonsure. Abbot Sergius did so, and gave him the name of Theodore; from his earliest years the boy had been taught abstinence, piety and chastity, following his uncle's precepts; according to some accounts he was given the tonsure when he was ten years old, others say twelve. People from many parts, towns and countries, came to live with Abbot Sergius, and their names are written in the book of life. The monastery bit by bit grew in size. It is recorded in the *Patericon* —that is to say, in the book of the early Fathers of the Church— that the holy fathers in assembly prophesied about later generations, saying that the last would be weak. But, of the later generations, God made Sergius strong as one of the early fathers. God made him a lover of hard work, and to be the head over a great number of monks. From the time he was appointed abbot, the holy Mass was sung every day. He himself baked the holy bread; first he flayed and ground the wheat, sifted the flour, kneaded and fermented the dough; he entrusted the making of the holy bread to no one. He also cooked the grains for the "kutia,"[9] and he also made the candles. Although occupying the chief place as abbot, he did not alter in any way his monastic rules. He was lowly and humble with all people, and was an example to all.

He never sent away anyone who came to him for the tonsure, neither old nor young, nor rich nor poor, he received them all with fervent joy; but he did not give them the tonsure at once. He who would be a monk was ordered, first, to put on a long, black cloth garment and to live with the brethren until he got accustomed to all the monastic rules; then, later, he was given full monk's attire of cloak and hood. Finally, when he was deemed worthy, he was allowed the "schema," the mark of the ascetic.

After Vespers, and late at night, especially on long dark nights, the saint used to leave his cell and go the round of the monks' cells. If he heard anyone saying his prayers, or making genuflections, or busy with his own handiwork, he was gratified and gave thanks to God. If, on the other hand, he heard two or three monks chatting together, or laughing, he was displeased, rapped on the door or window, and passed on. In the morning he would send for them and, indirectly, quietly and gently, by means of some parable, reprove them. If he was a humble and submissive brother he would quickly admit his fault and, bowing low before St. Sergius, would beg his forgiveness. If, instead, he was not a humble brother, and stood erect thinking he was not the person referred to, then the saint, with patience, would make it clear to him, and order him to do a public penance.[10] In this way they all learnt to pray to God assiduously; not to chat with one another after Vespers, and to do their own handiwork with all their might; and to have the Psalms of David all day on their lips.

In the beginning, when the monastery was first built, many were the hardships and privations. A main road lay a long way off, and wilderness surrounded the monastery. Here the monks lived, it is believed, for fifteen years. Then, in the time of the Grand-Duke Ivan Ivanovich (1353-59), Christians[11] began to arrive from all parts and to settle in the vicinity. The forest was cut down, there was no one to prevent it; the trees were hewn down, none were spared, and the forest was converted into an open plain as we now see it. A village was built, and houses; and visitors came to the monastery bringing their countless offerings. But in the beginning, when they settled in this place, they all suffered great privations. At times there was no bread or flour, and all means of subsistence was lacking; at times there was no wine for the Eucharist, nor incense, nor wax candles. The monks sang Matins at dawn with no lights, save that of a single birch or pine torch.

One day there was a great scarcity of bread and salt in the whole monastery. The saintly abbot gave orders to all the brethren that they were not to go out, nor beg from the laity, but to remain patiently in the monastery and await God's compassion. He himself spent three or four days without any food. On the fourth day, at dawn, taking an axe he went to one of the elders, by name Danila (Daniel), and said to him: "I have heard say that you want to build an entrance in front of your cell. See, I have come to build it for you, so that my hands shall not remain idle."

Danila replied, "Yes, I have been wanting it for a long while, and am awaiting the carpenter from the village; but I am afraid to employ you, for you will require a large payment from me."

Sergius said to him, "I do not require a large sum of money. Have you any mildewed loaves? I very much want to eat some such loaves. I do not ask from you anything else. Where will you find such another carpenter as I?"

Danila brought him a few mildewed loaves, saying, "This is all I have."

Sergius said, "That will be enough, and to spare. But hide it until evening. I take no pay before work is done."

Saying which, and tightening his belt, he chopped and worked all day, cut planks and put up the entrance. At the close of day, Danila brought him the sieveful of the promised loaves. Sergius, offering a prayer and grace, ate the bread and drank some water. He had neither soup nor salt; the bread was both dinner and supper.

Several of the brethren noticed something in the nature of a faint breath of smoke issuing from his lips, and turning to one another they said, "Oh, brother, what patience and self-control has this man."

But one of the monks, not having had anything to eat for two days, murmured against Sergius, and went up to him and said, "Why this mouldy bread? Why should we not go outside and beg for some bread? If we obey you we shall perish of hunger. To-morrow morning we will leave this place and go hence and not return; we cannot any longer endure such want and scarcity."

Not all of them complained, only one brother, but because of this one, Sergius, seeing they were enfeebled and in distress, convoked the whole brotherhood and gave them instruction from holy scriptures, "God's Grace cannot be given without trials; after tribulations comes joy. It is written, at evening there shall be weeping but in the morning gladness. You, at present, have no bread or food, and to-morrow you will enjoy an abundance."

And as he was yet speaking there came a rapping at the gates. The porter, peeping through an aperture, saw that a store of provisions had been brought; he was so overjoyed that he did not open the gates but ran first to St. Sergius to tell him. The saint gave the order at once, "Open the gates quickly, let them come in, and let those persons who have brought the provisions be invited to share the meal"; while he himself, before all else, directed that the "bilo" should be sounded,[12] and with the brethren he went into the church to sing the *Te Deum*. Returning from church, they went into the refectory, and the newly-arrived, fresh bread was placed before them. The bread was still warm and soft, and the taste of it was of an unimaginable strange sweetness, as it were honey mingled with juice of barley and spices.

When they had eaten the saint remarked, "And where is our brother who was murmuring about mouldy bread? May he notice that it is sweet and fresh. Let us remember the prophet who said, 'Ashes have I eaten for bread and mixed my drink with tears'." Then he inquired whose bread it was, and who had sent it. The messengers announced, "A pious layman, very wealthy, living a great distance away, sent it to Sergius and his brotherhood." Again the monks, on Sergius' orders, invited the men to sup with them, but they refused, having to hasten elsewhere.

The monks came to the abbot in astonishment, saying, "Father, how has this wheaten bread, warm and tasting of butter and spices, been brought from far?" The following day more food and drink were brought to the monastery in the same manner. And again on the third day, from a distant country. Abbot Sergius, seeing and hearing this, gave glory to God before all the brethren, saying, "You see, brethren, God provides for everything, and neither does He abandon this place." From this time forth the monks grew accustomed to be patient under trials and privations, enduring all things, trusting in the Lord

God with fervent faith, and being strengthened therein by their holy father Sergius.

According to an account by one of the elders of the monastery, blessed Sergius never wore new clothing, nor any made of fine material, nor coloured, nor white, nor smooth and soft; he wore plain cloth or caftan; his clothing was old and worn, dirty, patched. Once they had in the monastery an ugly, stained, bad bit of cloth, which all the brethren threw aside; one brother had it, kept it for a while and discarded it, so did another, and a third and so on to the seventh. But the saint did not despise it, he gratefully took it, cut it out and made himself a habit, which he wore, not with disdain but with gratitude, for a whole year, till it was worn out and full of holes.

So shabby were his clothes, worse than that of any of the monks, that several people were misled and did not recognize him. One day a Christian from a nearby village, who had never seen the saint, came to visit him. The abbot was digging in the garden. The visitor looked about and asked, "Where is Sergius? Where is the wonderful and famous man?"

A brother replied, "In the garden, digging; wait a while, until he comes in."

The visitor, growing impatient, peeped through an aperture, and perceived the saint wearing attire shabby, patched, in holes, and face covered with sweat; and he could not believe that this was he of whom he had heard. When the saint came from the garden, the monks informed him, "This is he whom you wish to see."

The visitor turned from the saint and mocked at him; "I came to see a prophet and you point out to me a needy looking beggar. I see no glory, no majesty and honour about him. He wears no fine and rich apparel; he has no attendants, no trained servants; he is but a needy, indigent beggar."

The brethren, reporting to the abbot, said, "We hardly dare tell you, revered father, and we would send away your guest as a good-for-nothing, rude fellow; he has been discourteous and disrespectful about you, reproaches us, and will not listen to us."

The holy man, fixing his eyes on the brethren and seeing their confusion, said to them, "Do not do so, brethren, for he did not come to see you. He came to visit me." And, since he expected no obeisance from his visitor, he went towards him, humbly bowing low to the ground before him, and blessed and praised him for his right judgment. Then, taking him by the hand, the saint sat him down at his right hand, and bade him partake of food and drink. The visitor expressed his regret at not seeing Sergius, whom he had taken the trouble to come and visit; and his wish had not been fulfilled. The saint remarked, "Be not sad about it, for such is God's Grace that no one ever leaves this place with a heavy heart."

As he spoke a neighbouring prince arrived at the monastery, with great pomp, accompanied by retinue of boyars, servants and attendants. The armed attendants, who preceded the prince, took the visitor by the shoulders and removed him out of sight of the prince and of Sergius. The prince then advanced and, from a distance, made a low obeisance to Sergius. The saint gave him his blessing and, after bestowing a kiss on him, they both sat down while everyone else remained standing. The visitor thrust his way through, and going up to one of those standing by, asked, "Who is the monk sitting on the prince's right hand, tell me."

The man turned to him and said, "Are you then a stranger here? Have you indeed not heard of blessed father Sergius? It is he speaking with the prince."

Upon hearing this the visitor was overcome with remorse, and after the prince's departure, taking several of the brethren to intercede for him, and making a low obeisance before the abbot, he said, "Father, I am but a sinner and a great offender. Forgive me and help my unbelief."

The saint readily forgave, and with his blessing and some words of comfort, he took leave of him. From henceforth, and to the end of his days, this man held a true, firm faith in the Holy Trinity and in St. Sergius. He left his village a few years later, and came to the saint's monastery, where he became a monk, and there spent several years in repentance and amendment of life before he passed away to God.

We will now turn to the miracles God performs through his elect. Owing to lack of water near the monastery, the brotherhood suffered great discomfort, which increased with their numbers and having to carry water from a distance. Some of the monks even complained to the abbot, "When you set out to build a monastery on this spot why did you not observe that it was not near water?" They repeated this query with vexation, often.

The saint told them, "I intended to worship and pray in this place alone. But God willed that a monastery such as this, dedicated to the Holy Trinity, should arise."

Going out of the monastery, accompanied by one of the brethren, he made his way through a ravine below the monastery, and finding a small pool of rain water, he knelt down and prayed. No sooner had he made the sign of the Cross over the spot, than a bubbling spring arose, which is still to be seen to this day, and from whence water is drawn to supply every need of the monastery.

Many cures have been granted to the faithful from the waters; and people have come from long distances to fetch the water and carry it away and to give it to their sick to drink. From the time it appeared, and for a number of years, the spring was called after Sergius. The wise man, not seeking renown, was displeased, and remarked, "Never let me hear that a well is called by my name. I did not give this water; God gave it to us unworthy men."

A certain devout Christian living close by the monastery, who believed in St. Sergius, had an only son, a child, who fell ill. The father brought the boy to the monastery, and entreated the saint to pray for him: but while the father was yet speaking the boy died. The man, with his last hope gone, wept and bemoaned, "It would have been better had my son died in my own house." While he went to prepare a grave, the dead child was laid in the saint's cell. The saint felt compassion for this man, and falling on his knees prayed over the dead child. Suddenly the boy came to life, and moved. His father, returning with preparations for the burial, found his son alive, whereupon, flinging himself at the feet of God's servant, he gave him thanks. The saint said to him, "You deceive yourself, man, and do not know what you say. While on your journey hither your son became frozen with cold, and you thought he had died. He has now thawed in the warm cell, and you think he has come to life. No one can rise again from the dead before the Day of Resurrection."

The man however insisted, saying, "Your prayers brought him to life again."

The saint forbade him to say this; "If you noise this abroad you will lose your son altogether." The man promised to tell no one and, taking his son, now restored to health, he went back to his own home. This miracle was made known through the saint's disciples.

Living on the banks of the Volga, a long distance away from the Lavra,[13] was a man who owned great possessions, but who was afflicted incessantly, day and night, by a cruel and evil spirit. Not only did he break iron chains but ten or more strong men could not hold him. His relatives, hearing tell of the saint, journeyed with him to the monastery, where dwelt the servant of the Lord. When they came to the monastery the madman broke loose from his bonds, and flung himself about, crying, "I will not go, I will not. I will go back from whence I came." They informed the saint, who gave the order to sound the "bilo," and when the brethren were assembled they sang the *Te Deum* for the sick. The madman grew calmer little by little, and when he was led into the monastery, the saint came out of church, carrying a Cross, whereupon the sufferer, with a loud cry, fled from the spot, and flung himself into a pool of rainwater standing nearby, exclaiming, "O horrible, O terrible flame." By the grace of God and the saint's prayers he recovered, and was restored to his right mind. When they inquired what he meant by his exclamation, he told them, "When the saint wanted to bless me with the Cross, I saw a great flame proceeding from him, and it seized hold of me. So I threw myself into the water, fearing that I should be consumed in the flame."

One day the saint, in accordance with his usual rule, was

keeping vigil and praying for the brotherhood late at night when he heard a voice calling, "Sergius!" He was astonished, and opening the window of the cell he beheld a wondrous vision. A great radiance shone in the heavens, the night sky was illumined by its brilliance, exceeding the light of day. A second time the voice called, "Sergius! Thou prayest for thy children; God has heard thy prayer. See and behold great numbers of monks gathered together in the name of the Everlasting Trinity, in thy fold, and under thy guidance."

The saint looked and beheld a multitude of beautiful birds, flying, not only on to the monastery, but all around; and he heard a voice saying, "As many birds as thou seest by so many will thy flock of disciples increase; and after thy time they will not grow less if they will follow in thy footsteps." Anxious to have a witness of this vision the saint called aloud for Simon, he being the nearest. Simon ran to him with all haste, but he was not found worthy to behold this vision; he saw no more than a ray of its light, but even so was greatly astonished. Filled with awe and wonder at this glorious vision, they rejoiced together.

One day some Greeks arrived from Constantinople, sent by the Patriarch to visit the saint. Making a deep obeisance they said to him, "The all-powerful Patriarch of Constantinople, Philotheus, sends you his blessing," and they presented him with gifts from the Patriarch, a cross and a "paramand,"[14] and also handed him a letter from him.

The saint asked, "Are you sure you have not been sent to someone else? How can I, a sinner, be worthy of such gifts from the most illustrious Patriarch?"

They replied, "We have indeed been sent to you, holy Sergius." The elder went then to see the Metropolitan, Alexis, and took with him the missive brought from the Patriarch. The Metropolitan ordered the epistle to be read to him. It ran, "By the Grace of God, the Archbishop of Constantinople, the Oecumenical Patriarch Philotheus, by the Holy Spirit, to our son and fellow-servant Sergius. Divine grace and peace, and our blessing be with you. We have heard tell of your godly life dedicated to God, wherefore we greatly praise and glorify God. One thing, however, has not been established, you have not formed a community. Take note, blessed one, that even the great prophet and our father in God, David, embracing all things with his mind, could not bestow higher praise than when he said, 'But now, however good and however perfect, yet, above all, is abiding together in brotherly love.' Wherefore I counsel you to establish a community. That God's blessing and His grace be always upon you." The elder inquired of the Metropolitan, "Revered teacher, what would you have us do?" The Metropolitan replied, "With all our heart we approve, and return thanks."

From henceforth life on the basis of community was established in the monastery. The saint, wise pastor, appointed to each brother his duties, one to be cellarer, others to be cooks and bakers, another to care for the sick, and for church duties, an ecclesiarch, and a subecclesiarch, and sacristans, and so forth. He further announced that the ordinances of the holy fathers were to be strictly observed; all things were to be possessed in common, no monk was to hold property of his own.

His community having been established with much wisdom, the numbers of his followers soon increased. Also, the larger the supply of offerings to the monastery, the more hospitality was extended. No person in need ever left the monastery empty-handed; and the saint gave orders that the poor and all strangers were to be allowed to rest in the monastery, and no suppliant to be refused, adding, "If you will follow my precepts and continue in them faithfully, God will reward you, and when I leave this life our monastery will prosper and continue to stand with the Lord's blessing for many years." And to the present day it has remained standing.

Before long dissension arose; the devil, hating goodness, put about the idea of disputing the authority of Sergius.[15] One Saturday, while Vespers were being sung, and the Abbot Sergius, wearing his vestments was in the altar, his brother, Stephen, who was standing by the choir, on the left, asked the canonarch, "Who gave you that book?" The canonarch replied, "The abbot gave it to me." The other said, "What has the abbot to do with it? Did not I sit in that place before?" and adding other silly remarks.

Although the saint was standing by the altar, he heard what was said, but he kept silence. When they all came out of church he did not go to his cell, he walked away from the monastery, unknown to all. When he arrived at the monastery of Makhrisch[16] he asked the abbot, Stephen, if one of his monks could lead him to some desert place. Together they searched and finally discovered a beautiful spot close to a river called the Kerzhach. The brotherhood, hearing about the saint, took to visiting him, in twos and threes, and more. Our father Sergius sent two of his followers to the Metropolitan Alexis, with the request for his blessing and permission to erect a church. Aided by divine favour, a church was erected in a short while, and many brethren gathered there.

Soon several monks from the Holy Trinity, unable any longer to bear the separation from their spiritual father, went to the Metropolitan and said, "Holy Lord, we are living like sheep without a shepherd. Command our abbot to return to his monastery, that he may save us from perishing and dying of grief without him."

The Metropolitan despatched two archimandrites, Gerasim and Paul, to the abbot with the message, "Your father, Alexis, the Metropolitan, sends you his blessing. He has rejoiced exceedingly to hear that you are living in a distant wilderness. But, return now to the monastery of the Holy Trinity; those persons who were dissatisfied with you shall be removed from the monastery."

Whereupon, hearing this, the saint sent reply, "Tell my lord the Metropolitan, all from his lips, as from those of Christ, I receive with joy and do disobey in nothing."

The Metropolitan, glad at his prompt obedience, instantly despatched a priest to consecrate the church to the Annunciation of the Immaculate and Blessed Virgin, Mother of God. Sergius selected one of his followers, called Romanus, to be the abbot of the new monastery, and sent him to the Metropolitan to be raised to the priesthood. The saint then returned to the monastery of the Holy Trinity.

When the news reached the monastery that the saint was returning, the brethren went out to meet him. On beholding him it appeared as if a second sun were shining; and they were so filled with joy that some of the brethren kissed the father's hands, others his feet, while others seized his clothing and kissed that. There was loud rejoicing and glorifying God for the return of their father. And what of the father? He rejoiced with his whole heart at seeing this gathering of his flock.

Now Bishop Stephen,[17] a god-fearing and devout man, had for St. Sergius a deep, spiritual affection. One day he was travelling from his episcopacy of Perm to the capital, Moscow. The road along which the bishop journeyed lay about seven miles from St. Sergius' monastery. When the godly bishop came opposite the saint's monastery he stopped and said, bowing low towards the direction of the saint, "Peace be with thee, brother in God!" The saint, at this hour, was seated at table with his brethren. Perceiving in spirit what Bishop Stephen was doing, he rose from the supper table, stood for an instant in prayer, then bowing, said aloud, "Be joyful, thou shepherd of Christ's flock; the peace of God be always with thee." At the end of supper his disciples inquired of him what he meant. He openly told them, "At that hour Bishop Stephen, going on his way to Moscow, did reverence to the Holy Trinity, and blessed us humble folk." He pointed out to them, also, where this had taken place.

One time, when Theodore,[18] son of Stephen, was with blessed Sergius in the monastery, he was taking part in the divine liturgy which was being sung by the saint, and with aforenamed Stephen, the saint's brother. Of a sudden Isaac, who had taken the vow of silence, saw a fourth person serving at the altar with them, of a bright, shining appearance, and in dazzling apparel. Isaac inquired of Father Macarius, who was standing by his side, "What miraculous apparition is this?" Macarius replied, "I do not know, brother, I see a fearful and ineffable vision. But,

I think, brother, that some one came with the prince." (Prince Vladimir was at this time in the monastery.) One of the prince's attendants was asked whether a priest had come with him; but, no, they knew of no one.

When the divine Mass was at an end, seizing a favourable moment, one of the brethren approached Saint Sergius and questioned him. But he, anxious not to disclose the secret, asked, "What wonder did you see, brother? My brother, Stephen, was saying the Mass, also his son, Theodore and I, unworthy as I am. No other priest whatever was serving with us." His disciples insisted, entreating the saint to reveal the mystery to them, whereupon he said, "Beloved brethren, what the Lord God has revealed can I keep secret? He whom you beheld was an angel of the Lord, and not only this time but every time I, unworthy as I am, serve with this messenger of the Lord. That which you have seen tell no one, so long as I am on this earth." And his disciples were astonished beyond measure.

A rumour spread that Prince Mamai was raising a large army as a punishment for our sins, and that with all his heathen Tartar hordes he would invade Russian soil. Very great fear prevailed among the people at this report. The puissant and reigning prince, who held the sceptre of all Russia, great Demetrius, having a great faith in the saint, came to ask him if he counselled him to go against the heathen. The saint, bestowing on him his blessing, and strengthened by prayer, said to him, "It behoveth you, Lord, to have a care for the lives of the flock committed to you by God. Go forth against the heathen; and upheld by the strong arm of God, conquer; and return to your country sound in health, and glorify God with loud praise."

The Grand-Duke replied, "If indeed God assists me, father, I will build a monastery to the Immaculate Mother of God." And with the saint's blessing he hurriedly went on his way. Assembling all his armies, he marched against the heathen Tartars; but, seeing the multitudes of them, he began to doubt; and many of his followers, not knowing what to do, were overwhelmed with fear. Of a sudden, a courier from the saint arrived, in all haste, with the message, "Be in no doubt, Lord, go forward with faith and confront the enemy's ferocity; and fear not, for God will be on your side." Forthwith, the Grand-Duke De-metrius, and all his armies, were filled with a spirit of temerity; and went into battle against the pagans. They fought; many fell; but God was with them, and helped the great invincible Demetrius, who vanquished the ungodly Tartars. In that same hour the saint was engaged with his brethren before God in prayer for victory over the pagans. Within an hour of the final defeat of the ungodly, the saint, who was a seer, announced to the brotherhood what had happened, the victory, the courage of the Grand-Duke Demetrius Ivanovich, and the names, too, of those who had died at the hands of the pagans; and he made intercession for them to all-Merciful God.

The Grand-Duke Demetrius returned to his country with great joy in his heart, and hastened to visit holy, venerable Sergius. Rendering thanks for the prayers of the saint and of the brotherhood, he gave a rich offering to the monastery and, in fulfillment of his vow, expressed his wish to build at once the monastery of the Immaculate Mother of God. After search-ing for a favourable place, venerable Sergius fixed upon one by the banks of the river Dubenka, and with the consent of the Grand-Duke a church to the Assumption of our Blessed Virgin Mother of God was consecrated by Saint Sergius. As abbot, the saint appointed one of his followers, Sabbas by name, a man of exceeding great virtue. A community was formed and many brethren joined it.

Once again the Grand-Duke Demetrius entreated Saint Sergius to come to Kolomna, to consecrate a site for the building of a monastery to be dedicated to the Holy Epiphany. It was the saint's custom to go everywhere on foot. Obedient to the Grand-Duke, he went to Kolomna, consecrated the site, and a church was erected and, at the Grand-Duke's request, he sent him one of his disciples for the founding of the monastery, a priest-monk, Gregory, a devout man and of great virtue. In time a stone church was built, which is standing to this day.

Another time the illustrious Prince Vladimir begged Saint Sergius, likewise, to come to his part of the country, to the town of Serpukhov, and consecrate a place by the river Nar, and dedicate a church to the Conception of the Immaculate Mother of God. Once again the saint obeyed the request. This god-fearing prince also begged him to send one of his disciples, Athanasius by name. Although the saint found it hard to grant this request, love prevailed, and he consented. Athanasius being a man of rare virtue, exceedingly learned in holy scriptures—many valuable writings by his hand bear witness to him to the present day—the saint loved him dearly. To him the saint entrusted the founding of the monastery, and the forming of the community. Aided by the prayers of the saint, the monastery was built, wonderful and beautiful, and named "On the Height."[19]

But why pursue further the saint's planting of ecclesiastical fruit? It is well known how many monasteries were founded by God's own chosen servant. And, offspring of his offspring, burning bright as stars, they are everywhere radiating a serene and wondrous life, and a blessing to all.

The Metropolitan Alexis, being old, and seeing his weakness increasing, sent for Saint Sergius. While they conversed the Metropolitan asked to have the cross with the "paramand" adorned with gold and precious stones brought to him, to give it to the saint; but he, bowing low in great humility, refused it, saying, "Forgive me, Lord, I have worn no gold ornaments since childhood, wherefore all the more do I wish in old age to continue in poverty." The bishop insisted, and said, "I know, beloved, that thou art fulfilling a vow, but be obedient, and take this which we offer thee with a benediction." Further, he said to the saint, "Dost know why I sent for thee? I desire, while I yet live, to find a man able to feed Christ's flock. I have doubted of them all, thee alone have I chosen as worthy. I know with all certainty that, from the puissant prince to the lowliest of his people, thou art the one they want."

On hearing this the saint was deeply grieved, regarding honour for himself as a thing of naught, and he pleaded with the bishop, "Forgive me, Lord, but this of which you speak is beyond my powers, and you never will find it in me. What am I but a sinner, and the least of men?" The bishop quoted many sayings from holy scriptures, but the saint, unyielding in his humility, said, "Gracious Lord, if you do not wish to drive away my poverty from your Holiness, speak no more about my poor self, nor permit any one else, for no one can make me otherwise."

The bishop, understanding that the saint would not yield, allowed him to return to his monastery. Before long the Metropolitan Alexis left this life, in the year 6885 (1378); and once more the princes implored the saint to accept the rank of bishop; but, firm as adamant, he would in no way consent. Then a certain archimandrite, Michael, was raised to the bishopric; but this man, with great presumption, not only invested himself with the episcopal robes, but also proceeded to plot against the saint, in the belief that the venerable Sergius would put a check on his audacity, wishing to occupy the episcopal throne himself. Blessed Sergius, hearing of Michael's threats against him, remarked to his disciples that Michael, vaunting himself of his sacred appointment, would not obtain his wish for, overcome by pride, he would not reach the imperial city. The saint's prophecy was fulfilled. On his way by boat to Constantinople[20] Michael fell ill and died. Thereupon everyone regarded Saint Sergius as one of the prophets.

One day the blessed father was praying, as was his wont, before the image of the Mother of our Lord Jesus Christ. Having sung the "Magnificat" of the Blessed Virgin he sat down to rest a while, saying to his disciple, Micah, "Son, be calm and be bold, for a wonderful and fearful event is about to happen." Instantly a voice was heard, "The Blessed Virgin is coming." Hearing this the saint hurried from his cell into the corridor. A dazzling radiance shone upon the saint, brighter than the sun, and he beheld the Blessed Virgin, with the two Apostles, Peter and John, in ineffable glory. Unable to bear so resplendent a vision, the saint fell to the ground. The Blessed Virgin, touching the saint with her hand, said, "Be not afraid, mine own elect, I have come to visit thee. Thy prayers for thy disciples for whom thou prayest, and for thy monastery, have been heard. Be not troubled; from henceforth it will flourish, not only during thy lifetime but when thou goest to the Lord, I will be with thy monastery, supplying its needs lavishly, providing for it, protecting it."

Having thus spoken, she vanished. The saint, in ecstasy, stood in trembling awe and wonder. Returning slowly to his senses, he saw his disciple, terror-struck, lying on the ground, whereupon he raised him up; but the other flung himself down at the feet of the elder, saying, "Tell me, father, for God's sake what miraculous vision was this, for my spirit almost loosed its bonds with the flesh from so resplendent a vision."

The saint, so filled with ecstasy that his face glowed therewith, was unable to answer other than a few words, "Wait a while, son, for I, too, am trembling with awe and wonder at this miraculous vision." They continued in silent adoration until, finally, the saint said to his disciple, "Son, call hither Isaac and Simon." When these two came he recounted to them all that had happened, how he beheld the Blessed Virgin with the Apostles, and what a wonderful promise she had given him. Hearing this their hearts were filled with indescribable joy, and they all sang the "Magnificat," and glorified God. All night long the saint remained in meditation on this ineffable vision.

After a while, a Greek bishop came from Constantinople to Moscow but, although he had heard a great deal about the saint, his doubts about him prevailed for, he reasoned, "How can such a light have appeared in this savage land, more especially in these latter days?" He, therefore, resolved to go to the monastery and see the saint. When he drew near to the monastery, fear entered his soul and, as soon as he entered the monastery and beheld the saint, blindness fell upon him. The venerable Sergius took him by the hand and led him to his cell. The bishop, with tears, confessed his doubts to the saint, and prayed for the recovery of his sight. The gentle lover of humility touched his blinded pupils and, as it were, scales fell from his eyes, and instantly he recovered his sight. The bishop proclaimed to all that the saint was indeed a man of God and that in God's mercy, he himself had been deemed worthy to behold a celestial man and an earthly angel.

A money-lender, living near the saint's monastery, and who, like the strong in all ages, oppressed the poor, ill-treated a certain poor orphan and, moreover, carried off his pig which was being fattened, and without paying for it had it killed. The ill-used orphan went to the saint in great distress and, weeping, begged for help. The saint, moved by compassion, sent for the offender, convicted him of wrongdoing and said, "My son, do you believe that God is a Judge of the righteous and of sinners; a father to widows and orphans; that He is quick to avenge, and that it is a fearful thing to come under the wrath of God?" Having reproached him and told him he must pay what he owed to the orphan, he added, "Above all, do not oppress the poor." The man, overcome by fear, promised to amend and to pay the orphan, then returned to his own house. Little by little the effect of the saint's rebuke grew faint, and he decided not to pay his debt to the orphan. And, thinking it over in his mind, he went as usual into his larder, where he found the pig half-devoured and swarming with maggots although it was mid-winter. He was stricken with fear, and without delay paid the debt; and ordered the pig to be thrown to the dogs and birds to eat, but they would not touch it and clear the usurer of his offence.

Now, again, one day, the saint was reciting the divine liturgy with one of his disciples, venerable Simon, the ecclesiarch, of whom we have already spoken, when a wonderful vision was vouchsafed to Simon. While the saint was saying the liturgy Simon saw a flame pass along the altar, illuminating it and surrounding the holy table; as the saint was about to partake of the Blessed Sacrament the glorious flame coiled itself and entered the sacred chalice; and the saint thus received Communion. Simon, who saw this, trembled with fear. The saint, when he moved away from the altar, understood that Simon had been deemed worthy of this miraculous vision, and telling him to approach, asked, "Son, why are you fearful?" The other replied, "Master, I beheld a miraculous vision; the grace of the Holy Spirit operating with you." The saint forbade him to speak of it, "Tell no one of this which you have seen, until the Lord calls me away from this life."

The saint lived a number of years, continually chastening himself with fasting, and working unceasingly. He performed many unfathomable miracles, and reached an advanced age, never failing from his place at divine service; the older his body grew, the stronger grew his fervour, in no way weakened by age. He became aware of his approaching end six months before, and assembling the brotherhood he appointed his dearest disciple to take his place, one perfect in all virtue, following his master in all things, small of stature, but in mind a continual blossoming, whose name was Nicon. The saint exhorted him to guide Christ's flock with patient care and justice. The great ascetic soon began to lose strength and in September was taken seriously ill. Seeing his end, he again assembled his flock and delivered a final exhortation. He made them promise to be steadfast in orthodoxy and to preserve amity among men; to keep pure in body and soul; to love truth; to avoid all evil and carnal lusts; to be moderate in food and drink; above all, to be clothed with humility; not to forget love of their neighbour; to avoid controversy, and on no account to set value on honour and praise in this life, but rather to await reward from God for the joys of heaven and eternal blessings. Having instructed them in many things, he concluded, "I am, by God's will, about to leave you, and I commit you to Almighty God and the Immaculate Virgin, Mother of God, that they may be to you a Refuge and Rock of Defence against the snares of your enemies." As his soul was about to leave his body, he partook of the Sacred Body and Blood, supported in the arms of his disciples and, raising his hands to heaven, with a prayer on his lips, he surrendered his pure, holy soul to the Lord, in the year 6900 (1392), September 25, probably at the age of seventy-eight. After his death an ineffable sweet odour flowed from the saint's body.

The entire brotherhood gathered around him and, weeping and sobbing, laid on its bier the body of him who in life had been so noble and unresting, and accompanied him with psalms and funeral oraisons. The saint's face, unlike that of other dead, glowed with the life of the living, or as one of God's angels, witnessing to the purity of his soul, and God's reward for all his labours. His body was laid to rest within the monastery of his own creation. Many were the miracles that took place at his death and after, and still are taking place, giving strength to the weaker members of the community, deliverance from the crafts and wiles of evil spirits, and sight to the blind. The saint had no wish during his life for renown, neither in death, but by God's Almighty Power he was glorified. Angels were present at his passing into the heavens, opening for him the gates of paradise and leading him towards the longed-for blessings, into the peace of the righteous, the ever-looked-for glory of the Blessed Trinity.

ST. NILUS SORSKY

THE TEACHER OF SPIRITUAL PRAYER

(About 1433-1508)

NILUS *The great monastery of the Holy Trinity founded by St. Sergius, although set in the midst of a virgin forest, was only fifty-odd miles to the North, from the city of Moscow. The disciples of St. Sergius took different directions, founding distinct schools of spiritual life which can even be located geographically. The school later called after the name of St. Joseph of Volotsk—ascetical, liturgical, social, and disciplinarian—built monasteries in and around Moscow, or in towns directly subject to the authority of the prince of Moscow. The lovers of silence and contemplation, on the other hand, withdrew into Northern Russia, where a vast territory, almost totally uninhabited, was open to their solitary settlements. Since the series of cells and monasteries which they built extended to the North, beyond the Volga River, the hermits were called Transvolga "startzy" ("elders"), or simply Transvolgians.*

The dwelling which they preferred was a solitary cell in the wood with a small chapel nearby. But the world from which they fled overtook them in the persons of their disciples and the peasants who would settle down close by the hermit's cell, which would be gradually transformed into a monastery; then a large settlement would arise, and even, in the course of time, a town. Yet the practice of contemplation and mystical prayer did not die out in these areas, but only receded deeper into the wilderness. By far the greater proportion of Russia's canonized saints of the fifteenth century belong to the Transvolgians. No one of them, with the exception of Nilus, left any writings; to St. Nilus' treatises only a few letters of St. Cyril of Belozersk can be added. The numerous Lives which have been preserved are, for the most part, only traditional accounts of their spiritual experience. Sometimes the occurrence in a Life of one or two sentences couched in the technical terminology of Greek mysticism leads the modern scholar to the conclusion that the subject belonged to the Hesychast school of prayer. The descriptions of celestial visions, such as those in the Life of St. Sergius, confirm the induction from the religious terminology. The true "holy Russia," the mystical one, remained silent, and in this she was faithful both to her deeply instinctive kenotic humility and to the mystical appreciation of silence as the necessary school of prayer.

The only exception to this rule is St. Nilus. He left a treatise on the spiritual life and prayer based upon the Greek fathers, and a short instruction or rule for the monastic life. Some personal letters are of further assistance in the reconstruction of his moral character and his religious ideal, but there is no extant biography of this saint; his Life is supposed to have been lost in the sixteenth century. This age, as we know, suppressed the school of Nilus and could have little interest in the preservation of his memory. Not until the nineteenth century was there a revival of his cult and a fresh interest in his literary remains.

Thus biographical data concerning Nilus are very scanty. He was probably of peasant origin and surnamed Maikov. After he had renounced the world and entered the famous monastery of St. Cyril, he journeyed to Greece in order to study monastic life at its sources. Here he was initiated into the Hesychast doctrine and practice. It is highly probable that he knew Greek, although the bulk of Greek ascetical and mystical literature had already been translated into Slavonic. He returned to Russia saturated with spiritual erudition; undoubtedly he was one of the most learned men in the Russia of his day. For a time Nilus lived again in the monastery founded by Sergius' disciple St. Cyril, which was second in greatness and influence only to the Holy Trinity of St. Sergius. St. Cyril's monastery, a large cenobitical brotherhood, was the center for the contemplative hermits of Northern Russia who settled down, nearby or at a distance, in the surrounding wilderness. Nilus chose for his solitary dwelling a wild and lonely spot in the forest bordering the River Sora (whence his monastic surname), about ten miles from St. Cyril's. A handful of his disciples, or "friends," settled in huts around him, forming what is called a "skete" (or "skit"). This was the type of life of which Nilus was most in favor: neither eremitical nor cenobitical, but a middle way which avoided the disadvantages of both.

In this retreat Nilus spent the remainder of his life. That his withdrawal from the world was not complete is evidenced by the letters which he addressed to disciples, some of whom were laymen, but the only established fact in his biography is his presence, towards the end of his life, at a council held in Moscow in 1503, to which he and the other outstanding abbots (St. Joseph among them), had been invited.

In the presence of this gathering, quite unexpectedly, Nilus began to inveigh against the holding of land by monasteries, declaring that it was contrary to the principle of spiritual poverty and labor. This daring attempt at reform was obstructed by Joseph and the majority of the other abbots, and the resentment which it aroused was the main reason for the subsequent persecution of the Transvolgian hermits.

The bulk of Nilus' literary work can only with reservations be considered original. He has composed a mosaic of quotations from the Greek fathers. He provides the framework, adds his own explanations of the difficult passages, especially of philosophic definitions, and some practical exhortations. He displays no inconsiderable art in achieving a unity of this heterogeneous material, so that it reads as the work of one mind and spirit. The author has a living knowledge of his sources; obviously, he has tested his authorities in practice, and he has given an unique form to the collective experience of the praying Church.

One can distinguish among the sources of St. Nilus those which belong to the ancient monastic tradition and those which represent the later Hesychast school of mystical experience. The former, of which Nilus' main teachers in the present work are John Climacus, Nilus of Sinai and John Cassian, laid the foundations of asceticism. The latter was the Latin intermediary of the Egyptian tradition in the West, particularly recommended by St. Benedict of Nursia in his rule. In accordance with these authorities, the Russian author emphasizes, not bodily asceticism, but the interior struggle against the passions and the temptations of the mind, in the perpetual spiritual work of self-examination.

The mysticism of the Hesychasts reveals to him the positive aim of the spiritual life—the ecstatic union with God achieved by a particular method of prayer, beginning with the constant repetition of a short invocation of Jesus and ending in prayer without words, purely of the mind or spirit. The necessary condition is a specific manner of controlling respiration and the beating of the heart (perhaps after the Indian pattern). It is accompanied by the experience of ineffable joy and the vision of uncreated light, all other visions being excluded. Simeon the New Theologian, a Byzantine mystic and poet of the eleventh century, provides Nilus with the most sublime expression of the mystical love attained in the union with Jesus.

What, then, can we determine to have been the spiritual character proper to the Russian Nilus himself? Without question, he is a strong personality. Although the very depth and complexity of his nature may give the reader the impression of sharp contradictions, his character presents a finely wrought integration, but of a kind remote from the experience of the modern mind.

On the one hand, Nilus is terribly aware of the reality of sin in all its ramifications in human nature. The most natural, innocent-seeming motions of the human heart contain mortal dangers for him: devout conversations with fellow-monks defile the soul; the soul, enraptured by Divine Love, longs to hide itself in a pit, burying itself alive in order to escape the world; not only is the possession of monastic property sinful, but even the delight of the senses in the beauty of church ornaments. In repudiating the spiritual value of estheticism in liturgical worship, Nilus is unique among the Russian saints. This is the most radical direction taken by kenoticism; it verges on iconoclasm.

On the other hand, this world-denying ascetic is a great friend of liberty. He protests against the persecution of heretics. He does not wish to be called teacher or abbot by his disciples; they are his friends; he speaks, not of teaching, but of sharing the spiritual experience. He does not think highly of living authorities; the only true authority for him is the "divine writings"— by which, however, he means not Scripture only but the whole Church tradition in written form. In transcribing the lives of saints, he even tries to exercise moderate criticism. He holds the human intellect of all his readers and followers in high esteem, and as for human charity, his letters are instinct with a fiery, vibrant love which is scarcely surpassed or even equalled in all Russian religious literature. It was such characteristics as these that made Nilus the favorite saint of the Russian liberal intelligentsia.

Nilus is the consistent representative of kenoticism among the saints of Russia, but as in the case of St. Sergius, his kenoticism was purified and elevated by the Divine Love, and ennobled by lofty conceptions of human dignity and freedom.

A. THE TRADITION TO THE DISCIPLES[1]

BY THE GRACE OF OUR LORD AND SAVIOR JESUS CHRIST, AND
WITH THE ASSISTANCE OF OUR LADY, I HAVE WRITTEN A
teaching for the profit both of my soul and the souls of my lords,
who are truly related to me in the brotherhood of one spirit. I
therefore call you brothers instead of disciples. We have but one
teacher, our Lord Jesus Christ, Who gave us the Scriptures and
sent the holy apostles and the venerable fathers to teach the
way of salvation to the human race. These saints began by doing
good, only afterwards did they teach. As for me, I have done
no good whatsoever, but I expound the teaching of the Holy
Scriptures for those who desire salvation.

A great number of the devout brothers who have come to me
with the desire to live here I have sent away, because I am myself
a sinful and ignorant man, full of infirmities of soul and body.
Nevertheless those whom I reject will give me no rest, but constantly return to harass me, and this is the occasion of great
distress.

It is my conviction that if it is by God's will that we are
gathered together, then we should be faithful to the traditions
of the saints and the holy fathers and to our Lord's commandments, instead of seeking to exempt ourselves by saying that
nowadays it is impossible to live according to the Scriptures and
the precepts of the fathers. We are weak indeed, but we must
nevertheless follow, according to the measure of our strength,
the example of the blessed and venerable fathers, even though
we are unable to become their equals. And anyone who does not
hold this principle must cease to harass me, wretched sinner
that I am. I send such persons away and give them nothing, as I
have said before. I have no desire to be their master, yet they
would force me to teach them. As for those who live with us,
if they do not attend to our teaching, which we derive from
Holy Scripture, I will not answer for them, for I am not respon-

sible for their self-will. But those who have the desire to follow
our way of life freely and without worldly care, I do accept, im-
parting to them the word of God, even though I do not accomplish it myself, in the hope that with God's grace and the
prayers of those who have profited by my words, I may be in a
condition comparable to that described by John Climacus of
the Ladder when he says: [2]"Men sunk in a mire warn passers-by
of their own danger, and for the sake of those who are thus preserved, Our Lord will rescue the fallen also."

If a brother falls away from the precepts through sloth or
negligence, he must confess this to a senior, who will then correct his fault in a suitable manner. This must be done whether
the sin is committed within the cell or outside it. When a
brother leaves his cell, he must be especially cautious and adhere
to the precepts more closely. But there are many who hate to
give up their own will in the name of God and seek to justify
themselves with evasions. Of these St. John of the Ladder says:
"It is better to send them away than to allow them to act according to their own will. For if you send such a man away, you will
humble him and teach him to give up his will; but if, under the
pretext of brotherly love, you treat him with indulgence, you
will be bitterly reproached by him at the hour of death."

We have been instructed by the holy fathers to gain our daily
bread and other necessities by manual labour, as Our Lord and
His Immaculate Mother have commanded. "If any man will
not work, neither let him eat," says the Apostle. This work must
be performed indoors, for Holy Writ[3] specifies that whereas
the monks of a community may drive a pair of oxen in the open
fields in order to plough the land, this is culpable in the case of
hermits living apart from other men. If, because of physical
disability, or for some other good reason, we cannot earn a sufficient livelihood by our own efforts, we may accept a few donations from laymen, but these alms must never be excessive. It
is not to be thought of that we should take the fruit of other
men's labor by force, for then how should we, who are a prey
to our passions, be able to keep God's commandment that "if
a man will contend with thee in judgment and take away thy

coat, let go thy cloak also unto him"? We must resist and avoid like deadly poison the desire to possess earthly goods.

In buying or selling necessary commodities, we should not bargain to the disadvantage of our brother, but should prefer to suffer a loss ourselves. If we employ laymen, we should never withhold what we owe them, but should give them their pay, with our blessing, and let them go in peace. It is not good to have anything in excess. As for giving alms or lending,[4] St. Basil stipulates that this is not expected of a monk, since a man who has nothing in excess of his needs is not obliged to give. And anyone who says, under such circumstances, "I have nothing to give," is not lying, according to Barsanuphius the Great.[5] True monks are dispensed from alms-giving, since they may honestly say: "We have given up all things to follow Thee." St. Isaac[6] writes: "Non-covetousness is above charitable gifts." The monk's alms are a helpful word spoken to his brother and the spiritual advice with which he gives comfort in the time of sorrow or any other necessity. And even this applies only to monks who are able to give as much. As for novices — "their patience in bearing with the annoyances, humiliations and rebukes inflicted upon them by their brothers will be spiritual alms of a higher order than any material offerings, in proportion as the soul is superior to the body," says St. Dorotheus.[7] If a traveler visits us, let us accommodate him as well as we can. After we have given him bread with our blessing, we should allow him to go his way.

As to leaving our hermitage, this should not be done indeliberately or in indulgence of a whim, but only in case of well-established necessity. It is not proper to leave our cell without a reason or inopportunely, St. Basil tells us: "It is the duty of the superior to assign each monk his task, and he may send on various errands such monks as he sees fit. The monk who receives a commission should not withdraw from obedience to God by making his journey the occasion for laxity, but should go on his way in a sober and God-fearing manner, for his own good and that of others."

All that I have said in the present writing I wish to be observed during my lifetime as well as after my death.

In our cells, brethren and visitors should be instructed only by monks of proved merit in whose capacity to direct souls we have complete confidence; let them be men who know the art of listening and of giving useful advice. All that I have written is to be done in so far as it is pleasing to God and helpful to souls; if such is not the case, let us do something better.

With regard to the decoration of churches, St. John Chrysostom writes: "If a man wishes to donate sacred vessels or other furnishings to a church, tell him to give them to the poor. "For," he adds, "no one has ever been condemned for not decorating a church." The teaching of other saints concerning this matter is the same. St. Eugenia the Martyr, for example, would not accept the sacred vessels of silver which were brought to her, for she said that it was not proper for religious to possess silver. Therefore neither should we have gold and silver and other unnecessary ornaments in our possession, but only what is necessary to the church. The great Pachomius[8] would not even allow the interior of a church to be decorated. After he had built the church of the Mochos monastery with brick pillars of great beauty, he came to the conclusion that it was not right to admire the work of human hands and to take pride in the beauty of a building, so he tied ropes around the pillars and kept exhorting the brethren to pull hard, until the pillars began to lean and the beautiful proportions were destroyed. And he then said: "This has been done so that our infirm spirit may not fall into the snare of the devil through vainglory." If so great and saintly a man spoke and acted in this fashion, how much the more should we, who are weak-minded and enslaved by our passions, do likewise?

With regard to eating and drinking, let the practice of each monk be adjusted to his physical and spiritual capacity, avoiding satiety and greediness. We should never seek intoxication in any kind of beverage. Those who are young and healthy should chastise their body as much as they can by abstinence from

food and drink and by work. The old and the infirm may permit
themselves some relaxation.

We should keep no vessels or other valuable objects in our
cells. Likewise the hermitage and other lodgings should be built
of poor materials and left undecorated, according to the instructions of Basil the Great; indeed every article should be made
of stuff that is easily purchased and everywhere available.
Women should not be allowed to enter our monastery, nor
should we keep within our enclosure any female beast for work
or other uses.[9] We should have no youths in our service and
should beware of all beardless and womanish faces.

B. THE MONASTIC RULE

INTRODUCTION

From the writings of the Holy Fathers on "mental doing."[10]
*Wherein its profit consists and how zealously we should seek
to attain to it.*

Many of the holy fathers have spoken of the "doing of the
heart," the "guarding of the spirit," and "mental concentration," each using the words which came to him under the inspiration of divine grace; but one thing is to be understood by
these various expressions, for the writers first of all received the
divine words: "from the heart come forth evil thoughts to defile
a man; therefore we must purify the inner vessel and worship
God in spirit and truth." St. Agathon[11] says: "Bodily action is
like a leaf; interior action—that is, spiritual labor—is the fruit."
Terrible are the pronouncements quoted by the saints with
regard to this. "Every tree that does not bring forth good fruit,
shall be cut down and cast into the fire." And the fathers say,
in addition, that if prayers are only uttered by the lips, while
the spirit is negligent, it is like offering prayer to the empty air;
for God listens to the spirit. The great Barsanuphius says: "If
interior action does not fortify a man with the help of God, his
exterior labors will have been in vain." And St. Isaac writes:

"Bodily action in the absence of spiritual action may be compared to barren loins and dry breasts, for God's wisdom is inaccessible to it." Many of the fathers have made similar observations, and all are in agreement upon this point. Blessed Philotheus of Sinai[12] describes certain monks who, owing to their lack of experience, are content with performing good works, but know nothing of spiritual contests, victories and defeats, and who therefore neglect the mind; and he counsels us to pray for these monks and to teach them, while they guard themselves against evil actions, to purify the mind, which is the eye of the soul.

In the past it was not only the holy fathers living as hermits in the solitude of the desert who kept themselves under spiritual restraints and attained grace and purity of soul; this discipline was likewise maintained by monks leading a community life, and even by those who had not removed from the world but lived in large cities, such as Simeon the New Theologian, and his staretz, Simeon the Studite, of the great Studion monastery in so vast and populous a city [as Constantinople], whose spiritual gifts shone like stars. Blessed Hesychius of Jerusalem[13] says: "Just as it is impossible to preserve life without eating and drinking, so it is impossible to achieve anything spiritual without that guarding of the mind which is also called 'sobering,' even for those who force themselves to avoid sin for fear of the pain of hell." The technique of this exquisite, light-giving action, according to Simeon the New Theologian, is communicated to many souls through instruction; but there are some who are enabled by ardent faith to receive it directly from God. The same statement is made by Gregory of Sinai[14] and by other fathers who say that it is no easy task to find a sure and trustworthy teacher to guide a soul in this wonderful operation; for a trustworthy guide, they explain, must be one who is grounded in practice and wisdom tested by the holy writings, and who has acquired spiritual discretion. Even in the days of those saints such teachers were hard to find, and in our sterile times they must be sought with even greater diligence. However, if such a teacher cannot be found, then the holy fathers order us to turn to the Scriptures and listen to our Lord Himself speaking. "Study the Scriptures, and you shall find eternal life in them." For the saints, who have labored bodily and have exercised themselves in the vineyard of the soul, and have purified their minds of sensuality, have found our Lord and attained spiritual wisdom. As for us, who are inflamed with desires, we are told to draw the waters of life from the sources of the divine writings, which will quench the fires of our concupiscence and guide us towards the grasping of truth. And so, although I am a sinner confirmed in my folly, I, too, have applied myself to the Holy writings in accordance with the advice of the god-inspired fathers. Like a dog picking up scraps from under the table, I have gathered the words uttered by those blessed fathers and have written all this down as a reminder to us to be their imitators, if only in a small way.

1.

Of the different spiritual battles waged against us, of our defeats and victories and how passions should be strenuously resisted.

The fathers describe a variety of conflicts by which the soul is engaged, with their victories and defeats. First there is the assault of thoughts and imaginings, then there is conjunction with them, then acceptance, then, enslavement, and finally, passion.[15]

The assault, say the fathers, John Climacus and Philotheus of Sinai and others, is a bare thought[16] or image concerning some object or event entering our heart and presenting itself to our mind; Gregory of Sinai says that such a thought may be inspired by the devil suggesting that we do this or that, as he tempted our Lord to command that stones should be turned into bread. In simpler words, this is an ordinary thought fleeting through our minds. Such a thought, the fathers say, is no sin, for it is impossible for us to be immune from the thoughts and imaginings inspired by the devil. It is the privilege only of those who have made great progress in perfection to remain unmoved, and even they are occasionally troubled.

"Conjunction" or "intercourse" the fathers tell us, occurs when a thought or image has been suggested by the devil to a man, and he enters wilfully, with or without passion, into conversation with it; in other words, when he ponders and reflects on a thought which may happen to enter his mind. Such intercourse, the fathers say, is not always sinless; however, it may be made the occasion of merit if discrimination is employed in making the issue pleasing to God. If we do not cut off the first impulse of the evil thought, but begin intercourse with it, and the enemy makes us think of it with passion, let us then strive to turn it to good. How this should be done, will be explained hereafter, with the help of God.[17]

"Acceptance" the fathers define as the voluptuous inclination of the soul towards the thought or image which has arisen; in other words, when, after the devil's suggestion has been received, we not only enter intercourse with it, but decide in some way that the conditions suggested by our adversary should take on reality. The degree of guilt in this acceptance, the fathers say, is to be judged according to the stage of spiritual advancement which the soul has reached. If a person is in a state of progress, enjoying divine assistance in preserving recollection, and yet grows slothful and negligent in turning away evil imaginations, he will not be without sin. But one who is still inexperienced and can make but feeble efforts to divert these imaginings, and who therefore accepts them momentarily, yet immediately confesses his sin to God, repenting and reproaching himself—such a person will be forgiven by God in the name of His mercy and because of human weakness. According to the fathers, mental acceptance of this kind means that a man has been defeated against his will while wrestling with the baneful thoughts; yet he remains firmly resolved in the depths of his soul not to sin and to abstain from evil in action; but, on the other hand, it often happens that a man wilfully accepts the thoughts inspired by the enemy, enters intercourse with them and is defeated by them; then, ceasing to resist passion, he makes up his mind to commit sin. Now even if it falls out that this man is prevented from realizing his intention, either by circumstances of time or place or by some other obstacle, his sin is a grievous one subject to excommunication.

As for "enslavement," this may be either an involuntary diversion of the heart or a sustained preoccupation with certain harmful thoughts, and this is most detrimental to our high purpose.

The first—that is, involuntary diversion—occurs when the mind is captured by a thought or image and is drawn into malicious reflections against its will, but, with the help of God, returns to itself. The second occurs when, as on the waves of a storm, we are carried away from our good dispositions into evil imaginations and are unable to return to peace and tranquillity. This is most often occasioned by idle conversations and useless sociability.

Now the first kind of captivation is judged according to whether it occurs during prayer, or outside the time of prayer, and whether it is inspired by thoughts which are essentially wicked or such as are of an inferior nature. If the mind becomes enslaved by evil thoughts during prayer, this is serious sin. For at such a time, we should hold our mind in attention to our prayer, turning away from all other thoughts. But if distraction occurs outside the time of prayer and concerns such matters as are necessary for our existence, it is no sin, for the saints themselves legitimately accomplished the actions essential to their livelihood. No matter what our thoughts may be, the fathers say, if the mind is in a pious disposition, it is with God; nevertheless we must drive away all evil thoughts.

The second form of enslavement—that is, passion—is when an evil thought becomes nested in the soul and, by force of habit, is made part of a man's nature. He has admitted it by his own choice, and now he is constantly disquieted by thoughts inspired by the enemy: again and again an image which exercises upon the agitated soul, willing or unwilling, an attraction above all others, is presented to it, and a spiritual defeat is sustained. Now this usually occurs when a man has attended to this thought through negligence and has entered intercourse with it—that is, has willingly given way to improper thoughts. This is a sin which incurs either repentance in proportion to its gravity or the torments of the future life. That is, we should repent and ask in prayer for deliverance from this perturbation. For our future punishment will be incurred by our failure to repent, and not by the fact that we have been assaulted by temptations. Otherwise no one could receive forgiveness unless he were perfectly impassible.[18]

A man who is attacked by a passion must resist it vigorously, and in a way which we shall describe in speaking of the passion of lust. If he is assailed by passion concerning anyone, he should avoid that person in every way—and this applies to the person's presence and conversation, the touch of the clothing or its very fragrance. A man who does not follow this rule yields to passion and commits fornication in his mind, kindling the fires of sensuality and allowing impure thoughts to enter into him like wild beasts.

2.

Of our struggle against these temptations of the mind, which are to be vanquished through the thought of God and through the guarding of the heart, that is, through prayer and spiritual silence. And furthermore of spiritual gifts.

The fathers counsel us to put forth a resistance equal to the force of the attack, whether we are to triumph or to suffer defeat. In other words, we should fight against evil thoughts with all the energies at our command. By conflict we shall either obtain the crown of life or be led to torment—the crown, to those who conquer; the torment, to those who have sinned and have not repented in this life.

A wise and excellent means of struggle, the fathers tell us, is to uproot at the very first impulse—that is, at the assault—the thought which comes to us. They also advise us to pray constantly. For by resistance in the beginning, we cut off the whole sequence. A man who struggles in this prudent manner, turns away the mother of all evil—that is, the baneful assault. Especially should he strive to render his mind deaf and dumb in prayer, as Nilus of Sinai[19] says, keeping his heart silent and aloof from any thought whatever, even if it be a good one. For after the dispassionate thoughts come the passionate, as experience demonstrates, and it is to the entrance of the former that the latter owe their admittance. It is for this reason that we should endeavor to maintain our mind in silence, remote even from such thoughts as may seem legitimate. Let us constantly look into the depths of our heart,[20] saying: "Lord Jesus Christ, Son of God, have mercy upon me."[21] Some of the time we should repeat only part of this prayer: "Lord Jesus Christ, have mercy upon me," then again, resuming, say: "Son of God, have mercy upon me"; since, according to Gregory of Sinai, this is easier for beginners. However, due order should be observed in this, and such alternations not made too frequently. The fathers in our day add still another sentence: "Lord Jesus Christ, have mercy upon me, a sinner." This is also good, and most appropriate for us sinners. Recite the prayer attentively in this manner, standing, sitting, or reclining. Enclose your mind in your heart and, moderating your respiration so as to draw breath as seldom as possible (as Simeon the New Theologian and Gregory of Sinai teach us), call upon God with fervent desire, in patient expectation, turning away all thoughts.[22]

The saints teach us to refrain from the frequent drawing of breath because, as experience will demonstrate, this exercise is most effective in bringing the mind under control. Nevertheless, if you are unable to pray without thoughts, in the silence of your heart, and are conscious of their increase, do not lose courage, but continue to pray. In the certain knowledge that we, who are wrought upon by passion, shall experience difficulty in conquering evil thoughts, Gregory of Sinai says that no beginner can hold his mind in check and turn away the thoughts which assail him without God's help. It is the privilege of the strong to preserve control over their minds and to divert imaginations, and even they do not deflect the attacks by their own strength, but with God's assistance, armed with His grace.

If you glimpse the impurity of malignant spirits in the representations of your mind, do not fear, do not wonder, and even though they seem good to you, pay no attention to them, but forcibly restraining your breathing and gathering your mind into your heart, call Jesus Christ to your aid, arming yourself with Him, appealing to Him frequently and laboriously, and the imaginations will dissolve, burnt invisibly by the Divine Name. But should these thoughts continue to harass you, then rise to your feet to pray against them, and resume your exercises with determination. How you should pray against your thoughts I shall now further describe with the help of God.

When, despite these exercises, thoughts develop and multiply, and your mind is powerless to defend your heart, you should recite an oral prayer with intense application and patience. And if you should grow weary and sluggish, then call upon God for help and compel yourself to go on praying with all your forces, never once turning from your purpose, and the imaginings will leave you immediately with the help of God.

When you are free from such delusions, then listen once more to your heart and do the prayer of the heart or mind. For although there are many good exercises, the good of the others is partial; the prayer of the heart is the source of all good, which refreshes the soul as if it were a garden, according to Gregory of Sinai. The achievement of this action — that is, this containing of the mind within the heart, free of all imaginings—is difficult not for beginners alone, but even for experienced and well-practised souls, if the latter have not yet received and preserved the sweetness of prayer in their hearts through the effects of grace. And we know from experience that, for weak souls, it is even more arduous and painful. But one who has acquired grace prays easily and lovingly, comforted by this very grace. And when the action of prayer begins to take effect, then, as the Sinaitas says, it encompasses the mind within the heart, making it joyful and free.

The fathers say that if the mind and the body nevertheless

grow weary, and the heart begins to ache from the effort of this continual invocation of our Lord Jesus, then we may sing a little, and this will provide some relaxation. This is, in fact, an excellent rule, prescribed by wise teachers both for those who pray in solitude and those who are attended by a disciple. If you do have a faithful disciple, let him recite the psalms while you listen in your heart. But pay no attention whatever to the dreams and images which may present themselves, lest you be seduced. For dreamlike fantasies occur even when the mind is motionless in the heart, generating prayer, and only the soul that is perfect in the Holy Spirit, having achieved freedom through Jesus Christ, can exercise control over them.

One of the saints tells us from his own experience that we should concentrate all our efforts on the prayer itself, reciting psalms only to dissipate accidie,[23] or dejection, with the addition of a few penitential *troparia*[24] but without any chanting. For "the pain of the heart born of piety will suffice for their joy," says St. Marcus,[25] "and the warmth generated by the spirit will bring them comfort." St. Marcus instructs us always to say the *trisagion* and *alleluia*. He also has given us a rule for these exercises; he tells us to pray for an hour, then read for an hour, and in this manner to spend the day. This is a good practice within the limitations of time and the resources of each monk. You may do as you think best, either observing the rules given above, or practising constant recollection, which is to pursue God's work always.

But if your prayer is filled with the sweetness of divine grace, and you are conscious of its action in your heart, then it is advisable for you to persevere in it. When you are aware of the continuous action of prayer in your heart, do not interrupt it or rise for singing, for fear that it should forsake you because of your own negligence. For to leave God within you in order to appeal to Him from without is like stooping from a height. Moreover, such a distraction agitates the mind and draws it away from silence. For silence is the absence of noise; it is attained through tranquillity and peace, and God is peace beyond all noise of utterance.

On the other hand, those who do not know this prayer, which is the source of all virtues and, according to the Ladder, waters the gardens of the soul, should practise singing frequently and live according to other rules and standards. For the action of prayer in monks observing silence differs from that in the monks of a community. There is a due measure in all things, according to the sayings of wise men. When the sails of a ship are filled with wind, no oars are required to bring it across the sea of passion. But when the ship is at a standstill, we must use oars or launch a rowboat for our passage.

To those who, for the sake of controversy, cite the holy fathers with reference to celebrating the all-night service or practising continuous chanting, Gregory of Sinai permits us to make this answer: "Not all souls attain perfection in all things because of the defects of our human nature, the lack of zeal, bodily exhaustion. But what is small in the great ones is not entirely small, and what is great in the small ones is not entirely perfect; indeed, not all the ascetics of present or past have walked the same way or followed it to the end." Those who are in progress and in a state of enlightenment are not asked to recite psalms; they must practise silence, abundant prayer, and contemplation, for such souls are united with God and should not detach their mind from Him and permit it to be troubled; for the mind which turns away from the thought of God and busies itself with inferior matters commits adultery.[26]

St. Isaac, speaking sublimely of such things, writes as follows: "When men are visited by this ineffable joy, it cuts the very prayer from their lips; the mouth and the tongue are stilled; silenced are the heart, guardian of imaginings, and the mind, guide of the senses, and the thoughts, swift as boldly soaring birds. Then thought does not govern prayer, nor has it any free movement, but instead of instructing, it is itself instructed by a power which holds it captive. It dwells on things ineffable and knows not where it is."

St. Isaac calls this the awe and vision of prayer and says that it is prayer no longer. For the mind no longer communicates itself by means of prayer but is lifted above utterance. Prayer is abandoned, a superior good having been attained. The mind is in ecstasy, and knows not whether it is in the body or out of the body, as the Apostle says. St. Isaac says moreover that prayer is the seed, and this the harvest; the harvesters are stunned at a vision so incommunicable, that from a seed poor and naked such fruit of grain should suddenly have sprung.

The fathers call such a condition prayer because this great gift has its wellspring in prayer and is bestowed on the saints during prayer, but no man knows the real name for it. For when, by this spiritual operation, the soul is drawn to what is divine, and through this ineffable union becomes like God, being illumined in its movements by the light from on high, and when the mind is thus allowed a foretaste of beatitude, then it forgets itself and all earthly things and is affected by nothing. And it is said elsewhere that during prayer the mind rises above desire, entering a realm of incorporeal ideas which are inaccessible to the senses. Of a sudden, the soul is infused with joy, and this incomparable feast paralyzes the tongue. The heart overflows with sweetness, and while this delight endures a man is drawn unwittingly from all sensible things. The entire body is pervaded with such joy as our natural speech is unable to describe; all that is earthly takes on the semblance of ashes and dung. When a man is conscious of this sweetness flooding his entire being, he thinks that this indeed is the kingdom of heaven and can be nothing else. And it is said in another place that one who has discovered this joy in God, not only knows no stirring of passion, but is forgetful of his very life, since the love of God is sweeter than life, and the knowledge of God sweeter than honey, and the honey-comb, and love is born of it.

"But this is incommunicable," says Simeon the New Theologian: "What tongue could express it? What words could describe it? This is formidable, indeed, formidable; it surpasses the understanding. I behold a light which the world does not see, glowing in my cell, as I sit on my couch. Within my own being I gaze upon the Creator of the world, and I converse with Him and love Him and feed on Him, am nourished only by this vision of God, and I unite myself with Him. And I rise above heaven: this I know surely and for certain. But where, at such a time, is the body? I do not know." And further, speaking of God, Simeon the New Theologian says: "He loves me and receives me unto Himself and folds me in His embrace; while He is in heaven, He is at the same time in my heart, and I behold Him, here and there." And Simeon addresses God: "This, O Lord, shows me to be equal to the angels, and even above them, for your substance is invisible to the angels, and your nature is inaccessible to them. Yet to me you are wholly visible, and your substance is fused with my nature." It is this that St. Paul describes when he says that "eye hath not seen, nor ear heard." In this state, not only am I without desire to leave my cell, but I long to hide in a pit deep in the earth, for there, removed from the whole world, I should gaze upon my immortal Lord and Creator."

In accordance with this testimony, St. Isaac also writes: "When the veil of the passions is lifted from the eyes of the mind and a man discerns this glory, he is elevated and filled with awe. If God did not place a limit to such a state, how long would one not dwell in it? And if it were permitted to last throughout a man's life, he would never wish to turn away from this wondrous vision." But God in his mercy diminishes His grace for a while in His saints, to let them care for the brethren through preaching and example, as St. Macarius says, speaking of those who have attained perfection. And he gives this illustration: "A man is ready to stand in the twelfth degree of perfection, but grace decreases, and so he descends and stands in the eleventh degree; full measure shall not be granted to such souls, in order that they may find time to attend to their brethren."

But what shall we say of those who, in their mortal body, have tasted immortal food, who have been found worthy to receive in this transitory life, a portion of the joys that await us in our heavenly fatherland? Such men no longer look for the pleasures and sights of this world, nor do they fear its sorrows and sufferings, for now they dare to say, with the Apostle: "Who then shall separate us from the love of Christ?"

But we who are burdened with many sins and preyed upon

by passions are unworthy even of hearing such words. Nevertheless, placing our hope in the grace of God, we are encouraged to keep the words of the holy writings in our minds, so that we may at least grow in awareness of the degradation in which we wallow: of the folly in which we are engrossed, squandering our resources in worldly purposes, exposing ourselves to the dangers of the world to obtain perishable goods; for the sake of these things, we are drawn into conflict and disorder, to the damage of our souls. And we think that this activity is good and praiseworthy! But woe to us if we neglect our souls and forget our calling, as St. Isaac says, and if we come to think that this life, its joys and sorrows, has some meaning. Woe to us if, because of our sloth and relaxation, we conclude that the way of life that was suitable for the saints of old is neither right nor possible for us. No indeed, this is not so. Such practices are impossible only to those who are engulfed by passions of their own will, who have not the desire to repent sincerely and labor for God, but are absorbed in the vain preoccupations of this world. But all who do repent sincerely, God will forgive, for he favors and glorifies those who seek this goal with great love and fear. Have this only before your eyes, and obey His commandments, living constantly in prayer.

It is most expedient that we should employ ourselves in this spiritual exercise during the night. For, as blessed Philotheus of Sinai tells us, it is especially at night that the mind is capable of purification. And St. Isaac teaches that prayer offered at night is the most salutary of all, for the joy which the penitent receives during the day has its source in nocturnal exercises. And other saints are likewise of this opinion. Therefore St. John Climacus instructs us to give more time to prayer at night and less to singing. And if we grow drowsy, we should rise to our feet for prayer.

Now in this prayer, too many words disperse the mind, but a few words assist in recollection. When we are assailed by imaginings, St. Isaac advises us to turn to reading. When our mind is scattered, we should occupy ourselves more with reading than with prayer, or we should apply ourselves to some manual work, as the angel taught the great St. Anthony.[27] Manual labor, or some other assigned task, is most profitable to souls who have not had much experience of the assaults of imaginations, and especially in the course of accidie. Blessed Hesychius of Jerusalem prescribes four methods of this mental exercise: to guard oneself consciously against the impetus of thought; or to keep the heart silent in its depths, free from all imaginings, and to pray; or to call Jesus Christ to one's aid; or to think of the hour of death. All these methods, says the father, conquer evil thoughts; whichever way is chosen, all of them are called "sobering,"[28] in other words, "mental doing." Examining all these methods, each of us has to fight according to his own way.

3.

Through what means we may be fortified in repelling the attacks of evil thoughts.

There is a way of fortifying ourselves in our struggle described in all writings, and that is to keep up our courage when we are most fiercely assailed by evil thoughts, not to yield in the midst of our conflict. For it is one of the malicious devices of the devil to fill us with shame at the prospect of being defeated by evil preoccupations, so that we shall be hindered from lifting our eyes to God in contrition and praying to be freed of them. But let us, by our continual repentance and uninterrupted prayer, conquer these delusions; let us never turn our back to the enemy, even if he deals us a thousand wounds each day. And let us firmly resolve never to give up this life-giving exercise, even to our death.

For along with these trials we receive secret visitations of God's mercy. Indeed it is not only those of us who are infirm and wrought upon by passions that are subject to falls in our mind; even souls who have reached a high degree of purity and lead most exemplary lives in the places of silence under the protection of God's wisdom are liable to these falls, followed by peace and comfort and by chaste and gentle thoughts, as St. Isaac tells us. How much the more, then, shall a man who is weak and ignorant be wounded and thrust to the ground and laid bare in his helplessness? But then will come the time when this man shall take the standard from the hands of giant warriors; on that day his name is to be praised above the names of men who have won brilliant military victories, the reward which crowns his endeavors is greater than that of his companions. Of this the saints assure us with complete certainty, removing all doubt, so that we shall not falter in the battle of our minds against wicked thoughts, or fall into despair.

When we are conscious of the infusion of grace, we should not grow careless or become too easily elated, but should turn to God and thank Him, recalling the sins he has allowed us to commit; we should remember how low we fell at such a time, how bestial our thoughts became. We should also remind ourselves of the wretched condition that our nature is in, considering the impure images and the hideous idols which arose before our disordered minds during that period so lately passed when our souls were racked in blind turmoil. Understand that all this has been brought upon you by Divine Providence, to humble you. For, as blessed Gregory of Sinai says: Until a man has experienced forsakenness and defeat, until he has been wounded and enslaved by every passion and conquered by the thoughts of his mind, so that he can find help neither in his own powers nor in God, nor in anything else, and is driven to the brink of despair with no avenue of escape: until then no man can have true contrition, nor can he realize that he himself is the least of slaves, more evil than the very fiends that have beset him and conquered him. But this is an exemplary humiliation effected by Providence for our instruction. And souls who have suffered it are granted a second favor: they are elevated by an infusion of power from God, in the name of which they can do all things, even to the working of miracles, always in the consciousness that they are His instruments. Take warning! If you will not humble your mind, grace will abandon you, and you will fall in real life after you have been tempted in your mind by mere thoughts. For it is not your doing that you stand in virtue, but the effect of grace, which holds you in God's hand and preserves you from all your enemies.

4.

General Conduct of Our Life

We must observe this general rule in our life: to be about the work of God perpetually, and in every undertaking, in body and soul, in word, thought, and action, according to the measure of our strength.

When we rise from sleep, we must first of all glorify God and make our confession to Him, and then we must turn to prayer, chanting, reading, manual labor, and various minor occupations. We must continually keep our mind in a disposition of great reverence, piety and trust in God, and do all we can to please Him, and not for the sake of vainglory or to please other men; for we know for certain that God is with us, since He is everywhere and fills everything. He Who has created the ear, hears all, and He Who has created the eye, sees all. If you enter into conversation, let it be one that will please God; refrain from murmuring, from judging others, from idle words and quarrels. Also, take food and drink with the fear of God. Most of all during sleep, be piously recollected, and let your body recline in decency. For our sleep is the fleeting image of the eternal sleep—that is, of death—and resting on your couch prefigures lying in your coffin.

Let him whose body is healthy mortify it with fasting, vigils and strenuous labor. Our movements during work, and our genuflections, must be made with energy, so that the body may be mastered by the soul and freed from sensuality by the grace of Christ. But if the body is sick, it should be treated according to its weakness. As for prayer, it should never be neglected, whether the body is healthy or ill. Even when we are engaged in necessary occupations, our minds should be secretly absorbed in prayer and filled with the fear of God. Physical work is required of those whose bodies are robust, according to the strength of the individual. But the work of the mind, which consists in preserving the disposition of fear and trust and love of God, should be pursued by everyone, even in the event of serious illness. Likewise we must love our neighbors in obedience to our Lord's commandments. To those who are close to us, we should show our love in word and deed, uniting it with our love of God. And to those who are far from us, we should unite ourselves spiritually, effacing all antagonism towards them; let us humble our souls before them and serve them by our good will. For if God sees this, He will forgive our sins and accept our prayers as worthy offerings, and He will send us the riches of His Grace.

5.

Of the different ways of fighting and conquering the eight principal temptations, those of the flesh and others.

The fathers tell us that there are various methods of resisting the temptations of the mind and various ways of defeating them, according to the strength of the one who struggles: one may either pray against evil thoughts or enter into contention with them, or else turn them away by contempt. The last method is that of the most perfect souls. As for contending with our thoughts, this too is a method suitable to those who are in progress. Beginners and weak souls should pray, evoking good thoughts against evil imaginings, for St. Isaac teaches that passions should be circumvented by the guile of virtues. When we are assailed by delusions, so that we cannot pray humbly and in interior silence, we should take arms against them, displacing evil thoughts by good ones. And how this can be done, we shall further explain from the holy writings. The fathers say[29] that there are eight principal vices of the soul, of which numerous temptations are the offspring; these are: Gluttony, Fornication, Covetousness, Anger, Sadness, Accidie, Vainglory, and Pride.

FIRST VICE: *Gluttony*

When we are besieged by thoughts tempting us to gluttony, either by the alluring imagination of various delicious foods or by the desire to eat more than we need and at improper times, we should first of all call to mind the words of Scripture which instruct us not to burden our hearts with an excess of eating and drinking. And we should pray, imploring God to come to our aid and pondering the writings of the fathers, who teach us that in a monk gluttony is the root of all other evils and especially of fornication.

Of the Measure To Be Observed in Food—The fathers teach us that the measure to be observed in food should be determined in the following way: if a monk discovers that the amount of food which he has permitted himself in the course of a day causes him any feeling of heaviness, he shall immediately reduce it. But if he sees that this quantity is not sufficient to sustain his energies, he shall increase it. And when he has gained the necessary experience in this manner, he should fix upon an amount of food that will preserve his body, eating not for the pleasure involved but out of strict necessity. And he should be satisfied with this and thank God for it. But at the same time he should realize that he has done nothing to merit even this small measure of bodily comfort. It is impossible to make one rule for everyone, since the physical capacities of individuals differ as sharply as copper and iron differ from wax. As a general rule, a novice should rise from his meal still somewhat hungry; yet if he feels satisfied, this is no sin. But if he has reached satiety, he should reproach himself for it and thus turn his failure into a victory.

Of the Time When Food Should Be Taken—Now with regard to the duration of the daily abstinence from food: the fathers prescribe fasting until the ninth[30] hour. Anyone who wishes to fast longer, may do so. As a general rule, we should wait until the decline of day—that is until two hours after noontime according to the sun. This is the ninth hour in spring and autumn, but in summer and in winter, in northern countries, the hours of sunrise and sunset are different from those in the countries around the Mediterranean, in Palestine and Constantinople. Therefore we should fast in accordance with the season and the rule of right reason. On the days when no fasting is prescribed, we may advance the hour of meals and if necessary partake of a small collation in the evening.

Of Different Kinds of Food—Concerning the various kinds of food: we should take a little of everything, even sweets. This is a wise rule, says Gregory of Sinai. We should never pick and choose or push our food aside, but should thank God for everything and perfect ourselves in humility. We shall thus avoid the pride which disdains the good fruit created by God. Nevertheless it is useful for those who are weak in faith or unstable to abstain from certain meats, especially the palatable ones, because they have not enough faith in the protection of God; the Apostle says: "For one believeth that he may eat all things, but he that is weak, let him eat herbs."

SECOND VICE: Fornication

The conflict which we must undergo with the vice of fornication is especially painful and fierce, for it engages both body and soul. Therefore we should strive ceaselessly and with all our strength to keep our heart sober and free of sensuality. This is most imperative during the Mass, when we are about to receive Holy Communion, for it is then that the enemy essays every sort of device in order to soil our conscience. When these thoughts of fornication attack us, we should hold ourselves fearfully in the presence of God, remembering that nothing, not even the subtlest movement of our heart, can be hidden from Him, and that He will be our judge and prosecutor. We should also keep in mind the vows we have taken before angels and men, to preserve purity and chastity. These vows bind us, not in our exterior conduct alone, but in the secret depths of our interior. A heart free from impure thoughts is most honorable and pleasing in the sight of God.

Those who permit the befouling thoughts of fornication to frequent their minds, fornicate in their hearts, the fathers assert. Moreover, it sometimes ensues that the sin is actually committed. In that event, the consequent disaster may well give us pause; for it is this sin, and no other, that is so often spoken of by the fathers, who call it the fall, because it deprives the sinner of hope and leads him to despair.

When we are harried by the temptation to fornication, I believe that it is salutary also to think of our monastic state; for we have assumed the form of angels,[31] and how can we trample on our conscience and defile this holy form with such an abomination? We may likewise picture to ourselves the shameful and scandalous example that we should present to the eyes of men, and this too might help us to resist these unworthy thoughts. For should we not rather die than be seen in this shameful condition? Thus the means by which, with zeal and perseverance, these wicked thoughts may be cut off are various.

When the assault is particularly violent, however, we should rise to our feet, and lifting our eyes and extending our arms, we should pray, as Gregory of Sinai instructs us, and God will disperse these evil imaginings. St. Isaac suggests the following prayer: "Thou art mighty, O Lord, and this is Thy battle. Do Thou wage it and gain the victory for us." It is with the name of Jesus that we must lay siege to our enemy, for no weapon is as powerful, either on earth or in heaven. The fiend selects for his most furious attacks the time when we feel unable to pray. Oh monk, take warning, and never fail to pray during these assaults in the manner we have described!

There are other times when, in remorse of conscience, we take these thoughts of fornication as a subject of meditation to reproach ourselves for having desires which bring us close to the beasts—although the unnatural lust by which we are worried is most uncommon among animals! However, novices should guard themselves even against these meditations, for fear that they should linger upon such thoughts in the belief that they are struggling against them, whereas in reality they are succumbing to passion. Therefore it is best to cut off all impulses to thoughts of this kind. Only the strong may entertain them for salutary examination.

Avoid all conversation with women, and indeed the very sight of them; shun youthful, beardless and effeminate faces, for the devil lays these snares for monks. If it can possibly be avoided, never be alone with such persons, however necessary it might seem, St. Basil the Great tells us. For, as the father goes on to explain, nothing is more essential than the soul for which Christ died and rose from the dead. Nor should we listen to improper conversations, for they stir the passions.

THIRD VICE: *Covetousness*

Covetousness, the fathers teach us, is contrary to nature; it issues from stupidity and lack of faith. Therefore it may be fought off without much difficulty by a man filled with the fear of God and sincere in his desire for salvation. Yet once covetousness has taken root in us, it is the worst of all vices; if we succumb to it, it brings us to perdition. Indeed the Apostle has said that it is not only the root of all sins—anger, sadness, and the others—but is in itself idolatry. The fathers say that a man who sets store by the gold and silver he can amass does not believe that there is a God who provides for him. And the holy writings declare that if a man is enslaved by pride or covetousness, the devil need seek no further weapon against him, for either of these passions will suffice to accomplish that man's destruction. We must restrain our desires not only for gold and other riches, but also for all other things beyond our essential needs. We must not covet clothes and footwear or the accommodations of our cells or vessels or any kind of implement. We may use only such things as have no intrinsic value, are unembellished and easily acquired. Nothing we have should be such as will give rise to comment, lest we be exposed to the seductions of the world. For covetousness has been genuinely conquered, not when we possess nothing, but when, in addition, we have no desire to possess anything. Thus do we learn to be pure of spirit.

FOURTH VICE: Anger

When the spirit of anger assails us, we are moved to remember the wrongs done us and to take revenge on the offenders. At such times we should bring to mind the divine words: if we will not forgive from our heart the brother who has wronged us, even so, our Heavenly Father will not forgive us our sins. Moreover, we should be aware that even though we believe ourselves to be acting justly, if we do not guard ourselves against anger, we offend God. For the fathers say that even if an angry man should bring the dead to life, his prayer would not be accepted. The fathers do not mean by this that an angry man actually could restore life to the dead; they are only trying to represent the abomination that such a man's prayer is. This is why we should not give way to anger or injure our brother by any word or action—not even by a look, for a mere glance may be an injury to him, according to the fathers. Therefore let us turn away all thought of anger from our mind.

"Now this is forgiveness from the heart; this, the great victory over the spirit of anger: to pray for the brother who has offended you," says Abba Dorotheus. And we should pray as follows: "O Lord, help my brother (name) and forgive me, a sinner, for the sake of that brother's prayer." It is an act of charity and mercy to pray for our brother; and to ask for the help of his prayers is humility. Furthermore, one should do him kindnesses, as far as possible. In this manner shall God's commandment be obeyed: "love your enemies; do good to them that hate you; and pray for them that persecute and calumniate you." To those who obey this commandment, God has promised a reward above all others: not only a kingdom in heaven or a particular comfort or gift, but the sonship of God: "That ye may be children of your Father who is in heaven." Our Lord Jesus Christ, Who gave us this commandment and promised us this great reward, has given us an example in order that we might imitate Him, each within the measure of his strength.

FIFTH VICE: *Sadness*

It is in no mean contest that we must engage the spirit of sadness, for this temptation can drive us to despair and perdition. Nothing that happens to us is contrary to the will of Providence, and everything that is sent us by God is for our good and the salvation of our soul. Even if it does not seem beneficial at the present moment, we shall understand later that it is what is willed by God, and not what we ourselves desire, that is useful to us. God sends us trials out of His mercy, so that after we have suffered these ordeals we may be crowned by Him. Without temptation, no one has ever been crowned. This is why we should offer thanks for all this to God, as our Benefactor and Savior. "Lips that utter frequent thanksgivings shall be blessed by God, and the grateful heart is visited by grace," says St. Isaac. We should abstain from murmuring against those who have offended us. Although God bears with all the weaknesses of men, he will not tolerate one who is forever complaining, but will punish him.

There is, of course, a wholesome kind of sadness which is inspired by our sins and is associated with contrition and trust in God. Since we know that there is no sin which overreaches God's mercy, which He cannot forgive in those who repent and pray, this sadness is shot through with joy; it prepares a man for all that is good and enables him to bear misfortune patiently.

The other kind of sadness, which is inspired by the devil, should be vigorously dispelled from our heart along with the other evil passions. If this sadness takes root in us, it will rapidly overwhelm the soul with despair, rendering it empty and dejected, impatient and weak, lazy in prayer and in reading.

SIXTH VICE: *Accidie*

When accidie has become firmly rooted in us, a great battle must be waged by the soul. This cruel, oppressive spirit is either combined with the spirit of sadness or follows after it, and its especial victims are the hermits. When fierce waves of this passion rise and sweep through a man's heart, he cannot think that he will ever be free of it; for the enemy inspires him with the thought that if he endures this suffering today, it will increase in the days that follow, because God has forsaken him and is indifferent to his need. Or else the man believes that he suffers this in spite of Divine Providence, that he alone suffers in this manner, no one else. But no, this is not so. Not on us sinners alone, but on His very saints, who have pleased Him, does God inflict this spiritual rod, like a loving father chastising his children in order to increase their virtue.

But presently a change comes, and we are comforted by the touch of God's mercy. And when this alteration comes about in a man, he realizes all the benefits he has received, and the sufferings he has undergone appear to him as nothing. He zealously sets about the task of growing in holiness, and wonders at his alteration and his progress. Now he fervently hopes never to stray from the path of virtue; he understands that God has sent him this ordeal for his profit and instruction, and out of His love. And so this man is inflamed with the love of God, since he knows for certain that God is faithful and never sends us a temptation which surpasses our strength. As to the enemy, he can do us no harm without God's permission.

Nothing furthers a monk's advancement in grace as much as the spirit of accidie, St. John of the Ladder declares, provided that he strenuously and unfalteringly pursues his spiritual exercises. But when the contest becomes fierce, we should strongly arm ourselves against the spirit of ingratitude and blasphemy. For at such a time the enemy avails himself of all these devices, so that a man is penetrated by doubt and fear. And the fiend whispers in his ear that it is impossible for him to obtain God's forgiveness and the remission of his sins, to be spared the pain of hell and gain heaven. And many other evil thoughts join forces in this assault, which cannot be recorded. These thoughts do not leave a monk, whether he reads or recites the Office.

It is now that we must resist despair with the utmost fortitude. and coerce ourselves into prayer, with all the forces at our command. If possible we should prostrate ourselves and pray in the fashion prescribed by the great Barsanuphius: "O Lord, behold my dejection and have mercy on me, a sinner." Simeon the New Theologian advises the recitation of the following prayer: "O Lord, do not permit temptations and sufferings to exceed my strength, but set me at liberty, so that I can endure this with gratitude." From time to time, raise your arms, extending your hands to heaven, praying in the way that Gregory of Sinai recommends for one in the grips of this passion. For he says that the spirits of fornication and accidie are the most savage of all.

Moreover, persevere in reading with as close attention as possible, and occupy yourself with manual labor, for this is of great help during such an ordeal. It sometimes happens, however, that accidie does not leave us even during this occupation. Then we must pour all our energies into our will to pray. Against the spirit of ingratitude and blasphemy, we should pray as follows: "Begone, Satan, I will adore my Lord God, and Him alone will I serve; I will accept with gratitude all the suffering and dejection sent to me for the healing of my sinfulness. May your ingratitude and blasphemy return to you, Satan. The Lord will say to you: 'Begone, God has created me in His image and likeness, that you may be destroyed.' "

God never abandons a soul that puts its trust in Him, even though it is overpowered by temptations, for He is aware of all our weaknesses. A man knows the weight that can be placed on the back of an ass, a mule or a camel, and burdens each beast with as much as it can carry; the potter knows how long he must keep his clay in the fire, for if he exposes it too long to the flames, the pot will crack, and if he does not bake it long enough, it will not be fit for use. Now if a man has judgment as precise as this, how infinitely greater is the wisdom of God in judging the degree of temptation which a soul is able to bear?

With this knowledge, we should suffer our trials courageously, within doors and in silence. Nevertheless there will be times when we need to converse with a man who is experienced in the spiritual life and prudent in his words. St. Basil the Great has this to say concerning the matter: "Often, when our heart is filled with accidie, we can disperse these thoughts by leaving our cell and entering into innocent and measured conversation.

Strengthened and refreshed, we may then return with greater zeal to our pious struggles." But if we are able to suffer this ordeal in silence and without leaving our cell, this is even better, the fathers assure us from their own experience.

SEVENTH VICE: Vainglory

We must exercise ourselves vigilantly against the spirit of vainglory, for it steals away our good resolutions with many allurements; it impedes the monk's progress by corrupting his actions, so that instead of being ordered to God, they are motivated by vanity and the desire to please men. That is why we should constantly probe our thoughts and feelings, so that our actions may be in harmony with God's will; we should shun what is human, keeping in mind the words of David: "God hath scattered the bones of them that please men."

This should be our method: when tempted to vainglory, we should weep and bring the Last Judgment to mind by special prayers if we know any; if not, we should think of the hour of death and repress all shameful ambitions. And if we are unable to do this, let us then think of the humiliation that follows upon ambition. For, as St. John of the Ladder remarks, he who exalts himself shall be humbled even in this life. If someone begins to praise us, or if our invisible enemy precipitates us into vainglory with the suggestion that we deserve the honors due to greatness and the position of highest authority, let us quickly recall the number and the gravity of our sins, or else select one sin in particular, which is especially serious, and ask ourselves whether anyone who has sinned in this way deserves to be praised. And if we have nothing with which to reproach our conscience, let us meditate on perfection, and we shall see ourselves as inadequate as a small fountain compared to the immensity of the sea. And so we must strive perpetually to guard ourselves against vainglory. If we are not sobered by our reflections, but are frequently stirred by vainglorious thoughts, our insolence will grow inveterate, giving birth to pride, which is the beginning and end of all evil.

EIGHTH VICE: *Pride*

What shall we say of arrogance and pride? Although the
terms which the fathers use in describing the sin of pride vary—
presumptuousness, haughtiness, conceit, and the like—they all
refer to the same thing. Whatever form this sin may take, it is
the greatest of iniquities. Holy writings say that God resists the
proud, that a haughty man is repulsive in His sight. Now if a
man has God for an adversary and is foul in his sight, from what
source can he hope to obtain any benefit? Who is there to forgive his sin and purify him? It is painful even to speak of this.
For anyone who falls prey to this sin is an enemy to himself,
a devil who carries his destruction inside him.

It is for this reason that we should tremble with fear of the
passion of pride and flee from it, taking refuge in the certitude
that no good whatever can be done without God's help. Remember that when God forsakes us we are like leaves, or dust,
swirling in the wind, in which the fiend buffets us with insults,
so that other men weep at the sight of us. Since we realize this,
it behooves us to preserve our humility.

And this is the very first rule: Let us consider ourselves to be
beneath everyone else, the least among men, the most perverse
of all creatures, since we are addicted to unnatural vices, in a
worse state than the devils who take us by force. And this is
what we should do: Choose the last place at meals and other
gatherings with our brethren; wear the poorest clothes and prefer the most menial tasks; upon meeting a brother, bow low and
devoutly before him; love silence; have no desire to shine in conversation, nor any delight in discussions; avoid insolence and
ostentation. Do not try to put in a word of your own, even if
you think it a good one. For the fathers say, in speaking of the
novice, that the inner man is formed according to exterior actions. And St. Basil the Great observes that when a man is unguarded as to his exterior, we have no reason to believe that his
interior disposition is good.

The pride of monks is discussed as follows in the holy writings: If a man has undergone considerable suffering for the sake

of his many undertakings and good works, he is tempted by the spirit of pride because of the piety of his life. And if pride is based upon the good name of the monastery[32] and the number of the brethren, the fathers call this worldliness. Pride may also be occasioned by the acquiring of land and other property, or even, in the case of certain monks today, by success in the world —what shall we say of them? Yet there are others who have nothing to be proud of but their proficiency in the art of chanting, reading aloud, or reciting the Office. But what praise do they deserve from God for the natural gifts which they could not have acquired by their own efforts? Then there are those who pride themselves on their handicraft, and they are like these others. Some monks are proud of belonging to families who are powerful in the world, or of being related to distinguished men, or of having enjoyed honor and rank themselves when they were still in the world. This is the height of folly. Such distinctions should be concealed. It is greatly to be deplored that those who have renounced the world should have an appetite for the honor and glory received from men. They should be ashamed instead of proud, for their prominence is disgraceful. But those who are harassed by thoughts of pride because of their pious life have no resort but the prayer: "My Lord God, take the spirit of pride away from me, and give Thy servant the spirit of humility."

6.

Of Vices in General

Against all harmful thoughts we should invoke God's assistance, for we cannot always resist them by force. Moreover this should be done deliberately, not in any way that occurs to us, but by the name of God and in accordance with the methods described in the holy writings. Addressing ourselves to each vice, we should say: "May God forbid you entrance." And again: "Depart from me, all of you, workers of iniquity. Turn back, all you wicked thoughts, so that I may be instructed in God's commandments."

Let us avail ourselves of the example of that holy staretz who used to say: "Depart, evil one; come, beloved!" Once a brother who overheard his words and supposed that the staretz was speaking to another man asked him: "With whom are you conversing, father?" And the staretz answered: "I am driving away evil thoughts and calling the good ones to my side." And so, if we are tempted, let us use the words of that staretz, or others like them.

7.

Of the Thought of Death and of the Last Judgment. How we should learn to keep this thought in mind.

The fathers say that in our mental prayer the thought of death and the Last Judgment is most salutary and effective. Philotheus of Sinai prescribes a definite rule. In the morning, we should spend the time before our meal in thinking of God—that is, in praying and holding our heart in recollection. Then, after we have said grace, our thoughts should turn to death and judgment. The Great Anthony, the first of the fathers, says that we should constantly preserve the disposition which we should have if we were not going to live through the day. And St. John of the Ladder says that if we think of our last hour, we shall never sin. And in another place he commands us to keep the thought of death always with us. St. Isaac the Syrian writes: "Man, may you always carry in your heart the thought that you will pass away. Not the fathers alone, but the teachers of profane philosophy also, teach us to remember death."

How can we, who are weak and sensual, learn to keep this thought in mind?—that is, so far as our human limitations permit, for, as St. Isaac says, to be fully occupied with this thought is a gift of God and a marvellous grace. I think that it helps if we bring to mind various deaths that we have witnessed or have heard of, or which have occurred in our time. For it is not only among laymen that unexpected death is common. Monks in excellent circumstances, who were attached to this life and hoped to live for a long time, since they had not yet reached old age, have been suddenly harvested by death. And some among them had no time in their hour of death to say even the prayers of the dying, but fell where they were standing or sitting; others died as they were eating and drinking; and still others were walking, and fell dead, or they passed away in their bed, where they were seeking a brief rest for their bodies and fell into eternal sleep. There were some who in their last hour were visited by awful visions. Such reflections will suffice to fill us with fear. They will inspire us with such thoughts as these:

"Where, at this hour, are the friends and acquaintances we made on earth? What if some of them were famous and eminent, rulers in this world? Has not all this corrupted into ashes and stench? This life is like a cloud of dust that is seen for a moment and then is gone, for it is less substantial than a cobweb, as St. Chrysostom says. Now a traveler, preparing for a journey, may wish to visit this or that country, and he goes there; and if he changes his mind, he does not go. And when he stops at an inn, he knows, when he enters it, at what time he intends to leave; he comes in the evening and goes in the morning; or, if he wishes, he may stay on at the inn. But whether we will it or not, we have to leave this life, and we know not when. Death's awful mystery comes upon us suddenly, and soul and body are violently severed, divorced from their natural union by the will of God.

What shall we do at that hour if we have not thought of it beforehand, if we have not been instructed concerning this eventuality and find ourselves unprepared? In that bitter hour we shall grasp in full the ordeal which the soul must undergo when it is separated from the body. Alas, what anguish it experiences at that hour, and there is no one to take pity on it. It looks up to the angels and prays in vain. It stretches out towards men and there is no one to help it; there is nothing but the good it has done in God's sight.

We look upon the coffin, and we see our created beauty become hideous and abominable, its shapeliness gone. And as we gaze at the naked bones, let us say to ourselves: "Who is this skeleton?—king or beggar, hero or outcast? Where is the beauty and delight of the world? Is not all become hideousness and stench? All that was honored and desired on earth has become useless. Like a flower withering, like a shadow passing, all that is human awaits destruction."

And we should also keep in our minds the thought of Our Lord's second coming and our resurrection and the Last Judgment, foretold in the very words of God by the inspired voice of St. Matthew: "And immediately after the tribulation of those days, the sun shall be darkened and the moon shall not give her light and the stars shall fall from heaven and the powers of heaven shall be moved. And then shall appear the sign of the Son of man in heaven. And then shall all tribes on the earth mourn; and they shall see the Son of man coming in the clouds of heaven with much power and majesty. And He shall send His angels with a trumpet and a great voice; and they shall gather together his elect from the four winds, from the farthest parts of the heavens, to the utmost bounds of them."

Brethren, what can plunge us into bitterer dread and remorse than the vision of that terrible judgment, when we shall witness the sinners who have never repented being sent to eternal torment by God's righteous judgment, trembling and crying out and weeping in vain. How can we restrain our own cries as we picture to ourselves the dreadful torments described in Scripture—everlasting fire, the outer darkness, the fathomless abyss, the dragon, cruel and ever-vigilant, the gnashing of teeth, all the tortures in store for those who have sinned and have angered God by their malicious dispositions, and I am the first among these wretches! My brethren, who can possibly describe the dreadful majesty of the second coming of our Lord and the horror of this unbribable judgment? Certain fathers have said that were it possible to die at that hour, then the whole world would die of fear.

It is for this reason that we should preserve holy fear and keep the thought of the judgment in our mind. And if our heart is reluctant to ponder upon these things, we should nevertheless constrain it to do so, addressing ourselves to our soul in the following words: "Alas, miserable soul, the time of your departure from this life is close by. How much longer will you defer the renunciation of your ways and lie in abasement? Why will you not ponder upon the terrible hour of death?"

O Lord, have mercy on my soul which has been wounded by the passions of this life, and receive it, cleansed by contrition and confession. And may Thy power conduct me until Thy judgment is at hand. When Thou shalt descend upon earth with glory, O Lord, and sit upon Thy throne, O merciful One, in order to execute Thy judgment, we shall stand before Thee, naked, like the condemned. On that day, most gracious One, do not expose my secret thoughts, do not disgrace me in the eyes of the angels and of men, but spare me, O God, and have mercy on me. For I meditate on Thy terrible judgment, most gracious Lord, and the day of my trial before Thee fills me with fear and trembling. My conscience condemns me and the evil I have done fills me with the sharpest remorse, and I am seized with confusion when I ask myself how I shall answer Thee, Immortal King, I who have incurred Thy wrath. How shall I dare to lift my eyes to Thee, base fornicator that I am? Yet, O Lord, Glorious and merciful Father, only-born Son and the Holy Ghost, do Thou forgive me and save me on that day from the undying fire; and mercifully permit me to stand at Thy right hand, O equitable Judge!

8.

Of Tears. What the acts should be of those who wish to acquire this gift.

Now if, in the course of the foregoing practice, and during other, similar exercises of prayer and meditation, we have been moved to tears by the grace of God, we should not restrain our

weeping. For the fathers tell us that by our tears we may be
preserved from the eternal fire and other torments. And if we
are unable to weep, we should at least seek painfully to shed a
few tears. Indeed, as St. John Climacus assures us, our good
Judge judges tears, like all other things, according to a man's
natural capacity: "I have seen men shedding a few tears as if
they were blood, with tremendous effort, whereas I have observed others whose tears flow painlessly, like a torrent. And I
judge not according to the tears, but by the effort entailed, and
it seems to me that God does the same."

Now if we cannot force out the smallest tear because of our
weakness or our negligence, or for some other reason, we should
not fall away or be discouraged. Let us grieve and sigh, deplor-
ing our insufficiency in this endeavor, but keeping up our hope,
for grief of mind is superior to bodily actions, as St. Isaac tells
us. It may be that the absence of tears is due to fatigue, as St.
Isaac goes on to say. This is experienced not only by those who
are seeking the gift of tears, but even by those who have acquired
it; the flow of their tears may stop, and their fervor may diminish because of bodily exhaustion. St. Simeon the New Theologian writes of these things with great subtlety: "It is not
salutary to war against nature; if you force the body to accomplish a thing that is above its strength, weakness ensues." "Confusion increases in the soul, and it grows more troubled than
before," writes St. Isaac, and many other fathers agree with him.

But what they mean is genuine weakness, not that false ener-
vation which has its source in our mind. It is good to employ
force against that, according to St. Simeon. This father, as well
as the others who have treated the subject, gives us the following instruction: "If our soul is in such a disposition, it will not
be impossible to produce tears. As to those of us who are incapable of attaining a great measure in these things, let us try
to accomplish at least a little, and let us ask this of our Lord
God with a contrite heart. For the fathers say that the grace
of tears is one of the greatest gifts, and that we should beseech
God to confer it on us." Blessed Nilus of Sinai teaches that we
should pray for this gift before all others, and blessed Gregory,

the most holy Pope of Rome, writes: "If a man has persevered in good deeds and has deserved other gifts, but has not received the gift of tears, he should pray to obtain it, either through the fear of judgment or through the love of the kingdom of heaven; for in the first case, those who have done evil shall weep, and in the second, those great souls who are filled with ardent love shall enter the heavenly kingdom." And other saints have written accordingly.

There are some men who have not yet acquired the gift of tears in its plenitude, and who may obtain it in different ways: either by contemplating the mystery of God's Providence, or by reading about the lives of the saints, their labors and teachings, or merely by reciting the prayer of Jesus or other prayers composed by the saints, for in this manner they will attain to contrition. Still others may reach this condition by reading the prayer-canons[33] and the *troparia*[34] or by recalling their sins, or by thinking of death and the day of judgment, or by longing for the joys of eternity, and in many other ways.

And if a man acquires the gift of tears by one of these methods, he should retain this disposition so long as the tears have not ceased to flow. Simeon the New Theologian says: "The virtues may be compared to an army, and contrition and tears to a king and a general; for they arm us and encourage us, and teach us to struggle against the enemy in all our enterprises, and they guard us against hostile forces. Even when our mind is absorbed in thoughts which are unsuitable or inspired by the enemy, or if we have been excited to tears by something heard or seen or by feelings of natural love and vain grief, we should convert these emotions into a salutary exercise: to praising God, to confession, or to the thought of death and judgment; and so doing, let us weep. For to pass from unvirtuous, or natural, tears to spiritual ones is a meritorious action."

Now if the movement of contrition arises spontaneously in the soul and tears likewise come without our willing them, this is God's action in us, and these are tears of piety. We should cherish them as the apple of our eye and yield ourselves to them until they leave us; for these tears have a greater power to destroy

sin and vices than the tears brought about by our own effort
and study. And when, as the result of concentration—that is,
keeping guard over the heart—spiritual action is manifested
in prayer by the grace of God, kindling the heart and diffusing
its glow throughout our being, comforting the soul, inflaming
us with an ineffable love of God and men, delighting the mind
and producing joy and interior sweetness—then tears flow
freely and without our effort, springing forth, as St. John
Climacus describes it, like those of an infant weeping and
smiling at the same time.

May God deign to send us such tears, for since we are beginners and inexperienced, there is no greater comfort for us
than this gift. And when it is increased in us, through the grace
of God, then our conflicts are eased and our imaginings quieted,
and the mind is abundantly fed and delighted with prayer, and
the heart distills an ineffable complacence which flows through
the whole body, and relaxes the pain of our limbs in sweet repose. "This is the comfort of mourning," says St. Isaac, in confirmation of Our Lord's words, "and it is given to each individual in the measure of the grace that is in him. Then a man
rests in a joy unattainable in this world, and no one can taste of
it, except those who have given all the powers of their soul to
this spiritual exercise."

9.

*Of renunciation and true detachment from all care, which
means dying to all things.*

The condition of this wonderful practice is the renunciation
of all care, which means dying to all things. According to the
great fathers, who have attained wisdom and are experienced
in the practice of prayer, it entails active concentration on the
task of God alone. St. Basil the Great says that the beginning
of purity of heart is silence. And St. John Climacus further defines silence as first of all, detachment from concern with regard

to necessary and unnecessary things; second, as assiduous prayer; and third, as the unremitting action of prayer in the heart.

Now St. John Climacus does not call necessary those things which are generally considered to be such in our time, as, for example the acquisition of land and the maintenance of many properties, and other worldly involvements; these in reality are unnecessary. By things necessary, St. John means conversations with good and spiritual fathers and brothers, which we may believe to be conducive to our spiritual improvement. But even conversations of this kind should be pursued within measure and at suitable times, for if we are unguarded in this matter, we shall involuntarily be drawn into needless turmoil. Nevertheless we do call these conversations necessary. Now unnecessary conversations are quarrels, discussions, complaints, accusations, humiliating remarks, rebukes, and the like which may arise during conversations of the previous sort—that is, the necessary ones.

St. Isaac gives the following instruction to those who want to observe true silence and to purify the mind through prayer: "Retire from the sight of the world and cut off conversations; do not let friends enter your cell, even under the pretext of a well-meaning visit, unless they have the same spirit and intention as yourself and are likewise practising mystical prayer. Fear promiscuity between souls—against this we can warn from experience. For after we have emerged from intimate conversations, even when they have seemed to be good, our souls are troubled against our will, and these preoccupations continue with us for a long time. Therefore it is unnecessary and imprudent, even in the case of persons whom we love and who are dear to us, to exchange words that may subsequently trouble us, disturbing our recollection and hindering the operation of mystical understanding."

O brothers, how many who break their silence are tempted! Even as a garden is withered by frost, so human conversations, though they be within bounds and seemingly good, wither the flowers of virtue that blossom tenderly in the atmosphere of silence, pervading with fragrance the garden of the soul which has been gently and freshly planted and watered with the rising fount of repentance. And if the conversation of those who are under discipline, yet deficient in it, troubles the soul, how much greater is the disturbance which results from our intercourse with the obtuse and uninitiated, to say nothing of the worldly. For just as wine loosens the tongue of a decent man, so that, forgetting his good reputation, he disgraces himself, and is laughed at for the outlandish thoughts which his intoxication causes him to express, so human entanglements diminish purity of spirit; the soul neglects to guard itself against desires, and its steadfastness is uprooted.

10.

Of the necessity of discretion in performing this exercise and of observing a fitting measure.

St. Basil teaches that this admirable exercise should be performed with discretion and within due measure. All our actions should be submitted to reason, for otherwise actions that are good in themselves can be turned to evil because they are done at the wrong time or in excess. But when reason fixes both the time and the measure, then the resulting benefit is truly marvelous. And St. John Climacus, echoing the Scriptures, says: "There is a time for everything under heaven: a time for silence and a time for quiet conversation, a time for ardent prayer and a time for the devout recitation of the holy Office. For if we are tempted by too great zeal, we seek to anticipate the right moment and have achieved nothing when the time is at hand. For there is a time to sow the seeds of labor and a time to harvest ineffable grace."

The great Barsanuphius relates how a brother had read in the *Patericon*, that one who desires salvation must first of all suffer at the hands of other men all vexations and insults and ignominies, and other tribulations, in the likeness of our Lord, and come in this manner to perfect silence, which is hanging on the Cross—in other words, complete mortification. And the staretz said to him: "The fathers have spoken well, and it is not otherwise." Yet to another man he said: "Silence breeds pride before a man has found himself." Now, to find oneself means to be perfect in humility.

Thinking of God, that is, mental prayer, is above all other actions and is the chief of all the virtues, for it is love of God; and those who have the temerity to introduce themselves into God's presence arrogantly, desiring to converse with Him often and to acquire friendship with Him by force, are quickly annihilated by devils if they are abandoned to them. It is the prerogative of the strong to draw the sword—that is, the word of God—and struggle in solitude against the demons. The weak and the beginners who take refuge in the fortress of holy fear and decline the contest until the time is ripe for it, avoid death.

This knowledge should preserve us from the error of seeking an elevation in advance of our progress, lest we wreak havoc in our soul and bring about our perdition. We should pursue the middle way, at a fitting time. The holy writings testify that the middle way has no pitfalls. And the fitting time is after we have acquired wisdom in the company of other men. For the middle way it is required that one, or at the most two, brothers share our abode, according to the teaching of St. John Climacus. He tells us that there are three excellent forms of monastic life; the life of solitude, cohabitation with one or two brothers observing silence, and community life. The middle way—that is, silence in the company of one or two brothers—is the most practicable, for it is perilous for a man to be alone. If he is plunged into accidie, or overcome by sleep or indolence or despair, there is no one to lift him up. And St. John Climacus quotes the words of our Lord Himself: "Where there are two or three gathered together in my name, there am I in the midst of them."

Those who are defeated by the spiritual passions should not undertake the life of silence, and even less that of solitude, the fathers say. Now, the spiritual passions are: vanity, conceit, malice, and others like them. "A man subject to these infirmities, who attempts to live in silence, is like one who leaps from a ship and tries to reach the shore on a plank," says John Climacus. And a man who is still unable to cleanse himself of dung—that is, the passions of the body—should likewise refrain from seeking solitude, except at a suitable time, and then only if he has a spiritual adviser, for solitude requires the power of an angel. We find that all the holy writings praise the life of silence with one or two brothers. I myself have witnessed it on holy Mount Athos, and in the country about Constantinople, and in other countries there are numerous examples of such a mode of life: a staretz, who is a spiritual guide, with one or two disciples—or sometimes three, if need be—living in silence and at no distance from him and coming to him to be instructed through spiritual conversations.

As for us beginners, who have not yet acquired wisdom, let us be edified and defended by each other, for it has been written that a brother aided by his brother is like a strongly fortified city. And may the holy writings be our unerring teacher.

Let us flee from all vain agitation, and from other things displeasing to God, and live according to His commandments, providing for our necessities by labor. And if we fail in this, we may accept small donations, seeing in them God's mercy, but shunning all excess. We should avoid like deadly poison all quarrels, disputes and lawsuits for the sake of material profit. And let us accomplish all the things that are pleasing to God: singing, prayer, reading, spiritual instruction, manual labor, and service of every kind, living in interior communion with God. Thus we shall glorify by our good works the Father, the Son and the Holy Ghost, One God in the Holy Trinity, now and for ever and ever, amen.

We the unwise have now written what is within the resources of our poor mind, as a memorandum to ourself and others like us who are in need of instruction, if they wish it. And as I have said above, it is not from my own wisdom, but from the God-inspired writings of the enlightened holy fathers that I teach. For what is set down here is not without authority from the holy writings. And if there is something here which is not pleasing to God or salutary to souls, owing to our lack of wisdom, let it not stand, but may God's perfect and beneficent will be done. As for myself, I beg forgiveness, and if anyone knows any better and more practicable ways of accomplishing these things, may he do as he sees fit, and we shall rejoice. And if someone finds this writing useful, let him pray for me, a sinner, that I may deserve mercy before God.

c. ST. NILUS' LAST WILL

In the name of the Father, and of the Son and of the Holy Ghost, I leave the following will to be executed by my lords and brethren who are of the same spirit as myself. I pray you, cast away my body in the desert, to be devoured by the beasts and birds, for that body has greatly sinned before God and is unworthy of burial. If you will not do this, then dig a pit on the grounds where we live and bury me in it with every kind of dishonor.[35] Take heed of the words with which the great Arsenius charged his disciples: "I will prosecute you if you give up my body to anyone; I have done all I could not to be granted fame and honor either in life or in death." I ask everyone to pray for my sinful soul, and I beg everyone to forgive me, as I myself forgive; may God forgive everyone.

I leave to my lords and brethren, who will continue to labor on these grounds, the large cross containing the passionstone, as well as the little books that I have written. I earnestly and humbly request that prayers be said for me until the fortieth day after my death. The small volumes of John Damascenus, the breviary, the *Irmologion*, [36] I also leave to them. The psalter in quarto copied by Ignatius shall be sent to the Kirillov monastery: other books and objects belonging to that monastery which were given to me for the love of God, should likewise be returned, and the rest distributed to the poor, to other monasteries, and to laymen; to whomsoever these things belong, let them be returned.

AVVAKUM: THE CONSERVATIVE REBEL

AVVAKUM As a representative of Muscovite spirituality St. Joseph Volotsky might have been chosen as the most venerated among the later Russian saints in Muscovy. We prefer, however, to select Avvakum, one of his remote descendants, and this for a number of reasons. First, Avvakum was an author of genius, undoubtedly the best writer among the Muscovites; and certainly, in the daring venture of writing his spiritual autobiography, unique in the Old Russia. Second, his spirituality, essentially of the Josephite type, was sublimated and reached true greatness through sufferings and persecutions. Avvakum was a martyr for his faith in an epoch wherein the ancient traditions were shaken, and what had been but yesterday the very foundation of Church and State had become the sign of schism: the conservative schism of the Old Believers. The millions of Old Believers who survive in Russia consider Avvakum as a canonized saint of the Church, and the majority of the members of the Orthodox (formerly the State or Synodal, now the Patriarchal) Church has ceased to look upon the martyrs of the old ritual with contempt. They have learned to respect the courage, the loyalty, and the moral standards of these schismatics; no one now denies the orthodoxy of their beliefs, and their final reconciliation with the Church is expected in the near future. Thus the inclusion of this one schismatic—an Orthodox schismatic—does not, perhaps, break the unity of the series of teachers of Russian spirituality.

The main facts of Avvakum's life are related by himself. What is to be added here, is the story of his beginnings and his end. In his youth Avvakum belonged to a group of conservative reformers consisting chiefly of Muscovite priests in the circle of the revered Archpriest Stephen Vonifatievich, the spiritual father of Tsar Alexis. At that time the decadence of religious and moral life in Muscovy was becoming evident, and to remedy such evils the group of zealots brought about the revival and enforcement of strict ecclesiastical rules of prayer, fasting and personal morality. Preaching and Confession were the main vehicles of the reform movement. Avvakum, then a country priest in Nizhny-Novgorod (now Gorky), gave his support to this program with an excessive pastoral zeal to which may be attributed all his early tribulations and persecutions.

Beginning in 1652, Nicon, the new Patriarch, took another view of the reform. He decided to lead Russia out of her religious and cultural isolation by bringing her closer to the Greek Orthodox Church. Himself a ritualist, as were all the Muscovites, he sought to achieve his end through the "correction" of the old Russian rituals, i.e., through their adaptation to contemporary Greek forms. Along with the reform of rites went the "correction" of the texts of sacred books, and this without a sufficient philological training on the part of the correctors. The national conservative party, of which Avvakum was one of the leaders, saw, in Nicon's reform, positive apostasy: beyond external alterations, through the symbolical interpretation of the rites, they discerned and denounced dogmatic errors. Their opposition brought upon them repressions ever increasing in severity. After the excommunication of the Old Ritualists, or Old Believers, by the Council of 1666-7, many thousands perished on the gallows or at the stake. For fifteen years Avvakum languished in the subterranean prison at Pustozersk, where he wrote his autobiography. Ten years after the completion of this work, on April 14th, 1682, he was burned at the stake.

Reading his Life, one is struck by the contradictions in this forceful character. Greatness of soul, narrowness of mind: acts of the sharpest violence and the tenderest movements of the heart proceed in rapid succession, or the violence and the tenderness are at once alive in him. Avvakum is unable to distinguish the essential from the secondary in religion. Everything is determined by the Law of God, subject to God's terrible judgment. Apart from his concept of God, there is something of the Old Testament character in Avvakum himself. He is constantly overwhelmed by the real, sensible presence of the Almighty. And, like the prophets of Israel, he feels that he is sent by God to announce His will to sinful men, without compromise or condescension to their weakness. Thus is opened to him a way of martyrdom which is inevitable and almost voluntary.

No mystical features can be discerned in this prophet-like personality. Avvakum is sensual in his approach to religion, in his esthetic appreciation of nature and of the spoken or written word—great master of the Russian word!—in his very austerities. Yet he lives in constant intercourse with the other world through visions and voices, demoniac or angelic; for him it is but an immediate continuation of this one. His prayer, for the most part the long and strictly canonical prayer of the service books, has a power, a dynamism, from which miracles proceed. To Avvakum a miracle is an ordinary, everyday thing, having no relation to holiness of life. Exorcisms and struggles with demons (characteristic phenomena of seventeenth-century Muscovy) are part of his pastoral duties.

But Avvakum—and with him Muscovite Russia as a whole—did not read the Gospels in vain. Despite their lack of psychological subtlety and their ideological narrowness, the image of the meek and loving Savior penetrated deeply into their consciousness. From this source flows the undercurrent of compassion and tenderness which sometimes wells up so unexpectedly in Avvakum's austere nature. After fits of anger and violence, he is stricken with compunction and asks pardon of God and his victims. He partakes in the Orthodox "charism of tears." And he knows how to find touching and affectionate words in the Russian style, such as "sweet," or, "my light," in which to speak, not only of his friends, but of Jesus Himself.

THE LIFE OF ARCHPRIEST AVVAKUM BY HIMSELF[1]

I WAS BORN IN THE REGION OF NIZHNY-NOVGOROD,[2] BEYOND THE RIVER KUDNA, IN THE VILLAGE OF GRIGOROVO. MY FATHER, Peter by name, was a priest. My mother, Maria, took the veil under the name of Martha. My father was given to drink, but my mother practised prayer and fasting and constantly taught me the fear of God. One day I saw a neighbor's ox fall dead, and that night I arose and wept before the holy icon, sorrowing for my soul and meditating upon death, since I likewise should die. From that time on it became my custom to pray each night. Then my mother was widowed and I became an orphan in my early days, and we were exiled by our kin. My mother decided that I should marry. I besought the Mother of God to give me a wife who would help me to attain salvation. In that same village there was a maiden, also an orphan, who was wont to go frequently to church, and whose name was Anastasia. Her father was the blacksmith, Marco, a rich man; but after his death his whole substance was wasted. The maiden lived in poverty, and she prayed to God that she might be united to me in marriage; and it was God's will that this should come about. Then my mother returned to God after a life of great piety, and as for me, being turned out, I went to live in another place. I was ordained deacon at the age of twenty and priest two years later. I exercised the functions of ordinary priesthood for eight years and was then made archpriest by the Orthodox bishops, and that was twenty years ago; and I have now been in holy orders for thirty years.

Since the early days of my priesthood I have had many spiritual children, until now, some five or six hundred. I, miserable sinner, labored without rest, in churches and in houses, at the crossroads, in villages and towns, and also in the capital of the Tsar and in the Siberian land, preaching and teaching the word of God for some twenty-five years.

During the time when I was a priest, a young woman came to me for confession, burdened with many sins, having committed fornication and all kinds of sins against purity, and she began to tell them to me in detail, weeping in the church before the holy Gospels. But I, thrice-accursed physician, fell sick myself and burned inwardly with lecherous fire; it was a bitter hour for me. I lighted three candles and fixed them on the lectern, and placed my right hand over the flame and held it there until the lust was extinguished in me. Letting the young woman go, I removed my vestments, and having prayed, I returned to my home in great sorrow and distress. It was about midnight, and entering my house, I wept before the icon of Our Lord until my eyes were swollen; and I prayed fervently that God should separate me from my spiritual children, for the burden was too heavy for me and too difficult to carry. And I fell with my face to the earth, weeping bitterly. Then I slumbered, not knowing how I was weeping, and the eyes of my heart looked upon the Volga. I saw two golden ships sailing majestically; they had golden oars and masts, all was of gold. And each was manned only by a helmsman. I asked "To whom do these ships belong?" And they answered: "To Luke and to Lawrence." These were two of my spiritual children who had led me and my household on the path of salvation and had died in God's favor. Then I saw a third ship, and it was not adorned with gold but painted many hues: red and white and blue and black and ashen, of a beauty and excellence which the mind of man could not conceive. A radiant youth sat at the helm, and I cried: "Whose ship is this?" And he who sat at the helm answered: " 'Tis your ship; you may sail on it with your wife and children if such is your prayer." I awoke all atremble, and sitting up I asked myself, "What does this vision mean, and whither will this voyage bear us?"

After a short time, as it has been written, "the sorrows of death compassed me, and the perils of hell found me. I met with trouble and sorrow." An officer took away a maid, the daughter of a widow, and I implored him to give the orphan back to her mother. But he disdained our importunities and raised a storm against me. His men came to the church and crushed the life out of me; I lay senseless on the ground for half an hour or more. I came back to life by the will of God, and he, seized with fear, gave up the maid to me. Then the devil prompted him and he came to the church and beat me, and dragged me, in my vestments, on the ground, and I recited a prayer all the while.

Afterwards another officer found occasion to be moved with fury against me; he came running to my house, beat me, and buried his teeth in my finger like a dog. And when his throat was filled with gore, he released my hand from the clutch of his teeth and, leaving me, went home. As for me, I thanked God, bandaged my hand with a piece of linen, and betook myself to Vespers. As I was on my way that same man attacked me once more, with two small pistols. Standing close to me, he fired one of them. By the will of God, although the powder exploded in the pan, the pistol did not go off. He flung it on the ground and fired the other pistol, and the will of God was exercised once more and the pistol did not go off. I continued on my way praying fervently, and raised my hand to bless the officer and bowed to him. He cursed me, and I said to him: "Let grace be on your lips, Ivan Rodionovich." He was enraged with me because of the chanting in church; he wanted it to be done with dispatch, and I sang the office according to the rule, without haste. Then he deprived me of my house and drove me out onto the road, plundering everything and giving me no bread for the journey.

At that time my son Procopy was born, the one who is now imprisoned underground with his mother.[3] I took my staff, and she the unbaptized child, and we went wherever God should speed us; on our way we baptized the child as, of old, Philip had baptized the eunuch.[4] When I arrived at Moscow and went to the Tsar's confessor, Archpriest Stephen, and to Archpriest John Neronov, they both told the Tsar about me, and from that time on the Tsar knew me. The Fathers sent me back with a certificate of safe-conduct, and I dragged myself home; but the very walls of my house were destroyed, and I began to establish myself afresh, and again the devil raised a storm against me.

To my village came dancing bears with tambourines and

lutes, and I, miserable sinner, full of zeal for Christ, drove them out. I broke the tambourines and lutes and smashed the clowns' masks out in the field, I alone, against a great number. I took from them two great bears; one I struck senseless, but he revived, and I set the other loose in the fields. Because of this Vasily Petrovich Sheremetev, who was sailing down the Volga to Kazan, to assume the office of governor, summoned me aboard his ship. He upbraided me and ordered me to bless his son Matthew, whose face was shaven. But I did not bless him and reprimanded him from the Scriptures when I looked upon his lewd countenance. In great wrath the nobleman commanded that I should be thrown into the Volga. After I had been dealt many injuries, they cast me out. But afterwards they were good to me; we were reconciled in the Tsar's antechamber, and Vasily's wife became my younger brother's spiritual daughter. Thus God leads his own.[5]

But let me resume my narrative. Later on, another officer was infuriated against me. He came with his attendants to my yard and laid siege with arrows and pistol-shots. Meanwhile I cried out to God, "O Lord, do Thou tame and appease him, through what means Thou knowest best." And he fled from the yard, driven by the Holy Ghost.

That night he sent his men to fetch me, and they cried out, weeping bitterly, "Father, Yefimy Stepanovich is close to death, and he is crying and moaning and beating his breast, saying, "I want Father Avvakum. God is punishing me on his account." Thinking that this was a trap, I was seized with fear and prayed to God thus: "O Lord Who hast taken me from my mother's womb, Who has brought me from nothingness into being! If I am strangled, do Thou sanctify me with Philip, Metropolitan of Moscow;[6] if they stab me, do Thou sanctify me with the prophet Zacharias; if they drown me, do Thou save me as Thou didst Stephen of Perm."[7] Praying in this manner, I went to Yefimy's house. As I was conducted into his yard, his wife Neonila came running out to meet me and seized my hand and cried, "Come, Father, my lord; come, our dear provider!" I answered, " 'Tis strange indeed! Yesterday I was 'son of a harlot,' and now I am 'Father.' Biting, in truth, must be the scourge of Christ! Your husband is quick to repent!"

She took me into his chamber. Yefimy leaped out of his feather bed and cast himself down at my feet, crying and muttering, "My lord, forgive me. I have sinned before God and before you!" And he was trembling all over. I said to him, "Do you want to recover your health?" He, lying at my feet, exclaimed, "Aye, my good lord." I said, "Arise, God has forgiven you." He was so badly stricken that he could not rise by himself. I lifted him and laid him on his bed, and confessed and anointed him with holy oil, and he was healed. Thus did Christ will it. In the morning he let me go with all civility, and he and his wife became my spiritual children, faithful servants of God. Thus does God scorn the scorners: and to the meek he will give grace.

Soon after this, others drove me out for the second time from this place. I dragged myself to Moscow, and by the will of God the Tsar ordered that I should be installed as Archpriest at Yurievets on the Volga. There too I remained but a short time, only eight weeks. The devil inspired the priests, the peasant folk and their women; so they came to the Patriarchal Chancery, where I was attending to ecclesiastical affairs, and they dragged me out of the chancery (they were about fifteen hundred strong); they beat me with rods in the middle of the street and trampled me on the ground, and the women beat me with oven-forks; for my sins I was beaten almost to death, and they threw me against the corner of the house. The governor came rushing up with his cannoneers and, seizing me, carried me off on horseback to my poor home; and he placed his men around the yard. Meanwhile the mob marched to the house, and they raised a great tumult in town; especially did the priests and the women whom I had warned against fornication shout, "Kill this thief and son of a harlot, and throw his body to the dogs in the ditch!"

As to me, having rested a while, I left my wife and children on the third day and fled by night up the Volga to Moscow with two companions. I should have liked to stop at Kostroma, but there too they had driven out Archpriest Daniel. Ah me, the devil stirs up trouble everywhere.

I got to Moscow, and went to Stephen, the Tsar's confessor: he too made a wry face, saying, "Why have you abandoned your church?" So there was more trouble at hand. Then, in the middle of the night, the Tsar came to visit his spiritual father and to receive his nightly blessing, and he found me there, and there was more woe, since he asked, "Why have you left your city?" My wife and children and some twenty retainers had remained in Yurievets; I knew not whether they were alive or dead, and that was another calamity.

Soon after this Nicon, our friend, brought the relics of Metropolitan Philip from the Solovki Monastery to Moscow. Before he arrived, Stephen, the Tsar's confessor, spent a week in prayer and fasting with the brethren on behalf of the patriarch (and I was with them), that God should grant us a pastor for the salvation of our souls.[8] Together with the Metropolitan of Kazan, we wrote, and signed with our own hand, a petition which we presented to the Tsar and Tsarina in favor of Stephen, that he should be made Patriarch. But Stephen would not have it so, and suggested Metropolitan Nicon. The Tsar followed his advice. He sent a letter, to be delivered on his way to Moscow: "To Nicon, the Most Reverend Metropolitan of Novgorod and Velikia Luki and of all Russia, greetings," and so on. And once he was there, he was all bows and compliments with us, like a fox. He knew that he was going to be Patriarch and feared lest some obstacle should arise. There would be much to tell about these wily dealings. And when he was installed patriarch, he would not even let his friends enter his chapel, and soon he spewed forth all his poison.

During Lent[9] he sent a letter to the Cathedral of Our Lady of Kazan,[10] addressed to John Neronov. The latter was my spiritual father; I lived at his church and took charge of it when he was absent. It was said that I should have been appointed to the post of the late Silas at the Savior's Church in the palace, but God had not willed it, and I myself had no great desire to be sent there. I loved the church of Our Lady of Kazan and was content to serve in it. I read holy books to the faithful, who came in great numbers. In his letter (dated such and such a year and month), Nicon wrote: "According to the tradition of the holy apostles and fathers, it is not fitting to make genuflections; suffice it to bow from the waist; and the sign of the cross must be made with three fingers."[11] We assembled and reflected upon this. We saw that winter was near; our hearts were frozen, and our limbs shaking. Neronov entrusted the church to me and hid himself in the Chudov Monastery, where, in a cell, he spent a week in prayer. As he prayed, a voice came from the icon: "This is the time of tribulation: you must suffer without weakening." He related this to me, weeping, also to Bishop Paul of Kolomna, whom Nicon afterwards had burned at the stake at Kostroma; then he likewise told all the brethren about it. With Daniel, I copied excerpts from the Holy Fathers concerning the fingers used in the sign of the cross and the bows to be made during prayer, and these were submitted to the Tsar. There were a great many of these excerpts, but I know not where the Tsar hid them; I believe he gave them to Nicon.

Soon after this Nicon ordered Daniel to be seized and had his head shorn[12] in the Monastery at the Tver Gates, in the Tsar's presence. They tore his cassock from his back, and, heaping insults on him, took him to the Chudov Monastery and locked him in the bakery. After many torments had been inflicted on him, he was banished to Astrakhan; there he was crowned with a wreath of thorns, and they let him die in a dungeon.

After Daniel was shorn, they seized another Daniel, Archpriest of Temnikov; he was locked up at the New Convent of Saint Savior. Likewise, Nicon himself tore the biretta off Archpriest Neronov's head and imprisoned him at the Simonov Monastery. Later on, he sent him to Vologda, to the Monastery of Saint Savior on the Rock, and then to Fort Kola. Because of the many sufferings he had endured, the poor man's strength failed him, so he accepted the sign of the cross with three fingers and died in this state. Oh, woe and misfortune. Let him who thinks himself strong fear lest he stumble. These are the evil days when in accordance with our Lord's words, even the elect shall be led astray by the Antichrist. We must pray to God most fervently that He may save us and forgive us, for He is full of mercy and loves mankind.

I too was arrested at Vespers by Boris Neledinsky and his musketeers. About sixty persons were arrested with me and taken to prison. As for me, I was put in chains and taken for the night to the Patriarch's Court. And on Sunday, as soon as it was day, I was placed in a cart with my arms outstretched and driven from the Patriarch's Court to the Monastery of Saint Andronicus. And I was thrown in chains into an underground cell. I spent three days in the dark, without food or drink, and in my chains I bowed in prayer, but whether to the west or to the east, I know not. Nobody came to my cell, only mice and cockroaches and chirping crickets and hordes of fleas. On the third day I was moved by the desire to eat—in other words, I was hungry—and, after Vespers, I saw someone standing before me; but whether it was man or angel I could not say, and cannot say even to this day, save that he uttered a prayer in the dark, and laying his hand on my shoulder, led me on my chains to a bench. He had me sit down and placed a spoon in my hand, and he gave me a little bread and some cabbage soup to eat, and it tasted good. Then, saying to me: "Enough. This will suffice for thy sustenance," he vanished: though the door did not open, he was no longer there. This would have been a strange thing, had it been a man, but for an angel 'tis no wonder, since he can be stopped by no barrier.

In the morning the Archimandrite and the brethren came to fetch me and led me out of the cell; they chided me for refusing obedience to the patriarch, and I condemned him and inveighed against him from the Scriptures. They removed the heavy chain and put a lighter one on me, and gave me into the custody of a monk, with orders that I should be dragged to the church. Close by the church, they pulled my hair and poked me in the ribs and jerked me around on my chain and spat in my eyes. May God forgive them in this world and the next. This was none of their doing, but the work of Satan, the malicious one. I spent four weeks in that place.

After me, they seized Longin, Archpriest of Murom; he was shorn at Mass in the cathedral, in the Tsar's presence. During the procession of oblation, the Patriarch took the paten with Christ's body from the archdeacon's hand and placed it on the altar; meanwhile Therapon, Archimandrite of Chudov, was standing with the chalice outside the altar, near the royal doors. Alas, such a division of Christ's body was worse than the doing of the Jews![13] Having shorn him, they tore his cassock and his kaftan off his back. But Longin was incensed with the fire of holy wrath; reproving Nicon, he spat into his eyes across the threshold of the sanctuary; undoing his girdle, he tore off his shirt and hurled it into Nicon's face. O wonder! The shirt spread and covered the paten on the altar like a corporal. The Tsarina also was in the Cathedral at the time. Longin was put into chains, dragged outside the church and beaten with brooms and whips all the way to the Monastery of the Epiphany. And he was thrown into a cell and musketeers were set to guard him. But during the night, God gave him a new fur coat and a hat. In the morning Nicon was informed of this happening and laughingly exclaimed: "I know these would-be saints!" He took the hat away from him but left him the fur coat.

Afterward I was taken from the monastery and led on foot, arms outstretched, to the Patriarch's Court. After a great deal of heckling, I was returned to my cell in similar fashion. On St. Nicetas' day there was a procession, and I was taken out in a cart to meet it; and I was brought to the cathedral to be shorn, and during Mass, they kept me for a long time on the parvis. The Tsar left his throne and, going up to the Patriarch, asked him not to have me shorn. I was taken to the Siberia Office, where I was placed in the custody of the secretary, Tretiak Bashmakov (now Father Savvaty), who today is also suffering for Christ's sake, imprisoned in an underground cell at the New Monastery of Saint Savior, may God save him. Even at that time he did me a kindness.

I was sent to Siberia with my wife and children. It would be a long tale, if I related all the tribulations we endured on our way; suffice it to say a little about them. During the journey Dame Avvakum gave birth to a child, and she was driven, sick, in a cart to Tobolsk. We travelled three thousand versts in thirteen weeks or so; we were dragged by cart, by boat or, half of the way, by sleigh.

In Tobolsk the Archbishop appointed me to a church,[14] and there I suffered great trials. In a year and a half, I was accused five times of treason against the Tsar. A certain Ivan Struna, secretary of the Archbishop's Chancery, persecuted me; while the Archbishop was away in Moscow, Struna was inspired by the devil to fall on me. Without cause he tormented Deacon Anthony, and the latter ran away from him and came to my church. Ivan Struna called his attendants and also came to the church on another day. I was singing Vespers, and he rushed into the choir and clutched Anthony by the beard, while I closed the church doors and let no one in. Struna was alone in there, carrying on like the devil. And I, interrupting the office, seated Struna in the middle of the church with the help of Anthony and thrashed him with a leather strap for disturbance in church. And the others, about twenty strong, fled, driven by the Holy Ghost. Having received Struna's repentance. I sent him home.

But Struna's kinsmen, monks and priests, set the whole city astir in order to bring about my undoing. At midnight they came in a sleigh to my door and tried to break in and seize me, in order to have me drowned; but the fear of God dispersed them and made them turn back. For a month I suffered, having to hide myself; I would sleep one night at the church and another night at the governor's house. I even begged to be locked in prison but was not admitted.

There came an ukase ordering that I should be taken away from Tobolsk, because I had condemned Nicon for his heresy, speaking from the Scriptures. At that time I received a letter from Moscow, informing me that two of my brothers, who lived in the palace in the Tsarina's apartments,[15] had died of the plague, with their wives and children; and many others among my kinsmen and friends had also died. God had let flow on the Kingdom the vial of His wrath, and the wretched ones did not repent; they continue to cause trouble in the Church. Neronov had often warned the Tsar: There will be three visitations resulting from the schism in the Church: plague, the sword, division. And this is what has happened today.

But the Lord is merciful; having punished us, so that we may repent, He forgives us; having cured the ills of our souls and bodies, He will give us peace. I hope and trust in Christ, I await His mercy and expect the resurrection of the dead.

Once more I sailed in my ship, as had been shown to me in the vision already described. I made my way to the Lena River. When we reached Yeniseisk there came another ukase ordering me to Dauria,[16] twenty thousand versts and more from Moscow; I was to be given over to Afanasy Pashkov and his regiment. He had six hundred men under his command. He was a rough man, for my sins, and he burned, flogged and tortured people unceasingly. I had often tried to stay him, but finally I had fallen into his hands. From Moscow he had received Nicon's orders to torment me.

After we left Yeniseisk, as we reached the great Tunguzka River, a storm almost wrecked my barge; it floated in midstream and filled with water, and its sails were torn. All but the deck was submerged. My wife, bareheaded,[17] pulled the children out of the water, and I, lifting my eyes to heaven, cried: "Lord, help us and save us!" By the will of God we were blown toward the shore. 'Tis a long story to tell. Two men in another barge were pitched overboard and drowned. And we, having regained our composure on shore, resumed our journey.

As we came to the Shaman rapids, we met other folk sailing on the river; among them were two widows, one about sixty and the other even more advanced in age; they were on their way to a convent to take the veil. And Pashkov wanted them to turn back and be compelled to marry. I said to him: "According to the law of the Church, it is not fitting to have them married." But instead of heeding my words, he became enraged and began to torture me. When we reached the Long Rapids, he started to push me out of the barge, saying: 'Tis because of you that the barge makes such slow progress, you are a heretic. Go into the mountains, your place is not among Cossacks."

Ah, poor me! the mountains were high, the forest dense; the cliffs stood like a wall, one could break one's neck looking up at them. In these mountains live great snakes, and geese and ducks with red feathers fly overhead, black crows and grey jackdaws. In these mountains there are also eagles and hawks and gerfalcons and guinea-fowl, pelicans and swans, and other wild birds of different kinds in great numbers. And many beasts roam likewise in these mountains: wild bucks and deer, aurochs, elks, boars, wolves, wild sheep, which are plainly to be seen but cannot be captured.

Pashkov wanted to cast me out into these mountains, to live among the birds and beasts. So I wrote him a short letter, and it started thus: "Man, fear God, Who sits on the Cherubim and Who watches over the abyss, before Whom tremble the heavenly powers and all creatures, including man. You alone despise Him and cause disturbance," and so on. There was much I wrote in that letter, and I had it taken to him. About fifty men came running, and they took my barge and towed it to where he was, about three versts away. I cooked some porridge for the Cossacks and fed them, poor souls; they were eating and trembling at the same time, and some of them wept out of pity for me.

When the barge was towed ashore, the executioners seized me and led me before him. He stood, sword in hand, and shaking. First he asked me: "Are you a true pope[18] or an unfrocked one?" I answered: "I am Avvakum, Archpriest. Speak, what is it you want of me?" He roared like a wild beast and struck me on one cheek and then on the other, and beat me on the head, and knocked me down, and seizing his battle-axe, he struck me three times on the back, as I lay there. Then, tearing off my garment, he applied seventy-two strokes of the whip on that very same back of mine. And I cried: "Lord Jesus Christ, son of God, help me!" And I repeated these words unceasingly, and he was sorely vexed, because I did not say: "Have mercy." At each stroke of

the whip, I recited the prayer; then, in the middle of the thrashing, I cried out: "Enough of this beating," and he ordered the
thrashing to be stopped. I asked him: "Do you know why you
beat me? Why?" And once more he ordered that I should be
struck in the ribs, and then they let me go. I trembled and fell.
And he had me placed in the ammunition-boat; they fettered
me hand and foot and threw me onto a beam. It was autumn,
and rain beat on me all night. I lay under the downpour. While
they had been flogging me, I had felt no pain, thanks to my
prayer, but now, as I lay there, a thought crossed my mind: "Son
of God, why didst Thou permit such a hard beating? Did I not
defend Thy widows? Who shall be the judge between Thee and
me? When I was committing evil Thou didst not afflict me so
cruelly. And now, I know not in what way I have sinned." Ah,
what virtue I displayed! I, another dung-faced pharisee, dared
to take issue concerning the Lord's justice! If Job could speak
thus, it is because he was just and sinless; moreover, he did not
know the Scriptures, for he lived outside the Law in the land of
barbarians, and knew God through the creation. As to myself,
I am first of all a sinner; and secondly, I am supported by the
Law, fortified in all things by the Scriptures, "We must through
much tribulation enter the Kingdom of God." And I had committed such folly. Woe to me! How was it that the boat did not
sink with me?

Then it was that my bones began to ache, and my veins grew
taut, and my heart failed me and I was near death. They blew
water in my mouth, and I breathed again and repented before
the Lord. The sweet Lord is merciful; he forgets our former
transgressions in view of our repentance. And once more nothing
pained me.

In the morning they threw me into a small boat and towed it
along. We reached the great Padun Rapids, where the river is
one verst wide. There are three steep reefs stretching across the
river. If you do not sail through the channel, your craft will be
smashed into splinters. I was brought to the rapids; it was raining
and snowing, and I had on nothing but a thin kaftan. The water
splashed over my back and belly. Great was my distress! They

took me out of the boat and dragged me in chains over the rocks round the rapids. It was painful, but good for the soul, and this time I did not murmur against God. I recalled the words of the prophets and apostles: "Whom the Lord loveth, He chastiseth: and He scourgeth every son whom He receiveth . . . For what son is there whom the father doth not correct?" And with these words I was comforted.

Then I was taken to Fort Bratsky and thrown into jail, and given a little straw. I remained there till St. Philip's fast,[19] in a frozen tower; it is already winter at that time in this land, but God warmed me in want of clothing. I lay like a little dog on the straw; some days they would feed me and some days not; there were a great many mice, and I hit them with my biretta— the fools would not even give me a stick. I lay all the time on my belly: my back was sore, and there were many fleas and lice. I wanted to cry out to Pashkov: "Pardon!" but God's will forbade it and ordered me to be patient. Later I was transferred to a warm house, and there I spent the winter in chains with the hostages[20] and the dogs. My wife and children had been sent far from me, some twenty versts away. And all that winter she was plagued and rebuked by her servant Xenia. My son Ivan, a small lad, came to stay with me for a while after Christmas. Pashkov had him thrown into the cold cell where I had lain. He spent the night there, poor dear lad, and almost froze to death. In the morning, he was sent back to his mother. He reached home with his hands and feet frozen.

In spring we went once more on our way. There was not much left of our supplies; all had been pilfered; even books and clothing and utensils had been stolen. On Lake Baikal again I came close to drowning. Pashkov made me pull the towing-rope on the Khilok River; it was a hard run, and no time for eating or sleeping. All summer I was tormented by this towing in the water. The men died, and my feet and belly were swollen. Two summers we towed in the water, and in winter we had to haul on dry land. It was on that river Khilok that, for the third time, I was nearly drowned. The boat was carried away; the other boats remained near the shore, but mine was seized and drawn by the current. My wife and children had remained on shore, but I was carried away with the helmsman. The stream was swift, it turned the boat upside down, and I crawled onto it, crying: "Our Lady, help! Our Hope, do not drown us!" Now my feet would be under water, and then again I would scramble onto the boat; we drifted a verst or so, and then the men caught us. Everything was soaked through and through. But what is to be done if such is the will of the Mother of God? I came out of the water laughing, but the men heaved many sighs and spread my clothing on the bushes: coats of satin and taffeta and some other trifles which still filled the chests and sacks. From that day on everything went to rot. We were without clothing. Pashkov wanted to give me another beating: "You have made yourself a laughing-stock!" But I once more entreated the good Mother: "Gracious Queen, stop that fool." And she, Our Hope, appeased him, and he took pity on me.

That spring we began to sail on rafts down the Ingoda River. This was my fourth year of navigation since I had left Tobolsk.

We floated lumber for the building of houses and forts. There was nothing to eat; men died of hunger, and from working in the water. Shallow was the river and the rafts heavy, the task-masters pitiless, the sticks hard, the cudgels knotty, the whips cutting, our sufferings cruel: fire and rack and people starving! One more stroke and a man would fall dead. Alas, what times were these! I know not how he could lose his mind in this way.

My wife had only one cloak left that had not rotted. It would have been worth twenty-five rubles in Russia, and more over here, but he gave four sacks of rye for it, and they lasted one or two years, while we lived on the river Nercha, eating mostly grass. He let all his men die of hunger; there remained a small troop, roaming through the steppes, digging for roots and grass, and we did as the others. In winter we fed on pine-bark, and sometimes, by luck, on horse flesh and the carcasses of beasts killed by wolves. What the wolves did not devour, we ate. And some would feed on frozen wolves and foxes and every other kind of filthy beast they could find. If a mare foaled, the foal was devoured in secret, together with the caul. When Pashkov heard about it, he would have them flogged to death.²¹ Sometimes the mare would die because she had not been allowed to foal naturally: they tore the foal out as soon as the head appeared, and they drank the foul blood. Ah, what sad times were these!

I also lost two small sons in those hard days. They roamed the hills with the others, naked and barefoot on the sharp stones, feeding on grass and roots as best they could. I myself, miserable sinner, had to eat that horse-flesh and the foul carcasses of bird and beast. Alas for my sinful soul! Who shall freshen my eyes with the source of tears, that I may weep over my poor soul, for having lost itself to the delectations of the world!

But we were helped in Christ by the lady Eudokia Kirillovna, daughter-in-law of Afanasy, the governor, also by his wife, Fekla Semenovna. They preserved us secretly from starvation and death by sending us, without his knowing anything about it, now a piece of meat, now a loaf of bread, sometimes a little flour and oats, whatever she could gather, ten pounds, and some money, and even sometimes as much as twenty pounds. Or else she would scrape up some food from the chickens' trough.

My daughter, the poor maid Agrippina, would secretly go up to her window. It made us feel like weeping and laughing at the same time. Sometimes they would drive her away, without the lady being warned, but sometimes she would come home with an armload. She was then but a small child; she is twenty-seven today and still a maid, living in Mezen with her two younger sisters, in grief and uncertainty. Her mother and brother are imprisoned underground. But what can be done about it? Let them all suffer bitterly for Christ's sake. So be it, with God's help. It is fitting to suffer for the Christian faith. This Archpriest formerly enjoyed intercourse with the great, and now, poor wretch, let him delight in suffering to the end; for it has been written: Blessed is not he who begins, but he who perseveres to the end. But enough on that subject. Let us resume our previous topic.

These great calamities lasted six or seven years in the land of Dauria, but sometimes there was a respite. Yet he, Afanasy, unceasingly sought to bring about my death, upon all kinds of charges. During this time of calamity he sent me two widows, Mary and Sophia, two women-servants of his, who were possessed by the devil. He had tried sorcery and spells of all kinds on them, but saw it was of no avail, that rather, a tumult was arising. They would shriek and writhe in convulsions. So he called me and, bowing to me, said: "Take these two and doctor them by prayers." I answered: "My lord, this is above my strength. But through the prayers of the holy fathers, everything is possible to God." So I took the poor women home, may it be forgiven me! I have had some experience of these matters in Russia, where three or four possessed would sometimes be brought to me, and through the prayers of the holy fathers, the devils would be cast out by the command and through the action of the loving God and our sweet Lord Jesus Christ: I would sprinkle them with tears and water and would anoint them with holy oil, and would chant some prayers in Christ's name, and the divine power would cast out the evil spirit, and the man would be healed, not through my own or any other person's merits, but because of these men's faith.

So the possessed women were brought to me. According to custom, I fasted and made them fast; I prayed and anointed them, and performed all that I saw fit. And the women were cured and became sound of mind. I confessed them and gave them Communion. They lived under my roof and prayed, and they loved me and did not go home. He learned that I had acquired two spiritual daughters, and was again greatly enraged against me; and, more than ever, he wanted to burn me alive: "You have extorted my secrets from them!" he cried. Now how could I have given them Communion without confession? And without Communion the evil one cannot be entirely cast out. The devil is not a poltroon; he does not fear the cudgel: he fears the Cross of Christ, holy water and holy oil, but he is completely routed before the body of Christ. I know not how to heal otherwise than by these sacraments.

In our Orthodox faith, Communion cannot be given without

confession; it is done in the Roman faith, where confession is neglected, but for us who practise Orthodoxy, it is not fitting; in any case we must seek penance.

Pashkov took the two widows away from me. Instead of thanks, all I received was abuse. He thought that Christ's work had been perfected, but the women carried on more evilly than before. He locked them up in an empty house, letting no one go near them, and summoned a monk to attend them, but they threw logs at him, so he dragged himself away. In my home, I wept, knowing not what I should do. I dared not go to his house, for his animosity towards me was very great. I sent them holy water in private, telling them to wash in it and drink it: so they, poor things, were somewhat relieved. Then they visited me secretly, and I anointed them in the name of Christ, and once more, thank God, they were healed, and they returned to their home; but they would come running to me under cover of darkness to pray to God. They became good spiritual children; all derangement left them, and afterwards they went to live with their lady at the Voznesensky Monastery. Glory be to God for them.

From the Nercha River we turned back once more to Russia. For five weeks we drove on icy roads in our sleighs. They gave me two nags to draw the children and the baggage. Dame Avvakum and myself journeyed on foot, stumbling on the ice. We travelled through a barbarous land, the natives were hostile; we dared not lag behind and could not keep up with the horses. We were hungry and weary. Dame Avvakum, poor thing, tramped on and on, and then she would fall. It was exceedingly slippery, and once another man, no less weary, stumbled over her and fell too. Both cried out and could not get to their feet again. The man cried: "Oh, good mother, dear lady, pardon me!" And she: "Do you want to crush me?" I came up to her, and she, poor lady, put all the blame on me: "How long, Archpriest, are we to suffer thus?" I answered: "Until our very death, Markovna!" And she replied, with a sigh: "So be it, Petrovich, let us plod on."

We had a little black hen that would lay two eggs a day for

the feeding of our children, by the will of God, helping us in our need. Thus had the Lord ordained. But during our journey by sleigh, the little hen was crushed to death, for our sins, and even today I am sorry for that fowl, every time I think of her. 'Twas no ordinary hen, but a real miracle-worker; she laid her eggs all the year round and every day; a hundred roubles for her? —spittle and trash! That little bird, a creature of God, fed us, and would peck in the pan where our broth of pine was cooking; or else, if we had fish, she would peck at it too, and she would give us two eggs a day. Glory to God, who has ordered all things well!

The way we got that little hen was extraordinary too. All our lady's hens had become blind and were dying; she placed them in a basket and sent them to me: "Let Father come and pray for the hens." And I said to myself, she is our provider and has small children, she needs these chickens. I chanted prayers, blessed the water, and sprinkled the hens with it and incensed them. Then I went into the woods and made them a trough to feed in, and sprinkled it and sent it to her. The fowl recovered and grew strong, by the hand of God and thanks to the lady's faith. Our hen was of that brood. But enough of this; 'tis nothing new, that Christ does these things. Cosmas and Damian in their day blessed and healed both man and beast in the name of Christ. All things are good in the eyes of God. Cattle and fowl have been made for the glory of the great undefiled Lord, and also for the good of man.

Then we journeyed back to the Lake Irgen. My lady took pity on us, and sent us a pan of wheat, and we had pudding to eat. Eudokia Kirillovna was our true provider, but with her too the devil prompted me to quarrel, and this is how it happened. She had a son, Simeon, who was born in that land. I had churched the mother and baptized the child, and each day she sent her son to me, that I should bless him; I would bless him with the cross and sprinkle him with holy water, and kiss him and let him go. The child was healthy and strong, but one day, when I was away, he became sick. The lady, angry with me and faint of heart, sent the baby to a witch-doctor. When I was informed of this, I was angry with her in turn, and so there was a bitter quarrel between us. The child grew worse, his right arm and leg became like sticks. Seized with remorse, she knew not what to do, and God struck even more heavily. The child was well-nigh dead, and the nurses came to me weeping, and I said: "Since she's a wicked woman, leave her alone!" And I waited for her repentance. I saw that the devil had hardened her heart, and I prayed for her, asking the Lord to bring her back to reason. And the Lord, God of mercy, freshened the arid fields of her heart; in the morning, she sent me her second son, John. Weeping, he begged my forgiveness for his mother, bowing low by my stove. I was lying on the stove, naked under some birch-bark; Dame Avvakum was in the stove, and the children lying about here and there. It was raining, and we had nothing to cover ourselves with, and water was leaking through the roof into our shack. We were managing as well as we could. In order to mortify the lady, I sent this message to her: "Tell your mother to beg Aretha, the witch-doctor, for this grace." Then they brought the child to me; she ordered him to be laid before me. They were all weeping and bowing. I rose, picked up my stole from the mud, and found the holy oil; having prayed and incensed the child, I anointed him and blessed him with the cross. And he—it was God's action—was healed, and his hand and leg became sound. I gave him holy water to drink and sent him back to his mother. Observe, you who listen to me, how great a virtue there is in a mother's contrition; she healed her own heart and restored her child's health. But what of that? 'Tis not only from this day that there is a God for penitents.

In the morning, she sent some fish and pies for us, who were starving; indeed it was a timely gift. From that day on, I made my peace with her. After she came back from Dauria, she died in Moscow, dear little lady, and I buried her in the Assumption Monastery.

Pashkov had heard the story of the child; she had told him about it. Then I went to him and he said, bowing low: "God save you, you have been a father to us, you have forgotten our evil doings." It was his favorite grandson; he had baptized the child and had been deeply grieved on his account. And at that time he sent us much food.

But soon he wanted to put me to torture once more; listen to the reason for this: He had sent his son Jeremy on a military expedition to the kingdom of the Mongols. There were seventy-two Cossacks and twenty native soldiers with him. And he ordered one of the natives to act as *"shaman"*—that is, a sooth-sayer: Would the campaign be successful and would they return victorious? Now one night this magician brought a live ram close to my hut and started to work his spell over it; he spun the ram round and round, twisted its neck off, and cast away its head. Then he started jumping and dancing and invoking the devils; with loud shouts, he flung himself on the ground, foaming at the mouth. The devils pressed upon him, and he asked them: "Will the campaign be successful?" And the devils answered: "You will return with great fame and much booty." The captains were delighted and they all joyfully declared: "We shall come back rich!"

Oh, my heart was bitter, and it has not yet softened! Bad shepherd that I was, I lost my sheep. In my grief I forgot what is said in the Gospels when the sons of Zebedee questioned Our Lord about the stubborn townsmen: "Lord, wilt thou that we command fire to come down from heaven and consume them? And turning, He rebuked them, saying: You know not of what spirit you are. The son of man came not to destroy souls, but to save. And they went into another town." But I, accursed one, did not do this! In my sheepfold, I cried out to God: "Hear me, Lord, hear me, radiant King of Heaven, let not one of them return! Prepare a grave for them all in that land. Visit evil upon them, visit them, O Lord; let them perish, so that the diabolical prophecy may not be fulfilled." And I uttered many other words to that effect, and in secret I prayed to God silently in like manner. They told him about these prayers I had said, but he was content with reproving me. He sent his son with the soldiers. They left by night, under the stars. Then I began to pity them; in a vision I saw, with the eyes of my soul, their defeat and massacre—and I had called down this disaster upon them! Some of them came to bid me farewell, and I said to them: "You shall perish in that land."

As they departed, their horses began to neigh and the cows to low, the sheep and goats to bleat, the dogs to howl, and the natives likewise began to howl like dogs. Panic had gripped them all. Jeremy sent me an urgent message—"Lord Father, pray for me"—and I was full of pity for him. He was my friend in secret and had suffered for me. When his father beat me, he had tried to stay his hand, and Pashkov had pursued his son with his sword.

And so they rode away to war. I had pity on Jeremy and began to solicit God most urgently to spare him. They were expected home, but on the appointed day they did not return. Pashkov would not let me come near him. He had a torture-chamber made ready and a fire lighted; he intended to torture me. I recited the prayer of the dying, for I knew his kind of cooking, and that few survived his fire. I waited for them to come and seize me; and sitting there, I said to my wife and children: "Let God's will be done. 'For whether we live, we live unto the Lord; and whether we die, we die unto the Lord.'" Marvellous are the works of God, and ineffable the ways of the Lord! For at that very moment Jeremy, wounded and accompanied by another horseman, rode past my house and yard. He beckoned to the executioners and led them away. Pashkov came out of the torture-chamber and went to meet his son like a man drunk with grief. Then, having exchanged greetings with his father, Jeremy related to him everything in detail: how his troops had been massacred to the last man and a native had helped him escape through desert country; how he had roamed for seven days over rocky hills and in the forests, without food (he had eaten one squirrel); and how in his sleep there had appeared to him a man resembling me, who had shown him the way and had blessed him; and joyfully springing to his feet, he had found the right way. As Jeremy was telling his story to his father, I came in to greet them both. And Pashkov, lifting his eyes to me—the very image of a white sea-bear he was—was ready to devour me alive, but the Lord would not deliver me to him.

He only heaved a sigh and said: "So that's what you've been doing! How many men have you destroyed?" But Jeremy said to me: "My lord Father, pray you, go home and say nothing." And I went away.

For ten years he tormented me—or I him, I know not which! God will decide on the day of judgment. Then he was appointed to a new post, and I received a letter; I was to return to Moscow. Pashkov left but did not take me with him. He said to himself: "If he journeys alone, the natives will kill him." He sailed in boats with men and weapons, and I learned from the natives that he was shaking with fear. One month after his departure, I gathered the old, the sick and the wounded, who were of no use over there, about ten men—with my wife and children, seventeen persons in all—and we got on a boat; trusting in Christ and with a cross on our prow, we sailed by the grace of God, afraid of nothing.

I gave the bailiff the Book of the Pilot (of the Canon Law), and he in exchange gave me a pilot to steer our boat. And I ransomed my friend Basil, the same one who, under Pashkov, had denounced his companions and shed their blood, and who had sought my own head. One day, after beating me, he was going to impale me, but once again, God saved me. After Pashkov left, the Cossacks wanted to kill him, but I obtained his pardon in the name of Christ, and I paid the ranson and took him to Russia, out of death to life. Let the poor wretch repent of his sins. And I took with me another lout of the same breed; they would not give him up to me, and he ran away into the woods to escape death; waiting until I should pass by, he threw himself weeping into my boat. They started in pursuit of him, and I knew not where to hide him. Then, may I be pardoned, I committed a sin; as Rahab, the harlot of Jericho, hid the men of Joshuah, the son of Nun, even so did I hide him in the bottom of the boat, and threw our bedding over him and told Dame Avvakum and my daughter to lie down. The men hunted everywhere for him but did not disturb my wife. They only said to her: "Take some rest, mother, you have suffered enough grief." And I, forgive me for the love of God, lied at that time, saying: "Nay, he is not here." I did not want to give him up to destruction. So, having looked all around, they went away, and I took him back to Russia.

The bailiff gave me some ten pounds of flour and a cow and six lambs and some dried meat. We lived on that all summer on the river. He was a good man, that bailiff. He had been godfather to my daughter Xenia. She was born in Pashkov's days, and he would not give me chrism and oil; so she had not been christened for a long time. I baptized her after he was gone. I myself churched my wife and baptized the children, with the bailiff as godfather and my elder daughter as godmother, while I acted as priest for them. In the same way I baptized my son Afanasy, and saying mass on the Mezen, I gave him Communion. I confessed my children and gave them Holy Communion, but could not do so for my wife, it is thus written in the Canon Law, and we must act accordingly.

Thus we left Dauria. Food became scarce, so I prayed to God together with my companions, and Christ sent us a buffalo, a huge beast. Thanks to this we reached Lake Baikal. A number of Russians had come to the shores of this lake, sable-hunters and fishermen. They were glad to welcome us, and they dragged our boat high onto the rocky shore. The good Terenty and his companions wept at the sight of us, and we looked at them. They gave us plenty of food, as much as we needed, about forty fresh sturgeons, saying: "Let this be your share, Father, God put them in our nets, take them all." I bowed to them, blessed the fish, and told the fishermen to take it back. What should I do with so much food? After we had stayed with them for awhile, I had to accept some of their supplies, and having repaired our boat and rigged up a sail with a woman's old smock, we started across the lake.

During the crossing the wind fell, and we had to use our oars. In that place the lake is not very wide, only eighty to one hundred versts or so. When we reached the other shore, a storm began to blow up, and we could scarcely land because of the waves. From the shore rose steep hills and sheer cliffs. I have dragged myself twenty thousand versts and more, but never have I seen such high mountains. And their summits are crowned with halls and turrets, pillars and gates, and walls and courts, all made by the hand of God. In those hills grow garlic and onion, the bulbs larger than those of Romanov onions, and very sweet. And there is also hemp, sown by God's hand, and in the courts, beautiful grass and sweet-smelling flowers. There are wild fowl in great number: geese and swans floating on the lake, like snow. And there are also fish: sturgeon and salmon-trout, sterlet and omul and white-fish, and many other kinds. This is a fresh-water lake, but great seals and sea-hares live in it. I never saw the like in the great ocean, when I lived on the Mezen River. And the fish is abundant; the sturgeon and salmon-trout are so fleshy, one cannot fry them in a skillet, it would be nothing but fat. And all this has been created by Christ for man, that he should find pleasure in it and praise God. But man, who is enslaved by vanity—his days pass like a shadow; he leaps, like a goat; he puffs himself out, like a bubble; he rages, like the lynx; seeks to devour, like a serpent; at the sight of another's beauty, he neighs like a foal; is wily, like the devil; having had his fill, he falls asleep without observing the rule of prayer. He puts off repentance until the day when he shall be old, and then he is vanished, I know not where, into the light or into the darkness. It shall be revealed upon the day of Judgment. Pardon me, I have sinned more than any man.

Then we reached the towns of Russia, and I became aware, concerning the Church, that "it prevailed nothing, but rather a tumult was made." I was saddened, and sitting myself down, I reflected: What am I to do? must I preach the word of Christ or go into hiding? For I was bound to wife and children. Seeing my distress, Dame Avvakum came up to me respectfully and asked: "What troubles you, my lord?" And I told her everything in detail: "Wife, what shall I do? 'Tis the winter of heresy. Shall I speak or be silent? You have shackled me." And she replied: "God forgive! What say you, Petrovich? Did you not read the words of the Apostle: 'Art thou bound to a wife, seek not to be loosed. Art thou loosèd from a wife? Seek no wife.' I and the children bless you. Continue to preach the word of

God as fearlessly as before, and be not concerned about us, as long as God shall allow it. If we are separated, then do not forget us in your prayers. Christ is mighty and will not abandon us. Go, go to church, Petrovich, and convict the heretics of their whoredom!"

At these words, I bowed to her, and, having shaken off my grievous blindness, I began once more to preach the word of God and to teach in towns and everywhere, and boldly to condemn Nicon's heresy.

I spent the winter at Yeniseisk; that summer I sailed once more, and I spent the second winter at Tobolsk. And on my way to Moscow, in all the towns and villages, in churches and in market-places, I cried out, preaching the word of God, teaching, and condemning the godless heresy. Then I arrived in Moscow. It had taken me three years to journey from Dauria; and to reach that land, I had toiled upstream for five years. In those days, I had been taken further and further east, amidst the camps and dwellings of the natives. It would take much telling. Several times I fell into the hands of the natives: on the great river Ob, twenty Christians perished before my eyes, and having taken counsel concerning me, they let me go. Another time, on the Irtish River, they assembled in wait for our men from Berezov and their boat, in order to slay them. Unaware of their designs, I went to them and landed on their shore. They surrounded us, armed with bows, and I went up to them and embraced them as if they were monks, saying: "Christ be with me and with you also." And their hearts softened toward me, and they brought me their wives. Dame Avvakum played the hypocrite with them, in the flattering way of intercourse in the world. So the women were coaxed into kindliness—and it is well enough known that when women are kind, then all are kind in Christ. So the men put away their bows and arrows. I bought some bear furs from them, and they let me go. When I arrived in Tobolsk, I related what had happened, and everyone marvelled, for throughout Siberia, Bashkirs and Tatars were at war in those days, and I, trusting in Christ, had journeyed among them. When I reached Verkhoturie, my friend Ivan Bogdanovich

Kaminin was also greatly surprised at seeing me. He asked me: "How did you pass through?" I answered: "God carried me through, and His most Holy Mother guided me. I am afraid of no one. I fear Christ alone."

Then I arrived in Moscow and the Tsar received me joyfully, as if I were an angel of God. I went to Fedor Rtishchev;[22] he came out of his chamber to meet me, asked for my blessing, and we talked for a long while: he would not let me go for three days and three nights, and then he announced my presence to the Tsar. The Tsar imme'diately received me in audience and spoke to me kindly: "How fares it with you, Archpriest? God has let us meet once more." I kissed his hand and pressed it, answering: "God lives and my soul lives, Tsar, my Lord! From now on, It will be as God ordains." And he, dear soul, sighed and went to attend to some business. We had spoken a few words more, but it is no use recalling them, it all belongs to the past. He ordered that I should be given lodgings in a monastery in the Kremlin; when he passed my house, he would bow to me, saying: "Bless me and pray for me." One day, as he rode by on horseback, he took off his hat. And when he drove in a carriage, he would lean out of the window to see me. And all the boyars did as much, each one bowing to me: "Archpriest, bless us and pray for us."

How should one not pity such a Tsar and such boyars? Yes, indeed, they are to be pitied. See how good they were, offering me parishes to choose from, and even suggesting that I should become confessor to the Tsar, if only I would consent to be reunited to them. I counted all this as dung, that I might gain Christ, thinking of death, for all these things pass away.

When I was still in Tobolsk, I had received a warning in a light sleep: "Beware that you be not slit in two by Me." Seized with great fear, I sprang to my feet and fell before the icon, saying: "Lord, I shall not go there, where they chant the office according to the new way." I had attended Matins at the Cathedral for the namesday of a princess; I had committed the folly of entering that church in the presence of the governors; and upon my arrival, two or three times I had watched the celebration of the oblation,[23] standing in the sanctuary near the sacrificial table; and I had reproved them for the way they celebrated, but when I grew accustomed to it, I did not scold any more. I was stung by the spirit of the Antichrist. And my dear Lord Christ put fear into my soul: "Do you want to perish after so much suffering? Beware lest I slit you in two." I did not go to the Mass, but I went to dine with the prince and told them everything. And the good boyar, Prince Ivan Andreievich Khilkov,[24] began to weep. Accursed am I, if I forget God's mercy.

They saw that I was not going to be reconciled with them. So the Tsar ordered Rodion Streshnev to persuade me to be silent. And I did so, in order to please him. He was the God-established Tsar, and good to me. I hoped he would advance little by little. On St. Simeon's day[25] I was promised an appointment to the Printing Office, to correct the books, and I was extremely pleased; I liked this better than being confessor to the Tsar. He did me a favor, sending me ten rubles, and the Tsarina gave me ten rubles; and Lucas, the Tsar's confessor, ten; and Rodion Streshnev, ten. As for my old friend Fedor Rtishchev, he told his treasurer to put sixty rubles in my bonnet—to say nothing of the others. Each one brought me something or other.

I spent all my time with my dear Feodosia Prokofievna Morozova, for she was my spiritual daughter; and so was her sister, Princess Eudokia Prokofievna, dear martyrs in Christ! I likewise visited Anna Petrovna Miloslavsky constantly, and I went to Fedor Rtishchev, to have disputes with the apostates. I lived in this manner for about half a year.

Then I saw that "it availed nothing" in the Church, "but that rather a tumult was made," and so I began once more to grumble. I wrote a long letter to the Tsar, asking him to reestablish the old ways of piety, to defend our common mother, Holy Church, against heresy, and to place on the patriarchal throne an Orthodox pastor instead of the wolf and apostate Nicon, scoundrel and heretic. When I had finished writing, I fell seriously ill; and I sent the letter to be given to the Tsar on his journey by my spiritual son, Theodore, fool in Christ, who was afterwards hanged by the apostates on the Mezen. Theodore boldly approached the Tsar's carriage, letter in hand, and the Tsar had him arrested and taken under the grand staircase of the palace. He did not know that the letter was from me. Then, taking it from Theodore's hands, he let him go.

From that time on the Tsar was hostile towards me. He did not like my speaking again. He wanted me to be silent, but this did not suit me. And the bishops sprang on me like goats. They wanted to exile me once more from Moscow, for many came to me in Christ's name, and, when they had heard the truth, gave up attendng their mendacious services. The Tsar reprimanded me: "The bishops complain of you, they say you have emptied the churches. You shall be exiled once more." It was Boyar Peter Mikhailovich Saltikov who brought me the message. They took me to Mezen. The good people had given me many things in the name of Christ, but I had to leave everything behind and was accompanied on my journey only by my wife, children and family. And again I taught the people of God in the towns and condemned the piebald beasts. So they brought me to Mezen.[26] After holding me there a year and a half, they took me back to Moscow with two of my sons, Ivan and Procopy. Dame Avvakum and all the others remained at Mezen. Having brought me to Moscow, they first took me to the Monastery of St. Paphnutius.[27] And there they sent me a message, always repeating the same thing: "How long will you torment us? Reunite yourself with us, dear brother Avvakum." I rejected them like the devils, and they flew into my eyes. And I wrote a long and wrathful declaration and sent it through Cosmas, deacon of Yaroslavl and clerk in the Patriarch's chancery. This Cosmas was I know not what kind of man. In public he tried to persuade me, and in private he upheld me, saying: "Archpriest, do not renounce the old (way of) piety. You will be a man great in the eyes of God if you suffer to the end. Do not heed us if we perish." And I said to him that he should return to Christ. He answered: "This I cannot do; Nicon has caught me in his snares." To say the truth, the poor man had renounced Christ for Nicon and could not get back on his feet. I wept, blessed him, poor wretch; that was all I could do for him. God knows how it will go with him.

Thus, after I had spent ten weeks in chains at the Monastery of St. Paphnutius they took me back to Moscow, an exhausted man an an old nag; a guard behind me, a guard in front of me. Whip your horse and on you ride! At times, the horse would fall into the mud, its four legs in the air, and I tumbling over its head. One day we galloped ninety versts and I was half dead at the end of it. In Moscow, at the Patriarch's chapel, the bishops held a disputation with me. Then I was led to the cathedral, and after the Great Entry I was shorn, together with Deacon Theodore; they cursed me, and I cursed them. Great indeed was the tumult at that Mass. Having stayed some time at the Patriarch's Court, I was taken by night to the Chamber of the Palace. There a colonel examined me and sent me to the Secret Gates on the Waterfront. I supposed that they would throw me into the river, but here Dementy Bashmakov, the man of Private Affairs and the agent of Antichrist, awaited me. He said to me: "Archpriest, the Tsar ordered me to tell you: 'Fear no one; place your trust in me.'" I bowed to him, saying: "My thanks for his favor. What security has he for me? My trust is in Christ." Then they led me over the bridge to the other bank of the river, and on my way, I said to myself: "Put not your trust in princes, in the children of men in whom there is no salvation."

Then officer Joseph Salov and his musketeers took me to St. Nicholas' Monastery at Ugresha.[28] They sheared off my beard, the enemies of God! And why not? They are wolves and have no pity for the sheep. They tore off all my hair—the dogs! —leaving but a forelock, such as the Poles have on their heads. They drove us to the monastery, not along the roads, but through marshes and mire, so that people should not see us. They were well aware of their folly, but were unable to give it up. The devil had clouded their minds. How can we blame them? Were it not they, it would be others. The time is at hand when, according to the Gospels: "It must needs be that scandals come." And the other evangelists teaches us: "It is impossible that scandals should not come. But woe to him through whom they come."

Take heed, you who listen to me: Our misfortune is inevitable, we cannot escape it. If God allows scandals, it is that the elect shall be revealed. Let them be burned, let them be purified, let them who have been tried be made manifest among you. Satan has obtained our radiant Russia from God, so that she may become crimson with the blood of martyrs. Well planned, devil! It pleases us, too, to suffer for our dear Christ's sake.

At St. Nicholas I was locked up in a cold hall above the ice-cellar for seventeen weeks. There I had a vision sent by God. You may read about it in my letter to the Tsar.[29] And the Tsar came to the monastery and walked around my prison and sighed, but did not come in to see me. They had prepared the road and sprinkled it with sand. He thought and thought, and did not come in. I think he pitied me, but such was the will of God. When I had been shorn, there had been a great dispute at the palace between the Tsar and the late Tsarina. The dear lady was at that time on our side, and she had preserved me from mutilation.[30] There would be much to say about that. May God forgive them. I do not hold them responsible for my sufferings, not even in the other world; it is fitting that I should pray for them, alive or dead. The devil has cleft us in two, but they were always kind to me. Enough of this.

Then they took me once more to the monastery of St. Paphnutius and locked me up in a dark hall and kept me in chains for a little less than a year. Here Nicodemus, the cellarer, was good to me in the beginning, but later he became cruel, poor wretch. He well-nigh suffocated me, blocking the windows and the door, so that there was no vent for the smoke. The nobleman Ivan Bogdanovich Kaminin, a good man, who provided an endowment for the monastery, came to see me; he reprimanded the cellarer and tore off the shutters of bark and all the rest, and from that day on I had a window and air to breathe. But why be surprised at that cellarer? He had drunk of that tobacco-plant, sixty pounds of which were discovered at the house of the Bishop of Gaza, together with a lute and other objects for merrymaking.[31] I have sinned, forgive me; 'tis none of my business, but his own; let him stand or fall before his Master. I just happened to mention it. Such were the teachers of God's law most favored among them.

On Easter day I asked this cellarer Nicodemus to let me breathe and sit awhile on the threshold before the open door. But he abused me and cruelly refused my request; such was his whim. Then, when he went to his cell, he was taken mortally sick, so that he was anointed and given Communion, and he could scarcely breathe. This took place on Easter Monday, and on Tuesday night, there came to him a man resembling me, holding a censer in his hand and clad in radiant vestments. Having incensed Nicodemus, he took him by the hand and raised him, and he was healed. That very night Nicodemus came to my dungeon accompanied by his serving-man. On his way, he said: "Blessed is this monastery for containing such a dungeon! Blessed is the dungeon for containing such sufferers! Blessed also are the fetters!" And he fell at my feet, seizing my chain and saying: "Forgive, in the name of the Lord, forgive me, for I have sinned before God and before you. I have offended you, and therefore God has punished me." I asked him: "Tell me, how did God punish you?" And he: "You, yourself, came, and having incensed me, you did me the favor of raising me. Why do you conceal this?" And the servant who stood at his side added: "Lord Father, I myself led you out of the cell, supporting you and bowing to you. And you came back here." I ordered that this secret should be revealed to no one. He asked my advice, how he should live from now on for Christ. Should I order him to go and live in the wilderness? I admonished him and bade him not to give up his functions of cellarer, but to observe, at least in secret, the old traditions of the Fathers. He, having bowed to me, retired, and next morning, at the refectory, he related everything to the brethren. Then people came to me boldly and openly, requesting my prayers and my blessing.

And I taught them from the Scriptures and healed them with the word of God. At that time, even such enemies as I had, made peace with me. Alas, when shall I emerge from this time of vanity? It has been said: "Woe to you when men shall bless you." In truth, I know not how I shall endure to the end. Good deeds there have been none, and yet God glorified me. He knows, 'tis His will!

There also came to me in secret, with my children, the late Theodore, the same that was to be hanged. He consulted me: "Shall I wear my shift, as before, or must I put on other garments? The heretics are after me, seeking to destroy me." And he said: "I was at Riazan, under penance, in the Archbishop's court, and he, Hilarion, tormented me cruelly. Few days passed without a thrashing, and he held me in chains, forcing on me the new sacraments of the Antichrist. I was exhausted, and in the night I prayed and wept, saying: 'Lord, if Thou dost not save me, they will defile me and I shall perish. What then wilt Thou do to me?' And thus I went on, weeping; and suddenly, Father, my chains fell rattling to the ground, and the door was unlocked and opened of itself. Bowing before God, I went forth; I came to the gates, and they too were open, so I took the Moscow road. At dawn they started in pursuit on horseback. Three men rode past me without seeing me. Trusting in Christ, I went my way. And soon they turned back and passed me once more, complaining: 'The son of a harlot has escaped us, where shall we find him now?' And again they rode by and did not see me. And finally I reached Moscow. Now I have come to ask you: Must I go on suffering tortures, or shall I put on garments and live in Moscow?" And I, miserable sinner, ordered him to put on garments and to live in obscurity among men. But I did not save him from the hands of the heretics. They had him strangled on the Mezen, hanging him on the gallows. Eternal remembrance to him and to Luke Lavrentievich. My dear little ones, they suffered for Christ's sake! Glory be to God for them!

That Theodore had led a life of great austerity. In the daytime he behaved like a fool in Christ,[32] and he spent the night in weeping and praying. I have known many a good man, but never such an ascetic. He stayed with me six months in Moscow; I was still sick at the time. We lived in the back room. He would lie down for not more than an hour or two, and then he would rise and make a thousand prostrations; and at other times he would sit on the floor, or stand, weeping for three hours at a time. Meanwhile, I would lie there, sleeping or restless with pain. And he, having wept his fill, would come up to me, saying: "Look here, Archpriest, how long will you lie there? Only think, you are a priest! Shame upon you!" And he would end by dragging me out of bed; and he made me say my prayers seated there, he doing the prostrations for me. He was my friend true of heart.

And now I shall tell you again about my tribulations. From St. Paphnutius, they took me back to Moscow and placed me in the court of the Monastery. And they dragged me many times to the Chudov Monastery, before the ecumenical patriarchs; and our bishops all sat there like foxes.[33] I discussed many things with the patriarchs in the words of the Scriptures. God opened my sinful lips and Christ confounded them. Their last words to me were: "Why are you stubborn? All our people of Palestine, and the Serbs, and the Albanians and Valachians and Romans and Poles, all cross themselves with three fingers. You alone in your obstinacy cross yourself with two fingers. This is not fitting." And I, miserable wretch, how bitter I felt! But I could do nothing. I reproved them as well as I could, and my last word was: "I am uncorrupted, and I shake the dust from my feet, for it is written: 'better is one that feareth God, than a thousand ungodly.'" So they cried out even louder against me: "Take him, take him, he has dishonored us all." And they began to shove me and beat me. And the patriarchs themselves rushed at me; about forty of them, I believe—'twas a great army of the Antichrist that had mustered. Ivan Uvarov seized me and dragged me along; and I cried: "Hy, wait, don't beat me!" They staggered back and I said to the interpreter, an archimandrite: "Tell the patriarchs: Paul the Apostle says: 'It was

fitting that we should have such a high-priest, holy, innocent,'
and so forth. But you, how shall you celebrate Mass after beating a man?" Then they were seated, and I retired to the door
and lay down on my side, saying: "Stay seated, and I shall lie
down for a while." They laughed and said: "This Archpriest is
a fool, without respect for patriarchs." I answered: "We are
fools for Christ's sake . . . we are weak but you are strong, you
are honorable, but we are without honor." Then the bishops
returned and began to discuss the *Alleluia*, and Christ helped
me to confound their Roman heresy with the help of Dionysius
the Areopagite. And Euthymius, the cellarer of the Chudov
Monastery, said to me: "You are right; it is of no use to discuss
anything further with you."

So they put me in chains; the Tsar sent an officer and musketeers, and they led me to the Vorobiev hills. With me were
the priest Lazarus and the monk Epiphanius, shorn and abused
as if they were village peasants, the dear souls! A man in his
senses could only weep at the look of them. But let them suffer,
why be troubled on their account? Christ was better than they,
and yet—our beloved!—He had to suffer as much from their
forefathers, Annas and Caiaphas. Why wonder at the men of
today? They imitate their model. It is on their account we
should be troubled, the wretches! Alas, poor Niconians! You
shall perish of your wicked and stubborn tempers!

Then we were returned to Moscow, to the court of the St.
Nicholas Monastery, and again they sought from us a profession of orthodoxy. And the gentlemen of the bedchamber,
Artemon and Dementy, were sent to me many a time, and they
repeated the Tsar's words to me: "Archpriest, I know your
innocent, spotless, and godly life. I ask your blessing, together
with the Tsarina and my children. Pray for us." Thus spoke
the messenger, bowing, and I always wept for the Tsar. I had
the greatest pity for him. And he went on: "I pray you, listen
to me, reunite yourself with the ecumenical patriarchs, at least
in part." I answered: "Let me die if God wills it so, but I will
not be reunited with the apostates. You are my Tsar—but they?

—what have they got to do with you? They have lost their own Tsar, and now they drag themselves here to devour you! I will not lower my arms, which are lifted to heaven, until God shall give you back to me!" There were many messages of this kind. One thing and another was discussed. Their last word was: "Wherever you are, do not forget us in your prayers." Even today, miserable sinner that I am, I pray for him as well as I can.

Then, after mutilating our brothers, but not me, they banished us to Pustozersk.[34] From there I wrote two letters to the Tsar, the first one short, and the second, longer. I told him various things, among them, of certain signs that God had shown me in my prisons. Let him who reads understand. Moreover, I and the brethren sent, as a gift to the followers of the true faith in Moscow, the Deacon's manuscript entitled *Answer of the Orthodox*, along with a condemnation of heresy and apostasy. It declared the truth about the dogmas of the Church. And two letters were also sent to the Tsar by the priest Lazarus. And for all this, we too received some gifts in return: in my house on the Mezen they hanged two men, spiritual children of mine, Theodore, the fool in Christ already mentioned, and Luke Lavrentievich, servants of Christ.

At that time came the order that my own two sons, Ivan and Procopy, should be hanged, but they, poor wretches, lost their heads and missed the chance to seize the crown of victory; fearing death, they made submission. So, with their mother, were they imprisoned underground. There you are: death in the absence of death! May you repent in your prison, while the devil thinks of some other device. Death is terrifying? Little wonder! There was a time when Peter, the dear friend of Christ, was a traitor, and went out and wept bitterly, and was forgiven because of his tears! So why should we wonder about these children! 'Twas because of my sins that their weakness was permitted. Well, so be it. Christ has power over our forgiveness and our salvation!

After that, the same officer Ivan Yelagin who had been with us at Mezen came to Pustozersk, and he received from us a profession which ran thus: "Such and such a year and month. We inalterably observe the traditions of the Holy Fathers, and we anathematize the heretical assembly of Païsius, the Patriarch of Palestine, and his followers." And this profession declared many other things, and Nicon, the maker of heresies, received his share in it. For this we were taken to the scaffold, and the verdict was read to us; I was taken to prison without mutilation. The verdict stated: "Let Avvakum be imprisoned in a wooden framework underground and be given only bread and water. In answer, I spat. I wanted to starve myself to death, and did not eat for eight days and more, until the brethren ordered me to eat again.

They took the priest Lazarus and cut his tongue out of his throat; there was little blood, and soon it stopped flowing. And he went on speaking, without a tongue. Then, placing his right hand on the scaffold, they cut it off at the wrist, and as the severed hand lay on the ground, the fingers disposed themselves for the sign of the Cross according to tradition—and the hand remained thus for a long time for people to see, making its profession of faith, poor thing! I myself marvelled at this; the lifeless condemning the living! On the third day I put my finger in his mouth; it was smooth, tongueless, but he felt no pain. God healed him in no time. In Moscow they had cut part of his tongue, some of it had remained. But this time, they plucked it out entirely. And for two years he could speak as clearly as though he had a tongue. After two years there was another miracle: in three days there grew in his mouth another tongue only a little blunt, but he praised God constantly and condemned the apostates.

Then they took the hermit from Solovki, a monk of strict observance, the elder Epiphany, and also cut out the whole of his tongue and severed four fingers from his hand. And at first he spoke with difficulty. Then he prayed to the immaculate Mother of God, and in a vision two tongues were shown to him: the tongue of Moscow and that of this land, suspended in mid-air. Taking one of them, he placed it in his mouth, and from that day on he could speak clearly and distinctly, and a perfect tongue grew in his mouth. Marvellous are the works of God and ineffable the ways of the Lord. He permits execution, and then again heals and forgives. But why speak of it at length? God is of old a miracle-worker.

Then they covered us with earth. They placed a wooden framework under the earth and another one nearby, and a common enclosure around them with four locks, and guards were placed before the prison doors. And we, imprisoned here and everywhere—sing before our Lord Christ, Son of God, a canticle such as Solomon sang as he looked upon his mother, Bathsheba.

Having first gone from us to Mezen, Pilate[35] journeyed to Moscow. And in Moscow the rest of us were roasted and baked. They burned Isaiah and they burned Abraham, and a great many other champions of the Church were annihilated. God will count their numbers. It is amazing that the Niconians refuse to regain their senses: they propose to establish the faith through fire, whip and gallows. Who were the apostles that taught them these things? I do not know. My Christ did not order His apostles to teach in this way, to lead men to the faith with fire, whip and gallows. He commanded the Apostles: "Go ye into the whole world and preach the gospel to every creature."[36]

Now I beg the forgiveness of every true believer: there are things concerning my life of which perhaps I ought not to speak. But I have read the Acts of the Apostles and the Epistles of Paul: the Apostles said of their deeds, when God was working through them: "Not unto us but to our God be the praise." And I am nothing. I have said and I repeat: I am a sinner, a fornicator and a ravisher, thief and murderer, friend of publicans and sinners, and to every man a wretched hypocrite. So forgive me and pray for me; and I must pray for you who read me or listen to me. I can do no better, and what I do, I relate to men; let them pray to God for my sake. On the day of judgment they shall know my actions, for good or evil. I am untaught in words, but not in knowledge; I am not learned in dialectic, rhetoric and philosophy, but I have Christ's wisdom within me. As the Apostle says: "Although I be rude in speech, yet not in knowledge."

Forgive me, and concerning my ignorance, I shall moreover tell you the following: yes, I foolishly transgressed my spiritual Father's law; and because of this my house was punished. Listen, for the love of God, how this came about: at the time when I was still an ordinary priest, the Tsar's confessor, Archpriest Stephen Vonifatievich, gave me as a blessing the icon of Metropolitan Philip and the book of St. Ephraem the Syrian, for my own profit and for that of others. But I, wretched one, ignoring the fatherly blessing and instructions, bartered that book against a horse of my cousin's, because of his insistent demands. At that time my brother Yefimy was staying with me; he was experienced in the reading of books and zealous for the Church. Later he became the chief lector of the elder Princess, but died of the plague along with his wife. This Yefimy fed and watered the horse and cared for it in every way, very often neglecting his prayers on that account. God beheld our unrighteous conduct: I bartering the book and my brother neglecting prayer and giving all his attentions to a beast. And the Lord deigned to punish us in the following manner: devils began to torment the horse day and night; it was continually in a sweat and a state of exhaustion, more dead than alive. I did not as yet understand why the devil was after us. Once on Sunday, after supper, my brother Yefimy was reciting, at Lauds, the 119th psalm. Crying out: "Look down upon me and have mercy on me," he dropped the book and fell to the ground, struck down by the devil, and he began to shriek and howl in dreadful tones, for the demons were tormenting him cruelly. I had staying with me two other brothers of mine, Cosmas and Gerasim, and although they were larger than he, they could not restrain him. And all those of my household, some thirty persons or so, were holding him and weeping and crying out: "Lord, have mercy upon us, we have sinned before Thee, we have outraged Thy bounty, have mercy upon us, miserable sinners! By the prayers of our Holy Fathers, forgive this youth!"

But he, even more bedevilled, howled and trembled and writhed in convulsions.

But at that moment, with the help of God, I did not let myself be troubled by that diabolical tumult. Having recited my Office, I prayed with tears to Christ and the Mother of God, saying: "Our Lady, most Holy Mother of God! Pray, show me for what sin I have deserved such punishment, so that knowing it, I may repent before your Son and you, and commit this sin no more!" And, weeping, I sent to the church, for the breviary and holy water, my spiritual son Symeon, about the same age as my Yefimy, fourteen years old or so; these two youths, Yefimy and Symeon were friends and associates, sustaining and comforting each other with books and prayer, both living in strict fasting and penance. Symeon wept over his friend, went to the church and brought back the book and the holy water. I started to recite over the bedevilled youth the prayers of Basil the Great, and Symeon assisted me; he tended the censer and the candles, and offered me the holy water; all the others held the possessed. I said the words of the prayer: "In the name of the Lord, I command thee, mute and deaf spirit, go out of this creature, do not reenter into him, but go into the deserts, where man liveth not, and God alone looketh down." But the devil did not obey and did not go out of my brother. And again I repeated these words, but the devil did not obey, but tormented my brother even more than before. Oh, misfortune upon me! How shall I tell this? I am ashamed and do not dare! But according to the orders of the elder Epiphanius, I shall describe the way in which it occurred.

I took the censer and incensed the icons and the possessed, and then I fell on the bench and wept for a long time. Then, rising, I repeated the prayer of St. Basil and cried to the devil: "Go out of that creature." The devil twisted my brother into a ring, and, writhing, went out of him and sat on the window; and my brother was like one dead. I sprinkled the window, and the devil came down and hid in the millstone corner; and my brother pointed at him, and again I sprinkled. The devil then climbed onto the stove, and my brother pointed there. Once more I sprinkled the holy water, and my brother pointed under the stove and crossed himself. I did not pursue the devil any further, but I gave my brother holy water to drink in the Lord's name. And he sighed from the very depths of his heart and spoke to me thus: "God save you, Father, for having freed me from the prince of devils and his two princelings. My brother Avvakum will thank you for your kindness. And God bless that youth who went to fetch the book and the holy water and helped you to fight them. He was in the likeness of my friend Symeon. They brought me to the river Sundovik, and there they beat me, saying: "You have been delivered to us because your brother Avvakum bartered his book against a horse and because you loved that beast. So tell your brother to take the book and pay back the money to his cousin." I said to him: "I, dear soul, am your brother Avvakum." And he answered: "How should you be my brother? You are my Father, you took me away from the prince and the princelings; as for my brother, he lives at Lopatishchi, and he will thank you."[37] I gave him some more holy water to drink, and he took the vessel from my hands and wanted to drain it, so sweet was that water to him. And when there was no more, I rinsed the vessel and again made him drink, but he rejected it. I spent all that winter night tending him. I lay a while at his side, and then I went to Matins; and in my absence, the devils once more assailed him, but less vigorously.

When I came back from church, I anointed him, and again the devils went out of him and he was sound of mind. But he was weak, broken by the devils; he would glance at the stove and become fearful; when I left, the devils would return. I fought the devils like dogs for three weeks for my sins, until I took the book back and paid for it with money. I went to see my friend, Abbot Hilarion; he offered a particle from the Eucharistic bread for my brother's recovery; in those days Hilarion led a good life, but since becoming Archbishop of Riazan, he has been a persecutor of the Christians. And I requested the help of other ecclesiastics for my brother; by their prayers they obtained forgiveness for us, miserable sinners, and my brother was freed from the devils. Such was the punishment for transgressing my father's commandment. How, then, shall we be punished for violating the commandments of the Lord? Ah, we shall deserve but fire and torment! I know not how to pass my days! I am full of weakness and hypocrisy and enmeshed with lies! I am clothed with hatred and self-love! I am lost because I condemn all men; I think of myself as something, whereas I—accursed!—am but excrement and rot, yea, dung! Foul of soul and body. 'Twould be good if I lived with pigs and dogs in their kennels; they too are evil-smelling, like my soul. Their stench is from nature, but I am evil-smelling because of my sins, like a dead dog left lying in the streets of the city. God bless the bishops who buried me underground; at least, giving out stench to myself for my sins, I offer no scandal to others. Yea, this is good.

And in Moscow also, upon my return from Siberia, I had with me a possessed man, Philip by name. He was chained to the wall in the corner of the house, for the devil in him was harsh and cruel, he beat and fought, and no one in my household could master him. And when I, miserable sinner, came up to him with the cross and holy water, he became obedient, and fell senseless before the cross of Christ and dared do nothing against me. And with the prayers of the Holy Fathers, the devil was cast out of him by the power of God, but his mind was not wholly restored. He was cared for by Theodore, the fool in Christ, who was afterwards hanged on the Mezen by the apostates. He recited the psalms over Philip and taught him the prayer of Jesus. I myself would be absent from my house in the daytime and could tend Philip only at night. One day I returned from Fedor Rtishchev filled with depression, for at this house I had engaged in much noisy quarreling with the heretics concerning the faith and the law. Meanwhile there was disorder in my own house: Dame Avvakum had quarreled with a servant-woman, the widow Fetinia; the devil had precipitated them into unreasoning anger against each other. When I entered the house, I beat them both and gave them great offence, because of my own sour temper: I sinned before God and before them. And then the devil was aroused in Philip and began to break his chain, raging and shrieking horribly. The servants were seized with panic, and there was a great tumult. I, without having repented, went up to him, wanting to tame him, but things did not go as usual. He seized me, and started to beat and thrash me, tearing at me as if I were a cob-web, crying out: "You have fallen into my hands!" I recited a prayer, but prayer without deeds is of no use. The servants could not tear me out of his hands; I gave myself up to him. I knew I had sinned, so let him beat me! But God works miracles: he beat me, but I felt no pain. Then he thrust me away from him, saying: "I do not fear you." And I was much aggrieved, saying to myself: "The devil has the better of me!" I lay down for a while and collected myself. Rising, I went and found my wife, and with tears asked her forgiveness, bowing to the ground before her and saying: "Nastasia Markovna, forgive me, miserable sinner. And she bowed to me in the same way. And I asked likewise Fetinia's forgiveness. Then I lay down in the middle of the room and ordered each man to beat me with a scourge, each giving me five strokes on my wretched back. There were about twenty people, and my wife and children, and they all lashed me, weeping. I said: "He, who does not beat me, shall have no share with me in the Kingdom of Heaven." And they beat me unwillingly and with tears, while I recited a prayer with each stroke. When every one of them had scourged me, I rose and asked their forgiveness, and the devil, seeing that it was inevitable, again went out of Philip. And I blessed him with the cross, and he was as before. Later, he wholly recovered, by the grace of God in Jesus Christ, Our Lord. Glory be to Him!

When I was an ordinary priest and had but begun my striving for perfection, this is the way the devil terrified me. My wife fell sick and her spiritual Father came to visit her. In the dead of night I went to the church to get the book for her confession. As I entered the porch, there was a small table there, which, by the devil's device, began to jump about where it stood. And I, fearing nothing, prayed before the icon, and going up to the table, I made the sign of the cross and put it back into its place, and it stopped dancing around. As I came to the nave, there was another trick of the demons: a corpse lay in its coffin on the bench, and through a device of the devil, the lid of the coffin was lifted, and the shroud began to wave about, filling me with fear. And I, praying to God, blessed the dead, and everything was as before. As I entered the sanctuary, I saw the chasubles and dalmatics flying around, to frighten me. But I prayed and kissed the altar and blessed the vestments, and going up, touched them, and they hung motionless as before. So I took the book and left the church. Such are the devices of the devil against us. But enough of this! What is the power of the cross and of holy oil unable to perform on the possessed and on the sick, by the grace of God! And we must remember this: not for our sake and because of us, but to His own name doth God add glory. I who am but mud, what could I do, were it not for Christ? It befits me to weep about myself. Judas was a miracle-worker, but because of his greed for money, fell into the devil's hands. And the devil himself was in heaven, but was cast out because of his pride. Adam was in paradise, but was driven out of it for his gluttony and condemned to hell for 5,500 years. Knowing this, let every man who believes he is able to stand, beware lest he fall. Clasp the feet of Christ and pray to the Mother of God and all the saints, and all will be well.

And so, my Elder, you have heard a great deal of my cackle. In the name of the Lord, I order you to write likewise for the servants of Christ, relating how the Mother of God broke that devil in her arms and gave him over to you, and how the ants devoured the secret part of your body, and how the demon set fire to your wood, and your cell was burned, but everything in it remained intact, and how you cried out to heaven, and what else you may recall for the glory of Christ and the Mother of God.[38] Listen, then, to what I say: If you do not write, I shall be angry. You listened to me with enjoyment—why, then, be ashamed? Relate it, if only a little. At the Council of Jerusalem the Apostles Paul and Barnabas told "what great signs and wonders God had wrought among the Gentiles by them." And the name of the Lord Jesus was magnified. And we find many instances in the Epistles and the Acts. And so, speak without fear, only keep a firm conscience. Say that you do not seek your own glory, but that of Christ and the Mother of God. Let the servant of Christ rejoice reading this account. When he reads us and we are dead, he will remember us before God. And we shall pray to God for those who read us and listen to us. They shall be our kin, there, at Christ's side, and we shall be theirs, for ever and ever, Amen.

ST. TYCHON

A WESTERNIZING KENOTIC

TYCHON The eighteenth century was no
more favorable to the spiritual life
in Russia than elsewhere: it was the period of eager and violent transplantation of Western civilization into Russia. These
influences of the West were avidly absorbed by the upper
classes, accepted only with reluctance by the common people.
Along with scientific and social influences, Russia received from
the West the "last words" of its modern thought: rationalism,
deism, materialism, atheism. The philosophy of the French
encyclopedists was very popular among the cultivated Russian
gentry. The peasants, cut off from educated society, adhered
to the old Muscovite traditions or listened greedily to the
apostles of secret, persecuted sects.

Between these two social strata the Church held a special
place. While preserving the Eastern liturgical and devotional
life, it modernized its theology in the school of the West. In the
seminaries which were founded in most dioceses, the teaching
was in Latin and the textbooks were those of Catholic and
Protestant theologians, adapted to the needs of the Orthodox
Church. St. Tychon was a student (and later a professor) in
one of these seminaries (in Novgorod), and he read the ancient
Fathers for the most part in Latin translations. The fundamental ideas of St. Augustine now made their first entrance into
Orthodox theology (with some mitigations, however) and
brought about a considerable rapprochement between the
Christian West and the East. A balance between Catholicism
and Protestantism was the mark of the new Russian theology,
the axis line passing nearer to Rome than to Geneva or Witten-
berg, although in the court circles of Catherine II, the opinion

was generally held that Orthodoxy was but an Eastern branch of Protestantism.

In the second half of the century, mystical currents in opposition to the dominant rationalism were infiltrating from the West. Along with the Free-Masonry movement in lay circles—and this movement had a Christian character in Russia at that time—Protestant pietism from Germany found its way into the Church. In Halle, Germany, a press was set up especially for printing pietist literature in Russian. The famous work of A. Arndt On the True Christianity, appeared in several Russian editions. Until the end of the century, a certain evangelical spirit coming from abroad mitigated and tempered the rather scholastic character of the theology prevailing in Russia.

In his writing and in his personality, St. Tychon (1724-83) reflects all the Western Christian influences of his time. Yet, deeply and fundamentally, his spiritual life was nourished from the source of Russian kenoticism. Of his two main theological works, one has, characteristically, the same title as Arndt's book, although the content is quite different: it is an essay in systematic theology which grew out of Tychon's lectures in the seminaries. Centered on the dogma of the Redemption, and rather emotional in style and devotional in purpose, this book, if translated into any European language, would betray in nothing its "oriental" origin, so completely does it fit into the pattern of Western evangelicism. The other book, A Spiritual Treasure Collected from the World, is an adaptation of a work in Latin by the seventeenth-century Anglican theologian Joseph Hall, Bishop of Norwich.

St. Tychon was a brilliant writer trained in a rhetorical school in which the traditions of later Hellenism (St. John Chrysostom) were fused with the Baroque of the seventeenth and eighteenth centuries. Although our age has lost the taste for the rhetorical "high style" of the past, the obvious defects of the literary school to which he belonged detract little from his work: the reader is always conscious of the personal vein, the cry of a heart deeply wounded by the love of Jesus.

Tychon's personality is much more interesting than his writings. *He is the first "modern" among the Russian saints, with his interior conflicts, his painful groping for his spiritual way— the constant shifting of light and shadow, of ecstasy and depression. The dramatic crisis of his life, the renunciation of his bishopric, finds no sufficient rational explanation. As Bishop of Voronezh, Tychon developed a great and fruitful activity: in preaching, in training the clergy, in organizing a seminary. Yet, after four years, he suddenly asked for permission to resign and retire into the solitude of a provincial monastery (at Zadonsk), and here he spent the remainder of his life. Tychon's first biographer, Bishop Eugene Bolkhovitinov, speaks frankly of the nervous illness which he calls Tychon's "melancholy."*

One of Tychon's "cellsmen" (monk servants) refers likewise to his "hypochondriacal and even choleric" temperament. A great irritability rendered intercourse with people difficult to Tychon until he overcame it by spiritual effort. But to the end the society of men was not easy for him. For the most part he shunned it, making exception chiefly of the simple people— peasants, beggars, and even imprisoned criminals. In this preference for the poor and oppressed and in his endeavors to protect them from cruel masters, in his voluntary poverty, Tychon is faithful to the Russian traditions of Sts. Theodosius and Sergius.

His spiritual life has two foci: the thought of death and the vision of the celestial world. He meditated constantly on this "double eternity." The fear of eternal torments was a mystical reality for him to as great an extent as were the visions of Christ, the holy Virgin, and the angels. In both these objects of contemplation, Tychon is the son of the Western Baroque rather than the heir of Eastern spirituality. Especially uncharacteristic of Russian religion is his continual concentration on the sufferings of the Crucified Savior. He had always before his eyes the icons—or, rather, pictures—portraying the various moments in the tragedy of Golgotha. These were obviously pictures after the Western pattern, the Eastern Church knowing no sacred models for them.

Thus St. Tychon united in his rather complex and tempestu-

ous spiritual life the Catholic devotion of the Crucified Lord, Protestant evangelicism, and Russian kenoticism—all three aspects of the confessional approaches to Christ.

Tychon was for long the most beloved saint of modern Russia. It is well known that Dostoevsky had him in mind (as well as Dostoevsky's contemporary, Ambrose, the staretz of Optina) when he endeavored to present the portrait of a saintly staretz in contrast to the figures of Russian nihilists. Yet close comparison of Zosima (The Brothers Karamazov) with Tychon reveals a disparity which is greater than the likeness. For Dostoevsky, in the attempt to reproduce the charitable and kenotic personality which attracted him in Tychon, introduced into his model a Christian humanism, a serene freedom and cosmic mysticism of Mother Earth, which were entirely foreign to the melancholy recluse of Zadonsk.

MEMOIRS BY CHEBOTAREV OF THE LIFE OF

ST. TYCHON OF ZADONSK

ALTHOUGH A LIFE OF THE LATE BISHOP OF VORONEZH, TYCHON, APPEARED UNDER THE TITLE OF *A Complete Account* AND the biographer[1] applied all his efforts to the task, he was unable to relate everything in full detail, having written his account from hearsay and as told by others. Whereas I, wretch that I am, lived at Tychon's side from 1770 onward and heard many things from his own saintly lips which he told me in conversation during his spare hours, speaking of his life, beginning with his early childhood and describing his various experiences. I was witness of his way of life, which was noble and of great virtue, and of this I shall have more to say further on. But here, truly and precisely rendered, are the Bishop's own words:

I first remember myself in our mother's house (I do not remember my father).[2] We were four brothers and three sisters. My eldest brother was a church cleric, the second was a soldier, and the other two, including myself, were very young and lived in great poverty, such that we had scarcely enough to eat and our mother was greatly concerned about our bringing-up. But in our parish there was a certain mail-coachman who was well-off and had no children. He visited us frequently, and he took a liking to me. Often he would beg my mother to let him adopt me, saying, "Give Timothy to me [Tychon's name before he became a religious was Timothy]. I will bring him up as my own son, and all I have shall be his."

Although my mother at first refused, not wishing to part with me, our dire want of food obliged her finally to give me to that mail-coachman. Taking me by the hand, she led me to his home. This I remember well. My eldest brother was away at the time, but when he returned, he asked my sister, "Where is Mother?"

My sister answered, "Mother has taken Timothy to the mail-coachman." My brother hurried after Mother, and having caught up with her, knelt before her, asking, "Where are you taking the boy? If you give him to the mail-coachman, the child also will become a mail-coachman. I should sooner be a beggar myself than give away my brother to this man. Let us teach him to read and write, and then he can become a church-reader or a sexton." This made my mother turn her steps homeward with me. But as there was nothing to eat in our house, I went to work on the farm of a rich peasant, harrowing or ploughing all day to earn my bread from that farmer. Such was the poverty in which I grew up. But when a seminary was founded in Novgorod and the children of clergymen were sought to enter classes there, my mother took me to the city and placed me in this seminary. Soon afterwards she passed away.

I pursued my studies at the State's expense and suffered great privations, for I was without personal means.[3] When I received bread at the seminary, I would keep half of it for my needs and sell the other half. With the money thus obtained, I would buy a candle, and sitting on the stove,[4] I would read a book. My classmates whose fathers were rich and who spent their time playing, would taunt me. Picking up an old shoe, they would wave it at me, shouting, "We salute you!"[5] Later on, when I was ordained suffragan bishop and returned to Novgorod, my classmates came to me asking for my blessing. But I said to them, "When we were small boys at the seminary you laughed at me and waved an old shoe. And now it is a censer that you would wave at me." (For at that time some of my former companions were priests or deacons.) They said, "Your Grace, forgive us." I answered, "I spoke in jest."

Now I shall relate how he was ordained bishop, for this was done by the special will of Providence, as I heard from His Lordship's own lips. Here are his words:

I had never thought of this high dignity [of becoming a bishop], but wanted to retire to some especially isolated monastery to receive the tonsure and lead a solitary life. But the Almighty willed that I should become a bishop—surely an unworthy one! At that time I was Archimandrite[6] in the city of Tver, where I was a member of the Consistory[7] and rector of the seminary. One day, it being the feast of Holy Easter, I was celebrating Mass together with Bishop Athanasius in the cathedral. And what should occur? During the hymn of the Cherubim, Most Reverend Athanasius was standing before the sacrificial table, cutting the particles of the holy bread and praying for the health of the living.[8] I went up to the sacrificial table and said, "Remember me in your prayers, Your Grace."

The Bishop meant to answer, "Your holy dignity of Archimandrite shall be remembered in heaven." But by mistake he said, "Your holy dignity of Bishop." He smiled, adding, "May God permit you to become a bishop!"

I was to learn afterwards that on that very day of Easter, in Petersburg, the first member of the Synod, Metropolitan Demetrius Sechenov, was casting lots[9] with Epiphanius, Bishop of Smolensk. There were seven candidates represented by these lots, but the Bishop of Smolensk said to the Metropolitan, "I beseech you, order Rector Tychon of Tver to be entered as a candidate."

But the Metropolitan answered, "He is young; there is yet time." Then, turning to his secretary, he added, "However, you may write down Tychon's name as a candidate."

My lot was the eighth. The lots were cast three times, and each time mine was drawn. So the Metropolitan said, "No doubt God wishes it to be so. Let Tychon be ordained bishop." The Metropolitan related this to me himself, adding that his intention had been to transfer me as Archimandrite to the Monastery of the Holy Trinity.[10]

At that time peasants were attached to the monasteries,[11] and there was in the neighborhood of Tver an estate belonging to one of these communities. There was a grove on that land, a place both beautiful and isolated. I planned to build a cell in that grove. On a Saturday in spring, having spare time on my hands, I visited the estate. The peasants were building a bridge across a small stream, and while I walked about I watched them at work. When I heard the cathedral bell ringing for Vespers, I ordered a carriage and drove to the monastery. Entering the church, I went and stood at my usual place. Presently a servant sent by the Bishop came to me and said, "Father Rector, please go to His Grace." I replied, "I shall first hear Vespers and shall then go at once to His Grace." But scarcely had the man left the monastery when another servant came to me, saying, "Please hurry." Without waiting for the end of Vespers, I went to the Bishop's house.

On the way I felt my heart filling with both joy and foreboding, for some persons belonging to the Bishop's household (such as the steward and a few others) were unfriendly towards me, and I wondered whether there had been some slander against me. When I arrived, I hurried into the Bishop's anteroom and asked the secretary to announce me to His Grace. At that very moment the Bishop appeared in person and said to me most affably, "I humbly request you to come in, Father Rector." Then, adding, "I offer you my congratulations for having been appointed Bishop," he showed me the order of the Synod and said, with tears in his eyes, "I am sorry to part with you. But do not tarry; give over the administration of the monastery and go to Petersburg."

When I had settled the affairs of the monastery, I went to Petersburg and was ordained bishop. After that I left at once for Novgorod, whither synodical instructions had preceded me, ordering that I should be met with the customary honors. This was done in a fitting manner, with the ringing of bells. During the ceremony, the inhabitants of the city came in great numbers, wishing to see me inasmuch as I had been educated at the Novgorod Seminary. And what should occur but that among the congregation in the church should be my own sister. She was a widow and extremely poor, earning her living by serving in the homes of the rich and scrubbing their floors. She worked in the city of Valday until the time when, having been ordained bishop, I had her stay in Novgorod and supported her on my income. On the morning following my own arrival I sent a carriage to fetch her, and she came, but dared not enter my apartment. I opened the door, saying, "Welcome, sister." So she entered and began to weep. I spoke to her: "Why are you weeping, sister?"

"Because of my great joy, brother!" she answered. "Remember in what poverty we lived in our mother's house. There were days when we lacked the most ordinary food, and now I see so high a rank bestowed on you. Yesterday I stood in the crowd and watched the reception given to you."

I said to her, "Sister, you must visit me often, and now you shall have the necessary transportation. There is a horse and carriage for you."

"Thank you, brother," she replied; "but my frequent visits may tire you."

"No, my dear!" I exclaimed. "I shall never tire of your visits. I love you with all my heart and respect you." (For she was my elder sister.)

But after I came to Novgorod, my sister lived only one month and then passed away. I myself performed her funeral service. In accordance with the bishop's ritual, I kissed the holy icons, went up to the coffin, uncovered it, and made the sign of the cross on her body. She seemed to smile at me. God alone knows whether this was an illusion of my eyes; I cannot vouch for it. On my way to the funeral and during the entire ceremony I could not restrain my tears and was as if outside myself because of my great sorrow. For my sister was a woman of good life.

In his will, His Grace wrote among other things the following: "I thank God that He protected me in the hour of calamity or mortal danger"; concerning which, this is what he told me:

When I was still a teacher[12] it happened that during vacation time the Archimandrite of the St. Alexander Monastery invited us teachers for a visit. When I arrived at the monastery I went forth alone and climbed into the bell tower, led by curiosity and wishing to survey the grounds about the monastery — a truly beautiful landscape. Without testing the solidity of the railings, I leaned on them, and suddenly they crumbled to the ground. At the same moment an invisible hand seemed to push me back, so that I fell at the foot of the bell, half-fainting. I regained my spirits with difficulty and went down the steps of the bell tower, groping my way until at last I reached the Archimandrite's cell. The persons there assembled exclaimed, "Why, you seem distraught! Look at yourself in the mirror; you are as pale as death."

I replied, "First give me some tea, and I shall then tell you why I am so distraught." After I had been given some tea, I led the way to the bell tower and we gazed at the railings, lying shattered on the ground. I said to those who accompanied me, "I too might have lain broken on this very spot." Later in Tver, when I was Archimandrite, and in Voronezh, when I was already diocesan Bishop, I was in mortal peril from runaway horses.

He also described to me a wondrous vision:

This was before I received the tonsure. When I was still a teacher, I had formed the habit (and I was much attached to it) of spending the night without sleep, either reading salutary books or pursuing edifying meditations. (But I tell you this in deep confidence; you must be silent concerning it.) This night in the month of May was very pleasant, mild and light. I left my room and went out onto the porch, which was on the north side, and standing there I meditated on eternal bliss. Suddenly the skies opened and were filled with a glow and a dazzling light such as mortal tongue is unable to describe: the mind is quite incapable of grasping it. This lasted but a moment, and then the skies regained their ordinary appearance, while I, who had beheld this wondrous vision, conceived an ardent desire to lead a life of solitude. And for a long time afterwards my mind recalled what I had seen, and even now, when I think of it, my heart is filled with joy and happiness.

Now I shall tell how His Grace lived in his cell at the monastery of Zadonsk. Likewise I shall describe his deeds and labors pleasing to God, for I, miserable man, was witness of these things.

First, at dinner it was his custom to listen to the Holy Scriptures of the Old Testament, which I read aloud to him. But what was remarkable in him was his great and ardent love of God. He rarely sat at table without tears of contrition, especially when he was listening to the reading of the book of Isaias. Sometimes he would say, "Read this chapter again"; and putting down his spoon, he would begin to weep. Remarkable also was the sincere love he bore his neighbor. Nearly every day, when sitting down to his meal, he would say, "Glory be to God!

What wonderful food I am tasting while my brothers suffer: one is imprisoned, another lives on poor fare, while a third is without salt." And he would add, "Woe to me, wretch that I am!"

In the evening I would read the New Testament to him, and sometimes this reading would be greatly prolonged, for he would ask, "Do you understand what you are reading?" If I answered, "No, I do not understand this or that," he would say, "I shall explain it." Sometimes this would take an hour.

He was wont to spend the night without sleep and lie down to rest at dawn. At night his exercises were prayer with genuflections and prostrations. These prayers were not cold but were filled with the greatest fervor, proceeding from a contrite heart, so that sometimes he would cry aloud, "Lord, have pity on me! Lord spare me!" And sometimes he would add, "My Benefactor, have pity on me!" And he would beat his head on the ground. And all this was wrought in him by the fiery love of God in his interior. As the hour of midnight struck, he would go into the anteroom of his cell, chanting the holy psalms in a gentle and contrite voice. When in a sombre mood, he would chant the psalm: "It is good for me that thou hast humbled me." When in a serene mood, he would chant: "Praise ye the Lord from the heavens," and other psalms of consolation. And this was always accompanied by tears and deep sighs.

After dinner he would take a short rest of an hour or more. Then, rising, he would read the lives of the holy fathers and other books. In summer it was his custom to take a walk in the monastery garden and beyond its grounds. He bade me not to approach him during these walks except in case of great necessity. "If you must come to me for some urgent matter," he said, "cough once or twice to make me turn around." This I would do, but one day when I had followed him into the garden, though I had coughed several times before coming upon him, so deeply was he engrossed in his meditations that he did not hear me. He was kneeling, his face turned to the east, his arms outstretched to the heavens. I went up to him and said, "Your Grace." He was so startled that he broke into perspiration. He said to me, "My heart is trembling like a dove. I have told you many a time to cough before coming up to me." Well, if I had told him that I had coughed, he would have answered that he did not hear me.

He never went forth without his psalter, which he carried in his breast-pocket (for it was a small book). In the end he could recite it by heart; he blessed me with it. When on a journey he always read the psalter, and sometimes he would chant the psalms aloud and teach me to chant them or explain to me some of the texts. He attended Mass every day, singing in the choir, and he rarely sang without weeping. It may truly be said that he had a special gift of tears granted by God. Two springs ever flowed from his eyes. Rarely did he smile at anything, and if he did so, he would say, "Lord, forgive me, wretch that I am, for I have sinned before you." He carefully avoided vain conversations, and his own speech usually concerned eternal torments and eternal bliss, also vices and Christian virtues. He was endowed with a remarkable memory, so that he knew by heart the Old and the New Testament; when speaking on any matter, he would quote the testimony of Holy Scripture, recalling what book and chapter contained the text he had mentioned. He also quoted from the lives of the saints such texts as fitted the matter treated. He rarely spoke of wordly matters, unless it were with noblemen, discussing military operations, and even then he seldom broached this subject, his discourse being above all concerned with eternity.

When visited by temptation, he would say, "I know not what to do with myself, brother." Or else, "Do you not smell an evil odor in this cell?" I would answer, "No," and he would say, "Go and fetch some tar and pour it on the floor." (For he liked the smell of tar.) Or else he would suggest going to Lipovka. This was an estate some fifteen versts from Zadonsk, belonging to the Bekhteiev gentlemen. There was a house on that estate, but the landlords did not live in it. His Lordship would sometimes visit the estate, remaining there two months or more attended only by the cook and myself. On that estate there was a priest who celebrated only Sunday and feast-day services, so the Bishop officiated on week days, singing Vespers, Matins, and the Day Hours, and I served him, reading the psalms and prayers.

Twice he visited the Tolshevsky monastery, in 1771 and 1776. I alone accompanied him, for I, the unworthy one, was entrusted with the affairs of his household. Once he had wished to settle down in that monastery for the remainder of his days, but the water in the neighborhood was polluted, the monastery being surrounded by swamps, and this caused him many ailments. Often during his stay there, he would say to me, "This indeed looks like a real monastery, and the life here is truly a solitary and monastic one. Ah!" he would add, "if it were not for that polluted water, I should never wish to live elsewhere." He always enjoyed more peaceful thoughts in this place and seemed more cheerful. Every day he went to the church for Mass and Vespers and sang in the choir, and on Sundays and feast days and throughout Easter week, he would partake of the refectory meal, eating with the monks (which he never did at the Zadonsk monastery). While staying at the Tolshevsky monastery, it was his custom to walk about the church at midnight and to pray on his knees before each of the doors, shedding burning tears, and I was witness thereof. Sometimes I would hear him praying aloud, "Gloria in excelsis," and reciting the holy psalms. Before the west doors, he would pray half an hour or more; then he would hurry back to his cell, where he would spend his time in greater labors. For sometimes he would chop wood with his own hands. He would say to me, "Sharpen the axe well and bring along your mittens, and I shall chop some fire-wood for my stove. This will stir up my blood, perhaps, and make me feel better." One day he went beyond the monastery grounds, and on returning to his cell, he said to me, "I have found in the woods a tree trunk large enough to make three cart-loads of firewood. Fetch the axe and let us go and chop up that tree trunk instead of buying our fuel." We went to the woods and began to chop the tree trunk. Throwing off his cassock, he worked in his shirt. Finally he said to me, "I am quite tired and thirsty. Go to the monastery and fetch me some kvas."[13] Thus he set me the example of industry. Nothing offended him more than to find us idle. At Zadonsk, for instance, he often said to us, "One who lives in idleness sins continually." He was never idle himself. In the morning before Mass he would occupy himself with the writing of edifying books, which are still in existence and prove most useful to those who seek the salvation of their souls. And I know of certain persons who, from reading these books, have perceived the vanity of the world, taken up their cross and followed Christ. How many craving for eternal salvation were fed from this spiritual spring in our fleeting life! Even after he had been translated to eternal bliss, his pious works remained to nourish many. His love for all was true and sincere. He told me that he had the impulse to embrace and kiss all mankind; nevertheless he would sometimes experience a repugnance towards everyone. This was a temptation which visited him not seldom.

His thoughts constantly reached out towards solitude and life in the wilderness, and he would often speak of this. "Were it possible," he said, "I would divest myself of my dignity, and not only of my dignity but also of the monk's hood and cassock, and would retire to the most deserted monastery and there give myself over to labor, carrying water, chopping wood, sifting flour, baking bread, and the like. It is most unfortunate that this cannot be done in Russia." He also spoke often of Mount Athos: "There," he said, "many of our brother bishops, having left their dioceses, live in solitude at the various monasteries." When Greek archimandrites from Mount Athos visited him, he conversed with them at length concerning their monasteries and their ascetic life, listening most attentively. And when they took leave of him, he gave them his blessing, saying, "Farewell, beloved. I pray, make known to the saintly fathers living at Mount Athos that I bow low before them; I beseech you, ask them fervently to remember my wretchedness in their holy prayers."

I shall also describe the life of poverty he led in his cell, for he retained there only such as was necessary and indispensable.

He had no bed, but only a small carpet and two cushions; he had no blankets, but used his coat of lambskin to keep himself warm at night. He girded himself with a leather belt. He had but one cassock, and it was made of worsted. He wore coarse leather shoes and thick woolen stockings, which he bound with leather straps. For two winters he was shod in shoes made of bark, although he wore these only in his cell. "How restful for my feet these bark shoes are," he would say. When he went to Mass or received visitors, he would put on his leather shoes. His beads were of the simplest kind, made of leather. He owned neither chest nor trunk, only an old leather bag into which he would pack his books and his comb when he travelled. These were all his commodities and all his clothes. It is true that Bishop Tychon[14] the Third presented him with a silk cassock, which for a long time he would not accept; only after many requests and much persuasion would he do so. Remarkable also was the fact that he took great care not to become attached to any material and corruptible object. When he returned from church, I would help him to take off his cassock and would start to fold it, but he would take it out of my hands and fling it on the floor, saying, "This is nonsense, brother. Quick, lay the table; I am hungry." There were no decorations in his cell, but only a few holy images representing our Savior's passion and other Gospel scenes. Everything was in accordance with his humility and his voluntary poverty.

He was of an hypochondriacal and somewhat choleric temperament. He would sometimes rebuke me with just severity, but he would soon repent, regretting his words; after an hour or so, he would call me and would give me a handkerchief or a cap or some other article, saying, "Take this for yourself," as a sign of comfort and encouragement.

For three summers he had a gig and a horse, which the Bekhteiev squire had given him; after dinner he would drive out in the gig for relaxation, visiting the surrounding fields and woods, and I was the only one to accompany him. He would say to me, "Go and get the gig ready, and we shall go for a ride. Take a cup and a scythe; we shall cut some grass for the Old

Man (meaning his old horse) and shall drink at the spring."

On the way he would talk to me, either using the leaves of grass as a parable or explaining some text from the Holy Scriptures, and always directing the conversation towards thoughts of eternity. Our usual excursion would take us along the Patriarch's Road, which runs beside the Don River; or we would go to the woods and he would stop to cut the grass in some meadow with his scythe, saying to me, "Put the grass in the gig; the Old Man will like it for his fodder." Sometimes he would drive to the spring, ten versts or so from Zadonsk, on the bank of the Don River, and there we would quench our thirst. He was fond of that spring, for its waters are very clear. He would take a short walk and then would bid me return to the monastery.

Not far from his cell there lived a monk, Theophanus by name, who was seventy years old. He was of free-peasant stock, uncouth and illiterate. But His Grace loved him so well that he would seldom take his meal without him. This monk was engaged in the humblest tasks, sewing and weaving bark shoes. When the Bishop was in a mood of dejection—that is, visited by temptation—Theophanus would give him much comfort by his plain peasant talk, for he spoke to His Grace as freely as to his own folk and never addressed him other than as "Father." As he listened to the old monk's discourse, the Bishop's mood would change; he would regain his peace of mind, and would exclaim, "Theophanus is my comfort, and I am well pleased with him! I praise him first for the simplicity of his heart, second because he is never idle but always busy with some blessed work." And truly this staretz was worthy of praise for his way of life. Almost daily His Grace would say to him, "Theophanus, it is time, indeed it is time, to return to the Fatherland. Truly I am weary of this life and would be glad to die this very day, provided I were not deprived of eternal bliss!" And he would continue, "How wretched and miserable we are! Today God's chosen ones are glad and rejoice, and shall do so throughout all eternity, while we who are but wanderers and strangers are suffering and fretting in this fleeting life." And he would add, "We should ever strive, Theophanus, after that other goal, in order not to be deprived of our share in it. Let the world love that which is of the world, but we shall seek that which belongs to heaven. That is the truth, little brother Theophanus!" he would conclude.

His thoughts and conversations were primarily concerned with death, and he had a picture painted of an old, white-haired man, clothed in black and lying in a coffin. This picture hung before the foot of his bed, and there was a wooden stand near the bed, on which some books were placed. He would often look at the picture, and sighing from the depths of his heart, he would say: "O Lord, make me know my end, And what is the number of my days: that I may know what is wanting in me." He was wont to chant this text night and day, always with deep sighs and tears of contrition.

I shall now speak of his mercy and charity. He lent an attentive ear to those who cried to him for help; he fed the orphans and the bereaved and had compassion upon poverty and wretchedness. In a word, he gave away all he possessed: he distributed the money which he received from the Treasury[15] or from the officers of the Don Cossacks. The noblemen and merchants of the cities of Voronezh and Ostrogozhsk likewise brought him considerable sums, but he gave away not only this money but also his underwear, keeping only such garments as he had on. He distributed the bread which the squires sent him, and even that was not enough, but he would purchase more to be given also to the poor, who moreover received from him shoes and clothing; he bought fur-lined overcoats for them as well as coats and linen; for others he acquired huts, together with cows and horses. He even went so far as to borrow money for the poor. When he had distributed everything in his possession, he would say to me, "You might go to the town of Yeletz and borrow money there from such and such a merchant. I shall repay him when I get my pension from the Treasury. For the present I have nothing; the poor brethren come to me and go away without having received any comfort. The very sight of them fills me with pity." Sometimes, having refused help to some beggar, he would begin to question him as to who he was and whence he came. And next day he would be seized with remorse, and calling me would say, "Yesterday I denied help to such and such a poor man. Take this money and bring it to him; perhaps we shall yet be able to comfort him." And all the poor who sought him had easy access to him.

His humility was astonishing. Old peasants were wont to visit him, and he would seat them by his side and talk to them for hours with gentle friendliness, discussing country life. Then, having received what they needed from him, they would depart joyfully. He also provided at his own expense for the poor State serfs who lived near the monastery, particularly widows and orphans, paying their taxes, giving them bread and clothing, and helping them in all their necessities. It was noticeable that on the days when he had received the greatest number of poor and distributed the greatest amount of money and other alms, he appeared especially cheerful and joyous. But on the days when he had been solicited only by a few or none at all, he would be sad and depressed. I may make bold to declare that he was like Job—the eye of the blind, the feet of the lame. His doors were always open to beggars and wanderers, who found food, drink, and rest under his roof.

He taught the small peasant children to go to Mass—and how did he proceed? When he left the church after Mass, all the children followed him. As he entered the anteroom, they would crowd around him, and making three genuflections and bows, they would say loudly in one voice, "Glory be to You, our God! Glory be to You!" And he would say to them, "Children, where is our God?" And they would answer all together, and in the same loud voice, "Our God is in heaven and upon earth."

"Very good, children," he would say, and stroking their heads, he would give them each a penny and a piece of white bread, or an apple if it were summer. When he did not go to Mass because of some bodily ailment, the children, seeing that he was not in church, would run away. After Mass I would return to him and he would ask me whether the children had attended the service. I would tell him that they had come to the church but had run home, declaring, "Our Bishop is not there." He would say, smiling, "This is indeed unfortunate! Poor creatures! They go to church because of pennies and bread. However, I am well pleased that they come to Mass!"

If the peasants who passed his house on their way to work were taken ill, they found rest and comfort under his roof. He waited upon them in person, lending them even his cushion and cap. He ordered that they be served more delicate food, and two or three times a day he himself would bring them tea. He would sit at their bedside for an hour or more, comforting and encouraging them with pleasing and wise words. Some of them died, and he surrounded the departing souls with Christian solicitude, bestowing the last sacraments upon them. He himself assisted them, and he likewise attended the funeral, ordering the cook and myself to dig the grave. As to the peasants who recovered, they would return to their homes laden with provisions.

In 1768 there was a great fire in the town of Livny. The Bishop did not neglect the victims of that fire. He sent the monk Metrophanus to Livny with a sum of money which the latter duly distributed. Another year, a fire occurred in the town of Yeletz. His Grace, moved by his usual compassion, proved his charity by betaking himself to the cities of Voronezh and Ostrogozhsk, where he collected money from his benefactors with which to rebuild the houses of the residents of Yeletz, thus greatly helping them.

Neither did he fail to visit prisoners. Twice he visited the Yeletz jail, comforting the incarcerated with salutary instructions and providing them with money and other necessities. When Zadonsk was reestablished as a town and prisoners were held in the town jail, he provided for them at his own expense.

At Yeletz he had a good friend Kozma Ipatievich Studenikin, the warden of the Pokrovsky Church, who was unmarried. His Grace was very kindly disposed towards this man and greatly trusted him, up to his very death. He always gave Studenikin the money to be distributed to the widows and orphans. As to the prisoners held in jail because of their debts—unpaid letters of exchange or other obligations—he would obtain their release and repay their creditors. His charity was not bounded by the neighborhood but extended to distant areas like Novgorod and Valday and his home village, Korotzk. At one time, in the month of May, he said to me, "It is written in the Acts of the Apostles that in Antioch the early Christians collected alms and sent them to the poor Christians of Jerusalem. I too wish to send you to Korotzk to my brother Euphemius in order to bring him some money; for in this our home village the people are exceedingly poor. You shall distribute the money through my brother, and God will reward you for your obedience."

And so I went on my way, taking with me a considerable sum of money. I was to give five rubles to his brother Euphemius and ten rubles to another of his brothers, Peter by name, who lived in Novgorod. And I did as I had been commanded. No sooner had I returned to Zadonsk, having spent scarcely two weeks with him, than he sent me on a fresh errand. This time I was to go on foot to Petersburg, not in order to serve his personal interests, but because of his charitable wish to help the widow of a cleric. This old woman's two sons had been forcibly enrolled in the army by Archbishop Tychon II, although they had committed no crime. His Grace entrusted me with personal letters addressed to the members of the Synod, and I also carried a petition written by the widow, which I presented at the Synod, together with the letters. The Bishop's request was granted, and the widow's sons, having been restored to her, resumed their positions as church clerics.[16] Then once more I was sent with funds to Novgorod and Korotzk, where with the assistance of His Grace's brothers, we distributed the money to the poor. In 1772 he sent me for the third time to his brother in Korotzk with funds for the poor, and in 1774 I went again to Petersburg, likewise on a mission of charity. The Bishop, however, ordered me to give no more than five rubles to each of his brothers, saying, "Let my brothers work for themselves instead of counting on me; the more money I should give them, the lazier they would grow." Before sending me on these errands, he would bid me close the door of the cell, and kneeling down he would tell me to do the same and to recite the psalm "Make haste, O God, to deliver me" and a prayer to Our Lady, followed by the blessing. Then he would give me his blessing and kiss me on the brow, saying, "May your guardian angel accompany you. I order you, brother, to recite the holy psalms on your way, as well as such prayers as you know. Thus you will feel more cheerful during your journey."

I shall now tell of his wondrous magnanimity and patience. He suffered many offenses from the Superior of the monastery and also from certain worldly monks, but he tried to overcome evil by good. The Superior was wont to visit the homes of the rich, and becoming intoxicated, he would speak of His Grace, saying, "He lives in my monastery more meanly than a monk." These words would be repeated to the Bishop, who would say, "Take a sugar loaf or a barrel of grape wine or some other provision and give it to the Superior, for he may not have any."

Perhaps some of the monks who harassed him would be sick, and he would visit them twice or three times a day, comforting and encouraging them with salutary and wise discourse, at the same time bringing them food and drink. He sometimes suffered persecutions even from the lay brothers, who laughed at him as he passed while they were engaged in their work. He would pretend not to have overheard their remarks, but later he would say, "It is God's wish that the lay brothers should laugh at me because of my sins—and even this is not enough. However," he would add, smiling, "how easy it would be for me to thrust at them, not the lay brothers alone but the Superior himself, on whom I could, if I chose, easily take revenge. But I do not wish to pursue vengeance against anyone: forgiveness is better than revenge." Even towards these lay brothers he was most charitable, bringing them bread, money, and other gifts. This is how he avenged himself of the insults and offenses suffered, according to the apostolic words: "If thine enemy be hungry, give him bread to eat." He fulfilled this literally.

He often wished to leave the Zadonsk monastery and to settle in the diocese of Novgorod, and on one occasion he wrote a request to this effect. That day I went for a walk outside the monastery grounds, and the monk Aaron joined me. I said to him that His Grace had firmly resolved to live in the diocese of Novgorod. Father Aaron exclaimed, "Are you mad? Our Lady forbids him to leave the monastery."

Now the Bishop had a great respect for Father Aaron because of the latter's austere life. Afterwards I reported to him what Father Aaron had said to me, and he asked, "Did the monk truly speak these words?" I insisted that he had. "In that case, I shall not leave this place," His Grace declared, and he tore up his letter of request.

He would often say, "I should like to leave the monastery, but I should be sorry to abandon Yeletz. I am very fond of the citizens of that town, and I see many charitable people among them. It is as if it were my home town." He was especially attached to the family of the merchant Gregory Fedorovich Rostovtzev, a pious and temperate man. His Grace would often say of him, "We religious should learn from the Rostovtzev household how to lead a pious life."

Rostovtzev had two sons, Demetrius and Michael, both of whom were unmarried. His Grace entrusted Demetrius with the selling of the silk which had been given him as material for his cassocks, and other articles. It was Demetrius, also, who bought the objects which His Grace needed for his cell. He placed great confidence in Demetrius and enjoyed his visits, holding long conversations with the young man about the duties of the Christian life. And when he betook himself to Yeletz, he went to see Demetrius in his cell (for the young man led the life of a monk). In 1779, on the occasion of his last visit to Yeletz, the Bishop even stayed in Demetrius' cell. At that time His Grace's health was already failing, and he could no longer keep up a conversation with the citizens. But in previous years, when he was still in good health, he used to have long talks with them and was pleased that they sought him in great numbers, hoping to receive from him salutary instructions. And to prove their zeal to His Grace the citizens brought him fish, bread, and other gifts. He accepted them but sent them to the prisoners in jail, retaining nothing for himself and only saying to me,

"Take some loaves for the journey. For myself I need nothing."

During that same year, 1779, in the last days of December, some noblemen came from Voronezh for the inauguration of the new town. On Christmas day, His Grace attended Mass for the last time. After the Epistle and the Gospel, I went up to him to receive his blessing. He gave it to me, saying, "Go ahead of me and open a passage for me" (for the church was crowded). I did as he bade me, and he went out onto the porch, saying, "Wait for me here." Then he went round the north side of the church and remained there a quarter of an hour or so. (Never before had he thus left the church during a service.) After that he returned to the church, telling me again to walk in front of him.

When Mass was ended the noblemen approached him to receive his blessing, and he blessed them all. But he looked most pitiful. When he had returned to his apartment, he ordered me to lock the door and to tell the noblemen, if they should want to see him, that His Grace was in extremely poor health. When they came to his door, I gave them his message, and they went away.

From that day on he did not return to church, nor did he betake himself to any other place up to the time of his holy death, but would only go out on the back porch. He would remain there, standing or sitting, for a short while. And he let no one enter his apartment, except some of his closest friends, such as were spiritual, and even these but for a brief time. For he observed profound silence and would speak only in cases of extreme necessity. Formerly, when I used to read to him from the Holy Scriptures, he would give me many explanations, but now he listened in silence. I would read him ten chapters or so, and he would say, "It is enough. Thank you. And now you may go." And that was all he would utter on those occasions.

He would often say, "Many tell me that I made a mistake when I left the diocese for a monastic cell. These are the reasons for my retirement: first, my poor health did not permit me to administer the affairs of the diocese; and second, the omophorium[17] in which a bishop is vested weighs heavily on his shoulders, and I did not have the strength necessary to wear it. Let those who are strong enough wear the omophorium. And this," he would repeat, "is why I am in retreat."

His Grace Bishop Tychon, great by his life and by many virtues, passed into eternal peace on August 13th, 1783. I have put down all this, not for the benefit of others, but in truth for myself, in order that I may remember his laborious and God-pleasing life and after the same manner myself reach eternal bliss.

FROM THE MEMOIRS OF IVAN YEFIMOV

St. Tychon had prepared a coffin for himself four or five years before his death. It was lined with a black fabric, and on the lid was a cross of white tape. Each day the Bishop would contemplate that coffin, which stood in a closet near his bedroom. Gazing at it, he would be deeply moved and would weep, bewailing the fall of the first man and of mankind, all the more because man is a reasonable being. On that subject he would often speak as follows to his attendants: "To what a state man has lowered himself that he must be buried in the earth like cattle, he who had been created sinless and immortal by God." Considering these things he would weep afresh and groan and retire to his cell, where his voice would be heard like that of a mourner. Then, seated on his couch, he would meditate on the two eternities, the one blissful, the other full of torments. So deeply would he be absorbed in these meditations that when his attendant (who was not always allowed to enter) would approach him, His Grace would neither see nor hear him but would remain motionless, his forehead in his right hand, sensing only as in a dream that someone had entered his cell. Afterwards doubting his senses, he would ask his attendant whether he had been in the cell at such or such a time.

Before his death, His Grace had given verbal instructions that his body should be buried on the south side of the path leading to the church, near the steps of the porch, and that it should be placed under a stone. Several years before his death, the Bishop had chosen this stone himself, desiring that all who went to church to pray should step on the stone beneath which his body lay. But out of respect for the saintly bishop, His Grace Tychon III placed his body under the altar.

Concerning his writings: as I heard from his own account, and also inasmuch as I observed these things myself when I took his dictation, his words flowed so rapidly from his lips that I scarcely had time to write them down. When the Holy Ghost became less active in him and he became lost in thought, he would send me away to my cell; kneeling, sometimes lying, with his arms extended in the form of a cross, he would implore with tears that God should send him the All-Activating One. Then, calling me back once more, he would begin to utter words in such abundance that I could scarcely follow him with my pen.

He was a great lover of the Holy Scriptures. At certain appointed hours he always read something from the Old Testament, and especially from the prophets. He read the New Testament at night, either alone or with the help of his attendant. Although I frequently worked with him in the evening, when the lamps were lit, I would for the most part write for him in the morning before the late Mass. Even during dinner the attendant always read to him from the Old Testament, in particular Isaias the Prophet. In the evening he himself would read some passage of the Lives of the Saints or of the Holy Fathers. At such times he would often say to me that if it were not for the temptations it might offer simple folk, and especially the sects, he would undertake the translation of the New Testament from the Greek into our modern Russian language, so that it would be accessible to the masses. For the benefit of such readers, he proposed that the texts should be rendered on one page into Church Slavonic, on the opposite page into simple language. He thought of submitting these suggestions to the Bishop of Novgorod and others, but his failing health caused him to set aside this most useful project.

While living at the Zadonsk monastery and writing his work in the six volumes entitled *On True Christianity*, he was lying one day on his couch when he was seized with a kind of ecstasy and heard overhead the singing of angels, the beauty of which he was afterwards unable to describe; neither could he at the moment grasp the words of that song but was aware of it only as the harmony of many voices. This lasted for about ten minutes, and then, with a sound like the tinkling of a small bell, the singing abruptly ceased. Recovering himself, he arose and was deeply grieved that it had been of such short duration. This happened during the second year of his stay at Zadonsk, as I often heard him relate. And in 1779, when I served him, he had retired one day to his private cell and was meditating, likewise stretched out on his couch, when, as it were in a light sleep, he beheld Our Lady floating in mid-air, and several figures standing nearby. He fell on his knees and saw four persons dressed in white who also fell on their knees around him. Who these persons were and what was the object of the prayer, His Grace did not see fit to tell me: it was something about a certain person, that he should not be parted from him until death. And Our Lady said: "It shall be done according to your prayer." Hearing this promise, His Grace awoke as from sleep, in joyful spirits.

In 1778, as in a light sleep, he had the following vision: while meditating on God, he beheld Our Lady seated on the clouds, and the Apostles Peter and Paul standing at her side. Kneeling before Our Lady, His Grace implored that the divine mercy should be extended to the whole world. And he heard the Apostle Paul saying in a loud voice: "When they proclaim peace and confirmation, then shall destruction suddenly assail them." He rose, and from the fear inspired by the Apostle's words, he felt himself trembling and in tears.

These visions incited him to express himself even more fervently in his writings. In 1770, at the time when he was writing *On True Christianity*, he had the following vision: he was meditating on the sufferings of Christ, the Son of God (for he had a great love and veneration of Our Lord's Passion, and this not only so far as he beheld it in his mind, for nearly all the scenes of the Passion were represented by pictures in his cell); thus, sitting on his couch before a picture showing the Crucifixion, the Descent from the Cross, and the Burial of Jesus, he was absorbed in deep meditation and, as it were, quite outside himself. Then he beheld Christ descending from Golgotha, having left that very cross, and walking toward him, his tortured body covered with wounds and blood. This vision at the same time filled his heart with joy and rent it with pity; he fell at Christ's feet so that he might kiss them, saying, "Is it You, my Savior, who have come to me?" And he really felt that he was at the feet of the Savior. From that day on he meditated even more deeply on the Passion and on the Redemption of mankind.

During the time of the yearly fair at the Zadonsk monastery, he did not go to church, but closeting himself in his cell, spent his time in devout meditation. When he left his cell and looked through the drawing-room window, he would observe the gentlefolk who had been at the fair and had come in pilgrimage to the monastery, the ladies dressed in fine clothes, strutting coquettishly, their faces covered with paint and powder. On such occasions, His Grace would say, "Poor blind Christians! They bedeck their mortal bodies but rarely trouble to bedeck their souls; these souls are as black as that of the Moor who knows not God nor believes in Our Lord Jesus Christ."

Some of these dressed-up ladies would seek his blessing. In such cases, if the ladies in question were not known to him personally, he would refuse to admit them under the pretext of ill health. In other instances, because of his deep humility, he would send the visitors word through me that they might receive the same blessing from the ordained monks of the monastery. But when he did receive the squires of the neighborhood, accompanied by their wives, these ladies would put away their finery, especially their bonnets and curls and their powder, and come to him in modest attire. When he was strong enough he admitted all, no matter of what rank or station, but most willingly he received clergymen, to whom he gave salutary instructions.

When, upon invitation, His Grace had visited the homes of the squires or of the Yeletz merchants, he would, upon returning to the monastery, devote two days or more to recalling his conversations and his very thoughts. If this examination of conscience revealed that he had fallen into some human error, especially in judging his neighbor, he would offer an act of contrition to God. Because of these scruples he often refused the invitations of people who asked him to their homes. He would say to his attendants, "He who leaves his solitude, even though it be for some salutary deed, does not return the same as he was before." And he would add, "Solitude collects spiritual treasures, a journey disperses them."

Sometimes the squires would insist on his visiting them, and the horses they sent to fetch him would wait for a whole day and night while he was considering whether or not the journey would do good. And if he did not feel impelled to go, he would send the horses back with a letter of excuse.

His Grace had given up his episcopal throne because of his poor health after he had experienced the difficulty of administering the affairs of a diocese. On his request he was permitted to retire. Living in the monastery of Our Lady of Zadonsk, he spent the first year in meditation, pondering on the vanity and the fleeting character of this world. After a year's seclusion he undertook his writings, which were to be profitable to the whole of Christian society. While he was composing these works, I saw no other books on his table than the Holy Bible and some writings of St. John Chrysostom. He wrote alone and with his own hand the six volumes entitled *On True Christianity*, which he finished in 1771. But even while engaged in this salutary task, he did not abandon the rule of prayers which befits a life of solitude, including bows and genuflections. Especially at night he would meditate on God, and in the morning he would read the psalms, standing and pacing about outside his cell, for he knew them all by heart, and the accompanying prayers as well. In meditation and prayer he had the gift of tears. While he meditated upon the two eternities he would be heard weeping and lamenting in the solitude of his cell: "Have mercy on us, O Lord! Have pity on us, O Lord! Have patience with our sins, our mercy! Hear us, O Lord, and do not cause us to perish with our iniquities!" And his weeping was like that of a friend mourning for a friend.

When he was absorbed in meditation, particularly if this occurred in the morning, nobody dared go near his cell, not even his attendants. Under no pretext whatever were they to announce to him the arrival of such squires as, moved by piety, had come to the monastery, nor that of other visitors asking for his blessing and his salutary instructions. In spite of their insistent demands, these visitors were not ushered in, and this rule was strictly observed by the attendants, not out of the fear of punishment but because of their devout respect for him and for his virtuous life.

That he might not be interrupted in his meditations, he would humbly petition his attendants, bowing to them and beseeching them not to disturb his peace of mind with these distractions. When his health permitted, he went to church for prayer, especially on feast days. On week-days, when there were but few people in the church, he attended early Mass, and he deigned to sing, chanting either with the right or with the left choir, according to the musical style of Kiev. With contrite looks and pious bearing, he would listen in ecstasy to the celebration of the sacred mystery hidden behind the veil of Christian faith in the Holy Eucharist. He was wont to exclaim, "Sing praises to our God, sing praises with understanding." But during the whole time that he lived at the Zadonsk monastery after having dedicated himself to solitude, he did not permit himself to celebrate Mass.

When he wished to receive Holy Communion, he would enter the sanctuary and approach the altar-table vested in the mantle and the omophorium, and the carpet decorated with eagles would be placed under his feet. During the early years of his life at Zadonsk, on the first day of Easter, he would celebrate solemn Matins and would also sing the *Te Deum* on solemn state feast days. But seeking greater solitude and deeper meditation, he was wont to make a summer and winter retreat in the isolated Tolshevsky monastery, which belonged to the same diocese. He had wished to reside there permanently, but had given up this plan because of the damp climate caused by the swamp surrounding the monastery. During his stay in the Tolshevsky monastery, as well as in Zadonsk, he practised his inherent charity, helping those who came to him, distributing alms and giving spiritual advice to men and women of all ranks and conditions. But he liked best to talk to simple folk. He would go out on the porch or await his visitors in his cell. Seating the peasants beside him, he would question them about their past, talking over old times with the aged. Often these peasants did not suspect with whom they were talking, for his simple attire disguised his bishop's rank. He was not loath to share the meal in his apartment with these uncouth visitors, eating out of the same dishes with them, suitable food being customarily provided for their refreshment.

When the courts were established at Zadonsk, a jail was built for criminals. St. Tychon was wont to betake himself there at nightfall to visit the sick prisoners and to distribute alms. On the first day of Easter, while visiting the jail, he gave the Easter kiss to all who were detained. Likewise in the town of Yeletz, to which he would betake himself at the request of the citizens, he deigned to visit the jail and the almshouse, concealing his high dignity under simple garb. In a word, all his life was founded on the holy Gospels, on the imitation of our Savior Jesus Christ, His Apostles and His disciples.

One day the saint heard of a squire who mistreated his serfs. His Grace intervened and betook himself to the lord of that estate in order to remonstrate with him. The hot-blooded nobleman started a dispute. The Bishop answered him gently but firmly. The anger of the nobleman grew, and finally he forgot himself so far as to strike the Bishop on the cheek. His Grace then left the nobleman's house. But on his way, true to the evangelical precept, he resolved to return to the man who had insulted him and to beg forgiveness for "having led him into such a temptation." So, going back, he fell at the feet of his host. The story goes on to say that this unexpected act of the pastor who knew no anger so deeply impressed the nobleman that he himself fell on his knees at the Bishop's feet, imploring forgiveness. From that day on his behavior towards his serfs was completely altered.

Progressing in humility and in charity, His Grace patiently suffered all kinds of temptation and courageously withstood the insidious attacks of the enemy who hated such a saintly way of life and who caused him many tribulations, especially through the lips of evil-speaking men. In order to repel these temptations, he would utter the following words of the Apostle Peter: "When he suffered, he threatened not, but delivered himself to him that judged him unjustly."

Although His Grace no longer permitted himself to celebrate Mass, he received Communion on Sundays and feast-days. As long as he was in good health and was not living in solitude, he partook of the holy sacraments vested in his episcopal robes. When he had retired into solitude, a monk brought him the chalice with the Holy Eucharist in his cell. During his illness he received the sacraments even more frequently, and with such fervor that he would not only shed tears but weep aloud. However, having partaken of the Holy Eucharist, he would be filled with gladness and joy. Sometimes when I entered his cell he would say to me, "I am drunk, Ivan," recalling, perhaps, the words "Drink, and ye shall be drunk."

When his mind was at peace, he would not only recite the psalms of David but would chant some of them as a diversion. And he would make me sing them too in his presence, but only for a short time.

One day in September or October of 1777 or 1778, he went to the back porch of his quarters, absorbed in meditation. Then, entering my cell, he ordered me to take pen and ink and began to dictate the following: "On such and such a day a great flood has devastated the city of Petersburg, causing the death of many people and the destruction of many houses." And this flood had truly occurred as he described it. Afterwards he was informed of the event by letter.[18]

For those who insulted and persecuted him, mocked and slandered him, he felt only remorse and pity; he considered that the sole mover in these evil occurrences was the Devil, the enemy of God and of Christianity. When one of the culprits, repenting, begged his forgiveness, His Grace would embrace him with tears of joy and would forgive him with a light heart. And his conversation at such a time would be so edifying and so pleasing that the former adversary would be turned into a friend. Read in the book entitled *Spiritual Treasures* the chapter "Waters Which Flow By," and you shall see how he describes the *friends* and the *enemies*, the enemies being turned into friends and the friends into enemies.

When assisting at Mass, the saint would sometimes be so deeply absorbed in the thought of God's love for the human race, of our redemption through the ineffable mystery of the incarnation of Christ, the Son of God, of His passion and the sacrament of the Eucharist, that he would shed many tears and even sob—and this in the presence of a large congregation. If he observed that at the moment when the celebrant invokes the Holy Ghost to descend upon the holy gifts, the faithful failed to pray with the priest during the chanting of the hymn "We praise Thee," he did not hesitate to rebuke them, calling them to due attention and prayer. And if, at Sunday and feast-day Mass, the Superior or the monks neglected to read the synodical sermon[19], he would interrupt the post-communion prayers and openly rebuke the religious, exhorting them to resume this salutary practice. And he so rebuked the Superior, Father Samuel, that one day the latter put on the stole and began to read himself.

The saintly Bishop was very much attached to Archimandrite Samson. One day when this Father Samson was talking with him alone in his cell, he began, among other things, to praise Tychon loudly for his pious life, hinting that after his death the Bishop would be glorified by his body's remaining incorrupt. His Grace was extremely vexed by these words and went so far as to believe that the evil spirit was speaking through the Archimandrite's lips. From that day on he complained bitterly of Father Samson, for he would suffer such words of praise from no one, recalling Lazarus the Just, the friend of Christ, whose body was decomposed on the fifth day after his death. This is an example of his deep humility.

Examining himself, he would analyze his thoughts, even such as were most salutary, with the attention one would employ in tracing the lines and furrows of a palm, and he taught all who sought salvation to do the like. On a day when no beggar came to him, he would be disturbed, as if grieved by the deprivation of some pleasure.

Now I shall recall the words which I heard from the saint's own lips. While he was writing the six volumes of his book entitled *On True Christianity*, he was troubled in his thoughts by the snares of the enemy. When he was absorbed in his work, especially if he were engaged in it at night, he would suddenly hear above his head a sound of thumping, jumping, and running as of human feet. Seized with fear, he would interrupt his writing, and calling his attendants, he would bid them climb to the attic and see whether some animal were there. The attendants would return saying that they had found nothing. This would also happen in the daytime: he would hear a rustling in the stove in which he was wont to throw bits of torn paper. He would be disturbed for a long time, so that finally he would open the stove, but he would find no vermin in it.

During the first year of his stay in the Zadonsk monastery (and this he often told me himself), he experienced dejection and melancholy. He would ask himself whether he deserved to receive a pension from the Crown. For an entire year he struggled against such thoughts as drew a picture of fame, honor, and respect and of the services he might have rendered to Christian society, and these thoughts made him wish to resume his episcopal functions. Such imaginings would daily inspire him with deep depression, and sometimes he would remain closeted in his cell for the whole day. Those who served him could hear his footsteps as he paced up and down, and the sound of his voice upraised in prayer and supplication to God. After a year had elapsed, it so happened that one day, lying on his couch, he was meditating on the melancholy of his life and struggling with great perturbation against the thoughts that were enticing him to return to his diocese. Finally, covered with sweat, he cried out in a loud voice, "Lord, I will die rather than go back!" From that hour he was no longer haunted by these thoughts and could live with a peaceful mind, filled each day with spiritual joy.

During the first years of his sojourn at the Zadonsk monastery, he was extremely strict with his attendants. He had a violent temper, and he punished them for the slightest fault, imposing on them many genuflections and bows during prayer. As the result of these severities he would sometimes lose those attendants who had served him most zealously but who would in the end leave him out of fear. Conscious of his intemperance, he began to petition God for the visitation of some ailment which should teach him patience and humility. And he obtained that for which he had prayed. He had a dream in which he beheld himself entering a church, and a priest emerged from the sanctuary carrying in his arms an infant whose face was covered with a piece of fine gauze. His Grace, who had a great love of little children (for Christ Himself had received them), approached the priest and asked him the infant's name. The priest replied that the child was named Basil (which in Greek means "king"). Removing the white cover from the infant's face, Tychon kissed him on the right cheek. But the child struck him with his right hand on the left cheek, with such force that the Bishop awoke. Rising, he observed that his left hand was trembling and his left leg was stricken with weakness. Meditating on the sign which had been sent him in his dream, he thanked God for this paternal visitation. From that time on, he began to acquire patience and deep humility. Indeed he learned so well that if he should rebuke his cook, the meanest of his servants, who was of peasant stock, and should see that he was offended, Tychon would bow before him, asking to be forgiven. With the help of divine grace, he made such progress that it was possible to behold in him all those fruits of the spirit of which St. Paul has spoken, such as charity, gladness, and peace.

CONFESSION AND THANKSGIVING

TO CHRIST, SON OF GOD,

THE SAVIOR OF THE WORLD

By ST. TYCHON

SINCE YOU CAME INTO THE WORLD FOR ALL, O SAVIOR, THERE-
FORE YOU CAME FOR ME, FOR I AM ONE OF ALL. YOU CAME
into the world to save sinners; therefore You came to save me
also, for I am one of the sinners. You came to find and to save
him who was lost; therefore You came to seek me too, for I am
one of the lost. O Lord, O my God and Creator! I should have
come to You as a transgressor of Your law. I should have fallen
at Your feet, cast myself down before You, humbly begging
forgiveness, pleading with You and craving Your mercy. But
You Yourself have come to me, wretched and good-for-nothing
servant that I am; my Lord has come to me, His enemy and
apostate; my Master has come and has bestowed His love of
mankind upon me. Listen, my soul: God has come to us; Our
Lord has visited us. For my sake He was born of the Virgin
Mary, He Who is born of the Father before all time. For my
sake He was wrapped in swaddling clothes, He Who covers
heaven with the clouds and vests Himself with robes of light.
For my sake He was placed in the lowly manger, He Whose
throne is the heavens and Whose feet rest upon earth. For my
sake He was fed with His mother's milk, He Who feeds all
creatures. For my sake He was held in His mother's arms, He
Who is borne by the Cherubim and holds all creatures in His
embrace. For my sake He was circumcized according to the law,
He Who is maker of the Law. For my sake, He Who is unseen
became visible and lived among men, He Who is my God. My
God became one like me, like a man; the Word became flesh,
and my Lord, the Lord of Glory, took for my sake the form of
a servant and lived upon earth and walked upon earth, He Who

is the King of Heaven. He labored, worked miracles, conversed with men, was like a servant, He Who is the Lord of all. He was hungry and thirsty, He Who provides food and drink for all creatures. He wept, He Who wipes away all tears. He suffered and mourned, He Who is the consoler of all men. He consorted with sinners, He Who alone is just and holy. He Who is omnipotent toiled and had nowhere to lay His head, He Who lives in light inaccessible. He was poor, He Who gives riches to all men. He wandered from town to town and from place to place, He Who is omnipresent and fills all space. And thus for thirty-three years and more He lived and labored upon earth for my sake—I who am His servant. O Son of God Who ceased not to dwell in His Father's bosom! What did You behold in me of merit? Why did You come to seek me in this vale of tears? Shepherds search for their lost sheep, but for their own profit. Men seek their lost property, but out of self-interest. Travellers visit foreign countries, but for their own benefit. Kings offer the ransoms of prisoners, but they pay it in gold and silver through their ambassadors, and largely for their own gain. But You, what was it that You found in me, my Lord? What use, what interest, what good did You behold in me that You came to seek me? And it was the King of Heaven and Earth Himself who came, not His ambassadors. God himself came to find and to ransom His servant, not with gold and silver but with His precious blood. Nothing indeed did you find but corruption, weakness, misery, disobedience and enmity towards Yourself. It would have been a deed sufficiently great, had You come to seek me because I had been lost through no will of my own, wrested from You by force and imprisoned by the enemy. But the marvel is that I, of my own will, am an apostate and Your enemy. I am ashamed to admit as much, but it is the truth: I am an apostate; I have followed in the path of Your enemy. I entered this conspiracy desiring to snatch Your divine honor. I, Your creature, not content that You have dignified me above the rest of Your creation by bestowing on me a rational soul and making me in Your own image, have desired to become

God! This great dignity has seemed too mean to me, and I have wanted to become God, to dishonor You Who have honored me, my Lord! I have provoked You exceedingly and insulted Your immeasurable greatness, and in this manner have I become Your enemy.

Thus I stand before You, I for whose sake You came to earth. Beholding in me nothing but my need of salvation, You have come to seek me. For You so looked upon me that my misfortune and my perdition became Your loss, my salvation Your gain. That I should be saved and should attain eternal happiness, this You considered to be Your gain. For Your generosity could not bear to see me in perdition; it impelled You, Invisible One, to descend and to seek me. Not a mediator, not an angel, but You Yourself, my Lord, came to me. You came to me, for I could not come to You. The Shepherd had to come and to labor in order to find the sheep lost in the hills. You showered upon me Your loving-kindness, my Lord. You sought me disinterestedly, my Shepherd. You loved me without profit, O my God! This indeed is true love: to love without profit, to do good without hope of recompense. Thus did You love me, my Lover: You came disinterested for my salvation. Oh, what kindness and love, Son of God, Son of the Ever-Virgin! Oh, how great is our joy, poor and wretched men for whose sake our Lord and King came to live among us. God likened Himself to men and came to us for our sake. Blessed is the womb that bore You, and the breasts which gave You suck! Son of God! Blessed are the swaddling clothes in which You were wrapped! Blessed, the crib in which You were laid! Blessed are the arms which sheltered the Infant Who was our God before all time! Blessed are the robes which clothed God Incarnate, Who was arrayed in garments of light! Blessed are the eyes that beheld You and the ears that heard You and the hands that touched You, Living Word and Giver of Life! Blessed is the time in which You, O Heavenly King, came down to earth! Yet, by far more blessed are those who see You, not walking on earth, but sitting at the right hand of the Father—Jesus, in Whom now, not seeing but believing, Your faithful on earth rejoice with an ineffable and glorious joy! Grant that I may see You now with the eyes of faith and honor You through love; that I may look upon You then face to face!

But look, O my soul, and see how the King of Heaven was welcomed by His subjects, in what manner they honored their God Incarnate: what offerings, what thanksgivings, what honors they bestowed on their Benefactor, Who had come to save them, Who performed miracles before them — Who cleansed the lepers, healed the sick, made the paralytic walk and the blind man see; Who straightened the lame and the crippled, Who raised the dead and fed the many thousands who were hungry. Oh, shame covers my face, awe grips my heart, and my tongue trembles to speak! His holy Evangelist cries out in grief: "He came unto His own, and His own received Him not." And they repudiated him, saying: "We do not wish this man to rule over us." Terrible and piteous are these words! God in flesh came to His people, and they did not receive Him. The King and Lord came to His servants, and they rejected Him. Listen, heaven, and harken, earth! Men did not accept their God; servants did not receive their Lord; subjects rejected their King! O, my God, all this You knew, and yet You came to save me, perishing; to find me, the lost! You were not turned away by the wickedness and the ingratitude of Your enemies; You surrendered Yourself to Your love and kindness; You were persuaded by my wretchedness.

It was not enough that ungrateful men should reject their Lord and Benefactor. They piled wickedness upon wickedness, cruelty upon hardness. They considered Your divine teaching to be inspired by the devil: "He hath a devil, and is mad: why hear you Him?" They attributed Your miracles to Beelzebub: "This man casteth not out devils but by Beelzebub the prince of the devils." Because you mingled with sinners, desiring to win their souls by Your compassion and to save them, they called You a glutton and a drunkard, the friend of publicans and sinners, and they vomited forth all manner of blasphemies against You, their Lord and Benefactor, against You Who are beyond all glory! Oh, the cruelty and ingratitude of men! Oh,

the patience and magnanimity that You showed, my Lord!
And more—they sought to kill You, their Savior. You beheld
their wicked plans, their hearts instinct with hatred. You looked
into them, Reader of hearts; yet You suffered in silence. They
found an instrument for their designs, Your ungrateful disciple.
And he sold them Him Who is without price for thirty pieces
of silver. He sold for this paltry sum Him Who is more precious
than the whole world, than a thousand worlds! You witnessed
this evil design, this iniquitous bargain; and You permitted it,
desiring to suffer for my sake, Your unworthy servant, to cleanse
me with Your blood, to give me new life by Your death, to
honor me through Your disgrace. Glory be to You for all, O
my Lover!

You were betrayed and sold; or, to speak more truly, You
gave Yourself up to them and freely went to them, knowing all
that would follow. And they bound You, the Lord inaccessible
to the Seraphim and the Cherubim! They judged You, the
Judge of the living and the dead! They insulted and dishonored
You, spat upon Your holy face, to which angels dare not lift
their gaze! And they buffeted Your cheek and condemned You
to death—You, the Life of all! They preferred a robber and a
murderer to You, the Son of God, the only good and just One!
The people cried with one voice: "Away with this man, and
release unto us Barabbas. Crucify him, crucify him." Oh
prodigy! Oh, fearful and unheard-of crime! They led Him out
of the city like a condemned criminal, and they hung Him like
a villain, between two villains. They put to death the Immortal
One, and as He hung on the cross they mocked Him and
wagged their heads. They fed Your hunger with gall and
quenched Your thirst with vinegar. They pierced Your hands
and Your feet and numbered all Your bones. And when You
expired, they pierced Your side. And then once more they
mocked You in death: "We have remembered, that that seducer
said, while he was yet alive: After three days I will rise again."
They placed a guard over Your most pure body and sealed Your
tomb. This is what Your people did to You, my Lord; to You
Who came to save them!

You suffered their fury, and like a lamb led to the slaughter, You did not open Your lips. The Lord suffered at the hands of His servants, the Creator at the hands of His creatures, the King at the hands of His subjects, the Benefactor at the hands of those who received from Him innumerable gifts, the Just and Innocent at the hands of the lawless. He suffered before Heaven and earth, in the sight of angels and men, before a great multitude of spectators, in the sight of friends and enemies. He suffered, naked and abandoned by all. And because He came into the world for the sake of all, He therefore suffered for me too, for I am one of all, O my Lord! For my sake did he bear so great a humiliation, O my Lord! And who am I, and what am I? Ashes and clay, a sinner and a worthless slave! Oh, new and unheard-of miracle! Oh, unutterable and ineffable mercy! Incomprehensible indulgence! Arise, my soul, arise! Be filled with awe; humble yourself, bow low and fall at the feet of your Lord! "Sing ye to the Lord a new canticle; because He hath done wonderful things." My Lord and Creator suffered, endured His passion, and died for His worthless servant and lawbreaker. I who broke the law, I the traitor; I who utter insults and blasphemies; I who have given myself up to my enemy, the Devil. I deserve to be spat upon by the Devil; I deserve to be mocked, insulted, buffeted, beaten, tortured, to die for all eternity! But You, my Lord and Sovereign, have suffered in my place. The servant sinned, but my Lord suffered the punishment; the servant erred, but my Lord was scourged; the servant stole, and my Lord offered compensation; the servant was indebted, but my Sovereign paid the debt. And in what manner did He pay it? Not in gold and silver but with His disgrace, His wounds, His blood, His death on the cross. For me, wretched and accursed, He bore the infamy, He Who is blessed throughout all eternity. For my blasphemies and my insults, He suffered disgrace, He Who is the Lord of Glory. For me—I who was held captive for sin—He was sold, He Who is beyond price. For me He stood trial and was condemned. For me He suffered death, my Lord and Creator! Glory be to You, glory be to You, glory be to You for all things! I have nothing else to bring to You but this: glory be to You! You lived on earth, King of Heaven, to lead me to heaven—I who had been cast out of paradise. You were born in the flesh of the Virgin to give me birth in the spirit. You suffered insults to silence the mouths of my enemies who calumniated me. You abased Yourself, You Who are higher than all honors, in order to honor me, the dishonored. You wept to wipe the tears from my eyes. You sighed, grieved, sorrowed to save me from sighing, grieving, suffering pain throughout eternity, to give me eternal joy and gladness. You were sold and betrayed that I might be freed, I who was enslaved. You were bound that my bonds might be broken. You submitted to an unjust trial—You Who are the Judge of all the earth—that I might be freed from eternal judgment. You were made naked in order to clothe me in the robes of salvation, in the garments of gladness. You were crowned with thorns that I might receive the crown of life. You were called king in mockery—You, the King of all!—to open the kingdom of heaven for me. Your head was lashed with a reed that my name should be written in the book of life. You suffered outside the city gates in order to lead me, one who had been cast out of paradise, into the eternal Jerusalem. You were put among evil men— You Who are the only Just One—that I, the unjust, might be justified. You were cursed, the One Blessed, that I, the accursed, should be blessed. You shed Your blood that my sins might be cleansed away. You were given vinegar to drink that I might eat and drink at the feast in Your kingdom. You died —You Who are the life of all—in order to revive me, the dead. You were laid in the tomb that I might rise from the tomb. You were brought to life again that I might believe in my resurrection. You ascended into heaven in order that I too might ascend into heaven and be glorified in Your kingdom. This You have done for me, Your servant, O my Lord! "What is man that Thou art mindful of him? or the son of man that Thou visitest him?" Man is dust and ashes and the destroyer of Your sacred law. Yet You have honored him, who has dishonored You, Lord and Creator! You have benefited Your creature, my Creator! You have forgiven Your servant, my

Master! You have found Your lost sheep, my Shepherd! You have called the one who had been rejected; You have released the one who was in chains, O my Liberator! You have restored to life the one who was dead, O my Life! You have raised the fallen one, O my Strength! You have honored the dishonored one and have defended the defenseless one, O my Intercessor! You have broken the chains that bound me! "I will offer to Thee the sacrifice of thanksgiving." I offer thanksgiving for Your grace. I kiss Your love of mankind. I adore Your kindness and Your mercy. I pay homage and sing praises to Your ineffable indulgence!

How shall I repay Your generosity, O my Lover? How shall I repay my God for all that He has given me? Had I died a thousand times for Your sake, it would be as nothing. For You are my Lord, my Creator and my God, and I am but clay and ashes, a sinner and a worthless servant, deserving of all manner of deaths, not alone in time but in eternity. How shall I thank You, my Lord, my Lover, my Intercessor, my Liberator, my Redeemer? How shall I reward You, Who did not spare Yourself, but for my sake gave Yourself up to dishonor, insult, mockery, infamy; to be spat upon, condemned, scourged, wounded, crucified, put to death that I, poor wretch, should be made joyful? How shall I reward You? I who possess nothing that is my own except for my corruption, my impotence, my sin. My soul and body—my nature—is from You—Yours, but alas, corrupted and spoiled by me. The counsel of the Evil One and my own will have corrupted me. I shall offer You a grateful heart, and that alone You desire of me. But even this thing I cannot do without You. For without You I cannot know You, or having known You, love You. Oh, how poor, how indigent I am! how weak, miserable, corrupt! Oh, how deeply my enemy has wounded, how he has broken me! But O my Liberator, forgive me! For You have loved me and have given Yourself up for me. Forgive me, and enlighten me, that I may know You in Whom is my life. Kindle the love of You in my heart; set my feet upon the rock; and straighten my steps, so that I may follow You, my Liberator and my only Leader, guiding me to heaven and to eternal life. Draw me after You, O burning Love! Let us run in the path You have trod! I will follow the scent of Your myrrh. For wherever You are, there shall I also be, I, the servant whom You have redeemed, so that I may behold Your glory. O Merciful, O Generous, O Lover of men, give me the heart that is able to follow You; guide me along Your ways, along the path of Your chosen ones; lead me after You by Your Holy Ghost! "Thy good spirit shall lead me into the right land."

You have accomplished a deed so sublime that my mind cannot grasp it! You, the Lord, the King of Heaven and Earth, have come down from Heaven, and have given Yourself flesh of the Virgin Mother of God, and have suffered, have been crucified, have shed Your blood, for me, for the sake of Your servant! What a sublime, a sublime wonder! I believe and I confess, I acknowledge and I preach, and I marvel that so great a love has been shown me! O Lover of men, my Lover, grant me, a sinner, yet another favor, I humbly implore You: cleanse me of all my sins with Your precious blood, the blood You have shed for the sake of Your sinning servant. Confirm me in fear of You, and in love of You. Grant that I may follow in Your steps through faith and charity. And guard me by Your strength from my enemies, who seek to stay my feet and to turn me from You, O Redeemer. "And Thy mercy will follow me all the days of my life": so that, being preserved by Your grace, I shall offer You thanksgiving, face to face, with Your chosen ones, and shall sing, and praise, and glorify You, with the Eternal Father and the Holy Ghost, for ever and ever. Amen.

STS. BORIS AND GLEB
SCHOOL OF SOUZDALE, XIIITH CENTURY
CATHEDRAL OF THE ASSUMPTION, MOSCOW

ICON OF ST. SERGIUS
XVITH CENTURY

ST. SAVIOR
OF THE CATHEDRAL OF ZVENIGOROD
XVTH CENTURY
MUSEUM OF HISTORY, MOSCOW

CHURCH (WOOD)
EARLY XVIITH CENTURY
TYPICAL OF THE CHURCH ARCHITECTURE OF NORTHERN RUSSIA

ST. TYCHON OF ZADONSK
AUTOGRAPHED

Изображеніе кончины
Іеромонаха Серафима
Пустынника и литвартика Сароевской пустыни
1833 года 2 Января.

THE DEATH OF ST. SERAPHIM
ENGRAVING

ARCHANGEL
(DETAIL OF THE ICON OF THE ORANTE-THEOTOKOS)
XITH CENTURY
MUSEUM OF HISTORY, MOSCOW

ALEXANDER YELCHANINOV

FROM THE LETTERS OF ST. TYCHON
OF ZADONSK

[1]

Noble Sir I. V. and dearest brother in Christ:

It is rumored that you brought a law-suit against Captain L. because he had dishonored you with some word of his, and this L. is dead long since. It is also rumored that before he passed away he sent a messenger to seek your forgiveness, but that you, not having granted this forgiveness, are now retaliating upon the son of the deceased. If this is true, I pray you to listen to me patiently and to follow my advice. Know, then, that rancor is the first of the Devil's lusts in man, for nothing pleases the Evil One more than a vindictive heart. Indeed a man filled with rancor will not be forgiven by God, inasmuch as this man himself has not forgiven. Thus Christ teaches us in the Gospels: "If you will not forgive men, neither will your Father forgive you your offences." And how shall you pray to God, saying: "Forgive us our debts, as we also forgive our debtors" if you will not forgive? Our brother is one like ourselves: he has dishonored, insulted us, with a word; but we—worms, dust, ashes, dung that we are—how many times a day do we offend God, our Creator, our great and awe-inspiring Lord, before Whom the heavenly hosts themselves tremble in fear? What forgiveness can we hope to obtain from God if we do not forgive others? We offend one another; therefore, we must forgive one another. Read the parable in St. Matthew, chapter the eighteenth; that which is written at the end of this chapter should fill with fear those who do not remit their neighbor's debts.

You know that you too will die, but you know not when—perhaps it will be today or tomorrow. And what if death overtakes you in this state of anger? L. showed humility and offered to make amends for the dishonor inflicted by asking your forgiveness; by this very act he paid his debt. What more do you want? It is upon you that now lies the obligation to forgive your brother. If you do not do so, and if you die burdened with this debt, what mercy can you expect from God? And how can L.'s son be blamed? If this were a debt of money, the son would indeed be held accountable, the father's estate having survived. But it was dishonor that the father inflicted, and you seek satisfaction from the son as if the latter had been an accomplice in the father's act and had inspired it, whereas this cannot be. I humbly pray you, leave all this; cut the knot of rancor, forgive your brother's debt, or, rather, acquit yourself of your own debt and do not remain bound by it until your death; for God's sake, make peace with that man's son, who is innocent.

Believe me, all this is the work of the Devil, who inspires men with enmity. Spit upon the Evil One, who is whispering in your ear and inspiring you with the thought of revenge. Listen instead to Christ, our Savior, Who promotes peace, Who prayed to His heavenly Father for those who crucified Him and told us to do likewise: "Love your enemies: do good to them that hate you: and pray for them that persecute and calumniate you."

Forgive your neighbor in order that you yourself may be forgiven. What pardon can you hope for if you will not pardon others? The man on whom you have turned your anger, the son of the deceased, will humbly visit you to beg your forgiveness. If you make peace with him, your love will be remembered until you die. Your peace will cause your friends to rejoice, your servants to love you, your other neighbors to praise you—and the Devil to suffer (for Christian love torments him, just as enmity fills him with gladness). I, your unworthy pastor, when I have heard of this, shall rejoice and inscribe your gracious name in my memory. Accomplish, then, this merciful act. First, you yourself will gain by it, inasmuch as you shall obtain God's mercy; second, it will benefit your brother, who humbly comes to you to find peace; and I, too, shall be mercifully benefited, inasmuch as you will fulfill my wish. May the merciful and peace-giving God soften your heart and incline it to forgiveness. I write you this inasmuch as it is my pastoral duty to do so. All shall receive the mercy that they seek. I send you the holy image of Him Who is both my Savior and yours. I plead with you in

His name. This name fills the angels with wonder, is beloved of the Apostles, the martyrs, the saints and the blessed, and is sweet to us sinners; for in it alone lies our hope and our assurance. Give up all rancor, I beseech you once more because of my duty as a pastor. If you do as I ask, you will grant me a favor, for if you make peace, I shall profit by it. But I conclude with what follows: this, my mean and unworthy writing, will be my testimony and the witness against you in the day of Christ's last judgment. And if someone should give you contrary advice, do not listen, for such advice is inspired by the Evil Spirit. Read all the Gospels and you shall see all. Expecting your answer, I remain Your Lordship's and most gracious Sir's unworthy intercessor and most unworthy Bishop of Voronezh.

Tychon

Voronezh, December 4, 1764

[2]

Answer to a man who asked St. Tychon where he should best live in order to attain salvation:

You wish that I should answer your question as to the events which lie in the unknown future. Considering man's infirmity and the snares of the Devil, who frequently offers evil under the semblance of good, like poison steeped in honey, I am unable to advise you as to things we cannot know, lest a bitter fate should befall you and I be led to grief because of it. Even if one should foresee all that is to occur, it is better to remain silent than to speak and proffer advice which will afterwards be regretted. Because of the reason known to you, it is dangerous for you to remain in your parents' home. And it is always safe for a man fearing God, seeking salvation, ever meditating on eternal torments and the future life and harkening to himself in silence, to live in any monastery whatever. I know that for one who wants to be saved, it is better to part with parents and relatives. There is only one suggestion I wish to make to you: if you retire to a remote monastery, you will suffer there from a great ennui. Therefore you will have to struggle and to overcome yourself. As for the Devil and wicked men, you will never escape from them, wherever you go. Like the shadow cast by the body in the sunlight, persecution and the hatred of evil persons follows him who seeks God. It seems to me that it is best to give yourself up to the will of God and to abide in some monastery, if only in order not to remain in your parents' house, and to stand firmly in that monastery, even if you suffer from ennui, finding comfort in the thought that death will put an end to everything: he who labors will soon be received into the realm of sweetness, joy, and glory. You will have to pray to God frequently, imploring his aid; you will have to work, never allowing yourself to be idle for a single moment. Thus shall you overcome your ennui. May God set your life right.

Seek salvation, and pray for me, a sinner.

Your well-wisher

Tychon (Episcopus)

[3]

Answer to a monk who suffered from the spirit of accidie.

I see from your letter that you have been assailed by the spirit of dejection. This is a grievous passion, against which Christians seeking salvation must struggle fiercely. Dejection assails even such as have bread and other objects of necessity ready at hand. How much the more, then, does it attack those who live in solitude? I commend to you the following practices:

1. Exhort yourself, force yourself, to prayer and every good work, however contrary be your inclination. As a lazy horse, driven by a whip, is compelled by man to walk and to trot, even so must we coerce ourselves into performing every kind of labor, and how much the more, to pray. God, beholding your efforts and your labor, will grant you zeal and inclination. Habit of itself creates the inclination, and, it might be said, attracts us towards prayer and good deeds. Learn to acquire this habit, and it will draw you to prayer and good deeds.

2. Zeal is also acquired by variety in our occupations—that is, by turning from one task to another. And so you must do as

follows: pray, then perform some manual task, then read a book, then meditate on your spiritual condition, on eternal salvation, and so on. And do these things alternately. If dejection grips you fiercely, leave your room, and walking up and down, meditate on Christ; lift your mind to God and pray. Thus dejection will leave you.

3. The thought of death, which perchance may cross your mind, the thought of Christ's judgment, of eternal torment and of eternal bliss, turns away dejection. Meditate on these things.

4. Pray and sigh, pleading with God Himself to grant you zeal and inclination: for without Him we are good for no task whatsoever.

If you follow these four instructions, believe me, little by little you will attain both zeal and inclination. God expects from us labor and courageous deeds; and He has promised to help those who labor. May you so labor that God may help you. He helps those who strive, not those who rest and slumber. Satan lies in wait to accomplish our perdition; nor should we slumber, but should stand erect and give battle to so fierce an antagonist; and this can be accomplished through prayer and reading and every kind of good work, so that when the Evil One visits us, he shall find no place.

"Resist the Devil and he will fly from you." No man is more easily approached by the Devil than one who lives in slothfulness and leisure; this is a house well swept and adorned for the Evil One. Meditate on these things and beware, and pray for me, a sinner.

Seek salvation in Christ.

[4]

My friend and brother in Christ:

I often hear the song of David: "There have they trembled for fear, where there was no fear." Before I had grasped the meaning of these words, I would often meditate on them. And then I realized in my spirit what this psalm meant: that men are afraid of man but are not afraid of God. They fear him who kills the body but who cannot kill the soul; but they fear not Him Who can throw both body and soul into the Gehenna: they dread the loss of temporal life but fear not to lose life eternal. They fear to lose their riches, fame, honors and comfort, but are not afraid of losing the eternal good; they fear the chains of imprisonment and exile in time, but have no fear of being bound and exiled for eternity. They fear temporal dishonor but not that which is eternal. And therefore this psalm befits them: "There have they trembled for fear, where there is no fear." And in the beginning of that psalm, it is said: "The fool hath said in his heart: There is no God," Now the characteristic trait of a man who says: "There is no God," is to fear not God but man: they tremble for fear where there is no fear. For he who does not fear the only God fears all: "The wicked man fleeth when no man pursueth." His conscience is more terrible than all his persecutors. But why should one fear that which is in itself not dreadful? Every man is like myself: subject to death and all kinds of misfortunes; he is weak, as I am; and everything in him corresponds to what is in me. Satan, the spirit of wickedness and my enemy, who is invisible to me but whom I know through the evil advice he gives me, is indeed to be feared; yet, without God's permission, he has no power, neither over me, a man, nor even over cattle and swine. And so it is with any man who is my adversary. Likewise, why should we fear the loss of that which we must lose of necessity? Riches, honors, fame and all the treasures of this world will be taken away from us—whether we dread it or not; death will take all these things from us. And whether or not you fear death, you will not avoid it. Without God, no one shall put me in chains, cast me into prison, or send me into exile. If these things are done to me, it means that God has consented to them. No one shall deprive me of riches, honor, fame, against God's will. And if I am deprived of these things, it means that such is God's pleasure. And if it is pleasing to God, then so be it. God holds all things in His hand, and nothing happens to us except through His will. And nothing occurs through God's will but what is good, even as light is generated by the sun, warmth by fire and mercy by love. God offers us His good, for He is good. He permits the Devil's attacks against us, as well as the attacks of evil men, and through them He permits misfortunes, disasters, and temptations, but He permits them according to the measure of our strength and inasmuch as we can bear them. He permits all this for our good. For from a God that is true and eternal, nothing but good can issue. Why should I fear that which is inevitable? If God will allow a misfortune to befall me, I shall not escape it; even though I fear it, it will nevertheless overtake me. But if God will not allow such a misfortune to occur, then even if all the Devils and all Evil Men and the entire world should rise against me, they can do nothing to me, because He, the Only One, Who is more powerful than them all, will divert the evil of my enemies. Fire will not burn, nor the sword cut, nor water drown, nor will earth swallow up, without God's permission, for that which is created can do nothing without the Creator. Therefore why should I fear anything but God? For that which God ordains is inevitable. And why should one fear the inevitable? Let us fear, my beloved, the One God, in order that we may fear no one and naught else. For such a man as truly fears God has fear of no one and nothing. The man who fears God finds everything in God. For him God is honor, fame, riches, comfort, life and joy, though men deprive him of these things. The God-fearing man enjoys God's mercy, for he fears to anger and insult God. And what has one who enjoys God's mercy to fear from the animosity and violence of his enemies? God is all, and without God, all is naught, and the wickedness of all Devils and all Evil Men is nothing. Let them gnash their teeth: naught can they do. Blessed is the man who fears God. Wretched and poor is the man who does not fear God, for such a man is afraid of everything: there does he tremble for fear, where there is no fear. This is what was sung by David, and his most sweet music has filled my spirit with joy. I send you this message from the desert. Receive it, beloved, and fortify your heart with hope in God.

[5]

My friend and brother in Christ:

Once more my ears are filled with the psalm of David: "What have I in heaven? and besides Thee what do I desire upon earth?"

I ask myself, What is the meaning of this psalm? and my spirit gives the following answer: not only upon earth, but even in heaven, the pious soul desires nothing except God. For such a soul, heaven itself, like earth, is naught without God. Upon earth, the evil and iniquitous find their pleasure; they have gold, silver, precious stones, diamonds and other gems, horses, carriages, fine houses, garments of byssine and other luxuries, in which they find their joy. But the soul enamoured of God rejects these things and tramples upon them as on dust and litter; it not only rejects earth and its treasures, but is ready to leave heaven itself in order to attain the One God, in Whom it finds all its joys and riches. Nothing can please it, neither heaven nor earth; neither heavenly nor earthly joys can bring it comfort, when it does not behold Him Whom it loves. Even as the friend enjoys nothing, whomsoever he may meet and in whatsoever intercourse he may be engaged, nor finds comfort or pleasure in anything, when he has not sight of his beloved; even so, no solace can be offered to the soul that loves God and does not see Him. "What have I in heaven? and besides Thee, what do I desire upon earth?" Let those who find their wisdom in earthly things find also their comfort in them: let some be pleased with gold and silver, some with fame and honors, some with the wisdom of our age, some with luxury and sweetmeats, some with other treasures. Let that be their comfort which they desire and consider to be their treasure. None of these things please me; my heart turns away from them. Not only do I seek nothing that is earthly, but I seek nothing even in heaven except You, my God and Creator!

[6]

This I write for you concerning the second coming of Christ, of which we spoke briefly when you visited me. I send you this letter and advise you to do that which is written therein.

Christians (especially in this last time, when 1,780 and more years have already passed since the first coming of Christ), Christians, say I, should every day expect the last judgment and prepare for it with fitting penitence. When an earthly king plans to visit a city, and the city is informed of his coming, all the citizens await him and prepare to receive him. The heavenly King, Jesus Christ, intends to descend to earth a second time. This He Himself declared when He lived on earth, and His servants, the holy Apostles, announced as much, and Holy Church awaits His coming. Therefore Christians, being informed of this second coming, must every day prepare themselves to receive Christ, for He will come when least expected. He will not come this time as He came before—that is, in poverty and humility—but in terrible glory. He will come, not to live on earth, to teach and to suffer (for this has already been accomplished), but to judge, and to render to each his due. If an angel should visit us and say to us that Christ would come one of these days, we should be seized with trembling and should turn to sincere repentance. We should guard ourselves from all sin and implore God's mercy with sighs and tears. But who knows how far off this coming of Christ is? It may occur any day now. For no one knows the counsel and intentions of God, and it has been said: "Wherefore be you also ready, because at what hour you know not the Son of man will come."

Truly our Lord will come. He will come to judge. He will come soon, and at a time when men do not expect Him. And he will render to each what he has merited. The greater the time which has elapsed since the first coming of Christ, the nearer draws His second coming; and the longer we live, the nearer we are to His universal judgment. Already we are closer to this day and hour of judgment than we were yesterday and before yesterday. Let us inscribe this in our memory and prepare for that day with true repentance. "Let us hold fast the confession of our hope without wavering (for he is faithful that hath promised), And let us consider one another, to provoke unto charity and to good works: Not forsaking our assembly, as some are accustomed; but comforting one another, and so much the more as you see the day approaching." Let us repent, beloved, in order that this day terrible to sinners may bring comfort to us instead of terror and despair: "Because he hath appointed a day wherein he will judge the world in equity." Hence we find comfort in the following: Christ Our Lord will judge the world; this is why God commands all men to repent, so that they may avoid that fearful condemnation: "Depart from me, you cursed, into everlasting fire which was prepared for the devil and his angels."

Let us turn, beloved, with all our love to God. Let us repent, and our sins will be forgiven, and we shall avoid condemnation; and Christ's judgment will not inspire us with fear and trembling but will give us comfort and eternal salvation. For Christ, Our Lord, will condemn not those who have sinned, but those who have sinned without repenting. He will forgive and will save those who have repented of their sin, for He has come into the world to save those who have sinned and have repented, and this I desire for you as well as for myself.

[7]

Now, in accordance with your desire, I shall write about man. But believe me, every time I think about man, I am filled with great wonder because of the kindness and love of God towards him; so that I exclaim with the psalmist: "What is man that thou art mindful of him? or the son of man, that thou makest account of him?" In truth man is a wondrous being. All God's creation is wondrous, but man above all else. Wondrous is the divine providence concerning him: he is created, not as other beings, but by the special decree of the Holy Trinity: "Let us make man to Our image and likeness." Man is created to God's image and likeness. All created things bear testimony to God's power, wisdom, and kindness; but man bears in addition God's image within himself. In truth, this is the greatest goodness, the most admirable beauty, the highest honor! Man is inferior to God, but he is above all other created things: man has been honored by God's image: beautiful are the skies, the sun, the moon and the stars, and all things made by God; but man is the most beautiful of all; for he bears within himself a beauty created to the image of God. Think and reflect on the beauty of God, Who is the Uncreated and Eternal Beauty! If God has so greatly honored man, who, then, can rise against him? The whole world, all hell and all the devils, can do nothing to man. God is within him and is his protector.

[8]

Sir Timofey Vasilievich,

I have heard that you have restored in Voronezh the amusement place[20] which had been destroyed. Do you not realize how many scandals and disorders occur about these premises because of irresponsible and shameless people? Beware, lest, in so far as you have offered the occasion for such disorders, all these scandals and licentious acts be imputed to you. Perhaps you seek your own profit in serving those human follies which God's word teaches us to uproot. It is iniquitous to seek one's profit in such things as are occasions for breaking the divine law, dishonoring the Law-Giver, and causing the loss of men's souls. The time in which we are now living in particular calls, not for amusement, but for tears of penitence. A man must be extraordinarily insensitive not to see God's hand on our fatherland: such a one is not merely asleep but spiritually dead. How many thousands of our brothers have been devoured by the Prussian War[21]! how many widows and orphans have been made! how, moreover, has the State Treasury been drained! Throughout the land fires have broken out and drought has spread. And scarcely have we had time to deplore this disaster when one even greater has befallen us. Once more our fatherland groans and sighs as foreign arms are turned against us: once more all are seized with confusion and fear; once more our brothers are wounded; once more is Christian blood shed; once more are thousands killed; once more is heard the weeping of fathers, mothers, wives, and children. The issue of this public calamity is as yet unknown, but I do know that without God's help we can expect no good. For we are saved, not by arms, but by God's omnipotent aid. But God has mercy upon those who repent, and saves them; He defends those who trust in Him and not in gold or other things, who appeal to Him with true devotion.

[9]

Christians, we now behold the hand of God punishing us; we see our fatherland sighing and groaning because of the bloody war in which we are engaged with the Moslems.[22]

To this calamity, another no less terrible has been added: the plague has gained ground; we hear of it spreading far and wide. We behold all this and sigh and weep, suffering our chastisement. But we must acknowledge that it is our fault, the consequence of our iniquity. We must bow our heads and confess to God: "To the Lord our God belongeth justice, but to us confusion of our face. Thou art just, O Lord, and all thy judgments are just, and all thy ways mercy, and truth, and judgment." If we examine our deeds, we shall realize our great shame and our great iniquity in God's sight. We make light of breaking the oath made with God as our witness on the holy Gospels. The courts of justice where God's judgment is delivered have been turned into markets for trading and barter. Truth and justice have been dethroned, and the voice of Mammon is heard in their place. It is useless to call upon the judge if you have no money, for you will get nothing from him. The landowner thinks nothing of taking five or six roubles a year from a peasant, and this in the Ukraine, where bread is cheap and money expensive. It is considered a slight matter to make peasants work three days a week for the landowner in addition to their other labors; and the poll tax besides is collected from them. This is great injustice and selfishness! How will those who are burdened with such labor and taxation earn the necessities of life? How will they provide for their wives, children, and other dependents? Where will they get bread and other food, clothing, shoes, and shelter? How will they find rest for their weakened bodies? Some of them groan under the yoke of the landlords, others under that of unjust and corrupted judges, and their cries resound in the ears of God. And like iniquities are committed by merchants, by peasants, and among all other classes. It is deemed a small sin, or no sin at all, to cheat, seduce, steal; to defile our neighbor's bed; to act in anger and take revenge; to hurt a neighbor's reputation by calumny, or to bring about his ruin. These are our deeds! This is our Christianity! God calls upon us to repent. We do not hear Him.

[10]

Remember that to those who want to be saved God says: "In your patience you shall possess your souls." Read the Apocalypse, chapters 2 and 3, and chapter 7, verse 9 to the end. Suffer all that befalls you, so that you may find refreshment in eternal life. (And pray diligently for your parents, that God may forgive them.)

In order to strengthen your small courage, let me tell you that this week one in our monastery heard a certain voice when, having retired for rest, he fell asleep at midnight. To wit: he heard above his head such singing that his heart melted like wax from joy and sweetness. And when the singing had ceased, he awoke and felt that joy and sweetness in his heart, where it remained for a short time and soon left him. And a great sadness assailed him because of the joy that had gone from him.[23] Meditate on this and tell it to your brethren in Christ. Even here, God does not leave us without comfort, and how much the more shall he comfort us in the future life. Suffer all things and strive to please Christ.

Your well-wisher and servant,

Tychon, Bishop of Voronezh
September 1773.

[11]

Living in your cell, conduct yourself as follows: rising from sleep, thank God and pray. Coming back from church, read some book salutary for your soul, then undertake some manual labor. Having performed part of this work, rise and pray; and having prayed, return to your reading. If you do all these things alternately, you will experience great devotion and zest as the result of the variety in your occupations. In the same manner do men walk from place to place and take their exercise; and so also is a variety of food more palatable than if we always partake of the same fare. When dejection, ennui or sadness troubles you excessively, leave your cell and walk about in whatever place is accessible, and while walking, sigh after Christ, that He may help you. Think often of death, of Christ's judgment, and of eternity. These thoughts, like a whip, drive away all dejection, ennui, and melancholy. All that is temporal is brief and soon finished. That which occurs after death endures for ever. The day passes, and with it everything that is sad or joyful. And in the same manner, all our life passes away, drawing nearer and nearer to death. And with that occupation in which a man is engaged when death overcomes him shall he appear in eternity.

P.S. Beware of going on visits, lest you disperse among men that which you have gathered in solitude. It is rare that a man returning to his cell is the same as when he left it. The desert and the cell accumulate riches, but the temptations of the world disperse them. In the cell man gathers up his whole past life in his thoughts, and contemplating it, turns to Christ with sighs and asks for His mercy. Nothing causes a man to sin so often as his tongue. In seeking solitude, he flees the occasion of sin. Our eyes and ears are like windows through which temptations penetrate to our heart and strike at it. In solitude this is avoided and temptation refused. One who is young and unmarried and in the full tide of life must observe solitude in order neither to offer the occasion of, nor to accept temptation. Listen attentively and meditate upon that of which I write. We read in history how pillars fell because of the flesh; how, then, shall reeds hope in themselves? The desert and solitude preserve us from this weakness with the help of God. A certain saint heard a voice crying "Flee men, that you may be saved."[24] Let this voice re-echo in our ears. However, if we flee men, it must not be because of men, but because of sin. We must hate sin, not men: men we must love, and we must pray for them. It is our need which moves us to pray for ourselves, but love persuades us to pray for our neighbors.

Your well-wisher,
The humble Tychon,
March 23, 1780.

[12]

Christians:

Christ's judgment draws near; like a thief in the night this day will come unexpectedly, and with whatever it shall surprise each of us, with that shall each appear at this dreadful trial. One man shall be surprised during fornication, and he shall appear with it. Another shall be surprised in murder, and he shall appear with it: another still in evil utterances or calumny or lying, plotting or hypocrisy, or insult to his neighbor; and each shall stand trial with these sins. Some shall be surprised during feasts and banquets, or at card-playing, or at the opera or a masquerade; and they shall stand there for trial. Others again shall be surprised in quarrels and disputes and shall thus appear at their judgment. Still others shall be surprised in bribery and corruption, or during dancing and revelling and other licentious amusements and excesses, and shall face judgment under these circumstances.

I implore you, beloved, I implore you in the name of the gentleness and meekness of Christ, to spare your souls and repent, that you may not be lost for all eternity. God still waits for us, still has patience with us.

Listen to one who desires your salvation, and especially, listen to Christ Himself, Who hungers and thirsts for our salvation, Who came because of it into this world, Who suffered and died in order to see our salvation.

FROM ST. TYCHON'S WILL

Glory be to God for everything! Glory be to God for having created me to His image and likeness. Glory be to God for having redeemed me, the fallen. Glory be to God for having extended his solicitude to me, the unworthy. Glory be to God for having led me, the sinner, to repentance. Glory be to God for having offered me His holy words, like a lamp in a dark place, thus setting me on the path of righteousness. Glory be to God for having illumined the eyes of my heart. Glory be to God for having made known to me His holy name. Glory be to God for having washed away my sins through the bath of baptism. Glory be to God for having shown me the way to eternal bliss. The way is Jesus Christ, Son of God, Who says of Himself: "I am the way and the truth and the life."

Glory be to God, that He has not brought me to perdition through my sins, but suffered them because of His kindness. Glory be to God for showing me the vanity and emptiness of the world. Glory be to God for helping me in various temptations, misfortunes, and calamities. Glory be to God for protecting me in accidents and mortal dangers. Glory be to God for defending me against the Devil, who is the enemy. Glory be to God for raising me when I was prostrate. Glory be to God for comforting me in my sorrow. Glory be to God for converting me when I was erring. Glory be to God for punishing me as a father. Glory be to God for announcing to me His last Judgment, that I might fear it and repent of my sins. Glory be to God for revealing to me eternal torment and eternal bliss, that I might flee the one and seek the other. Glory be to God for offering to me, the unworthy one, food which strengthened my body, clothing which covered my nakedness, a house wherein I found shelter. Glory be to God for all the other benefits He granted me for my comfort and sustenance. I received benefits from Him as often as I breathed.

Glory be to God for everything!

Now, my brethren, I address my words to you. I cannot speak

to you as I did formerly, with my voice and my lips, for I am silent, and my breath is spent. But I can talk to you by means of this short letter.

1. The temple of my body has been destroyed, and earth returns to earth, according to the word of God: "Dust thou art, and into dust thou shalt return." But with the holy Church, I expect resurrection from the dead and the life of the world to come. My hope is sitting at the right hand of God, Jesus Christ, my Lord and God. He is my life and resurrection. He says to me: "I am the resurrection and the life. He who believes in me shall not die but live." With His voice will He awaken me from my sleep.

2. I have gone away from you according to the way of earthly things; I have departed, and we no longer see each other as we did before. But we shall see each other in that place where shall be gathered all the nations that have lived from the beginning of the world and to its very end. O God, grant that we may see each other there, where God is seen face to face, and gives new life to those who see Him, and comforts and gladdens them, and gives them ineffable joy for all eternity. There do men shine like the sun; there is true life; there is true honor and glory; there is true joy and gladness; there is true ecstasy, and all that is eternal and endless. "Let thy mercy, O Lord, be upon us, as we have hoped in thee."

3. I greatly thank my benefactors, who did not forsake me in my weakness and misery, but out of their mercy and love, provided me with their goods. May God render to them their kindness on the day when all shall be rendered their due.

4. I have forgiven, and I forgive, all who have offended me; may God forgive them in His gracious mercy. I too pray to be forgiven wherein I have offended anyone, being a man. "Forgive, and ye shall be forgiven," God has said.

5. As I have no belongings, nothing remains after me. I pray that those who lived at my side and served me may want nothing.

Pardon, my beloved, and remember Tychon!

ST. SERAPHIM, MYSTIC AND PROPHET

SERAPHIM In presenting the latest, and perhaps the greatest, of Russian saints, we make our only departure in this work from the principle of selecting primary sources. The pamphlet of A. F. Dobbie Bateman is here reprinted almost in its entirety, together with the only original document concerning the saint, one which is, however, of the highest importance.

Mr. Dobbie-Bateman, an English student of Russian Orthodoxy, has brought to the difficult task of presenting this remarkable Russian saint to the Western world an insight uncommon in European interpreters of Eastern spirituality. The sources of the saint's life upon which his account is based consist of a mass of recollections transmitted by oral tradition traceable to the time immediately after Seraphim's death and stories told of him by disciples and admirers, particularly by the nuns of the Diveyev Convent. These documents are of unequal value as historical evidence: some of them are testimonies of first order, others belong to the category of legend. A judicious critical sifting has still to be made, and the general impression conveyed is so much that of the miraculous, the "medieval," that there is some danger of their being received with scepticism by modern readers. Yet it must be borne in mind that in Seraphim we are presented with a personality of extraordinary spiritual endowments, with gifts of a higher order than can be tested by the religious historian with purely rational methods.

The only work composed by the saint, which was published after his death as his "Instructions," is rather disappointing. It contains only traditional maxims of the Eastern authorities on spiritual matters and is devoid of any personal element. It is conjectured by some that a benevolent censorship was exercised upon the book by the Metropolitan Philaret of Moscow, who might have thought it prudent to expurgate all paradoxical elements in the mystical experience of the elder, had the latter really dared to expose them to the world. Mr. Dobbie-Bateman quotes some excerpts from this work.

In the personality of the hermit of Sarov one is struck by the blending of features which are traditional, medieval, and prophetical gifts which evoke all the strangeness of a soul working directly under the inspiration of grace. His life in the virgin forests of Sarov, where he stood night after night, praying on a stone, his solitude broken only by stalking beasts, his fifteen years of complete seclusion, recall the life of a saint of medieval Russia; Seraphim seems like a contemporary and the closest spiritual relation of Nilus Sorsky. Seraphim was well-read in the ascetical literature of the Greek fathers, but nothing about him suggests that he was acquainted with the modern secular literature of Russia. He lives and thinks in isolation from his time and from modern culture.

A period of the severest asceticism, lasting for many years, served as Seraphim's preparation for the life of mystical prayer. He had his terrible struggles with the temptations of the flesh and the spirits of evil, but all this experience was behind him when, at the age of sixty-six, he emerged from his secluded cell and turned to the suffering world as a seer, a healer, and a spiritual guide.

Unlike other startzy (elders) of modern Russia, Seraphim had no teacher in the art of spiritual guidance: it was his personal gift, and one which he did not transmit to any successor. In his novel The Brothers Karamazov Dostoevsky has described this new institution of startzy (monks as the spiritual guides of laymen), and in the figure of Zosima has given his own conception of the ideal staretz. Seraphim is the first known representative of this class of spiritual elders in Russia. But this is not his only original contribution to the spiritual life; he was the prophet of a new era, his approach to the world is unprecedented in the Eastern tradition.

Seraphim knew how to be extraordinarily severe in his demands upon a soul in the grips of demonic forces, but when the tide of human suffering flowed to his threshold he would go to meet it with the radiance of life: "My joy," was his usual greeting; or he would address his visitor with the paschal exclamation, "Christ is risen!" Sometimes he would know, without being told, the names and private circumstances of the supplicants, and he would give them sound advice concerning their domestic and vocational problems in terms of the deepest tenderness.

Even in his personal appearance and his attire he broke with the monastic tradition: instead of the black cassock obligatory for Eastern monks he usually wore a white peasant's costume. He would reveal to no one, not to his most intimate friends, his experience with evil spirits, but he described readily and graciously his visions of the celestial world in which he lived almost continuously; for him it was such an ever-present reality that with the utmost naturalness he could give a friend an apple or a leafy branch as a gift from paradise, received through the courtesy of Our Lady.

Since his mystical spirituality was little understood by the brethren of his monastery, it was in the guidance and instruction of the sisters of the nearby Diveyev Convent that Seraphim's paternal love found its deepest expression, and they were his confidantes concerning the most mystical of his visions and prophecies. His religious admiration of virginity—a feature not characteristic of the Russian religion—was such that he separated the virgins from the widows in the convent. The theme of virginity runs through his visions. Our Lady once appeared to him in the company of twelve virgin saints, and it is also, perhaps, in this sense that her words concerning him: "He is one of our family" are to be interpreted. It is not without significance that Seraphim's favorite icon, before which he prayed even at the hour of his death, was not one of the classical Byzantine-Russian madonnas representing the Divine Mother but one of the Western type representing a Holy Virgin of "Tenderness."

When Seraphim defined the aim of the Christian life as "the acquisition of the Holy Spirit," he repeated the words of

Macarius of Egypt (or, at least, of the writer whose homilies are ascribed to St. Macarius). And yet this formula was unusual in Russia; not only to his disciple Motovilov, but to the vast majority of spiritually minded people in Russia, it was in the nature of a revelation. The highest gift of the spirit which Seraphim acquired in the spiritual school of the Hesychasts (known to him through the Philocalia) he boldly offered to laymen as something accessible to them and destined for all Christians.

Peculiar to Seraphim were likewise the extraordinary physical manifestations which accompanied the gifts of the Holy Spirit, the effects of which were witnessed and described by Motovilov. This blending of the highly spiritual and the delicately sensible in Seraphim's mystical life exercised a powerful attraction upon the generation of the Orthodox Renaissance, the last before the Revolution (1900-17). For these groping, creative minds, seeking to interpret and express through esthetic media their eschatological apprehension of the approaching crisis, St. Seraphim was the prophet of the expected revelation of the Holy Spirit and the forerunner of the new form of spirituality which should succeed merely ascetical monasticism: in symbolical terms, the white, spirit-bearing flame of mystical prayer, embracing the hearts of all men in the unity of the love of God, which should succeed the black night of austerity.

ST. SERAPHIM OF SAROV

By A. F. DOBBIE-BATEMAN

SERAPHIM OF SAROV IS ONE OF THE GREAT SAINTS OF THE RUSSIAN CHURCH AND MOREOVER ONE WHO IS NEAR TO US IN time. He was born at Kursk in central Russia on 19th July, 1759, died at the Sarov Monastery on 2nd January, 1833, and was canonised on 19th July, 1903, seventy years after his death. His life coincided with a period of war, revolution and change, the period of the French Revolution and Napoleon's invasion of Russia. Within his own Russia it was the honeymoon period of vigorous and insurgent Europeanisation with its alternations of Encyclopedist Enlightenment and military reaction; his age saw the birth and golden youth of the modern Russian literature and the spread of new economic theories which preceded the emancipation of the serfs. It was the age of free masonry and of the new education, which laid the foundations of the new intelligentsia. In the Church also the spirit of the times was stirring between obscurantist reaction on the one hand and on the other the dayspring of the new theology and the Bible in Russian; it was the age of the reactionary priest Photius, of the Russian Bible Society, and of Philaret, greatest of the Metropolitans of Moscow. The modern age of Europe had begun and with it the characteristic vacillation of men's minds before seemingly limitless possibilities, which led the young mind of Russia from pillar to post, and finally to that disaster which Seraphim foretold.

Was Seraphim aloof from all this? Did he reject and condemn this modern life of progress? Neither the one nor the other. "Poor Seraphim" was neither hostile nor critical; he simply lived in another world, in direct contact with the patristic age of the Church and with the primitive monks of Egypt and Syria who first instituted Christian ascesis. He was not touched by this unquiet, mobile world, which found him, and still finds him, scarcely intelligible. Was he then remote? To most men he was remote; yet he stood close to numbers of those who flocked to him and to those few whose inspired, naive and possibly credulous narratives give all that is known of this almost legendary saint and seer.

Known in the world as Prochor Moshnin, Seraphim was the son of Isidor Moshnin, a building contractor of Kursk, and Agatha, his wife. While Prochor was still a child, his father died, leaving his widow to complete the construction of the church to the Mother of God in Kursk. The building of this church was one of the child's early memories; he played about the growing structure and from it at the age of seven he fell to the ground fortunately without injury. At the age of ten he began to read and made rapid progress; too rapid, for he soon fell seriously ill. But even at this tender age he showed spiritual gifts; during this illness he had a vision of the Mother of God, who promised him restoration of health. His complete recovery followed the reception in his mother's courtyard of a famous icon which he was taken down to see. He made rapid progress once more with his studies and zealously took to reading the Hours, the Psalter, the Bible and other spiritual books. For a time he also helped his older brother, Alexis, in business; but business did not attract him. Already he had formed a friendship with a certain "holy fool" who promised great things of him. By the age of eighteen he had decided to become a monk and enter the Sarov Monastery. Full of this idea he went with five other sons of Kursk business families on a pilgrimage to the relics of the saints in the Pechersky (or Cave) Monastery at Kiev, and there an elder named Dositheus approved and blessed his intention. Two years later, being then nineteen, on 20th November, 1779, he was received into Sarov.[1]

There Prochor was handed over to the care of Joseph, the bursar. For a time he served in the two bakeries, baking bread for the brethren or sacred bread for the Eucharist, and worked in the joiner's shop, where he showed particular proficiency. He also had to perform the duties of watchman and sexton. Meanwhile he maintained his habits of prayer and study, reading the Scriptures together with patristic, ascetic and hagiological literature, the *Hexaemeron* of St. Basil, the Homelies of St. Macarius, the *Ladder* of St. John, the *Philocalia*, etc. The New Testament he used to read standing in the attitude of prayer before icons. He ate but once a day, and not at all on Wednesdays and Fridays, when he would obtain permission to disappear into the woods, there to practise the ancient "rule" (that is, the order of prayers) of St. Pachomius, the Egyptian founder of the first Christian coenoby. In 1780 he fell ill and for three years spent most of his time on his back; but he refused medical aid and devoted himself to spiritual remedies. As before during an illness he was visited by the Mother of God. The Blessed Virgin appeared to Prochor in the company of St. Peter and St. John the Divine, to whom she turned and said: "He is one of our family." Then she stroked Prochor's head and touched his side with her staff. After his recovery Prochor bent his energies to the endowing of a hospital church for the monastery. It was founded in 1784, and he visited the neighbouring towns collecting for it. On 13th August, 1786, at the age of twenty-seven, he was at length tonsured a monk and given the name of Seraphim. In the autumn of 1786 he was ordained a deacon by Victor, Bishop of Tambov. The new deacon gave himself up to his duties of prayer and service in church, where his spiritual powers manifested themselves in visions of angels and finally of the Son of Man Himself in glory, blessing the worshippers at the Eucharist on Holy Thursday. On 2nd September, 1793, at the age of thirty-four, Seraphim was ordained a priest by Theophilus, Bishop of Tambov, and there followed a year of service in his new order with daily communion. At this time the superior of the monastery, Pachomius, also citizen of Kursk, died, and his death made a great impression on Seraphim. With the authorization of the new superior Seraphim removed into the solitude of the "wilderness" towards which he had long since turned.

The next ten years, from 1794 to 1804, were spent alone in

a hut in the woods. For food he grew vegetables in a small garden or gathered grasses. His daily life of prayer was governed by the long and severe rule of St. Pachomius, and in addition he continued his studies of the Bible, patristic, ascetic and hagiological literature. But now he held an area of woodland in the immediate control of his fantasy and invested its different places with the names of the sacred sites, Jerusalem, Nazareth, Bethlehem, Tabor, Golgotha, Jordan and so on, reliving the Gospel scenes. Here he entered into silent intercourse with all kinds of wild animals, bears, wolves, foxes, hares, seeking neither to tame them nor constrain them, but feeding them when they came to him. It was a time of prayer, study and discipline; it must also have been a time of intense and stubborn wrestling with all the claims of mind and body. It came to an end on 12th September, 1804, when the hermit was knocked senseless by two footpads. He offered no resistance and refused to countenance their prosecution. But the assault left him shocked in spirit, ill and permanently bent in body. And again in his illness came Mary in a vision with Peter and John, to whom she spoke the same words: "He is one of our family."

For five months Seraphim could not return to his wilderness, and then it was for a renewal and accentuation of the fight for self-mastery. His experience had made him even more drastic with himself. Thus began the stylite period of his life, which lasted from 1804 to 1807. With the exception of short respites for such necessary offices as feeding himself, he stood in the attitude of prayer for 1,000 days and nights on a large stone in the woods, using one stone by day and another stone by night. His prayer was the prayer of the publican.

In 1807 the superior of the monastery died, and the succession was offered to Seraphim. He refused the offer and instead began a period of complete silence. He no longer went out to greet visitors, and, if he met passers in the woods, turned away; he did not even speak with the brother who brought him food from the monastery. But by 1810 his legs were seriously weakened, and on 8th May he had perforce to return to the monastery, where on the following day he shut himself up in his cell in order to preserve and continue his silence. He did not leave his cell even in 1815, when the Bishop Jonah visited Sarov. In the cell there was a single lamp before a single icon, the icon of the Blessed Virgin alone without the child, known by the name of "Tenderness."² There was no heating and no bed. He rarely lay down to sleep, taking such sleep as he needed either sitting on the ground against the wall or on his knees and elbows with face to floor. Each day he completed his rule of prayer, and in addition on Mondays read St. Matthew, on Tuesdays St. Mark, on Wednesdays St. Luke, on Thursdays St. John, on Fridays the office of Holy Cross, and on Saturdays the office of All Saints. Each day he made a thousand obeisances. On Sundays and feast days the consecrated "gifts" were brought to him from the early Eucharist. Then at last, in September, 1815, he opened the door of his cell and blessed the Bezobrazov pair, husband and wife, who had come to visit him. Even so the long silence was not brought to a final end. A further vision of Theotokos, accompanied on this occasion by St. Peter of Alexandria and St. Clement of Rome, finally closed the period of silence and opened the period of "elderhood," the crowning period of a lifetime's discipline. Seraphim entered on his spiritual maturity on 25th November, 1825, at the age of sixty-six, and continued therein until his death in 1833, a period of a little over seven years.

The Western reader will find the type of the elder or *staretz* in the character of Father Zosima, described in Dostoevsky's *Brothers Karamazov*. It is not an undisputed likeness of the particular elder, Ambrose of Optina (†1891), whom Dostoevsky had in mind; it contains an element of romanticism and has been criticised on this ground. Perhaps something of the atmosphere of St. Seraphim's age and circumstance (as also of the function and meaning of the Jesus Prayer which he practised) may be more readily obtained from the anonymous and more nearly contemporary *Way of a Pilgrim*.³ Elderhood is not an appointment in the Church which can be made and filled, nor is it an order in the hierarchy which can be conferred in ordination. It expresses a spiritual authority which arises from the inner life of the elder himself; it can be revealed and recognized but not claimed or given. Without being, therefore, individualist, elderhood is individual and personal. The old monk, whose spiritual powers are thus manifested, retains his own character, transfigured, or, if you like, sublimated; his own, but informed by a higher power. St. Seraphim was one single and very vital personality, combining and fusing in himself many facets of religious enlightenment. The touch of the healer, the insight of the seer, the eccentricity of the Fool in Christ, the glow of the mystic, the obedience of the son by adoption and the perfect dignity and humility of God's instrument—all these may be seen in him.

The healings had already begun during the long and slow process during which Seraphim outlived his silence before finally emerging from his cell. The sickness of M. V. Manturov was complicated beyond the resources of contemporary medicine, but in 1823 Seraphim healed him. The healed man threw himself at the feet of the recluse, but Seraphim restrained him: "Is it Seraphim's work to kill and to make alive, to bring down to hell and to raise up again? Nay, son, it is the work of the one Lord, who does the will of them that fear Him and hears their prayer. To the Almighty Lord and His spotless Mother give the thanks." In 1829 the boy Korsakov went to him almost blind. The saint breathed on the boy and signed him with the sign of the cross. "Thou wilt be well," he said; then a moment later, as the boy turned to go, added the words: "And wilt wed Seraphima!" It is Seraphima herself who years later tells the story. In 1831 Seraphim cured the pious landowner, Nicholas Motovilov, of rheumatism and sores. "Do you believe," he asked, "that the Lord Jesus Christ is God and Man, and that His spotless Mother is ever Virgin? . . . Then, if you believe, you are well already." Seizing Motovilov by the shoulders, he slowly and firmly made him walk; then stopped him. "That is enough," he said. The scalded and suffering child, Natalia Evgrafova, dreamed of Seraphim and after her recovery was taken to visit him. "Aha! the child has come!" he exclaimed; then with surprise he heard of the cure. Suddenly and unexpectedly he turned to her. "Wouldst have an onion?" he said. "Mine are sweet!" Years afterwards the riddle was solved; the life was bitter-sweet. In May, 1829, the wife of A. G. Voroshilov lay dying and the husband hastened to the elder. The reply was that she must die. Overcome by grief, Voroshilov threw himself at the elder's feet and besought his prayers. Seraphim became lost in mental prayer; then at last opened his eyes and said: "Come, my joy, the Lord will give to thy partner life; go home in peace." From that moment the sick woman recovered.

His words were accepted prophetically, such was the impression of meaning and insight which he succeeded in conveying. They were simple and unexpected words arising out of the circumstances of each individual suppliant, whose needs he knew before they told them or before their letters were opened. Why did he speak suddenly to this woman about Job—St. Job the Sufferer—who lost children and all? How did he know that as Job suffered, so would she? What power enabled him to read the mind of this merchant, to link unmentioned griefs with unmentioned passions in caressing rebuke? Were all things clear to him? "Say not so, my joy. The heart of man is open to the Lord alone and only God sees what is in the heart; but man comes and the heart is deep. . . . What the Lord bids His servant say, I give to the suppliant, the first thought that arises in the soul." . . . And sometimes Seraphim becomes self-conscious and makes mistakes. But Seraphim's supreme prophecy must be deferred for later mention.

Of Seraphim's own human heart it is possible to know only by inference; these secrets of his struggle for self-mastery he has not divulged. Had he any special temptations? There are indications in the things that he avoided and taught others to avoid; but for himself he is silent. In his later years he was asked whether he had ever seen devils. "They are foul," was the reply. But if the facts of his inner life remain his own secret, the methods whereby he mastered his secret are known: by the ordering of his whole life in the Church and above all by prayer. He was steeped in the traditional prayer-life of the Church and in the rich and meaningful services of the Orthodox East. His own prayer rule for use in his cell consisted of long and expressive sequences from the services of the Church woven round the Psalter; it is not a rule for ordinary men, but the prayers throughout were the prayers of the ordinary Christian. At bottom the principle was simple. Seraphim held that the veriest layman in his daily life could achieve Christian perfection and the Divine love in the use of three fundamental prayers: the Lord's Prayer, which the Lord Himself gave as a pattern of all prayers; "Hail, Mary," the greeting brought by the Archangel Gabriel from heaven as the cornerstone of the New Testament;[4] and the last the Nicene Creed, which summarises the whole dogmatic content of the Christian faith. Everything else that can be added from sacred literature is a gift to be received with humility and thanksgiving. But to one prayer he gave special attention, the Jesus Prayer, which can be used at study and at work. He schooled himself to the ceaseless and, as it were, consciously subconscious repetition: "O Lord Jesu Christ, thou Son of God, be merciful to me a sinner." "In this be all thine atten· tion and learning," he said. "Walking and sitting, working and standing in church, coming and going, let this unending cry be on thy lips and in thy heart. With it thou shalt find peace, thou shalt acquire spiritual and physical purity, in thee will abide the Holy Spirit, the fount of all good things, who will guide thy life in holiness, in all piety and purity." So Seraphim prayed as he went; he was himself a living prayer. The strength of his prayer infected his visitors. "Now thou wilt chatter to all that Sera· phim is a holy man, he prays in the air. The Lord forgive thee! See that thou keep it to thyself and tell no man until my death, or thy sickness will return." That was an occasion in his cell. At another moment, in the woods, three nuns were certain that they had seen him walking through the air above the ground.[5]

It is not surprising that he was a happy man, with no room for depression and grief. As two monks wandered through the woods, sharing their troubles, Seraphim suddenly advanced upon them through the trees with his smock trussed up round him like a workman and a large scarf around his head. He sang a verse of a hymn and, stamping with his foot, said to them:

"We have no road for depression, for Christ has subdued all things, has raised up Adam, set Eve free, and slain death." Such a man could never be lonely with himself. In the privacy of his cell he had his own visitors, spiritual visitors. He spoke of such visitations with Father Basil Sadovsky, the chaplain of the Diveyev Convent. Then, his face radiant with joy, he filled the priest's handkerchief with biscuits. "See, father," he said, "the Queen has been with me and these are left over after the guests!" The priest was to taste them himself and give them to his wife, to the nuns of Diveyev—yes, to the women living near the convent. "They will all be ours!" And so it proved to be, but Father Basil did not comprehend. "The Queen of Heaven, father, the Queen of Heaven herself has visited poor Seraphim," the elder told him; "see, what a joy this is for us! The Mother of God has cast her veil round poor Seraphim!" . . . And poor Seraphim had prayed to her for his orphans.

The "orphans" were the nuns of the Diveyev Convent. They had been placed under his spiritual charge, and it was a duty which he deeply loved, organising, advising, commanding and inspiring. The convent was a small community founded in 1780 by the nun Alexandra (Melgunova). On her death she handed her charge over to Father Pachomius of Sarov, and he in turn in 1794 to Father Seraphim. His every care for his charge was inspired by his own devotion to Theotokos; here he found a special vehicle for expressing his own virginal mysticism. So sensitive was the elder that he even separated the virgins at Diveyev from the widows, forming them into a new community with the Blessed Virgin herself as their abbess. The experiment did not long survive Seraphim, and in 1842 the two communities were amalgamated to form the Seraphimo-Diveyev Convent. The name itself shows how far the elder entered into the tradition of this community. The reformed convent maintained the rules laid down for them by him according to his will, where it is interesting to note that the expert in solitude forbade solitude to the sisters even in their walks.

His spiritual daughters responded with a perfect filial devotion. There was no limit to their obedience. On the nun Helena, sister of M. V. Manturov, Father Seraphim laid the ascetic discipline of death, that she should die instead of her sick brother Michael, whose work was not yet done. Helená was frightened, but Seraphim comforted her; so she died, fortified by the last sacrament and with faith in her lot. Such familiarity with ultimate destinies was terrifying, and the dead woman's sister Xenia abandoned herself to grief. Seraphim sent her away to communicate daily until the requiem on the fortieth day. For long he paced his cell. "They understand nothing! They weep! They should have seen how her soul flew, how the bird took wing! Cherubim and Seraphim made way for her! She has been found worthy to sit near the Holy Trinity as a virgin!" He especially cherished the nun Mary. The child Mary Melyukova entered Diveyev at the age of thirteen; she died at the age of nineteen on 21st August, 1829. To her he confided his secret hopes and revelations regarding the convent; her death he treated as a festival. "See, my joy!" he said to her brother, "what mercy has been vouchsafed her from the Lord! In the heavenly kingdom at the Throne of God, near the heavenly Queen with the holy virgins she stands! For all your family she makes her prayers!" She is a nun of the severest order now, a schimnitsa, and has received the name Martha; Seraphim had shorn her. "When thou art at Diveyev, go not by, but kneel at her tomb and say: 'Lord and mother Martha, remember us at the Throne of God in the kingdom of Heaven!'" In 1836, after the elder's death, came to Diveyev the Fool in Christ, the woman Pelagia (†1884); as a young and unhappy wife she had come to Sarov, and Seraphim held her in conversation for six hours. She never forgot him and on her tomb it was written: "Seraphim's Seraphim."

The nun Eupraxia of Diveyev was the invited witness of Father Seraphim's last and supreme vision of the Blessed Virgin. On 25th March, 1832, Theotokos came to him in the company of two angels, of the two Johns, the Baptist and the Divine, and twelve virgins. The elder stood before her as a privileged friend and they communed together of his coming death. The nun was terrified; but the Queen of Heaven, resplendent as on an icon, comforted her. The twelve virgins related to her their lives, as they are written in the Book of the Saints. This vision was vouchsafed to her by the prayers of Father Seraphim, of Mark, of Nazarius and of Pachomius. . . .

So Seraphim turned towards death. He grew weaker and began to weary. There was some suggestion of disappointments. In his cell was his coffin, the work of his own hands. He thought of death and wept. "My life is shortening!" he said. "In spirit I feel as if I had just been born and to everything bodily I am dead." He wished his bishop, Arsenius, farewell and gave him the candles for the requiem. Early on the morning of 2nd January, 1833, his cell was found on fire from an overturned candle. The fire was extinguished and Seraphim was found kneeling before the icon "Tenderness"—dead. But he had not abandoned his orphans. "When I am no more, come to my grave. As you have time, come. The oftener the better! All that is on your soul, whatever may have befallen you, come to me and bring all your grief to my grave. Bending to earth, as to a living thing, tell all and I shall hear you. All your sorrow will fly away and pass! As you ever spoke with the living, speak here! For you I live and shall live for ever!"

To those who know the Russian mind only in its historic disquiet St. Seraphim brings a new experience, an experience perhaps of that Holy Russia which many writers have sought and never found. There are obvious dangers in rationalising an experience; still more so, when it comes to extracting a teaching from the life of one who never stood forth as a teacher. For this it is necessary to plot the graph through the scattered sayings of the saint and to thread on a string the tissue of his visions. The task is impossible and inevitable. The Conversation of St. Seraphim with Nicholas Motovilov forms the central point of his teaching; it also contains within itself a warning against any purely intellectual interpretation. His experience occupies the whole mind and soul; understanding certainly, but understanding through the ear, through the touch, through smell and through sight. Words alone are not sufficient. Yet St. Seraphim's words are already much.

"God is the fire," he said, "which warms and ignites the heart and the inward parts; when we feel in our hearts the chill which is of the devil (for the devil is cold), let us call on the Lord and He will come to warm our heart with perfect love, not only to Him but to our neighbour."

"True hope seeks only the Kingdom of God, and is convinced that all earthly things necessary for this life in time will without doubt be given. . . . The heart cannot have peace until it acquires this hope."

"Many words with those whose ways are opposed to ours are enough to disorganise the inwardness of an attentive man."

"Those who have truly decided to serve the Lord God must have practice in the remembrance of God and in ceaseless prayer to Jesus Christ. . . . When the mind and heart are united in prayer and the thoughts of the soul are not scattered, then the heart is warmed with a spiritual warmth, wherein shines the light of Christ, filling with peace and joy the whole inner man."

"The heart of him in whom flow tears of tenderness is lit by rays from the Sun of Righteousness."

"He who has overcome passion has overcome also melancholy."

"Boredom is cured by prayer, by abstention from vain speech, by working with the hands according to our strength, by reading the Word of God and by patience; for it is born of a faint soul, of idleness and vain speech."

"It is a mercy of God when the body is worn out by illness, since thereby the passions weaken and man comes into himself."

"We must always bear something for God's sake with gratitude. . . . Bear in silence when the enemy disparages, and open thy heart to the Lord."

"Behave kindly with a neighbour, giving not even the appearance of scorn."

"God has enjoined on us enmity against the serpent alone, against him who in the beginning deceived man and drove him from Paradise, against the killer-devil. We are also commanded to war with the Midianites, the impious spirits of impurity and lust, who sow in the heart filthy and unclean thoughts."

"Strive only for the soul and strengthen the body inasmuch as it may strengthen the soul. If we wilfully mortify the body until spirit also is mortified, such mortification is unreasonable, even though done in pursuit of virtue."

"We must so train ourselves that the mind, as it were, swims in the law of God, under the guidance of which our life must be governed. It is very useful to be occupied with reading the Word of God in solitude and to read the whole Bible through with understanding. . . . When a man so equips his soul with the Word of God, then is he filled with understanding of what is good and what is evil."

"It is the sign of a reasoning soul when a man sinks his mind within himself and his workings in his heart."

"Try in every way to preserve the peace of the soul and not to be disturbed by the insults of others. Likewise avoid judging others. By not judging and by silence the peace of the soul is preserved. When a man is in such a frame of mind, he receives Divine revelations."

"But though the devil be transformed into an angel of light and suggest thoughts of a good appearance, the heart will still feel an ambiguity, some agitation in the thoughts and disturbance of feelings."

"In order to receive and observe in the heart the light of Christ, we must abstract ourselves as much as possible from visible objects. Having first purified the soul by repentance and good works, and with faith in the Crucified having closed the bodily eyes, immerse the mind within the heart and there call on the name of our Lord Jesus Christ. Then, by the measure of his zeal and warmth of spirit towards the beloved, man finds in the summoned name a sweetness which prompts in him a will to seek the highest enlightenment."

"When a man contemplates inwardly the eternal light, the mind is pure, and has in it no sensuous images, but, being wholly immersed in the contemplation of uncreated beauty, forgets everything sensuous and does not wish to see even itself; but would rather hide in the heart of the earth than be deprived of this true good—of God."

"The mind of an attentive man is the sentry, the sleepless guardian, placed over the inner Jerusalem."

"Man must be lenient with his soul in her weaknesses and imperfections and suffer her failings as he suffers those of others, but he must not become idle, and must encourage himself to better things."

"Most of all must he adorn himself with silence. As Ambrose of Milan says, by silence have I seen many saved, by many words not one. Again one of the fathers says: Silence is the sacrament of the world to come, words are the weapons of this world."

"At thy handiwork or being somewhere on thy set task, make unceasingly the prayer: 'O Lord Jesu Christ, be merciful to me, a sinner!' In prayer be attentive to thyself, that is, gather the mind together and unite it to the heart. At first for a day or two or more make this prayer with the mind alone, separately, noting specially each word. Then, as the Lord warms thy heart with the warmth of His grace and unites it in thee into one spirit, this prayer will flow in thee unceasingly and will be ever with thee, regaling and nourishing thee. This is that of which the prophet Isaiah said: The dew that is of Thee, is to them a healing."

These excerpts may serve to illustrate the quality of Seraphim's own self-training; they are the preparation and introduction to that process of which the *Conversation* is the product. The *Conversation* itself must be left to create its own effect, though even so the inadequacy of the title must be noted, since it is something more than a rational discourse which leads to the transfiguration of every thought and sense. Here both thought and sense unite in the communication of an experience which is not intellectual and equally is not irrational. It overrides that antithesis and leads up to the consideration of other no less valid expressions of Seraphim's spiritual life with the warning that his visions are not mere sensory or emotional images but the vehicles of meaning and understanding. There

is in them a dogmatic core which in turn must be related to the
common inheritance of Catholic Christianity. For though to
the empirical mind the elder may seem by virtue of his moral
and mystical eminence to be beyond, he is never in fact outside,
the corporate consciousness of the Church. The contrast between personal and institutional faith was not alien to Russia,
but it was utterly alien to Seraphim; only within the Church is
he to be interpreted.

"Do you believe that the Lord Jesus Christ is God and Man?"
he asked Nicholas Motovilov. Two of Ostashov's sketches of
Seraphim in his cell place the icon "Tenderness" on a table
prominently in the corner of the room. Above it in the more
usual position on a small corner shelf is another icon, which in
the second sketch, the elder's death, is flanked by yet other
icons of two saints. This other icon depicts the face of the Suffering Lord imprinted on the napkin.[6] Again, in the short
prayer rule for laymen are included both the Lord's own prayer
and the Nicene Creed. Thus the divine-human person of the
God-Man is in the centre of Seraphim's contemplations, and
it would not be legitimate to impute to him any semi-mono-
physite concentration on the deity of Christ. At the same time it
is impossible not to notice in him an almost deliberate reticence
regarding the human history of Christ. Possibly by way of contrast there is in turn something Nestorian in modern problems
of historicity with their major emphasis on Christ's humanity.
It is perhaps a matter of emphasis only; yet as between the
divine humanity and the human divinity the distinction is, to
say the least, important. It will be necessary to return to this
point. Meanwhile to Seraphim as to Russian Orthodoxy generally the appeal comes rather from the risen and glorified Christ
than from the example of His earthly career; Seraphim's vision
was of the Son of Man in glory, blessing the worshippers. Does
this then mean that the elder neglected or underrated the
Gospel story? The question answers itself. His very diction was
instinct with the spirit of the Gospels; in the *Conversation* he
moulds them creatively to his theme. Again and again in gesture
and in act he recalls the gestures and acts of the Master. One

would expect this of the student who for a lifetime had soaked his memory in the Bible and of the visionary who could conjure up a whole Holy Land within a small area of Russian forest. But it makes his reticence about the human life of Christ the more emphatic. The man who could dramatise the Gospel story through the long years of his ascesis is silent about it. For he did not expound the Gospel, but lived it, as after the pattern of his Lord he grew in stature and in the grace and mind of God. He has indeed shared that secret, but as a secret of solitude and silence; and the father confessor who could show great candour in many intimate relations of the spirit showed as great a restraint in this central focus of his faith, where God and man is one Christ.

"Do you also believe that His spotless Mother is ever Virgin?" Then Mary is in no sense substituted for her Son, but because of Him and by reference to her own part in His Incarnation she is named by the Church both Theotokos and ever-Virgin. She is, as it were, the human obverse of the Incarnation; because of her and of her substance the Son of God is also the Son of Man. Her two titles contain the whole dogmatic basis for all the highly wrought poetry of the Eastern hymns to the Mother of God, which are hymns of the Incarnation, wherein she too is seen as the meeting-place of the human and the divine. The Blessed Virgin in her own person is the flower of mankind, the human side of the Church, the human soul, the Bride of the Lamb, the mystical figure of sister and bride in the Song of Songs. The Virgin without the Child, crowned as by an aureole by the refrain of many hymns: "Hail, Virgin Bride!"—this is the Mary of the icon "Tenderness" before whom Seraphim prayed and died. Finally, in her assumption and exaltation by her own Son, Mary becomes the Queen of Heaven, the representative and advocate of a creation which through the God-Man has been redeemed and renewed; this is the Mary who appeared to Seraphim in vision and claimed him as one with her in the company of the saints. It is but a short step to envisage Seraphim's own passion for virginity and his own tender care for his "orphans." But it is necessary to go yet further.

The Son has ascended unto the Father, and has sent the Holy Spirit, the Comforter, who will testify of Him. As Mary is the human side of the Church, the Holy Spirit is the divine life in the Church. Moreover it was the Holy Spirit who overshadowed the Blessed Virgin at the Incarnation; and by the tradition of the Church, Mary was present in the upper room at Pentecost when the Holy Spirit descended in tongues of fire on all there and on her also. Thus the Holy Spirit and the Mother of God, as it were, enclose the whole Gospel story and the mystery of the two natures in the God-Man. From a purely human standpoint it was natural that Seraphim should have found a living kinship with the one person in the whole history of the Church who was most closely concerned in the life of Christ and the most completely silent about it; she was the Mother who had given all, her Son above all, and had understood. But in the divine-human economy of the Church it means more; for though the Bridegroom tarrieth, still yet in Mary the Church is overshadowed by the "Comforter and Spirit of truth, who is everywhere and filleth all things, Store of all gifts and Giver of life."[7] It is the eternal Nativity.

The message of St. Seraphim is this message of the eternal Nativity in the bosom of the Church and in the soul of every humble believer. It is the promise and the unfathomable potentiality of union in the two natures, divine and human, the marriage of Heaven and Earth. Herein then is disclosed at its source the transfiguration of humanity, the *theosis* of man, which is the theme of the *Conversation* of St. Seraphim with Nicholas Motovilov, the revelation of the simple human soul as the bearer of the Spirit. Divine humanity or human divinity? It is necessary to contemplate the divine-human process also in the person of Theotokos, for it is also the revelation of sonhood by adoption through the Spirit. There is and must be a qualitative distinction between the manifestation of God-Manhood in Christ and the derivative apotheosis of manhood in His Church, which excludes any one-sided historicity with regard to the person of the Only-begotten Son of the Father. For He was not just the righteous man found acceptable to God and there can be no reincarnation of the Divine Word. But every Christian soul is called to its own transfiguration and to be the vehicle of the Christ-life in the Church. It is the universal message of man's self-realisation in Christ. And then within the Russian Church, which had been supposed to have sacrificed the practical to the contemplative, arises the further message that the Christ-life is made manifest in man, not by any unsolicited and unwanted gift of grace from on high, but through the activity of man, freely given, freely accepted and by grace made effective; for the divine-human relationship demands no less. The son of the contractor jested with the landowner about the acquisition of the Holy Spirit, and thereby the saint brought home to his follower and friend this essential part of his theme:

> All good deeds done unto the Lord,
> And purity of virgin souls.

"The Holy Spirit itself enters our souls, and this entrance into our souls of Him, the Almighty, and this presence with our spirit of the Triune Majesty is only granted to us through our own assiduous acquisition of the Holy Spirit, which prepares in our soul and body a throne for the all-creative presence of God with our spirit according to His irrevocable word."

There is the man and the message, and it would be difficult to assert that either was typical of the Russian mind through its century and a half of secular humanism since the days of Catherine II. He was afflicted neither by psychological revolt nor by discursive introspection; but there was in him an uncommon zeal for godliness and holiness, and a great love for the simple man. The self-conscious members of the intelligentsia could not have appreciated him, even had they heard of him. When they did hear, when Seraphim was canonised in 1903, this solemn act was dismissed and condemned as a mere "canonisation of peasant ignorance" at the instance of the statesman Pobedonostsev in the interests of poltical reaction. Not until a new movement had matured in the "return of the intelligentsia" to the Orthodox Church was the elder seen at anything like his full stature. And then in the hour of political and social ruin they found that Seraphim could speak to them on the very subject that had vexed the intellectuals for generations—God in the world and the meaning of the world for God which is the whole destiny of man.

The tribute that has since been paid to Seraphim has been wholehearted, for Seraphim has justified Russian Christians to themselves in the hour of secular judgment. Naturally enough it has been a human and personal vindication. Professor Lossky contrasts Seraphim with the medieval St. Sergius and the period when the Russian Church exercised a creative influence in Russian social organisation. "Seraphim of Sarov," he says, "is the inexhaustible source of a warm and intimate caress in the *individual* relationships of men." Professor Ilyin sees in the elder a revelation of some secret concerning the maturing of the individuality in time. "Individuality is apophatic,[8] closed; it is the 'non-ego' and bears in itself the seal of God the Father, the Lord of Hosts, the Absolute Individuality." These are vast phrases, but the theme is great, greater even than the collapse of liberal individualism. For the elder was no individualist, as he also was no subjectivist. His sense of human social relations also was creative. He was a churchman and a monk in his community at Sarov; but his great creation in this sphere was his organisation of the social and mystical life of the community at the Diveyev Convent, which gladdened the sensitive mind of Nicholas Fedorov as he pondered over his hopes for an active social participation in the "common task" of the resurrection.[9] Fairest of all perhaps is the appreciation of Fr. Sergius Bulgakov: "The saint has shown the fulfilment of the first commandment, of love of God with the whole heart, but he has also fulfilled the second commandment, which is *like* unto it, of love for one's neighbour . . . not the love of human sentimentality, which can be impotent, blind and prejudiced, but a spiritual, jealous love; and in this love became known to him the revelation concerning *man*, how God has loved and revered him, setting in man His own image and making the supreme delight of His Wisdom in the sons of men."

The official mind of the Russian Church was not necessarily

more appreciative of St. Seraphim than were the intellectuals of 1903. The initiative in the act of canonisation was not taken by the Over-Procurator of the Holy Synod, Pobedonostsev, but by the Empress Alexandra Fedorovna. Pobedonostsev vigorously opposed this "Saint-making" at the behest of a princess of Hesse-Darmstadt. But it is necessary to understand the fact of a Church which has been externally aggrandised and internally restrained and repressed by a State which intended to seize, and thought that it had seized, the task of civilisation into its own hands, for such was the position of the Russian Church from the suppression of the patriarchate by Peter the Great until the days of the Provisional Government in 1917, when the legal separation of Church and State made possible the liberation of the Church. The revolt against the State of the intellectual class created by the State is the story of the Russian Revolution, and with the State fell the administrative apparatus of the State Church—and more besides in the modern tragedy of Russia, for the whole mind of Russia was in revolt.

Was there then revolt within the Church? Not revolt, but perennial dissonance from the days of Peter to the days of Philaret of Moscow[10] and down to the attempt to regain the Church's conciliar autonomy in 1906, while Russian churchmen elaborated in opposition their doctrine of *Sobornost*, of a conciliar Catholicity, which has since become classical. But dissonance in Seraphim? No, the elder was not concerned with policies. Nevertheless, as the seer gazed in solitude into the depths of the forest beneath the trees that screened the outer, superficial world, it was granted to him to see some factor in the destinies of his land which was to leave its tracks in Russian history right down to the Council *(Sobor)* of the Church in 1917 and beyond. He expressed his vision in words of unsurpassed prophecy. "See, mother!" he said. "When we have a Council, then the Moscow bell, Great John[11] himself, will come to us. When they hang him and toll him for the first time and he rings out, then you and I will waken. Aha, mother mine! What joy there will be! In the middle of summer they will celebrate Easter! To the people, yes, the people from all sides, from all sides!" Father Seraphim became silent awhile, then added: "But that joy will be for a very short time. Something beyond that, mother! There will be such tribulation as has not been from the beginning of the world!" The elder's bright countenance was darkened and he burst into tears. And on another occasion: "Mother," he said, "the time will come for us when the angels will not be quick enough receiving souls!"

In a Church which statesmen and intellectuals have exiled and trampled down, St. Seraphim has come into his own, making manifest her reserves of grace and truth. He has been one of the stable influences in the Russian religious consciousness of the post-revolutionary period. "My joy!" he said. "Thou thinkest much of poor Seraphim. Is it for me to know when will come the end of this world and that great day in which the Lord will judge the quick and the dead and will reward each according to his works? Nay, this I cannot know!" In limited historical perspectives the hour of fulfilment may not be foreseen. But the elder of Sarov has lit the way, "an angel upon earth and in the flesh Seraphim."

A CONVERSATION

OF ST. SERAPHIM OF SAROV

WITH NICHOLAS MOTOVILOV[12] CONCERNING

THE AIM OF THE CHRISTIAN LIFE.

It was Thursday. The day was gloomy. Snow lay deep on the ground and snowflakes were falling thickly from the sky when Father Seraphim began his conversation with me in the plot near his hermitage over against the river Sarovka, on the hill which slopes down to the river-bank. He sat me on the stump of a tree which he had just felled, and himself squatted before me.

"The Lord has revealed to me," began the great elder, "that in your childhood you longed to know the aim of our Christian life and continually asked questions about it of many and great ecclesiastical dignitaries."

Let me here interpose that from the age of twelve this thought had ceaselessly vexed me, and I had, in fact, approached many clergy about it; but their answers had not satisfied me. This was not known to the elder.

"But no one," continued Father Seraphim, "has given you a precise answer. They have said: Go to church, pray to God, fulfil the commandments of God, do good; such is the aim of the Christian life. Some were even irritated against you as being occupied with irreverent curiosity and told you not to seek things higher than yourself. But they did not answer as they should have. And now poor Seraphim will explain to you in what really this aim consists. Prayer, fasting, watching, and all other Christian acts, however good they may be, do not alone constitute the aim of our Christian life, although they serve as the indispensable means of reaching this aim. The true aim of our Christian life, is to acquire the Holy Spirit of God. But mark, my son, only the good deed done for Christ's sake brings us the fruits of the Holy Spirit. All that is not done for His sake, though it be good, brings neither reward in the life to come nor in our life here the grace of God. Wherefore our Lord Jesus Christ has said: He that gathereth not with me scattereth abroad. Not that a good deed can be called anything but 'gathering,' since even though it be not done for Christ's sake, yet is it good. The Scripture says: In every nation he that feareth God and worketh righteousness is so pleasing to God that the Angel of the Lord appeared at the hour of prayer to Cornelius, the God-fearing and righteous centurion, and said: Go to Joppa to Simon the tanner; there shalt thou find Peter and he will tell thee the words of everlasting life, whereby thou shalt be saved and all thy house.

"Thus the Lord uses all His Divine means to give such a man for his good works the opportunity not to lose his reward in the future life. But to this end we must begin here by a right faith in our Lord Jesus Christ, the Son of God, who came into the world to save sinners, and by winning for ourselves the grace of the Holy Spirit, who brings into our hearts the Kingdom of God and lays for us the path to win the blessings of the future life. The acceptability to God of good deeds not done for Christ's sake is limited to this, that the Creator gives the means to make them effective; it rests with man to make them effective or not. Wherefore the Lord said to the Hebrews: If ye had not seen, ye would have had no sin; but now ye say, we see, and your sin remaineth with you. A man like Cornelius finds favour with God for his deeds, though done not for the sake of Christ; let him then but believe in the Son of God and all his works will be accounted as done for Christ's sake just for faith in Him. But in the opposite event a man has no right to complain that his good has had no effect. It never does, unless the good deed be done for Christ's sake, since good done for Him both claims in the life of the world to come a crown of righteousness and in this present life fills men with the grace of the Holy Spirit; as it is said: Not by measure doth God give the Holy Spirit; the Father loveth the Son and giveth all things into His hands.

"So it is, my little lordling of God! In acquiring this Spirit of God consists the true aim of our Christian life, while prayer, watching, fasting, almsgiving and other good works done for Christ's sake are only the means for acquiring the Spirit of God."

"How do you mean acquire?" I asked Father Seraphim. "I do not somehow understand."

"To acquire is the same as to gain," he answered. "You understand what acquiring money means. Acquiring God's Spirit, it's all the same. You know well enough what it means in the worldly sense, my son, to acquire. The aim in life of ordinary people is to acquire or make money, and for the nobility it is in addition to receive honours, distinctions and other rewards for their services to the government. The acquisition of God's Spirit is also capital, but grace-giving and eternal, and it is gained in very similar ways, almost the same ways as monetary, social and temporal capital.

"God the Word, the God-Man, our Lord Jesus Christ, likens our life to a market, and the work of our life on earth He calls buying, and says to us all: Buy till I come, redeeming the time, because the days are evil. That is to say, economise the time for receiving heavenly blessings through earthly goods. Earthly goods are virtuous acts performed for Christ's sake and conferring on us the grace of the Holy Spirit, without whom there is not and cannot be any salvation; for it is written: "By the Holy Spirit is every soul quickened and by purity exalted, yea, is made bright by the Three in One in holy mystery."[13] The Holy Spirit itself enters our souls, and this entrance into our souls of Him the Almighty and this presence with our spirit of the Triune Majesty is only granted to us through our own assiduous acquisition of the Holy Spirit, which prepares in our soul and body a throne for the all-creative presence of God with our spirit according to His irrevocable word: I will dwell in them, and walk in them; and I will be their God, and they shall be My people.

"Of course, every virtuous act done for Christ's sake gives us the grace of the Holy Spirit, but most of all is this given through prayer; for prayer is somehow always in our hands as an instrument for acquiring the grace of the Spirit. You wish, for instance, to go to church and there is no church near or the service is over; or you wish to give to the poor and there is none by or you have nothing to give; you want to preserve your purity and there is not the strength in you to succeed because of your own constitution or because of the insistent snares of the enemy, which on account of your human weakness you cannot withstand; you wish to perform some other virtuous act for Christ's sake and the strength or the opportunity is lacking. This in no way affects prayer; prayer is always possible for everyone, rich and poor, noble and simple, strong and weak, healthy and suffering, righteous and sinful. Great is the power of prayer; most of all does it bring the Spirit of God and easiest of all is it to exercise. Truly, in prayer it is vouchsafed to us to converse with our Good and Life-giving God and Saviour, but even here we must pray only until God the Holy Spirit descends on us in measures of His heavenly grace known to Him. When He comes to visit us, we must cease to pray. How can we pray to

Him, Come and abide in us, cleanse us from all evil, and save
our souls, O Gracious Lord,[14] when He has already come to us
to save us, who trust in Him and call on His holy name in truth,
that humbly and with love we may receive Him, the Comforter,
in the chamber of our souls, hungering and thirsting for His
coming?"

"Yes, father, but what about other virtuous acts done for
Christ's sake in order to acquire the grace of the Holy Spirit?
You speak of prayer alone."

"Acquire, my son, the grace of the Holy Spirit by all the other
virtues in Christ; trade in those that are most profitable to you.
Accumulate the capital of the grace-giving abundance of God's
mercy. Deposit it in God's eternal bank, which brings you un-
earthly interest, not four or six per cent, but one hundred per
cent, for one spiritual shilling and even more, infinitely more.
Thus, if prayer and watching give you more of God's grace,
pray and watch; if fasting gives much of God's Spirit, fast; if
almsgiving gives more, give alms. In such manner decide about
every virtue in Christ.

"Trade thus spiritually in virtue. Distribute the gifts of the
grace of the Holy Spirit to them that ask, as a candle, burning
with earthly fire, lights other candles for the illumining of all
in other places, but diminishes not its own light. If it be so with
earthly fire, what shall we say about the fire of the grace of
God's Holy Spirit?"

"But, father," said I, "you continue to dwell on the acquisition of the grace of the Holy Spirit as the aim of the Christian
life. How and where can I see it? Good deeds are visible. Is the
Holy Spirit then to be seen? How am I going to know whether
He is with me or not?"

"At the present time," the elder replied, "thanks to our almost
universal indifference to the holy faith in our Lord Jesus Christ
and thanks to our inattentiveness to the working of His Divine
purpose in us and of the communion between man and God,
we have come to this, that one might say we have almost entirely
departed from the true Christian life. Those words seem strange
to us now that the Spirit of God spake by the lips of Moses:

And Adam saw the Lord walking in paradise; or those words which we read in the Apostle Paul: We went to Achaia and the Spirit of God came not with us, we returned to Macedonia and the Spirit of God came with us. More than once in other passages of Holy Scripture is told the story of God's appearance to men. Some people say these passages are incomprehensible; could men really see God? But there is nothing incomprensible here. This failure to understand comes about because we have wandered from the spacious vision of early Christians. Under the pretext of education we have reached such a darkness of ignorance that now to us seems inconceivable what the ancients saw so clearly that even in ordinary conversation the notion of God's appearance did not seem strange to them. Men saw God and the grace of His Holy Spirit, not in sleep or in a dream, or in the excitement of a disordered imagination, but truly, in the light of day. We have become very inattentive to the work of our salvation, whence it comes about that many other words also in the Holy Scriptures we do not take in the proper sense; and all because we do not seek the grace of God, because in the pride of our minds we do not allow it to enter our souls, and therefore we have no true enlightenment from the Lord, which is sent into the hearts of men, to all who hunger and thirst in heart for God's truth.

"When our Lord Jesus Christ had accomplished the whole work of salvation, after His resurrection, He breathed on the Apostles to restore the breath of life which had been lost by Adam, and gave them that same grace of the Holy Spirit of God which had been Adam's. On the day of Pentecost He triumphantly sent down on them the Holy Spirit in the rushing of a mighty wind like tongues of fire, which sat upon each one of them and entered in and filled them with the strength of Divine flame-like grace; whose breath is laden with dew, and it creates joy in the souls partaking of its power and influence. And, when this same fire-inspired grace of the Holy Spirit is given to all the faithful in Christ in the sacrament of Holy Baptism, they seal it in the chief places appointed by the Holy Church on our flesh, as the eternal vessel of this grace. The words are: "The

seal of the gift of the Holy Spirit."[15] On what do we miserable
creatures set our seal except on the vessels which preserve some
precious treasure? But what can be higher and more precious
in the world than the gifts of the Holy Spirit sent us from above
in the sacrament of Baptism? For this baptismal grace is so
great, so necessary, so life-giving for man, that it will never be
taken away even from the heretic until his very death; that is,
until the term which has been set by the Providence of God to
man's earthly trial—for what will he be of use and what will he
accomplish in the time and with the grace given him by God?
If we were never to sin after our baptism, we should remain
for ever holy, spotless, exempt from all foulness of flesh and
spirit, like the saints of God. But the trouble is that, though
we increase in stature, we do not increase in the grace and mind
of God, as our Lord Jesus Christ increased; but on the contrary,
growing dissipated bit by bit, we are deprived of the grace of
God's Holy Spirit and become sinners of many degrees and
many sins. But, when a man, stirred by the Divine Wisdom
which seeks our salvation, is resolved for her sake to rise early
before God and keep watch for the attainment of his eternal
salvation, then must he in obedience to her voice hasten to
repent truly of all his sins and to perfect the virtues that are
their contrary, and thus by virtuous acts done for Christ's sake
to acquire the Holy Spirit, which works in us and sets up in
us the kingdom of God. Notwithstanding man's repeated falls,
notwithstanding the darkness around the soul, the grace of the
Holy Spirit which is given at our baptism in the name of the
Father and of the Son and of the Holy Spirit shines still in the
heart with the Divine immemorial light of the precious merits
of Christ. When the sinner turns to the way of repentance, this
Christ-Light smooths out all trace of past sin and clothes the
former sinner once more in a robe of incorruption woven from
the grace of the Holy Spirit; about the acquisition of which, as
the aim of the Christian life, I have been speaking so long.

"Still more will I tell you, that you may the more clearly
know what to understand by the grace of God, how to recognise
it and how in particular its actions are revealed in those enlight-

ened therewith. The grace of the Holy Spirit is the light which lighteneth man. The Lord has more than once revealed for many witnesses the working of the graces of the Holy Spirit in those whom He has sanctified and illumined by His great outpourings. Think of Moses after his talk with God on Mount Sinai. People were unable to look on him, with such unwonted radiance did he shine; he was even forced to appear before the people under a veil. Think of the Lord's Transfiguration on Mount Tabor: His garments were glistering like snow and His disciples fell on their face for fear. When Moses and Elias appeared to Him, then, in order to hide the effulgence of the light of God's grace from blinding the eyes of the disciples, a cloud, it is written, overshadowed them. Thus the grace of God's Holy Spirit appears in light inexpressible to all to whom God reveals its power."

"How then," I asked Father Seraphim, "am I to know that I am in the grace of the Holy Spirit?"

"It is very simple, my son," he replied; "wherefore the Lord says: All things are simple to them that get understanding. Being in that understanding, the Apostles always perceive whether the Spirit of God abideth in them or not; and, being filled with understanding and seeing the presence of God's Spirit with them, they affirmed that their work was holy and pleasing to God. By this is explained why they wrote in their epistles: It seemed good to the Holy Spirit and to us. Only on these grounds did they offer their epistles as immutable truth for the good of all the faithful. Thus the Holy Apostles were consciously aware of the presence in themselves of God's Spirit. And so you see, my son, how simple it is!"

I replied:

"Nevertheless I do not understand how I can be firmly assured that I am in the Spirit of God. How can I myself recognise His true manifestation?"

Father Seraphim replied:

"I have already told you, my son, that it is very simple and have in detail narrated to you how men dwell in the Spirit of God and how one must apprehend His appearance in us. What then do you need?"

"My need," said I, "is to understand this well!"

Then Father Seraphim took me very firmly by the shoulders and said:

"We are both together, son, in the Spirit of God! Why lookest thou not on me?"

I replied:

"I cannot look, father, because lightning flashes from your eyes. Your face is brighter than the sun and my eyes ache in pain!"

Father Seraphim said:

"Fear not, my son; you too have become as bright as I. You too are now in the fulness of God's Spirit; otherwise you would not be able to look on me as I am."

Then, bending his head towards me, he whispered softly in my ear:

"Give thanks to the Lord God for His ineffable mercy! You have seen that I did not even cross myself; and only in my heart I prayed mentally to the Lord God and said within myself; Lord, vouchsafe to him to see clearly with bodily eyes that descent of Thy Spirit which Thou vouchsafest to Thy servants, when Thou art pleased to appear in the light of Thy marvellous glory. And see, my son, the Lord has fulfilled in a trice the humble prayer of poor Seraphim. Surely we must give thanks to Him for this ineffable gift to us both! Not always, my son, even to the great hermits, does the Lord God show His mercy. See, the grace of God has come to comfort your contrite heart, as a loving mother, at the intercession of the Mother of God herself. Come, son, why do you not look me in the eyes? Just look and fear not! The Lord is with us!"

After these words I looked in his face and there came over me an even greater reverential awe. Imagine in the centre of the sun, in the dazzling brilliance of his midday rays, the face of the man who talks with you. You see the movement of his lips and the changing expression of his eyes, you hear his voice, you feel someone grasp your shoulders; yet you do not see the hands, you do not even see yourself or his figure, but only a blinding light spreading several yards around and throwing a sparkling radiance across the snow blanket on the glade and into the snowflakes which besprinkled the great elder and me. Can one imagine the state in which I then found myself?

"How do you feel now?" Father Seraphim asked.

"Unwontedly well!" I said.

"But well in what way? How in particular?"

I answered:

"I feel a calmness and peace in my soul that I cannot express in words!"

"This, my son," said Father Seraphim, "is that peace of which the Lord said to His disciples: My peace I give unto you; not as the world giveth, give I unto you. If ye were of the world, the world would love its own; but because I chose you out of the world, therefore the world hateth you. But be of good cheer; I have overcome the world. So to them that are hated of the world but chosen of the Lord, the Lord gives that peace which you now feel, the peace which, in the words of the Apostle, passeth all understanding.—What else do you feel?" asked Father Seraphim.

"An unwonted sweetness!" I replied.

He continued:

"This is that sweetness of which it is said in Holy Scripture: They shall be satisfied with the plenteousness of Thy house, and Thou shalt give them drink of Thy sweetness as out of the river. See, this sweetness now overflows and pours through our veins with unspeakable delight. From this sweetness our hearts melt and we are filled with such blessedness as tongue cannot tell. What else do you feel?"

"An unwonted joy in all my heart!"

Father Seraphim continued:

"When the Spirit of God descends to man and overshadows him with the fulness of His outpouring, then the human soul overflows with unspeakable joy, because the Spirit of God turns to joy all that He may touch. This is that joy of which the Lord speaks in His Gospel: A woman when she is in travail hath sorrow, because her hour is come; but when she is delivered of the child, she remembereth no more the anguish, for the joy that a man is born into the world. In the world ye shall be sorrowful; but when I see you, your heart shall rejoice, and your joy no one taketh away from you. Yet however comforting may be this joy which you now feel in your heart, it is nothing in comparison with that of which the Lord Himself said by the mouth of His Apostle that this joy neither eye hath seen, nor ear heard, neither have entered into the heart of man the good things which God hath prepared for them that love Him. The earnest of that joy is given to us now, and, if from this there is sweetness, well-being and merriment in our souls, what shall we say of that joy which has been prepared in heaven for them that weep here on earth? You too, my son, have had tears enough in your life; see now with what joy the Lord consoles you while yet here! What else do you feel, my son?"

I answered:

"An unwonted warmth!"

"But why warmth, my son? See, we sit in the forest, the winter is out and about, the snow is underfoot, there is more than an inch of snow on us and still the snowflakes fall. What warmth can there be?"

I answered:

"Such as there is in the bath-house, when they pour the water on the stone and the steam rises in a cloud."

"And the smell?" he asked me. "Is it the bath-house smell?"

"No!" I replied. "There is nothing on earth like this fragrance. When in my dear mother's lifetime I was fond of dancing and used to go to balls and parties, my mother would sprinkle me with scent which she had bought at the best fashion-shops in Kazan. But those scents did not give out such fragrance!"

Father Seraphim, smiling kindly, said:

"My son, I know it just as you do, and I purposely ask you whether you feel it so. It is the very truth, my son! No pleasure of earthly fragrance can be compared with that which we now feel, for the fragrance of God's Holy Spirit surrounds us. What earthly thing can be like it? Mark, my son! You have told me that around us it is warm as in the bath-house; but look, neither on you nor on me does the snow melt, and above us it is the same. Of course this warmth is not in the air but in us. It is that very warmth about which the Holy Spirit in the words of the prayer makes us cry out to the Lord: Warm me with the warmth of Thy Holy Spirit! Warmed therewith the hermits have not feared the winter frost, being clad, as in warm coats, in the cloak of grace woven of the Holy Spirit. So in very deed it must be, for the grace of God must dwell within us, in our heart, because the Lord said: The kingdom of God is within you. By the kingdom of God the Lord meant the grace of the Holy Spirit. See, this kingdom of God is now found within us. The grace of the Holy Spirit shines forth and warms us, and, overflowing with many and varied odours into the air around us, regales our senses with heavenly delight, as it fills our hearts with joy inexpressible. Our present state is that of which the Apostle says: The Kingdom of God is not meat and drink, but righteousness and peace in the Holy Spirit. Our faith consists not in persuasive words of human wisdom, but in the demonstration of the Spirit and of power. In this condition we now find ourselves together. Of this condition the Lord said: There are some of them that stand here, which shall in no wise taste of death, till they see the Kingdom of God coming in power. Of such unspeakable joy, my son, the Lord God has now thought us worthy! This is what it means to be in the fulness of the Holy Spirit, about which St. Macarius of Egypt writes: I too was in the fulness of the Holy Spirit. With this fulness of the Holy Spirit the Lord now has filled us to overflowing, poor as we are. Come now, there is no more need to ask, my son, how men may be in the grace of the Holy Spirit! Will you remember this manifestation of God's ineffable mercy which has visited us?"

"I know not, father," I said, "whether the Lord will grant me always to remember this mercy of God as vividly and clearly as now I feel it."

"I think," Father Seraphim answered me, "that the Lord will help you always to retain it in your memory, since otherwise His goodness would not have bowed so instantly to my humble

prayer and would not so readily have anticipated hearkening to
poor Seraphim; the more so that not for you alone is it given
to understand this, but through you to the whole world in
order that you yourself might be confirmed in God's work and
might be useful to others. The fact, my son, that I am a monk
and you are a layman need not keep us. God requires a right
faith in Himself and His Only-begotten Son. For this the grace
of the Holy Spirit is given abundantly from above. The Lord
seeks a heart filled with love of God and neighbour: this is the
throne whereon He loves to sit and whereon He appears in the
fulness of His heavenly glory. My son, give me thine heart, He
says; and all the rest I Myself will add unto you. For the Kingdom of God is in the human heart. The Lord is nigh unto them
that call upon Him in truth, and there is in Him no respect of
persons; for the Father loveth the Son and will give all things
into His hands, if only we too love our Heavenly Father truly
as sons. The Lord hears equally the monk and the simple Christian layman, so be they are both right believers, and both love
God from the depth of their soul, and both have faith in Him,
if only as a grain of mustard-seed; and they both shall move
mountains. One shall move thousands and two shall move multitudes. The Lord Himself says: All things are possible to him
that believeth. Father Paul the Apostle exclaims with his whole
voice: I can do all things in Christ who strengtheneth me. But
surely more wonderfully even than this does our Lord Jesus
Christ speak of them that believe in Him: He that believeth
on Me, the works that I do shall he do also; and greater works
than these shall he do; because I go unto My Father and will
pray to Him for you, that your joy may be fulfilled. Hitherto
have ye asked nothing in My Name; ask and ye shall receive.
Thus, my son, whatever you may ask of the Lord God, you will
receive all, provided only that it were for the glory of God or
the good of your neighbour; for He relates the good of a neighbour to His glory, wherefore He says: All that ye have done
unto one of the least of these, ye have done unto Me. Then have
no doubt that the Lord God will fulfil your petitions, if only
they are to God's glory and the good and edification of your

neighbours. But, even if something were necessary for your own need or good or profit, that too just as quickly and graciously will the Lord God send you, so be that extreme need and necessity insist. For the Lord loves them that love Him; the Lord is good to all men and will do the will of them that fear Him and will hear their prayer."

THE PILGRIM The Candid Narrations of a Pilgrim to His Spiritual Father *was first printed in Kazan' in 1884. It soon became a rare book, considered to be almost esoteric and held in high esteem by all searchers into the ways of Orthodox mysticism. Only recently, through reprinting in Western Europe and translation into English, has this precious little book become accessible to the wide circle interested in Russian religious life.*

Nothing is known of the author. Written in the first person singular, the book presents itself as the spiritual autobiography of a Russian peasant who lived at about the middle of the nineteenth century, related in intimate conversations. The social conditions depicted in the story represent Russia during the last decades of serfdom, under the severe autocratic government of Nicholas I. The mention made of the Crimean War (1853-54) permits an exact chronological placement.

There are, however, many factors which do not allow us to accept literally the anonymous author's description of himself. Although the style of the book has somewhat the flavor of the popular Russian idiom, it is essentially in the elaborate literary manner characteristic of the Russian spiritual writing of the middle of the nineteenth century. There are even many traces of the epoch of Alexandrian mysticism (Alexander I, 1801-1825) which deeply influenced the religious mentality and style of the Russian Church. Quite apart from the style, we come across many profound theological and philosophical digressions and comments which would be inconceivable in the mouth of a Russian peasant, even one well read in the Philocalia. The traces of a romanticism of Western origin are undeniable.

On the other hand, the many incidents related in detail, and even the confused order of the narrative, prevent us from dismissing the autobiographical form of the narration wholly as a literary convention. Probably a real experience of the pilgrim is the basis of the composition. Some educated person may have worked over the original oral confessions, either his actual "spiritual father," a priest or monk in Irkutsk (Siberia), or some monk on Mount Athos, whence the manuscript is supposed to have been brought to Kazan' by the abbot Païsius.

These critical remarks are intended to warn the reader not to accept the mystical life of the Pilgrim as reflecting Russian popular religion. On the contrary, it is the product of a fine spiritual culture, a rare flower in the Russian garden. Its main value consists in a convincingly detailed description of mental prayer as it was or could be practised, not in a monastic cell, but by a layman, even under the peculiar conditions of a wandering life.

From another point of view, the book is a work of propaganda, designed to popularize in lay circles the mystical prayer of the Hesychasts as embodied in an ascetic-mystical anthology entitled the Philocalia. The first Greek edition of this anthology, the work of an anonymous compiler (probably Nicodemus of Mount Athos), was printed in Venice in 1782. The Slavonic translation by Païsius Velichkovsky was printed in 1793. Most of the Greek fathers of this collection were already known in Russia to Saint Nilus Sorsky in the fifteenth century. But from the sixteenth century onward, the mystical movement in Russia was suppressed until the time of the revival effected by Païsius. This Russian monk was an emigré living in the Balkan monasteries of Mount Athos and Rumania, where he imbibed the mystical tradition at its sources. The whole monastic revival which took form at the end of the eighteenth and the beginning of the nineteenth century in Russia is attributable to Païsius and his disciples. The Optina cloister in Russia (in the province of Kaluga), with its unbroken line of startzy, held itself to be the heir and depository in a special sense of Païsius' tradition. That this tradition was not held within the confines of monasteries is demonstrated by the Pilgrim's book. It is his aim to convince us that mental prayer is possible in every condition of life. True, he admits that complete solitude is for him the most favorable condition for the practice of continual prayer: he often feels uneasy in human society when suddenly the prayer of Jesus begins to "act of itself" in his heart. Yet the conditions under whch a wanderer lives are as suitable for mystical prayer as is the cell of a monk.

The wandering life (this is a more correct English equivalent of the Russian phrase than "pilgrimage") is characteristic of Russian spirituality. Very often, as in the case of the present author, the wandering has no visit to a place of devotion as its object but is a way of life in which the early Christian ideal of spiritual freedom and detachment from the world is grafted onto the Russian feeling for the religious significance of nature as Mother Earth, and the truly Russian rejection of civilization out of religious motives. Yet, reading the tales of the Pilgrim, we realize that the mystical life of the author is moving against a background of the external manifestations of Christian charity. Some of his tales have little or nothing to do with the prayer of Jesus, but portray ideal types of the evangelical life, found in all strata of society—among the gentry, the army, the clergy, the simple peasantry. These portraits of secular, uncanonized, and even unknown, lay saints are, as it were, a counterpoint to the scenes of cruelty, violence, and despotism which we are not spared. What is lacking is rather the average level of Russian life. The author has not the intention of depicting life around him as it is, but that of selecting instructive examples of Christian virtue.

A reader who would like to get a more adequate idea of Russian life under Nicholas I can be guided by many of the classical works of Russian literature: Gogol's Dead Souls, Turgenev's Memoirs of a Sportsman, the short stories of Leskov. The anonymous Pilgrim gives us rather exceptional specimens of Russian piety, authentic in themselves but inadequate as a basis for generalization.

THE WAY OF A PILGRIM

I

B Y THE GRACE OF GOD I AM A CHRISTIAN, BY MY DEEDS A GREAT
SINNER, AND BY CALLING A HOMELESS ROVER OF THE LOWEST
status in life. My possessions comprise but some rusk in a knapsack on my back, and the Holy Bible on my bosom. That is all.

On the twenty-fourth Sunday after Pentecost, I went to
church to hear Mass. The first Epistle of St. Paul to the Thes-
salonians was read. In it we are exhorted, among other things,
to *pray incessantly*, and these words engraved themselves upon
my mind. I began to ponder whether it is possible to pray without ceasing, since every man must occupy himself with other
things needed for his support. I found this text in my Bible and
read with my own eyes what I had heard, namely that we must
pray incessantly in all places, pray always in spirit, lifting up
our hands in devotion. I pondered and pondered and did not
know what to think of it.

"What am I to do?" I mused. "Where will I be able to find
someone who can explain it to me? I shall go to the churches
known for their famous preachers; perhaps there I shall hear
something that will enlighten me." And I went. I heard a great
many very good sermons on prayer in general, how one ought
to pray, what prayer is and what fruits it bears, but no one
said how to succeed in it. There were sermons on spiritual
prayer, on incessant prayer, but no one pointed out how it was
to be accomplished.

Thus my attendance at the sermons failed to give me what
I sought. Therefore, after having heard many of them, I gave
them up without acquiring the desired knowledge of incessant
prayer. I decided to look, with the help of God, for an experienced and learned man who would talk to me and explain the
meaning of incessant prayer since the understanding of it
seemed most important to me.

For a long time I went from one place to another, reading my Bible constantly, and inquiring everywhere whether there was not a spiritual teacher or a pious and experienced guide. Finally, I was informed that in a certain village there lived a gentleman who had, for many years, sought the salvation of his soul. He had a chapel in his house, never left the premises and spent his days praying and reading religious books. Upon hearing this I well-nigh ran to that particular village. I got there and went to the owner of the estate.

"What is it that you want?" he asked.

"I was told that you are a pious and intelligent man," I said. "For the love of God enlighten me in the meaning of the Apostle's utterance 'pray incessantly.' Is it possible for anyone to pray without ceasing? I wish I could know, but I do not seem to understand it at all."

The gentleman remained silent for a while, looking at me fixedly. Finally he said: "Incessant inner prayer is a continuous longing of the human spirit for God. But in order to succeed in this sweet practice we must pray more and ask God to teach us incessant prayer. Pray more and with fervor. It is prayer itself that will teach you how it can be done without ceasing; however, it will require some time."

Having said this he ordered that food be brought to me, gave me money for my journey and dismissed me. And in the end he had explained nothing at all.

Once more I set out. I pondered and pondered, read and read, and my thoughts dwelt constantly upon what this man had told me, though I could not understand what he meant. Yet, so ardently did I wish to fathom this question, that I could not sleep at night.

I traveled two hundred versts on foot and reached a large city which was the capital of the province. There I saw a monastery, and at the inn where I stayed I learned that the abbot was a kindly man, at once pious and hospitable. When I went to see him he received me in a friendly fashion, asked me to sit down and offered refreshments.

"Holy Father," I said, "I do not want any food, but I beg you, enlighten me in spiritual matters. Tell me how I can save my soul."

"How can you save your soul? Well, live according to the commandments, pray and you will be saved."

"But it is said that we should pray incessantly. I do not know how this can be done for I cannot even get the meaning of it. Father, I beseech you, explain to me what incessant prayer means."

"I do not know, dear brother, how to explain it to you! But wait a moment . . . I have a little book which will enlighten you." He handed me St. Demetrius'[1] book, called *The Spiritual Education of the Inner Man* and said: "Here, read this page."

I read the following statement: "The words of the Apostle 'pray incessantly' should be interpreted as referring to the prayer of the mind, for the mind can always be soaring to God and pray without ceasing."

"But," I said, "won't you indicate to me the means by which the mind can always be directed to God without being disturbed in its incessant prayer?"

"This, indeed, is very difficult, unless God Himself bestows upon one such a gift," answered the abbot, and he offered no further explanations.

I spent the night in his monastery. The following morning I thanked him for his kind hospitality and went on my way, though I did not know myself where I was going. I was saddened by my incapacity to understand and read the Holy Bible for consolation.

In this wise I followed the main road for about five days when, one evening, I was overtaken by an elderly man who looked as though he belonged to the clergy. In reply to my question he answered that he was a monk from a monastery situated some ten versts off the main road and extended to me his invitation.

"In our guesthouse," he said, "we offer rest, shelter and food to pilgrims and other pious people." I did not care to go with him and replied that my peace of mind did not depend upon my lodging, but upon finding spiritual guidance. Neither was

I concerned about my food, for I had a provision of rusk in my knapsack.

"What kind of spiritual guidance are you seeking? What is it that troubles you?" he asked. "Do come for a short stay, dear brother. We have experienced elders who will guide you and lead you to the true path in the light of the word of God and the teaching of the Holy Fathers."

I told him what was troubling me. The old man crossed himself and said: "Give thanks to God, my beloved brother, for he has awakened you to the irresistible longing for incessant, inner prayer. Acknowledge in it the voice of our Lord and be calm in the assurance that all that has happened to you hitherto was the testing of the compliance of your own will with the call of God. You have been given the privilege of understanding that the heavenly light of incessant inner prayer is not found in wordly wisdom or in mere striving for outward knowledge. On the contrary, it is attained in poverty of spirit, in active experience and in simplicity of heart. For this reason it is not astonishing that you have not been able to learn anything about the essential work of prayer or to attain the skill by which incessant activity in it is acquired. What is prayer and how does one learn to pray? Though these questions are vital and essential, one gets only rarely a true enlightenment on that subject from contemporary preachers. It is because these questions are more complex than all the arguments they have at their disposal. These questions require not merely academic achievements, but mystical insight. And one of the most lamentable things is the vanity of elementary knowledge which drives people to measure the Divine by a human yardstick. Only too often wrong reasoning is applied to prayer, for many believe that preparatory steps and great virtues lead us to prayer. In fact it is prayer that gives birth to all the virtues and sublime deeds. The fruits and consequences of prayer are wrongly taken for the means of attaining it. This attitude belittles the value of prayer, and it is contrary to the statements of the Holy Scripture. The Apostle Paul says: 'I desire therefore, first of all, that supplications be made.' Here the main thing that the Apostle stressed in his words about prayer is that prayer must come before anything else: 'I desire therefore, first of all'.... There are many virtues that are required of a good Christian, but above all else he must pray; for nothing can ever be achieved without prayer. Otherwise he cannot find his way to God, he cannot grasp the truth, he cannot crucify the flesh with all its passions and desires, find the Light of Christ in his heart and be united to our Lord. Frequent prayer must precede all these things before they can be brought about. I say 'frequent' because the perfection and the correctness of prayer is beyond our power. 'For we know not what we should pray for as we ought,' says the Apostle Paul. Therefore we ought to pray often, to pray at all times, for this alone lies within our power and leads us to purity of prayer, which is the mother of all spiritual good. As St. Isaac the Syrian says: 'Win the mother and she will bear you children,' so must you first of all attain the power of prayer, and then all other virtues will be easily practised afterwards. All this is scarcely mentioned by those who have had no personal experience, but only a superficial knowledge of the most mysterious teaching of the Holy Fathers."

While he talked to me, we reached the monastery without noticing it. In order that I might not lose contact with this wise elder, and to get further information more quickly, I hastened to say: "Reverend Father, do me a favor: Explain to me what incessant prayer is, and how I am to learn it. As I see, you are deeply versed in all these matters."

It was with kindness that he granted my request and taking me to his cell, he said: "Come in, I shall give you a book written by the Holy Fathers. With God's help you may get from it a clear and definite idea of what prayer is."

As we entered his cell he began to speak again: "The constant inner prayer of Jesus is an unbroken, perpetual calling upon the Divine Name of Jesus with the lips, the mind and the heart, while picturing His lasting presence in one's imagination and imploring His grace wherever one is, in whatever one does, even while one sleeps. This prayer consists of the following words: — 'Lord Jesus Christ, have mercy on me!' Those who use this prayer constantly are so greatly comforted that they are moved to say it at all times, for they can no longer live without it. And the prayer will keep on ringing in their hearts of its own accord. Now, do you understand what incessant prayer is?"

"Yes, I do, Father. In the Name of God explain to me how to achieve the mastery of it," I said, feeling overwhelmed with joy.

"You will learn how to master it by reading this book, which is called the *Philocalia*; it comprises the complete and minute knowledge of incessant inner prayer, as stated by twenty-five Holy Fathers. It is full of great wisdom and is so useful that it is regarded as the first and best guide by all those who seek the contemplative, spiritual life. The reverend Nicephorus said once: 'It leads one to salvation without labor and sweat.'"

"Is it then loftier and holier than the Bible?" I asked.

"No, it is not, but it sheds light upon the secrets locked up in the Bible which cannot be easily understood by our shallow intelligence. Let me give you an analogy: the largest, the brightest and at the same time the most wonderful of all luminaries is the sun; yet you must protect your eyes in order to examine it, or simply to look at it. For this purpose you use artificial glass, millions and millions of times smaller and darker than the sun. But through this tiny piece of glass you can contemplate the sublime king of all stars with its flamboyant rays. Thus the Holy Scripture is like the resplendent sun, while this book—the *Philocalia*—may be compared to the piece of glass which permits us to contemplate its lofty magnificence. Now, listen; I shall read you the instructions on incessant prayer as they are given here."

He opened the book, and after having found the instruction by St. Simeon the New Theologian, he began to read: "Take a seat in solitude and silence. Bend your head, close your eyes, and breathing softly, in your imagination, look into your own heart. Let your mind, or rather, your thoughts, flow from your head down to your heart and say, while breathing: 'Lord Jesus Christ, have mercy on me.' Whisper these words gently, or say them in your mind. Discard all other thoughts. Be serene, persevering and repeat them over and over again."

The elder did not limit himself to mere explanations, but made them clear by examples. We read passages of St. Gregory of Sinai, St. Callistus and St. Ignatius[2] and he interpreted them to me in his own words. I listened to him attentively, overwhelmed with gladness, and did my best to store every detail in my memory. Thus we stayed up the whole night together and went to Matins without having slept at all.

When the elder dismissed me with his blessings, he told me that while I was learning the ways of prayer I must return and relate to him my experiences in a full and sincere confession; for this work cannot be crowned with success except with the attentive guidance of a teacher.

In the church I felt a burning zeal to practise incessant prayer diligently and asked God to help me. Then I began to ask myself how I could visit the elder for guidance and confession, since it was not permitted to remain in the monastery guesthouse for more than three days, and there were no other houses nearby.

However, I soon discovered a village situated about four versts from the monastery. When I went there in search of living quarters, God led me to the right place. A peasant engaged me for the whole summer to take care of his kitchen garden; he placed at my disposal a hut where I could live by myself. Praise be to God! I came upon a quiet place! I took up my dwelling and began to learn inner prayer in the manner I had been told and went to see my elder from time to time.

Alone in my garden, I practised incessant prayer for a week as the elder had directed me. In the beginning things went very well. But soon I began to feel tired, lazy and bored. Overcome by drowsiness, I was often distracted by all kinds of thoughts that came upon me like a cloud. I went to see my elder in great anxiety and told him of my plight.

He received me cordially and said: "The kingdom of darkness assails you, my dear brother. To it nothing is worse than a prayer of the heart. And the kingdom of darkness uses every means at its disposal to hold you back and to prevent you from learning prayer. Nevertheless the fiend can do no more than God will permit, no more than is needed for our own good. It seems that your humility needs more testing; it is too soon for you to approach with intemperate zeal the sublime entrance of the heart, lest you fall into spiritual covetousness. Let me read you an instruction from the *Philocalia* about this case."

The elder found the teaching of ·Nicephorus the monk, and began to read: "If after some efforts you do not succeed in reaching the region of the heart in the manner you have been told, do what I am about to tell you, and with the help of God you will find what you are seeking. The faculty of speech is located in the larynx, as you know. Drive back all other thoughts—you can do it if you wish—and use that faculty in saying constantly the following words: 'Lord Jesus Christ, have mercy on me.' Make yourself do so at all times. If you persist in it for a while, your heart by this means will be open to prayer without doubt. This is known from experience."

"Here you have the teaching of Holy Fathers dealing with these cases," said the elder. "Therefore you must accept it with confidence and repeat the oral Jesus Prayer as often as possible. Take this rosary. Use it in saying three thousand prayers every day in the beginning. Whether you sit or stand, walk or lie down, constantly repeat: 'Lord Jesus Christ, have mercy on me.' Do it quietly, without hurrying, but say it exactly three thousand times a day, neither increasing nor diminishing the number of prayers of your own accord. By this means God will help you to attain also the incessant action of the heart."

With joy I accepted this instruction and returned to my lodging, where I began to carry out faithfully and exactly what the elder ordered me to do. It was somewhat hard for two days. Later it became so easy and pleasant that I felt something like a longing for the prayer; I said it willingly and cheerfully, and not under compulsion as before.

I told my elder of this and he decreed that I recite six thousand prayers a day: "Be calm," he admonished me, "and try to say as faithfully as possible the fixed number of prayers. The Lord in His mercy will give you His grace."

In my solitary hut I said for a whole week the Jesus Prayer six thousand times a day, forgetting all cares and discarding all other thoughts, however much they assailed me. I had in mind but the one aim of fulfilling the bidding of the elder faithfully. And, behold! I got so used to my prayer that when I stopped for a short time I felt as if I was missing something, as if I had undergone a loss. And the minute I started it all over again I had the joyous sensation of freedom. When I met people, I did not care to enter into conversation at all, for all I desired was to be left alone and to say my prayer, so accustomed had I grown to it during that week.

The elder, who had not seen me for about ten days, called on me himself. I told him how I was getting along. He listened attentively and then said: "Now that you have become accustomed to prayer, persist in this habit and strengthen it. Waste no time, and with the help of God say precisely twelve thousand prayers a day from now on. Keep to yourself, get up early, go to bed later than usual, and come to me for advice twice a month."

I did as the elder ordered me to do. On the first day I had barely finished my twelve thousand prayers by the late evening. But the following day they flowed with greater ease and joy. At first the incessant saying of the prayer wearied me to a certain extent; my tongue was somewhat numbed and my jaws stiff. My palate, too, hurt a little, but this was not unpleasant at all. I felt a slight pain in the thumb of my left hand, which I used for counting my beads. A minor inflammation developed in my left arm from the wrist up to the elbow. The sensation it caused was most pleasant; it stimulated and urged me to the frequent saying of the prayer. Thus for about five days I said faithfully my twelve thousand prayers, and as the habit became fixed I did it willingly and with joy.

Early one morning I was, so to speak, aroused by the prayer. When I began to recite my morning prayers, my tongue refused to utter the familiar words with ease. My only desire was to go on with the Jesus Prayer, and no sooner had I started it than I felt joyfully relieved. My lips and my tongue recited the words without any effort on my part. I spent the whole day experiencing great happiness and a complete detachment from earthly things, as though I were living on another planet. Easily did I finish my twelve thousand prayers by the early evening. I wished I might keep on, but I dared not to increase the number fixed by my elder. The following day I continued in the same way, calling on the name of Jesus Christ, and did it with readiness and facility. Then I went to see the elder and, opening my heart, I told him everything in detail.

He listened to me attentively and then began to speak: "Thank God for having discovered in yourself the desire and facility for prayer. This is a natural result that crowns continuous efforts and action. It is like this: a machine operates for a while if its principal wheel is given a push; however, if it is to operate still longer, that wheel must be oiled and given another push. And so is the sensual nature of man, which God in His loving mercy has endowed with great capacities. You have yourself experienced what a feeling can be born in a sinful soul not yet in the state of grace, not yet purified from all sensuality. But how comforting, wonderful and sublime it is when God in His benevolence cleanses the soul of man from passion and bestows upon him the gift of self-acting, spiritual prayer! This state is impossible to describe, for the revelation of the mystery of prayer foretells here on earth the bliss of heaven. That kind of happiness is granted to loving hearts which seek after God in simplicity. Now I authorize you to recite the Prayer as often as you wish, the more the better. Give it all your waking hours, and from now on call on the name of Jesus without counting. Submit yourself to the will of God in humility, looking to Him for assistance. I firmly believe that He will not abandon you but direct your steps."

Following these instructions I spent the whole summer in incessant oral prayer to Jesus, enjoying peace of mind and soul. I often dreamt in my sleep that I was reciting the Prayer. If during the day I happened to meet people, I felt that I liked them as though they were my closest relatives, but I wasted none of my time on them. My thoughts calmed down by themselves. I was concerned with nothing but my Prayer, to which my mind was beginning to listen; and from time to time the sensation of delightful warmth was sweeping over my heart. Whenever I went to church the long monastic services seemed short to me and failed to tire me out as had happened before. And my lonely hut had for me all the splendor of a palace. I did not know how to thank God for having guided me, a miserable sinner, to that saving elder who became my master.

However, I was not long to profit by the instructions of my beloved teacher, who was blessed with divine wisdom. At the end of the summer he passed away. I bade him my last farewell in tears and in profound gratitude for the fatherly guidance he had given to a poor wretch like myself. For a blessing I begged permission to keep the rosary which he had been using in his prayers.

Thus I remained alone. Summer passed and the work in the kitchen garden came to an end. My peasant dismissed me, giving me two rubles for my work as a watchman and filling up my knapsack with rusk for my journey. Once more I set off on my wanderings to various places. But now I was no longer alone and in want as before. Calling upon the Name of Jesus brought cheer to me on my way. People I met were kind to me as if they liked me.

Thus I began to wonder what to do with the money I had earned for my work in the kitchen garden. What was it good for? "Look here," I said to myself. My elder was gone. I had no one to guide me. Why not buy the *Philocalia* with the purpose of learning from it more about inner prayer.

I made the sign of the cross and went on my way reciting my Prayer. When I came to a large province town I began to look for the *Philocalia* in all the stores. Finally I found the book, but they asked me three rubles for it, whereas I had only two in my possession. I haggled and haggled over the price, but the shopkeeper would not give in. In the end he suggested: "Go to that church nearby and speak to the warden. He has a very old copy of this book and may be willing to sell it to you for two rubles." I made my way there and lo! for my two rubles I bought the *Philocalia*. It was an old copy, much damaged by use. Overjoyed with my purchase, I repaired it as well as I could, made a cloth cover for it, and put it into my knapsack with the Bible.

And now, I am wandering about repeating incessantly the Prayer of Jesus. To me it has greater value than anything else on earth. Occasionally I walk seventy versts or so and do not feel it at all. I am conscious of only one thing, my Prayer. When bitter cold pierces me, I say it more eagerly and warm up in no time. When I am hungry I begin to call on the Name of Jesus more often and forget about food. When I am ill and rheumatic pains set in in my back and legs, I concentrate on the Prayer and no longer notice the discomfort. When people do me wrong, my wrath and indignation are quickly forgotten as soon as I remember the sweetness of the prayer of Jesus. In a way I have become a half-witted person; I have no anxiety and no interest in the vanities of the world, for which I care no longer. I am longing by habit for only one thing, to be left alone and to pray incessantly. When I am doing this I am filled with joy. God knows what is going on within me. It is sensuous, no doubt! As my departed elder explained to me, this is natural and artificial at the same time, as a consequence of my daily practice. But I realize my lack of merit and of intelligence and dare not proceed further in learning and mastering the spiritual prayer within my heart. God will enlighten me at the same time. Meanwhile, I hope that my late elder prays for me. Though I have not yet reached the state in which ceaseless spiritual prayer is self-acting in the heart, I do understand, thank God, the meaning of the Apostle's words in the Epistle: "Pray incessantly."

I I

I roamed about through many different places for a long time with the Prayer of Jesus as my sole companion. It gladdened and comforted me in all my wanderings, my meetings with other people and in all the incidents of the journey. Soon, however, it occurred to me that it would be better to take a fixed abode so as to be alone more often and study the *Philocalia* more easily. Though I read this book whenever I could in all the refuges I was able to find for the night's or day's rest, I felt that I ought to dedicate more time to it. With faith and concentration I wished to gather from its instruction more information about the truth that would save my soul by means of inner prayer.

But despite my sincere desire I could not find any work whatever, for my left arm was crippled from early childhood. Because of this I·was not able to make a permanent home for myself. Thus I made up my mind to go to Siberia and to visit the tomb of St. Innocent in Irkutsk.³ I thought that I would travel in the great silence of Siberian forests and steppes in a manner that was more suitable for praying and reading. I set off and on my way recited the Prayer without ceasing.

At the end of a short period I began to feel that the Prayer had, so to speak, passed to my heart. In other words I felt that my heart in its natural beating began, as it were, to utter the words of the Prayer. For instance, one "Lord"; two "Jesus"; three "Christ," and so forth. No longer did I say the Prayer with my lips, but listened attentively to the words formed in my heart, remembering what my departed elder told me about this state of bliss. Then I began to feel a slight pain in my heart, and my whole being was glowing with so great a love for Jesus Christ that it seemed to me if only I could meet Him, I would fall to His feet, embracing them and kissing them in tenderness, tears and gratitude for His love and mercy which gives such comfort in calling on His Name to me, His unworthy creature. A pleasant warmth was filling my heart and spreading through my whole bosom. This urged me to a more eager reading of the *Philocalia*, so as to test my emotions and to study further the effects of inner prayer. Without this test I might have fallen a victim of delusion, or might have taken natural results for the manifestation of grace, and prided myself at the quick mastering of the Prayer. My late elder had warned me of this danger. I decided therefore to walk more at night and to devote my days mainly to reading the *Philocalia*, sitting under the forest trees. Ah! A wisdom so great that I had never thought it possible was revealed to me in this reading. As I went on, I felt a happiness which, until then, had been beyond my imagination. Although many passages were still incomprehensible to my dull mind, the prayer of the heart brought the understanding I wanted. Besides, on rare occasions, I dreamt of my late elder, who explained many things to me, and, above all, led my dormant soul to the path of humility.

Thus, blissfully happy, I spent more than two months of the summer. As a general rule I made my way through the forest, choosing byways. Whenever I entered a village I asked only for rusk and a little salt. With my bark jar filled with water I made another hundred versts.

Summer was drawing to a close as I was assailed with trials and temptations. Were they the consequence of sins weighing on my wretched soul? Or was something lacking in my spiritual life which required other experiences? I do not know. This is what happened: One day, at twilight, when I reached the main road, two men looking like soldiers caught up with me and demanded money. When I told them that I had not a penny on me, they refused to believe me and shouted rudely: "You are lying. Pilgrims always collect plenty of money."

"What is the use of talking to him," said one of them, and he hit me on the head with his club with such force that I fell senseless to the ground. How long I remained unconscious I do not know, but when I came to myself I was lying by the forest road, robbed. My knapsack was gone from my back; only the cords which had fastened it and which they had cut, remained. Thank God! they had not taken my passport, for I kept it in my old cap, ready to show it at a moment's notice. I rose, shedding bitter tears, not so much on account of the pain in my head, as for the loss of the Bible and the *Philocalia*, which were in the stolen bag.

I did not cease to mourn and to wail day and night. Where was my Bible, which I had carried with me all this time and read since my early youth? Where was my *Philocalia*, which gave me so much enlightenment and consolation? Alas, I had lost my first and last treasures in life without having enjoyed them fully.

It would have been better for me to have been killed on the spot, than to exist without spiritual food. There was no way of replacing these books now.

Heavily I dragged myself for two days, overcome by my calamity. Exhausted at the end of the third day, I fell to the ground and went to sleep in the shelter of a bush. And then I had a dream. I saw myself in the monastery cell of my elder, lamenting over my loss. In his endeavor to console me the old man was saying: "You must learn therefrom detachment from worldly things for your greater progress towards heaven. All this has been allowed to come to pass so as to prevent you from slipping into mere enjoyment of spiritual sweetness. God wills that a Christian relinquish his desires, his attachments and his own will, so as to give himself entirely to the Divine Providence. God directs all events for the good of mankind, for 'He wills that all men should be saved.' Be of good cheer and trust that along with the temptation God provides also a way of escape. In a short time you will rejoice more than you grieve now."

As these words were spoken, I woke up, my strength returned and my soul was at peace, as though filled with the brightness of dawn. "God's will be done," I said, and, crossing myself, got up and went on my way. Once more the Prayer was self-acting in my heart as it had been before, and I walked serenely for three days.

All of a sudden I met a group of convicts escorted by soldiers. When I came closer I saw the two men who had robbed me. As they were in the outside row, I fell to their feet and asked them urgently to tell me where my books were. In the beginning they paid no attention to my plea; finally one of them said: "If you'll give us something, we'll tell you where your books are. Give us a ruble."

I swore that I would gladly give them a ruble, even if I had to beg it for the love of God, and offered to leave with them my passport in pawn. At this, they told me that my books might be found in one of the carriages that followed the convicts with other stolen things which had been found on them.

"Well, but how can I get them?"

"Speak to the officer in charge."

I rushed to the officer and told him what had happened. "Do you mean to say that you can read the Bible?" he asked. "Indeed, I can," I replied. "Not only can I read everything, but I can also write. You will see my name written on the Bible, which proves that it belongs to me. And here is my passport bearing the same name and surname."

The officer told me that the two villains were deserters and lived in a forest hut. They had plundered many people until a quick-witted driver, whose *troika* they were about to steal, had caught them the day before. "Very well," he added, "I will return your books if they are there, but won't you walk with us as far as our stopping place for the night? It will save me from halting men and carriages on your account." I willingly agreed to this, and while I walked at the side of his horse, we fell into conversation.

The officer impressed me as being a kind and upright man, no longer young. He wished to know who I was, where I came from and where I was planning to go. To all his questions I gave a frank reply, and so we came to the house which marked the journey's end for that day. The officer got my books, and, returning them to me, said: "Now that it is night, stay here; you may sleep in my entrance-hall." I stayed.

I was so happy to have my books again that I did not know how to thank God. I pressed them to my chest for such a long time that my hands got quite stiff. I wept from exultation, my heart beating with gladness. The officer looked at me fixedly and said: "I see that you are very fond of your Bible." My happiness was so great that I was not able to speak. He continued: "I, too, read the Gospel every day, brother." He took from his breast pocket a small book of the Gospels bound in silver. It was printed in Kiev. "Take a seat," he said. "Let me tell you what happened to me."

"Hey, there! bring us some supper," he ordered.

We sat down to the table and the officer told me his story.

I have been in the army since my early youth — not in a garrison, but in the field service. My superiors liked me, for I knew my business and fulfilled my duties as a second lieutenant conscientiously. But I was young and had many friends. Unfortunately, I took to the bottle so that my passion became a disease. As long as I remained sober, I was a reliable officer, but when I yielded to temptation I was good for nothing, sometimes for a period of six weeks. They stood me for a long time, but in the end, when, in a state of intoxication, I insulted my commanding officer, I was degraded and transferred to a garrison as a private soldier for three years. And I was warned that a still more severe punishment was in store for me if I did not reform and give up drinking. I was so miserable that all my efforts to control or to cure myself proved vain. When I was told that I was to be sent to prison, I did not know what to do with myself. As I sat in the barracks plunged in my bitter thoughts, a monk came in. He was making a collection for a church. We gave him what we could.

The monk approached me and asked why I looked so sad. We began to talk and I told him of my misery. He said compassionately: "My brother had the same experience. And what do you suppose has cured him? His spiritual father provided him with a copy of the Gospels and bade him to read a chapter as soon as he felt the urge to drink. If it persisted he was told to read the second chapter, and so forth. My brother did so, and before long he stopped drinking altogether. Now, for fifteen years he has never touched as much as a drop of alcohol. Won't you try the same cure? You'll see that it will help you. I have a copy of the Gospels and will bring it to you."

I listened to him and said: "How can your Gospels help me when my own efforts and medical treatment have failed to stop me from drinking?" I spoke in that way because I never read the Gospels.

"Don't say that," answered the monk. "I am sure it will help you." And he brought me this very book the following day. As I glanced at it and tried to read a little, I said to the monk: "No, I won't take it. I can't understand it and I am not familiar with Church Slavonic." The monk, however, insisted that there is a grace-giving power in the words of the Gospels, for they relate what our Lord Himself had said. "It is unimportant if you do not understand; just go on reading," he urged me. "A saint said once upon a time: 'you may not understand the Word of God, but the devils do, and tremble.' And the poison of drunkenness is, certainly, incited by devils. Let me tell you another thing: St. John Chrysostom writes that even a lodging in which there is a Gospel wards off the spirits of darkness, for it proves to be a wrong place for their deceiving tricks."

I forget how much money I gave the monk, but in the end I took his Gospel, packed it into my trunk with my other belongings and did not give it another thought. Sometime later when I was overcome by an insurmountable urge to drink, I opened my trunk hastily, so as to take out some money and dash to a tavern. Then I saw the book of the Gospels and the words of the monk came back to my mind. I came across a chapter of St. Matthew and began to read; though I did not understand a word of it, I finished it remembering what the monk had said: "It is unimportant if you do not understand, just go on reading."

"Well," I said to myself, "I will read the second chapter." As I did so, I realized that I understood it somewhat better. So I began reading the third chapter, until the barracks bell rang the signal for retreat, after which no one was permitted to go out. So I stayed where I was.

The following morning, upon rising, I was just about to get myself a drink when I thought of reading another chapter at the Gospels. What was the result of it? Well, I read and did not go to the tavern. As soon as I craved a drink I read a chapter and felt somewhat relieved. This gave me confidence, and from that time on, whenever I felt like drinking, I resorted to the Gospels. Things improved greatly in a while. When I had finished the four Gospels my drunkenness was completely gone. I felt nothing but disgust for alcohol and for twenty years have never tasted a drop of it.

I was so greatly changed that everyone noticed it with surprise. Three years later my commission was restored to me. In due time I got a promotion and finally rose to the rank of a captain. I am married. My wife is a good woman. We are well provided for and live comfortably, thank God! We help the poor as far as our means permit and shelter the pilgrims. My son is also an officer now — a good boy. Note this, after I was cured of alcoholism, I vowed to read the Gospels every day as long as I lived — one Gospel in every twenty-four hours, allowing nothing to stop me from doing it. When I am very busy and too tired to do it myself, I relax and ask my wife or my son to read one Gospel to me, so that I may avoid breaking my vow.

I ordered a binding of pure silver for this copy of the Gospels. This I did for the glory of God and by way of thanksgiving, and I keep it constantly on my breast.

I listened to the Captain's story with pleasure and said: "I also happen to know a similar case. There was a workman at our village factory, a nice fellow, very clever at his work. Unfortunately he used to drink, and not infrequently. A certain God-fearing man had suggested that whenever a craving for alcohol gripped him he should recite the Prayer of Jesus thirty-three times for the glory of the Holy Trinity and in remembrance of the thirty-three years of the earthly life of Jesus Christ. The workman paid heed to this advice and carried it out. In a short while he was no longer drinking at all. And what is more, he entered a monastery three years later."

"Which do you think is best?" asked the captain, "the Prayer of Jesus or the Gospels?"

"It is quite the same thing," I answered. "What the Gospel is, so is the Prayer of Jesus, for the Divine Name of Jesus Christ contains all the truth of the Gospel. The Holy Fathers tell us that the Prayer of Jesus summarizes the whole Gospel."

We set out to say the prayers after our conversation. The Captain started on the Gospel of St. Mark from the beginning. I listened to it and recited the Prayer in my heart. After one o'clock in the morning he finished his reading and we retired to rest.

I got up at day-break as usual, when everybody was still asleep. When it began to dawn I got hold of my beloved *Philocalia*. With what joy I opened it! It was as though I had seen my own father returning from a distant land, or a dead friend who had just risen. I covered it with my kisses, thanking God for having returned it to me. Wasting no time, I opened the

second part of the book and began to read Theoliptus of Phila-
delphia. His instructions startled me, for he suggests that one
and the same person do three different things at once. "Seated
at the table, give nourishment to your body, fill your ears with
reading and your mind with prayer." But when I remembered
the happy evening I had spent the day before, I understood from
my own experience what was the real meaning of this thought.
And here I got the revelation that mind and heart are not one
and the same thing.

When the Captain rose I went to bid him farewell and to
thank him for his kindness. He treated me to tea, gave me a
ruble and said good-bye. Joyfully, I started on my way. I had
gone scarcely a verst, when I recalled that I had promised to
give the soldiers a ruble which had come into my possession
in an unexpected way. At first I wondered whether I should give
it to them or not. After all, they had beaten me and robbed me;
besides, money would be of no use to them since they were
under arrest. Then another thought coursed through my mind.
I remembered what the Bible says: "If thy enemy be hungry,
give him to eat." And Jesus Christ bade us "to love our enemies"; and "if any man will take away thy coat let him have thy
cloak also." Thus, the question was settled in my mind. I re-
traced my steps and came just in time, when the prisoners were
about to start on their march. Quickly I approached one of the
soldiers and slipped the ruble into his hands, saying: "Repent
and pray. Jesus Christ is merciful. He will not forsake you." I
left them with these words and went on my way in another
direction.

I walked for some fifty versts along the high road. Then I
decided to take a side-road so as to be alone and read in peace.
I was going through a dense forest for a long time. Only rarely
did I come upon even small villages. Occasionally I would spend
nearly a whole day sitting in the forest and attentively reading
the *Philocalia*, which to me was an inexhaustible source of
knowledge. There was in my heart a burning desire to unite
with God by means of inner prayer, and I was anxious to learn
it, using my book as a guide. I could not help regretting that I

had no abode where I could read in peace all the time.

Meanwhile I was also reading my Bible and became aware of a clearer understanding of it than before, when I had failed to grasp a multitude of things and had many perplexities. The Holy Fathers were right in their assertion that the *Philocalia* represents a key to the mysteries of the Scripture. It helped me to understand, to a certain degree, the Word of God in its hidden meaning. I began to perceive the significance of the following sayings: "The inner secret man of the heart," "true prayer," "worships in the spirit," "the kingdom of God within us," "the intercession of the Holy Spirit with unspeakable groanings," "abide in Me," "give Me thy heart," "to put on Christ," "the betrothal of the Spirit to our hearts," the cry from the depths of the heart, "Abba, Father," and so forth. And when I prayed in my heart bearing all this in mind, everything about me appeared to be pleasing and lovely. It was as though the trees, the grass, the birds, the earth, the air and the light were saying that they existed for the sake of man, in testimony and proof of the love of God for mankind. It was as if they were saying that everything prayed and praised God.

In this manner I began to get the meaning of what the *Philocalia* describes as "the understanding of the language of the creation" and I saw that there were ways of conversing with all the creatures of God.

Thus I wandered about for a long time. Finally I came to a district so isolated that for three days I saw no villages at all. My provision of rusk was exhausted, and I was disheartened at the thought that I might perish from hunger. Then I prayed in my heart, intrusting myself to the divine will, and my anxiety left me at once. My mind was at peace again and I regained my good spirits. As I walked farther along the road bordered by a vast forest, a dog ran out of it and trotted in front of me. When I called him, he came up to me in a friendly fashion. I was very happy at the thought that this was another proof of God's mercy. Surely there was a flock grazing in the forest and this dog belonged to the shepherd. There was also a possibility that a hunter was in the neighborhood. At any rate I would be able to ask for bread, if nothing else, for I had gone without food for twenty-four hours. At least they would be able to tell me where the nearest village was.

The dog jumped around me for a while, but seeing that I was not going to give him anything, he ran back to the narrow path by which he had come. I had followed him for a few hundred yards among the trees when I noticed that he ran into a burrow, looked out and barked. And then out from behind a large tree came a middle-aged peasant, gaunt and pale. He wanted to know where I came from: In my turn, I asked him what he was doing there, and a friendly conversation began. The peasant invited me to his hut, explaining that he was a forester in charge of this particular section which had been sold for timber. As he placed bread and salt in front of me, we began to talk once more. "I just envy you," I said. "Aren't you lucky to live here quietly, all by yourself. Look at me, I ramble from place to place and rub shoulders with all kinds of people."

"You may stay here if you wish to," he said. "The old dugout of the former forester is not far from here. It is in bad condition, but still good enough to live in in summer. You have your passport. Don't worry about bread; we shall have enough for both of us. My village supplies me with it every week. This little brook here never dries up. This is all I need, brother. For the past ten years I have lived on bread only and drunk nothing but water. That's how it goes. In the fall, when the farmers have finished tilling the land, some two hundred workers will come to fell these trees. Then my business here will come to an end, and you will not be permitted to remain either."

As I heard all this I well-nigh fell to his feet from sheer joy. I knew not how to thank God for His mercy. My greatest desire was fulfilled in this unexpected way. There were still over four months at my disposal before the next fall. And during that time I could give myself to attentive reading of the *Philocalia* in my endeavor to study and to master the incessant prayer of the heart. Thus, I stayed there with joy and lived in the dugout he had shown me.

I often talked with this simple-hearted brother who had

sheltered me, and he told me the story of his life and of his thoughts.

"I enjoyed a good position in our village," he said. "I owned a workshop where I dyed red and blue linens. My life was easy but not without sin. I cheated, swore in vain, used foul language, drank to excess and quarreled with my neighbors. There lived in our village an old church-reader who had an ancient book on the Last Judgment. He used to go from house to house reading from it and thus earning a few pennies. Occasionally he would come to me. For ten kopeks he would read all night long till cock-crow. While working, I often listened to his reading about the torments of Hell, about the living who will be changed and the dead who will rise from their graves, about God who will judge the world with the angels sounding their trumpets. I learned about fire and pitch and the worms which will eat up sinners. One day as I listened I was overcome by horror at the thought that these torments might be in store for me. Stop! I decided to work for the salvation of my soul, hoping that I would be able to pray my sins away. I pondered over the whole matter, then I quit my work; and since I was all alone in the world, I sold my house and took the job of forester here. All I ask of the village assembly is bread, a few clothes and candles for my prayers. I have lived in this manner for over ten years. I eat once a day and my meal consists of bread and water only. I get up with the roosters, make my morning devotions, burn the seven candles in front of the holy icons and pray. When I make my round in the forest I wear sixty pounds of iron chains under my clothes. I never use bad language, never drink wine or beer and no longer come to blows. As for women and girls, I have been avoiding them all my life.

"At first I was very pleased with my existence, but now other thoughts begin to assail me, and I cannot be rid of them. Only God knows whether I will be able to atone for my sins in this way. And my life is hard. I cannot help wondering if everything written in that book is true? Is it possible for the dead to rise again? And what if a man has been dead for over a hundred years, and even his ashes exist no longer? Who can tell whether there is a Hell or not? Why, no one has returned from the Beyond! It seems that when a man dies and rots, he is gone forever. That book might have been written by priests and lords so as to frighten us poor fools, and keep us quiet. Perhaps we torment ourselves in vain and forsake our pleasures and happiness for nothing at all. What then, if there is no such thing as an after-life? Would it not be better to enjoy what we have on earth and take things easy? I am often disturbed by such thoughts now. I don't know. Maybe some day I shall return to my former work."

I listened to him with compassion. They say, I thought, that only educated and intelligent men have no faith whatever. Well, here was one of ourselves, an ordinary peasant, and what impious thoughts he had! It looks as if the kingdom of darkness finds access to everyone, and perhaps the simple-minded are its easiest prey. Let us seek wisdom and strength in the Word of God and brace ourselves for the fight with the enemy of our souls.

It was my sincere desire to help this brother in strengthening his faith. With this intention I took the *Philocalia* out of my knapsack, opened it and read to him the 109th chapter of Saint Hesychius. I tried to explain that it was worthless and vain to keep away from sin merely from fear of Hell and told him that the only way to relieve our souls from sinful thoughts is to guard our mind and purify our hearts by means of inner prayer. The Holy Fathers tell us that those who seek salvation from the mere fear of Hell are regarded as slaves, and those who perform glorious deeds in order to be rewarded with the Kingdom of Heaven are simply mercenary. God wills us to come to him in the manner of sons. He wishes us to lead honorable lives for the love of Him and from the eagerness to serve Him. He wishes us to seek felicity in uniting ourselves to Him in mind and heart.

"However difficult may be the physical tasks which you impose upon your body, it is a wrong way to strive for peace," I said. "Without God in your mind and the incessant Prayer of Jesus in your heart, you are almost certain to slip back into sin on the slightest provocation. Start to work, brother, make up your mind to say the Jesus Prayer incessantly. You have here, in this remote place, a unique opportunity to do it. And you will profit by it in a short time. Godless thoughts will assail you no longer. The faith and the love of Jesus Christ will be revealed to you. You will be given to understand how the dead rise and what the Last Judgment is in reality. You will be amazed at the sense of lightness and bliss that follows the Prayer. Boredom will fade away and will not trouble your solitary life."

Then I began to explain as well as I could how one is to proceed with the incessant prayer of Jesus, what is said about it in the Word of God and in the instructions of the Holy Fathers. He seemed to compose himself and to agree with me.

After this we separated and I locked myself in the old dugout he had given me. Almighty God! How happy and calm I was when I crossed the threshold of my cave, which looked more like a tomb. To me it was a splendid royal palace filled with comfort and delight. Shedding tears of joy I offered thanksgiving to God and thought that in this peaceful and quiet place I must start to work at my task and beg God for enlightenment. So, once more I began to read the *Philocalia* from the first page to the end, with great attention. Before long I had finished the entire book and realized how much wisdom, sanctity and profound insight it contained. But it dealt with such a vast variety of subjects and so many instructions of the Holy Fathers that it was beyond me to understand all and to summarize all I wished to know, particularly about inner prayer. Yet I ardently longed for it, in accordance with the divine bidding in the words of the Apostle: "Be zealous for the better gifts," and further, "extinguish not the Spirit." I pondered over it for a long time. What was I to do? The task was beyond my reason and my understanding, and there was no one who could have explained it to me—I resolved to beset the Lord with my Prayer. He could enlighten me somehow or other. And for twenty-four hours I did nothing but pray, without ceasing for a moment. At last my thoughts stilled and I fell asleep.

I dreamt that I was in the cell of my departed elder who was explaining the *Philocalia* to me. He was saying: "There is a deep wisdom in this holy book. It is the hidden treasury of the meanings of the mysterious ways of God. The access to this treasury is not revealed everywhere and to everybody. And the guidance given here is subordinated to individual needs: the wise receives from it a subtle guidance, the plain man a simple one. Therefore you, simple-minded, must not read the chapters in succession as they appear in this book. It was meant for those who are versed in theology. Those who are not thus instructed but wish to learn inner prayer, should read the *Philocalia* in the following order: (1) the book of Nicephorus the Monk (part two must be read first of all); (2) then take the entire book of Gregory of Sinai, leaving out the short chapters; (3) read the Three Forms of Prayer by Simeon the New Theologian and his sermon on Faith; (4) then comes the book of Callistus and Ignatius. These Fathers give full guidance and instruction in the inner prayer of the heart, couched in words accessible to everyone. If you desire a still clearer understanding of prayer, open part four and read of the way of prayer as it was summarized by the most holy Callistus,[4] Patriarch of Constantinople."

In my dream, still holding the book in my hand, I was trying to find this particular instruction but failed. Then the elder went through a few pages himself, saying, "Here it is. Let me mark it for you." And with a piece of charcoal picked up from the floor he indicated with a mark on the margin the chapter he had found. I listened to him carefully, trying to remember, word for word, what he had been saying.

It was still dark when I woke up. I lay quietly thinking of my dream and of the words of my elder. "God alone knows," I said to myself, "whether I have really seen the spirit of my departed teacher or only imagined it in my mind, for it is constantly riveted on the *Philocalia* and on him." Prey to this doubt, I rose at daybreak. And behold! The book lay on a stone which I used as a table in my dugout; it was open at the very page which my elder had indicated to me, with the charcoal mark on the margin, just as I had seen it in my dream. And the charcoal lay next to the book. I looked in amazement, for the book had not been there the evening before. On that point my recollection was clear; I had closed it and slipped it under my pillow; neither had there been the charcoal on it. I was quite sure of that, too.

This strengthened me in my belief that my dream was true and that my beloved teacher of blessed memory was agreeable to the Lord. I started to read the *Philocalia* just as he had bidden me to do. I read it once, then again, and my soul was aroused by an ardent longing to experience in practice what I have been reading about. Now I understood clearly the meaning of inner prayer, how it may be attained and what the fruits of it are. I also was given to see how it filled the heart with sweetness and how one was to recognize whether that sweetness came from God, from natural causes, or from delusion.

I began to seek the place of my heart in the manner Simeon the New Theologian taught. With my eyes closed I looked upon it in thought, *i.e.*, in imagination. I tried to see it as it is in the left side of my breast and to listen attentively to its beating. At first I did it several times a day for half an hour, and failed to see anything but darkness. Then I succeeded in picturing my heart and the movement in it, and I learned how to bring in and out of it the Jesus Prayer, timing it with my breathing. In this I followed the teaching of Sts. Gregory of Sinai, Callistus and Ignatius. While inhaling, I saw my heart in my mind and said: "Lord Jesus Christ." In breathing out, I said: "Have mercy on me." This I did for an hour at a time, later for two hours, then as long as I was able to. Finally, I succeeded in doing it almost all day long. If things were hard to manage and I fell prey to laziness and doubt, I hastened to open the *Philocalia* and to read passages dealing with the action of the heart, and then once more I felt a fervent and eager desire for the Prayer.

About three weeks later I noticed that my heart ached. Afterwards this pain was transformed to the delightful sensation of warmth, comfort and peace. This incited me still further and urged me to the saying of the Prayer with greater care. My thoughts dwelt constantly on it and I felt a great joy. From that time on I began to experience occasionally a great many different sensations in my heart and my mind. Now and then my heart would brim over with happiness overwhelmed by such lightness, freedom and solace that I was all changed and enraptured. At times I felt a glowing love for Jesus Christ and all

God's creatures; and my eyes filled with tears of gratitude to God, Who poured His grace on me, a great sinner. As for my mind, so dull before, it sometimes received such an enlightenment that I was able to understand easily and to meditate upon things which hitherto had been beyond my comprehension. Now and then a sensation of delightful warmth would spread from my heart throughout my whole being, and I would be profoundly moved in recognizing God's presence in all things. Again, when I called upon the Name of Jesus I would be overwhelmed with bliss, and the meaning of "The Kingdom of Heaven is within you" would become clear to me.

From these and other, similar, comforting experiences I drew the conclusion that the results of inner prayer are threefold: it manifests itself in the spirit, in feelings and in revelations; the *spirit* is filled by a mellowness that comes from the love of God, inward calmness, exultation of mind, purity of thoughts and sweet remembrance of God. The *feelings* convey to us a delightful warmth of the heart, a joyful exultation, lightness and vigor, enjoyment of life and insensibility to pain and sorrow. The *revelation* brings us enlightenment of the mind, understanding of the Holy Scriptures and of the speech of all creatures, freedom from vanities, awareness of the sweetness of the inner life and cognizance of the nearness of God and of His love for mankind.

After having spent some five months in solitude and prayer which filled me with sweet sensations, I grew so used to it that I practised it constantly. In the end I felt that it was going on by itself in my mind and heart, not only while I was awake but also in my sleep. It never ceased for a single moment in whatever business I might have been doing. My soul gave thanks to God, and my heart melted away in continuous joy.

The time came for the felling of the trees. People began to arrive in great numbers, and I was compelled to leave my silent abode. I thanked the forester, prayed, kissed the plot of land on which God had showed his grace to me, unworthy of His mercy, donned my knapsack and set off. I wandered for a long time in different places until I reached Irkutsk. The self-acting Prayer of the heart comforted and braced me on my journey. Wherever I found myself, whatever I did, it was never in my way, nor was it hindered by anything at all. When I was working at something with the inner prayer of the heart, my business progressed more readily. Whether I was listening to something attentively or reading, the Prayer still went on at the same time. I was cognizant of both things simultaneously, as though my personality had been split and there were two souls in my body. Almighty God! How mysterious is the nature of man. "How manifold are Thy works, O Lord! In wisdom hast Thou made them all."

On my way I met with many adventures and happenings. If I were to relate them I should not finish in twenty-four hours. Here is an example of it! One winter evening I was walking alone through the woods towards a village about two versts away, where I was to take a night's rest, when a big wolf sprang at me all of a sudden. I held in my hand the wooden rosary of my elder, which I always carried with me, and made the motion of striking the animal with it. The rosary somehow or other encircled the neck of the wolf and was pulled out of my hand. As he leapt away from me, the wolf caught his hind paws in a thorny bush. Furiously he dashed about but failed to extricate himself, for the rosary, also caught on the branch of a dead tree, was tightening around his neck. I crossed myself in faith and went to set him free, mainly because I feared that if the rosary snapped, he might run off with my precious possession. And sure enough, scarcely had I got hold of the rosary when he broke free and darted away, leaving not a trace. I gave thanks to God and thinking of the elder on my way, I came hale and hearty to the village inn, where I asked for shelter.

At the corner table in the inn two men sat drinking tea. One of them was old, the other middle-aged and stout. They did not look like ordinary folk, and I asked the peasant caring for their horses who they were. He said that the old man was a teacher in the elementary school, and the other a clerk in the district court. Both belonged to the gentry. The peasant was taking them to the fair some twenty versts away.

After sitting there for a while I borrowed a needle and thread from a woman, drew closer to the candle-light and began to mend my broken rosary.

The clerk noticed it and said: "You've been praying so hard that you broke your rosary?"

"It was not I who broke it, it was the wolf," I answered.

"What! A wolf? Say, do wolves pray too?" he said humorously.

I told them the whole story and explained why the rosary was so dear to me. The clerk laughed: "To you bigots," he said, "miracles seem always to happen. What is miraculous about all this? The wolf was frightened and ran off simply because you hurled something at him. It is a known fact that wolves and dogs are scared by the gesture of hurling, and getting caught in the thicket is also quite common. Many things happen in the world. Shall we see miracles everywhere?"

Hearing this the schoolteacher shook his head: "Don't say that, sir," he replied, "you are not expert in science. As for me, I can readily see in this peasant's story the mystery of nature, which is sensuous and spiritual at the same time."

"How is that?" asked the clerk.

"It is like this. Though you have not received any higher education, you are nevertheless familiar with the sacred history of the Old and New Testaments through the catechetical instructions we use in our schools. Do you remember that when Adam, the first man, still enjoyed the state of holy innocence all animals were obedient to him, approached him in reverence and received their names from him? The elder who owned this rosary was a saint. And what is sanctity? It is the return of the sinner to the innocence of the first man. When the soul is holy, the body too becomes sanctified. This rosary had always been in the possession of a saintly man. Thus the touch of his hands and the emanations of his body had endowed it with the holy power of the first man's innocence. This is a mystery of spiritual nature. Now then: all animals in succession, down to our own times, have experienced this power naturally by means of the sense of smell, for in all animals the nose is the main organ of the senses. This is the mystery of sensuous nature."[5]

"You learned men are always talking about forces and wisdoms. For my part, I take things more simply. Fill your tumbler with vodka and send it down, and you'll have all the force you want," said the clerk, and he went to the cupboard.

"That is your business. As for the learned matters, pray, leave them to us," said the schoolteacher.

I liked the way he talked, so I approached him and said: "May I tell you, sir, a few more things about my elder?"

And I told him how the elder appeared to me in my dream, how he had instructed me, and made the charcoal mark in the *Philocalia*. The schoolteacher listened attentively, but the clerk, who had stretched out on the bench, grumbled: "It is true enough when they say that people go out of their mind from reading the Bible too often. That is what it is! What devil would come up at night to mark your book? You let it drop down yourself in your sleep and got it soiled with soot. There is your miracle. Ah, you cunning old fox! I have come across plenty of your kind!"

Mumbling this, he rolled over to the wall and fell asleep.

At these words, I turned to the schoolteacher and said: "I'll show you, if I may, the very book, which was really marked and not just soiled with soot." I took the *Philocalia* from my knapsack and showed him. "What amazes me," I said, "is how a disembodied spirit could have picked up a piece of charcoal and written with it."

The schoolteacher looked at the mark and began to speak: "This, too, is a mystery of the spirit. I will explain it to you. You see, when spirits appear in a physical form to a living man, they compose for themselves a palpable body from the air and the particles of light. After their appearance, they return to the elements what they have taken out for the composition of their bodies. And since the air possesses elasticity—a capacity of contraction and expansion—the soul vested in it can take anything and act and write. But let me see your book." He took it and chanced to open at the sermon of St. Simeon the New Theologian. "Ah," he said, "this must be a theological book. I have never seen it before."

"This book, sir, consists almost entirely of instructions on inner prayer in the Name of Jesus Christ. It is revealed here in full detail by twenty-five holy fathers," I told him.

"I also know something about inner prayer," said the schoolteacher.

I bowed before him to the ground and asked him to tell me what he knew of it.

"Well, the New Testament tells us that men and all creation 'are subject to vanity not willingly,' but sigh and long for the liberty of the children of God. This mysterious sighing of all creation, the innate longing of souls for God, is inner prayer. There is no need to learn it, for it is inherent in everything and everyone."

"But how is one to find it, to discover it in one's heart, to take it by one's own will that it may act manifestly, give gladness, light and salvation?" I asked.

"I don't remember whether there is anything concerning this subject in theological treatises," said the schoolteacher.

"Oh, yes, there is. Everything is explained here," I said, pointing at the book.

He took out a pencil, wrote down the title of the *Philocalia* and declared: "I shall most certainly have a copy sent me from Tobolsk, and examine it." After that we separated, and when I started off, I thanked God for this conversation with the schoolteacher. As for the clerk, I prayed that our Lord would cause him to read the *Philocalia*, be it only once, and let him find through it enlightenment and salvation.

Another time, in spring, I came to a village, and it so happened that I stayed in the house of a priest. He was a kindly man, living quite alone. I spent three days with him. When he had observed me for that length of time, he said: "Stay here; you will be paid. I am looking for a dependable man. We are building a new stone church near the old wooden chapel. I need a trustworthy person to keep an eye on the workmen and stay in the chapel to take care of the collection for the building fund. It is just the sort of thing you can do, and will suit your way of life perfectly. You will sit alone in the chapel and pray. There is a quiet little room for the watchman there. Do stay, please, at least until the church has been built."

I refused repeatedly, but finally I had to yield to the priest's urging, and I remained there until fall, taking up my abode in the chapel. In the beginning it seemed to be quiet and suitable for prayer, though a great number of people came to the chapel, particularly on holy days. Some of them came to say their prayers, others to fritter away time and still others with the hope of filching money from the collection plate.

Sometimes I read the Bible and the *Philocalia;* some of the visitors saw this and started a conversation; others asked me to read aloud for them.

After a while I noticed a young peasant girl who came frequently to the chapel and spent a long time in prayer. Giving ear to her mumbling, I discovered that some of the prayers were very strange and the others were completely distorted. I asked her where she had learned them; she said that it was from her mother, who belonged to the church. Her father, however, was connected with a sect that had no priesthood. I felt sorry for her and advised her to say the prayers correctly, according to the traditions of Holy Church. Then I taught her the right wording of the Lord's Prayer and of the Hail Mary, and finally told her: "Say the Prayer of Jesus as often as you can, for it reaches God sooner than any other and will lead you to the salvation of your soul."

The girl heeded my advice and followed it carefully. And what happened? A short while afterwards, she told me that she had grown so accustomed to the Jesus Prayer that she felt an urge to say it all the time. She was filled with gladness and the desire to recite it over and over again. This made me very happy, and I advised her to go on with the Prayer in the name of Jesus Christ.

Summer was ending. Many of the visitors to the chapel wished to see me, not only for the sake of the reading and advice, but also to tell me all their worldly troubles and even to find out about things they had lost or mislaid. It seemed as though some of them took me for a sorcerer. The girl I had already mentioned also came to me in a state of great distress to ask advice. Her father wanted her to marry, against her will, a man of his sect. The wedding was to be performed not by a priest, but by a simple peasant. "But this marriage cannot be lawful," cried the girl. "Is it not the same thing as fornication? I will run away some place."

"But where?" I asked. "They will find you anywhere. Nowadays you can hide nowhere without a passport. They'll find you! You had better pray to God fervently to change your father's mind and to safeguard your soul from heresy and sin. This is a much better plan than flight."

As time went on I began to feel that all this noise and confusion were more than I could endure. Finally, at the end of summer, I determined to leave the chapel and go on with my wanderings as before. I told the priest of my plans: "You know my condition, Father! I must have peace for my prayers. This place is disturbing and harmful to me. Now that I have shown you my obedience, and stayed here the whole summer, let me go with your blessings on my solitary journey."

The priest did not wish to let me go. He tried to change my mind: "What hinders you from praying here? Apart from staying in the chapel, your work amounts to nothing, and you have your daily bread. You may say your prayers day and night if you wish, but stay here and live with God, brother. You are of great help to me. You do not go for foolish talk with visitors, you are scrupulous with the collection money, and are a source of profit to the House of God. This is worth more than your solitary prayer. Why do you wish to be always alone? Community prayers are pleasanter. God did not create men to live only to themselves, but to help each other and lead each other on the path of salvation. Think of the saints and the Church Fathers. Day and night they worked hard, cared for the needs of the Church and preached in many places. They didn't sit down in solitude, hiding themselves from people."

"God gives everyone a special gift, Father," I said. "There have been many preachers, but also many hermits. Each has done what he could in his own way and in faith that God Himself was showing him the path of salvation. How do you explain the fact that many of the saints gave up their work as bishops, priests or abbots and retired into the desert to get away from the confusion which comes from living with other people? Thus, Isaac the Syrian, who was a bishop, left his flock. The venerable Athanasius of Athos abandoned his large monastery; and just because their places became a source of temptation to them. For they firmly believed in our Lord's saying: 'What shall it profit a man if he gain the whole world and lose his own soul?' "

"To be sure," said the priest, "but they were saints!"

"If saints must guard themselves from the hazards of mingling with people, what else can a weak sinner do?" I answered.

In the end I bade farewell to the kindly priest, who sent me on my way with the love in his heart.

Some ten versts further on, I stopped in a village for the night. At the inn there was a peasant so gravely ill that I recommended that those who were with him should see that he received the last sacraments. They agreed with me, and towards the morning they sent for the parish priest. I remained, for I wished to worship and pray in the Presence of the Eucharist. While waiting for the priest, I went into the street and sat on the bench there. All of a sudden I saw running towards me from the backyard the girl who used to pray in the chapel.

"What are you doing here?" I asked.

"They have set the day for my betrothal to the sectarian, so I ran away." Then she knelt before me and said: "Have pity on me. Take me along with you and put me in a convent. I do not wish to marry. I wish to live in a convent and recite the Prayer of Jesus. They will listen to you and receive me."

"Look here," I said. "Where do you want me to take you? I don't know a single convent in the vicinity. Without a passport, I can't take you anywhere! No one would receive you. It would be quite impossible for you to hide at a time like this.

They will get you at once. You would be sent home and punished as a tramp besides. You had better go home and pray. If you do not want to marry, pretend that you are ill. It is called a saving dissimulation. The holy mother Clementa did it, and so did Saint Marina, when she took refuge in a monastery of men, and many others."

While we sat there discussing the matter, we saw four peasants driving up the road with a pair of horses. They came straight to us at a gallop, seized the girl and placed her in the cart. One of them drove off with her. The other three tied my hands together and forced me back to the village where I had passed my summer. In answer to all my objections they yelled: "We'll teach you, you fake saint, not to seduce girls."

In the evening I was brought up into the village court. My feet were put in irons and I was left in the prison to await my trial the next morning. The priest, upon learning that I was in jail, came to see me. He brought me some supper, consoled me and promised to intercede for me as a spiritual father by saying that I was not the kind of man they believed me to be. He sat with me for a while and then left for home.

The district police officer came late in the evening. He was driving through the village on his way somewhere else and put up at the deputy's house. They told him what had happened, and a peasant meeting was called. I was brought again to the village court. We went in and stood there waiting. In came the officer in a tipsy swagger, sat on the table with his cap on and shouted: "Hey, Epiphan! Did the girl, that daughter of yours, swipe anything from your house?"

"No, sir!"

"Has she been caught in doing anything wrong with that blockhead there?"

"No, sir!"

"Very well: this is what our judgment and decision will be. You manage your daughter yourself. As for this fellow, we'll give him a good lesson tomorrow and banish him from the village with strict orders never to return again. That is all."

So saying, the officer got down from the table and went off to bed, while I was put back in prison. Early in the morning two village policemen came, whipped me, and let me go.

I went my way thanking God for having esteemed me worthy to suffer in His Name. This thought consoled me and infused a new glow into my incessant prayer. None of these incidents touched me very deeply. It was as if I had seen them happen to somebody else, being myself a mere spectator of it all. Even when I was whipped, I had the power to bear it; the Prayer that gladdened my heart made me unaware of anything else.

When I had gone about four versts, I met the girl's mother, who was driving from the market with her purchases. She saw me and said that the bridegroom had turned her daughter down. "You see," she added, "he was angry with Akulka for having fled from him." Thereupon, she gave me bread and a pie and I went on.

A long time after this another thing happened. I may tell you about it too. It was the 24th of March—I felt an irresistible desire to make my Communion the following morning, which was the Feast of the Annunciation of our Lady. I asked for the nearest church and was told that there was one some thirty versts away. So I walked the rest of that day and the whole night in order to arrive in time for Matins. The weather was very bad; a cold wind blew strongly; it was snowing and raining in turn. On my way I had to cross a brook; just as I got to the middle, the ice broke under my feet and I fell into the water up to my waist. Drenched as I was, I came to Matins, stood through it and through Mass, at which I made my Communion, by the grace of God. As I wished to spend a peaceful day in order to enjoy my spiritual happiness, I asked the warden permission to stay in his guard-room until the following morning. My heart was filled with indescribable happiness and joy. I lay there on the planks in the unheated room, as happy as if I were resting on Abraham's bosom. And the Prayer was surging in my heart. The love of Jesus Christ and His Blessed Mother swept over me in waves of sweetness and immersed my soul in rapture and delight. At nightfall, however, a sharp pain set in in my legs, and I remembered that they were wet. I paid no attention to it, but listened attentively to the prayer in my heart and was no longer conscious of the discomfort. But in the morning when I tried to get up, I found that I could not move my legs. They were paralyzed and weak as bits of straw. The warden dragged me down off the plank bed. Motionless, I sat in the guard-house for two days. On the third day he began to drive me out saying: "Should you die here, think of the mess I would be in."

I crawled out on my arms with great difficulty and made for the church. There I lay on the steps for another couple of days. The people who passed by paid no attention to me or my pleading. Finally, a peasant came up, sat beside me and talked. After a while he asked, casually: "What will you give me if I cure you? I used to suffer from exactly the same thing, and I know a drug for it."

"I have nothing to give you," I answered.

"What do you have in your bag?"

"Just some rusk and books."

"Well, maybe you'll work for me at least one summer if I cure you?"

"I can't do that either. See, I can use only one arm, the other is almost completely withered."

"What can you do then?"

"Nothing much, except read and write."

"Ah, you can write! Well then, teach my little boy to write. He can read a little, and I wish him to know how to write. But the masters are dear. They ask twenty rubles to teach him."

I consented to do it. With the help of the warden, he dragged me to his backyard and installed me in an old and empty bath-house there. Then he began to treat me. He picked from the fields, yards and cesspools all sorts of putrid bones of cattle and birds, washed them carefully, broke them up with a stone and put them in a large earthen vessel. This he covered with a lid having a small perforation in it and placed upside down on an empty jar sunk in the ground. He covered the upper vessel with a thick layer of clay, and put a pile of wood around it which he kept burning for twenty-four hours. "We'll extract some tar from these bones," he said, as he was feeding the fire. The following day, when he raised the jar from the ground, there was in it about a pint of thick, oily, reddish liquid, which dripped through the perforation in the lid of the upper vessel. This liquid had the strong smell of fresh raw meat. The bones in the earthen vessel were no longer black and decayed, but looked white, clean and transparent, like mother of pearl. With this liquid, I rubbed my legs five times a day. And what happened? In twenty-four hours I was able to move my toes. On the third day I could bend and unbend my legs. On the fifth day I stood on my feet and walked through the yard, leaning on a stick. In a word, within a week my legs had become as strong as they were before. I gave thanks to God, musing upon His wisdom and the mysterious power hidden in all creation. Dry, decayed bones, almost completely disintegrated, keep in themselves vital force, color and smell, and can act upon living bodies, communicating life to those which are already half-dead. This is a pledge of the future resurrection of the flesh. I wished that I could point this out to the forester with whom I had lived, remembering how uncertain he had been about the resurrection.

Having in this manner recovered from my illness, I began to teach the lad. I wrote out the Jesus Prayer as a sample of calligraphy, and made him copy the words carefully. To teach him was a restful occupation, for during the day he worked for the bailiff of the estate nearby and came to me while the latter slept —that is, from dawn to late Mass. The youngster was bright and soon began to write fairly well. When the bailiff found that he could write, he asked who his teacher was.

"A one-armed pilgrim who lives in our old bathhouse," the boy told him. The bailiff, who was a Pole, took interest in me and came to look me up. He found me reading the *Philocalia*, and he started a conversation by asking: "What are you reading?" I showed him the book.

"Ah," he said, "the *Philocalia!* I saw it in the house of our priest[6] when I lived in Vilno. I was told, however, that it contains all sorts of tricks and artifices for prayer laid down by Greek monks. It is like those fanatics of India and Bokhara who sit and inflate themselves trying to get a ticklish sensation in their hearts and in their foolishness take this purely physical reaction for prayer, considering it to be the gift of God. One must pray simply so as to fulfill our duty to God, stand and recite Our Father as Christ taught us. That will put you in the right groove for the whole day, but not the repetition of the same thing over and over again. That, I dare say, might drive you mad and injure your heart besides."

"Don't speak that way about this holy book, my dear sir!" I said. "It was not written by simple Greek monks, but by great and holy men of ancient times, by men revered by your own church, such as Anthony the Great, Macarius the Great, Mark the Hermit, John Chrysostom and others. The 'heart method' of inner prayer was taken over from them by the monks of India and Bokhara, who spoiled and distorted it, as my elder told me. In the *Philocalia*, however, all the instructions concerning the action of the prayer in the heart have been taken from the Word of God, from the Holy Bible in which the same Jesus Christ who commanded us to recite the Our Father taught also the incessant prayer of the heart. He said: '*Thou shalt love the Lord thy God with all thy heart and with all thy mind*'; '*Watch and pray*'; '*Abide in Me and I in you.*' And the holy Fathers, referring to the holy words of the Psalms, '*O taste, and see that the Lord is sweet,*' explain this passage in the following way: 'A Christian must seek and find, by every possible means, delight in prayer. He must look constantly for consolation in it and not be satisfied by merely saying "Our Father" once a day.' Now let me read to you how they censure those who do not try to find the happiness of the prayer of the heart. The wrong of such is threefold: (1) because they contradict the Scripture inspired by God; (2) because they do not strive for the higher and more perfect state of the soul, but are satisfied with outward virtues, and neither hunger nor thirst for truth, thus depriving themselves of blessedness and joy in the Lord; (3) because, in constantly thinking of themselves and their outward virtues, they often lapse into temptation or pride and thus fall into danger."

"What you are reading is too lofty," said the bailiff; "for us worldly people, it is hard to grasp."

"Well, let me read you something easier about men of good-will, who, though they lived in the world, had learned how to pray incessantly." I found in the *Philocalia* the sermon by Simeon the New Theologian on the youth George and read it to him.

The bailiff was very pleased and said: "Lend me this book for a while. I will read it some day at my leisure."

"I may give it to you for twenty-four hours, but not for longer," I answered, "for I read it every day myself and can't live without it."

"Well, then, at least copy out for me what you have just read. I'll pay you."

"I don't want you to pay me. I will make a copy for you in brotherly love, and in hope that God will grant you a desire for prayer."

It was with pleasure that I copied for him the sermon at once. He read it to his wife and they both liked it. Thus it came to pass that they would send for me now and then, and I would take the *Philocalia* and read to them while they sat drinking tea and listening. One day they kept me for dinner. The bailiff's wife, a kindly old lady, sat with us at the table and ate fried fish. By some mishap, she swallowed a bone, which got stuck in her throat, and all our efforts to relieve her failed. She suffered a great ache, and in an hour or so was compelled to lie down. They sent for a doctor who lived thirty versts away. In the evening, feeling very sorry for her, I went home.

While I was sleeping lightly that night, I heard the voice of my elder. I did not see him but heard him speak to me. "Your landlord cured you; why, then, don't you try to cure the bailiff's wife? God has bidden us to feel pity for our neighbors."

"I would have helped her gladly, but how? I do not know!" I answered.

"Well, what you must do is this: from her early youth she had an aversion for olive oil, not only when she tastes it, but even its smell makes her very ill. Let her drink a spoonful of it.

She will be nauseated, the bone will come out, but the oil will have a soothing effect on the sore in her throat and she will recover."

"And how am I to give it to her since she dislikes it so? She won't swallow it."

"Let the bailiff hold her head and pour it in her mouth even though you have to use force."

I woke up, rushed to the bailiff and told hem all this in detail.

"Of what use can your oil be now? She is wheezing and delirious, and her neck is swollen. However, we may try, even if it doesn't help. Oil is a harmless medicine."

He poured some into a wine glass and we made her swallow it. Seized with nausea at once, she ejected the bone along with some blood and was greatly relieved. Soon she fell into a profound sleep. In the morning I came to inquire about her health and found her sitting peacefully at the tea table. She marvelled with her husband at the way she had been cured. But what surprised them even more was the fact that her dislike of oil that had been told me in a dream was not known to anyone except to themselves. At that time the doctor drove up and the bailiff's wife told him of her experience. For my part, I told him how the peasant had cured my legs. The doctor heard us through and said: "I am not surprised at either of the cases, for the forces of nature operated in both of them. However, I shall take note of it." And he wrote with the pencil in his notebook.

After this the rumor quickly spread throughout the neighborhood that I was a seer, a doctor and a healer. People streamed to me from all parts to consult with me on their affairs and their troubles. They brought me presents, treated me with reverence and pampered me. I endured all this a week. Then, fearing that I might succumb to the temptation of vainglory, I left the place in secrecy at night.

Once more I started on my lonely journey, feeling as light as if a heavy load had been lifted off my shoulders. The Prayer comforted me more than ever, and at times my heart was glowing with boundless love for Jesus Christ. This joyous bubbling seemed to send flows of consolation through my whole body.

The mental representation of Jesus Christ was so vivid that when I meditated on the events related in the Gospel, I seemed to see them before my very eyes. Moved to tears of joy, I sometimes felt such happiness in my heart as I have no words to describe.

It happened at times that for three days or more I came upon no human habitations, and in the exaltation of my spirit I felt as though I were all alone on this earth, just one miserable sinner before the merciful and man-loving God. This sense of complete solitude comforted me, and the rapture I experienced in my prayers was much stronger than when I was among many people.

At last I reached Irkutsk. When I had made my prostrations and said my prayers before the relics of St. Innocent, I began to wonder: "Where shall I go now?" I did not care to stay there for a long time, for it was a large and crowded city. I was going along the streets, deep in my thoughts, when a local merchant stopped me and asked: "You are a pilgrim, aren't you? Won't you come to my house?" He took me to his wealthy home and asked me where I came from. I told him all about my beginnings. He listened and said:

"You should go to Jerusalem on a pilgrimage. That place is more sacred than any other site on earth."

"I should be only too happy to do so," I said, "but I haven't the means of going there. I could get along until I reached the sea, but I cannot afford the voyage. It costs a great deal."

"If you wish me to, I can get the money for you. Last year I sent an old man there, one of our townspeople," said the merchant.

I sank to his feet in gratitude. "Listen," he continued, "I'll give you a letter to my son who lives in Odessa. He has business connections with Constantinople and sends his own ships; he will be pleased to arrange your transportation on one of his boats there. One of his agents will book a passage from Constantinople to Jerusalem for you. He will pay; it does not cost much."

When I heard this I was overcome with happiness and

thanked my benefactor for his kindness. Even more did I thank God for the fatherly love and care He showed to me, a wretched sinner, who did no good either to himself or to men, but ate in idleness the bread belonging to others.

I stayed with the generous merchant for three days. He wrote me a letter to his son as he had promised. And now, here I am on my way to Odessa with the intention of reaching the Holy City of Jerusalem. Yet, I do not know whether the Lord will permit me to pray in reverence at His life-giving tomb.

I I I

Just before leaving Irkutsk I called on my spiritual father with whom I had had so many talks, and said to him: "Now, that I am ready to go to Jerusalem, I have come to take leave of you and to thank you for your love for me in Christ, unworthy wanderer that I am."

"May God bless your journey," answered the priest. "But tell me about yourself—who you are and where do you come from? About your travels I have already heard a great deal. Now, I should like to know more about your life before you became a pilgrim."

"Well, I'll gladly tell you about that also. It is not a long story," I answered.

I was born in a village in the province of Orel. After our parents died, there were just the two of us left, my elder brother and I. He was ten years old and I was two. We were adopted by my grandfather, an honorable man, quite well-off. He kept an inn on the main road, and because of his kindness many people stayed in his place. My brother, who was a high-spirited boy, spent most of his time in the village. I preferred to stay near my grandfather. On Sundays and holy days we would go to church together, and at home my grandfather would read the Bible — this very Bible I carry with me now. My brother grew up and turned bad. He began to drink.

Once, when I was seven years old and we were both lying in bed, he pushed me down; I fell and injured my left arm. Never since have I been able to use it; it's all withered up.

My grandfather, seeing that I should never be able to work in the fields, taught me to read from this Bible, for we had no spelling-book. He pointed at the letters, made me learn them and form the words. I can hardly understand it myself, but somehow or other by repeating things over and over again, I learned to read after a while. Later, when his eyesight grew weak, he often bade me read the Bible to him, and corrected me as he listened. A certain village clerk often put up at our inn. He wrote a beautiful hand. I watched him write and liked it. Then I began to copy words at his direction. He gave me paper and ink and quill pens. Thus I learned to write. My grandfather was very pleased and admonished me: "God has given you the knowledge of reading and writing, which will make a man of you. Give thanks to the Lord and pray often."

We used to attend all the services at church, and at home said our prayers frequently. I was always made to read the fifty-first psalm, and while I did so, grandfather and grandmother knelt or made their prostrations.

My grandmother died when I was seventeen years old. After a while my grandfather told me: "There is no longer a mistress in this house, and that is not right. Your brother is good for nothing, and I am going to look for a wife for you." I refused, saying that I was a cripple, but my grandfather insisted, and I got married. My wife was a quiet and good girl about twenty years old. A year later my grandfather fell hopelessly ill. Feeling that death was near, he called me, bade me farewell, and said:

"My house and all I have is yours. Live according to your conscience; deceive no one, and above all, pray, for everything comes from God. Trust in Him only. Go to church regularly, read your Bible and remember your grandmother and me in your prayers. Here, take this money. There are a thousand rubles here; be thrifty, do not waste it, but don't be stingy either; give to the poor and to God's church." Soon after this he died and I buried him.

My brother begrudged me the property, which was left entirely to me. He grew more and more angry, and the Enemy incited him against me to such an extent that he even planned to do away with me. Finally, this is what he did one night while we slept and no guests stayed in the inn. He broke into the store-room where the money was kept, took it from the chest and set fire to the store-room. The flames spread rapidly through the whole house before we were aware of them, and we barely escaped with our lives by jumping from the window in our night-clothes. The Bible was lying under our pillow. We grabbed it, and took it with us. As we looked at our burning home, we said to one another: "Thank God, we saved the Bible. This, at least, is a comfort in our misfortune."

Thus, all we possessed burned to ashes, and my brother had disappeared without a trace. Later on we learned that while on a spree, he was heard to boast that he had stolen the money and set fire to the house.

We were left naked and bare-foot, like beggars. With some money we borrowed, we built a little hut and set out to lead the life of landless peasants. My wife was a nimble-fingered person. She knew how to knit, spin and sew. People gave her work; she toiled day and night and supported me. For my part, I was not even able to make bast shoes. My crippled arm made me quite useless. And while my wife was knitting or spinning, I would sit next to her and read the Bible. She would listen to me, but sometimes she would begin to weep. When I asked her: "Why are you weeping? We are still alive, thank God!" she would answer: "It is that beautiful writing in the Bible. It moves me so deeply!"

Remembering my grandfather's bidding, we fasted often, said the *Acathistos*[7] to Our Lady every morning, and at night made a thousand prostrations to keep away from temptation. In this manner we lived for two years in peace. But this is what is really astonishing; although we had no idea of the inner, heart-acted prayer, but prayed with our lips only and made senseless prostrations, turning somersaults like fools, we nevertheless felt the desire for prayer, and the long ones we recited without understanding did not seem tiring; quite the contrary — we enjoyed them a great deal. It must be true, as a certain teacher once told me, that secret prayer is hidden deeply in the heart of man, though he may not know about it. Yet, it acts mysteriously within his soul and prompts him to pray according to his power and knowledge.

After two years of that kind of life, my wife suddenly fell ill with a high fever. She received Communion and passed away on the ninth day of her illness. Now I was left completely alone. Unable to work, I was compelled to beg, though I was ashamed of it. Besides, I was grief-stricken at the loss of my wife and did not know what to do with myself. If I happened to enter our hut and see her dress, or maybe a kerchief, I would cry out or even faint away. Life at home was beyond my endurance. Therefore I sold my hut for twenty rubles and gave to the poor whatever clothes my wife and I had possessed. Because of my withered arm, I was given a passport which exempted me for good from public duties. And taking my beloved Bible I left, neither caring nor even knowing where I was going. But after I had set off I began to wonder where I should go. "First of all," I said to myself, "I will go to Kiev. There I will pray at the shrines of saints and ask for relief in my sorrow." As soon as my decision was made, I began to feel better, and reached Kiev greatly comforted. Since then, for the last thirteen years I have been going from place to place. I have visited many churches and monasteries, but now I prefer to wander in the steppes and the fields. I don't know whether God will let me go to Jerusalem. There, if it is His Divine will, it is high time for my sinful bones to be laid to rest.

"And how old are you now?"
"I am thirty-three years of age."
"The age of our Lord Jesus Christ."

I V

"Tell me more about the edifying experiences you have encountered in your wanderings," said my spiritual Father. "It was with great pleasure and interest that I listened to what you told me before."

"I shall do it gladly," I answered, "for I have lived through many things, good and bad. But it would take a long time to tell of them all; besides, I have already forgotten a great deal; I have always tried to remember only that which guided and urged my indolent soul to prayer. All the rest I remember but rarely Or rather, I try to forget the past, as the Apostle Paul bids us. My late elder of blessed memory also used to say that forces opposed to the prayer in the heart assail us from two sides, from the right hand and the left. In other words, if the enemy cannot distract us from prayer by means of vain and sinful thoughts, he brings back edifying reminiscences into our minds, or fills them with beautiful ideas so that he may draw us away from the Prayer—a thing which he cannot bear. This is called 'a theft from the right side,' where the soul, forgetting its intercourse with God, revels in a colloquy with itself or with other created things. Therefore, he taught me to shut myself off from even the most sublime spiritual thoughts whenever I am at prayer. And if at the end of the day I remembered that more time had been given to lofty ideas and talks than to the essential secret prayer of the heart, I was to consider it a sign of spiritual covetousness and immoderation.

"Yet, one cannot forget everything. An impression may have engraved itself so profoundly in one's memory that although it seems to be gone, it comes back in all its clarity even after a long while. Such are, for example, the few days God deemed me worthy to stay with a certain pious family:

One day as I was wandering through the province of Tobolsk, I found myself in a certain district town. My provision of rusk had run low, so I went to one of the houses to ask for some bread for my journey. The owner of the house told me: "Thank God you have come at the right time. My wife has just taken the bread out of the oven. Here you are, take this warm loaf. Remember us in your prayers." I thanked him and was putting the bread into my knapsack when his wife saw it and said: "Your knapsack is pretty worn-out. I'll give you another instead," and she gave me a new and a stout one. I thanked them again from the bottom of my heart and went away. Before leaving the town I asked in a little shop for a bit of salt, and the shopkeeper gave me a small bag of it. I rejoiced in spirit and thanked God for letting me, unworthy as I was, meet such kind people. "Now," I thought, "I have not to worry about food for a whole week and shall sleep in peace. 'Bless the Lord, O my soul!'"

About five versts or so from that town, I passed through a poor village where I saw a little wooden church with lovely paintings and ornaments on its façade. I wished to honor the house of God and went up to the porch to pray. On the lawn beside the church, two little children, five or six years old, were playing. They might have been the parish priest's children, except that they were too well-dressed for that. After I had said my prayer, I went away. Scarcely had I gone a dozen steps when I heard them shout: "Dear beggar, dear beggar, stop!" The two mites I had just seen, a boy and a girl, were running after me. I stopped. They came up to me and took me by the hand. "Come with us to Mummy; she likes beggars," they said. "She will give you money for your journey."

"Where is your mummy?" I asked.

"Over there, behind the church, behind that little grove."

They led me to a beautiful garden in the midst of which stood a large manor-house. We went inside. How clean it was, and so beautifully furnished! In ran the lady of the house to greet me. "Welcome, welcome! God sent you to us. Where are you from? Sit down, sit down, dear." She took off my knapsack with her own hands, laid it on the table, and made me sit in a very soft chair. "Wouldn't you like something to eat, or perhaps some tea? Is there anything I can do for you?"

"I thank you most humbly," I answered, "but my bag is filled with food. As for tea, I do take it occasionally, but in our peasant way I am not used to it. But I shall pray that God may bless you for your kindness to strangers in the true spirit of the Gospel." As I said this I felt a strong urge to retire within myself. Prayer was bubbling in my heart and I needed peace and silence to give an outlet to its rising flame. I also wished to hide from others my sighs and tears, and the movements of my face and lips — these outward signs which follow Prayer. Therefore I got up and said: "Excuse me, Lady, but I must go now. May the Lord Jesus Christ be with you and your dear little children."

"Oh, no! God forbid that you should go now. I won't let you. My husband will be back in the evening. He is a magistrate in the district court. How delighted he will be to see you."

So I stayed to wait for her husband, and gave her a short account of my journey.

Dinner-time came and we sat down to table. Four other ladies came in, and we began our meal. When we had finished the first course, one of them got up, bowed to the icon and then to us. Then she went out; she returned with the second course and sat down again. Then another of the ladies in the same manner fetched the third course. Seeing this I asked: "May I venture to ask if these ladies are related to you?"

"Yes, indeed! They are my sisters. This is my cook and this is the coachman's wife; that one is the housekeeper; the other is my maid. They are married, all of them. We have no unmarried girls in the house."

The more I heard and saw all this, the more I wondered and thanked God for having brought me to these pious people. The Prayer was working strongly in my heart, and I wished to be alone, so as not to hinder its action. As we rose from the table, I said to the lady: "Surely you will want to rest after dinner, and I am so used to walking that I shall go to the garden for a while."

"I don't need a rest," said the lady. "Tell me something edifying, I will go to the garden with you. If you go alone the children will give you no peace. The moment they see you, they will not leave you at all. They have such a liking for beggars, brothers of Christ and pilgrims."

There was nothing I could do but go with her. We entered the garden. In order to remain silent myself, I bowed down to the ground before her and said: "Pray, tell me in the name of our Lord if you have lived that pious life very long. How did you come to it?"

"I will tell you the whole story," she answered: "My mother was a great-granddaughter of the bishop Joasaph, whose relics you may see in Belgorod. When she gave my husband and myself her motherly blessing, she bade us live as good Christians, to pray fervently but above all to carry out the greatest of all God's commandments, which is to love our neighbors, to feed and help beggarly brothers of Christ in humble simplicity, to bring up our children in the fear of God, and to treat the serfs as our own brothers. That is how we have been living here in retirement for the past ten years, trying to fulfill my mother's last wishes. We have a guesthouse for beggars. A few sick and crippled people are living there now. We may visit them tomorrow."

After we had gone indoors, her husband arrived. When he saw me, he greeted me with kindness. We kissed each other in a Christian and brotherly fashion. Then he led me to his own room, saying: "Come to my study, dear brother; bless my cell." We entered his study. How many books there were! and beautiful icons, too, and the life-giving Cross in full size, with a copy of the Gospels lying nearby. I said my prayer and turned to my host: "This is God's paradise here!" Then I asked what kind of books he had.

"I have a great many religious books," he replied. "Here are the lives of the Saints for the whole year, the works of St. John Chrysostom, Basil the Great and of many other theologians and philosophers. I also have many volumes of sermons by famous contemporary preachers. My library cost me five thousand rubles or so."

"Do you have anything on prayer?" I asked.

"Yes," he said, "I like very much to read about prayer. This is the very latest book on that subject written by a priest of St. Petersburg." He took out the book on the Lord's Prayer, and we began to read it with interest. After a while the lady came in and brought us tea, and the little ones dragged a silver basket full of cakes such as I have never eaten before in my life. The gentleman took the book from me and handed it to his wife, saying: "Now, we'll make her read, she does it very well. And we shall have tea meanwhile." The lady began reading and we listened. As I did so the prayer became active in my heart, and I listened to it. The longer she read, the more intense became my prayer, and it filled me with joy. Suddenly I saw something flickering quickly before my eyes in the air, and I thought that it was my late elder. I gave a start, but tried to hide it and said by way of apology: "Pardon me, I must have dozed off for a moment." Then I felt as if the soul of my elder had penetrated into my own or was giving light to it. There was a sort of light in my mind and a great many thoughts concerning the Prayer came to me in a flash. I crossed myself, trying to drive them away with my will as the lady finished the book and her husband asked me whether I liked it. We began to talk again.

"I liked it very much," I answered, "and 'Our Father' is the most sublime and the most precious of all the written prayers we Christians have, since it was given to us by our Lord Jesus Christ Himself. And the interpretation of the prayer which has just been read is a very good one, but it emphasizes mainly the active phase of Christian life, whereas in my reading of the Holy Fathers I have noticed a stress upon the speculative and mysterious side of it."

"In which of the Holy Fathers' works did you read this?"

"Well, for example, in the works of Maxim the Confessor and of Peter the Damascene as given in the *Philocalia*."

"Can you recall what they say? Do tell us."

"Why, certainly! The very first words of the prayer — 'Our Father who art in Heaven' are interpreted in your book as an appeal to the brotherly love we must feel for each other since we all are children of the same Father — and this is quite true. The Holy Fathers, however, give to them another explanation which is more spiritual and profound. They say that we should lift our mind upwards to the Heavenly Father and remember every moment that we find ourselves in the presence of God.

"The words 'Hallowed be Thy Name' are explained in your book in the following manner: we must be careful not to utter the Name of God without reverence, nor use it in false oaths; the Holy Name of God ought to be spoken in devotion but never in vain. Yet the mystical interpreters see here a direct call to inner prayer, so that the Most Holy Name of God may be engraved in the heart and hallowed by the self-acting prayer, and at the same time hallow all the feelings and powers of the soul. The words 'Thy Kingdom come' they interpret as a call to inward serenity, peace and spiritual contentment. Further, your book says that the words: 'give us our daily bread' must be understood as a request for the needs of our physical life, not in superfluousness, of course, but just that which we need for ourselves and for the help of our neighbors. But Maxim the Confessor understands by 'daily bread' the nourishment of the soul with the heavenly bread which is the Word of God and the union of the soul with God by meditation upon Him and praying to Him incessantly in the heart."

"Ah! This is a great thing. But for lay people the attainment of inner prayer is well-nigh impossible," exclaimed the gentleman. "We may deem ourselves fortunate if God helps us to say our ordinary prayers without laziness."

"Don't think that, father. If it were impossible, or too difficult, God would not have bidden us all to do it. His strength manifests itself in weakness. And the Holy Fathers, rich in experience, show us easier ways to attain to inner prayer. Naturally, to the hermit they point out special and higher methods of procedure. But lay people also find in their writings convenient means which truly lead them to inner prayer."

"I have never read anything about the matter," he said.

"Well, if you wish to hear it, I will read to you from the *Philocalia*," I said, taking out my book. I found in part three, page 48, the treatise of Peter the Damascene and began to read: "One must call upon the Name of God even more often than one takes a breath, at all times, in all places in any kind of work. The Apostle says: 'Pray incessantly,' that is, he teaches men to remember God always, everywhere and in all situations. Whatever you do, keep in your mind the Maker of all things. When you behold light, remember who gives it to you; when you see heaven and earth and sea and all that they contain, be in awe and give praise to their Creator. When you put on your clothes, remember whose gift they are and give thanks to Him who takes care of your needs. In a word, remember and praise God in all your actions, and then you will be praying incessantly and your soul will be filled with gladness."

"Now, you see yourself how simple and easy the way of incessant prayer is," I said. "It is within the reach of everyone who still retains some sort of human feelings."[8]

They were greatly pleased with this. My host embraced me and thanked me again and again. In a while we went to supper and the whole household of men and women sat down to table as before. How reverently quiet and silent they were during the meal! After we finished, all of us, including the children, prayed for a long time.

They had me read the *Acathistos* to Jesus the Most Lovable. Thereafter, the servants retired and the three of us remained alone. The
lady went out of the room for a while and then came back with a
pair of stockings and a white shirt which she gave me. I bowed
down to the ground before her and said: "I won't take stockings,
my dear Lady; we peasants are used to leg-bands." She left again and
this time brought one of her old dresses of thin, yellow material and
cut it into two leg-bands. Her husband observed: "O, my poor man!
his footwear is almost falling apart." In his turn he brought me his
large, new overshoes which are worn over the boots. "Go to the next
room," he said, "there is nobody there, and you can change your
shirt." I did so, and when I returned they made me sit down on a
chair to put on my new footwear. He wrapped my feet and legs in
the leg-bands, and she put on the shoes. At first I would not
let them, but they said: "Sit still and don't protest. Christ washed
the feet of His disciples." There was nothing I could do but obey,
and I began to weep. And they were weeping, too. After this the
lady retired for the night to the children's apartment and her husband took me to the summerhouse in the garden. There we had
a long talk, after which we slept for an hour or so till we heard the
Matins bells. We got ready and made our way to the church. The
lady of the house and her little children had already been there
for some time. We heard Matins; Mass began soon afterwards. I
could not help weeping when I saw the light on the faces of my
host and his family as they prayed and knelt in devotion.

After the service the masters, the priest, the servants and all the
beggars went to the dining room together. There were about forty
beggars, some of them crippled and sickly-looking. Among them
were children, too. All of us sat down at the table, and the meal
was silent and peaceful as usual. Summoning my courage, I whispered to my host: "In convents and monasteries they read lives of
the saints during meals. This could be done here. You have a set of
volumes of the lives of the saints for the whole year round."

My host nodded: "Yes, indeed!" and turning to his wife said:
"Let's do that, Masha. It will be most edifying! I will begin to read
at the next dinner, then it will be your turn, after you the Reverend
Father's and then all the brothers who can read will come next."

The priest, who had already begun his meal, said: "I'd love to listen. As for reading, with all respect, I should prefer not to. At home I am so busy that I don't know which way to turn from worries and obligations of all kinds. With that host of children and animals I must attend to my day is filled up. There is no time for reading or preparing sermons; I long ago forgot what I learned in the seminary."

Upon hearing this I shuddered, but the lady who was sitting beside me patted me on the hand and said: "Father talks like that out of sheer humility. He always belittles himself, but he is a most kindly and saintly man. He has been a widower for the last twenty years, and now takes care of his grandchildren, besides holding services very often." At these words I remembered the saying of Nicetas Stethatus in the *Philocalia:* "He who attains true prayer and love has no discrimination between things and sees no difference between the righteous man and a sinner, but loves them all and condemns no one, as God makes the sun shine and the rain fall upon both the just and the unjust."

Silence fell again. Opposite me sat a beggar who lived in the guest-house. He was quite blind and the host took care of him. He cut fish for him, handed him a spoon and poured his soup.

As I looked at the beggar closely, I noticed that his mouth was always open and his tongue was moving as though it were trembling. I wondered if he wasn't one of those who recite the Prayer, and I went on observing him. At the end of dinner an old woman fell suddenly ill; it must have been a serious attack, for she groaned from pain. The masters of the house took her into their bedroom and laid her on the bed. The lady remained there to look after her, and while the priest went to get the Reserved Sacrament, our host ordered his carriage and dashed to town to fetch a physician.

I felt as if I were hungry for the Prayer. The urge to pour out my soul was strong, yet I had had no privacy and peace for nearly forty-eight hours. There was in my heart something like a flood that was about to burst out and overflow all my limbs. My attempt to hold it back caused me a sharp, though delightful, pain in my heart— a pain that could be soothed and calmed only in prayer and silence. Now it became clear to me why those who truly practise self-acting inner prayer avoid men and flee into the solitude of unknown places. I understood also why the venerable Hesychius considers even the most spiritual and useful talk to be but idle chatter if it is too prolonged, just as Ephrem the Syrian says: "Good speech is silver, but silence is pure gold."

Musing upon the matter, I went to the guesthouse, where everybody was resting after dinner. I went up to the attic; there I calmed down, rested and prayed.

When the beggars got up, I found the blind man and led him to the kitchen garden; we sat down alone and began to talk. "Pray, tell me for the love of my soul," I said, "do you recite the Prayer of Jesus?"

"Yes, indeed! I have been saying it without ceasing for a long time."

"What do you feel when you do so?"

"Only this, that I cannot live without praying day or night."

"How did God reveal it to you? Tell me about it in detail, dear brother."

"You see, I am a craftsman here. I used to earn my living by tailoring. I journeyed to other provinces, going from village to village and making peasant clothes. It happened that I lived for a long time in one village in the home of a peasant for whose family I was working. On some feast day I noticed three books lying by the icons and asked, 'Who is it can read them?'—'No one,' I was told. 'These books belonged to our uncle, who was very proficient in reading.' I took out one of these books, opened it at random and read the following words which I remember to this day: 'Incessant prayer is calling upon the Name of God at all times. Whether one is talking or sitting down, walking, working or eating, or whatever one may be doing, it is meet that one should call on the Name of God in all the places and at all times.' When I read this I thought how easy this would be for me, and I began to do it behind my sewing machine and liked it. People who lived with me noticed it and made fun of me: 'What are you whispering all the time?' they asked. 'Are you a witch-master trying to cast a spell over someone?' I stopped moving my lips so as to hide what I was doing and continued saying the Prayer with the tongue only and grew so accustomed to it that my tongue says it by itself day and night. I went about my business for a long time and then all of a sudden I became completely blind. In my family almost everyone got 'dark water' in the eyes. Because of my poverty our people placed me in the almshouse at Tobolsk — the capital of our province. I am on my way there now, but our hosts have kept me here, for they want to give me a cart to Tobolsk."

"What was the title of the book you read? Wasn't it called the *Philocalia?*"

"Frankly I couldn't tell. I did not look at the title page."

I brought my *Philocalia* and found in part four those very words of the Patriarch Callistus which the blind man recited by heart, and read them to him.

"Why! these are exactly the same words," he exclaimed. "Go on with your reading, brother. Isn't it wonderful!"

When I came to the line that "one must pray with the heart," he asked me with surprise: "What does it mean? How can this be done?"

I told him that a complete instruction on the prayer of heart was given in the same book, called the *Philocalia*, and he urged me to read it to him.

"Well, this is what we ought to do," I said. "When are you planning to leave for Tobolsk?"

"Right away, if you wish me to."

"All right, then. I am starting on my way tomorrow. We'll go together; I will read you all the passages which deal with prayer of the heart, and I will tell you how to find your heart and enter it."

"But how about the cart?" he asked.

"Ah, what do you need the cart for? Tobolsk is not too far, a mere hundred and fifty versts. We'll walk by easy stages, all by ourselves, you and I, talking and reading about the Prayer as we go." So, our plans were made.

In the evening our host himself came to call us to supper. After the meal, we told him, the blind man and myself, that we were starting on our journey together. We explained that we did not need a cart, for we wished to read the *Philocalia* with more leisure.

The next morning we took the road after thanking our hosts most warmly for their great kindness and love. Both of them came with us about a verst from their house, and then we parted, bidding farewell to each other.

We walked in a leisurely fashion, the blind man and I, doing from ten to fifteen versts a day. And the remainder of our time we spent in lonely spots reading the *Philocalia*. When we had finished the required passages, he begged me to show him the means by which the mind may find the heart, and the divine Name of Jesus may be brought into it so that we could pray sweetly with the heart.

"Well," I said, "when you fix your eyes upon your hand or your foot, can't you picture them as clearly as if you were seeing them, although you are blind?"

"Indeed, I can," he answered.

"Then try to imagine your heart in the same way; fix your eyes upon it as if they were looking through your breast; picture it as vividly as you can, and listen attentively to its beating. When you have grown used to it, begin to time the words of the prayer with the beats of your heart. Thus, say or think 'Lord' with the first beat, 'Jesus' with the second, 'Christ' with the third, 'have mercy' with the fourth and 'on me' with the fifth. Repeat it over and over again. This you can do easily, for you have already made the preparation and the beginning of the prayer of the heart. Later, you must learn how to bring in and out of your heart the whole Prayer of Jesus, timing it with your breathing, as the Fathers taught. While inhaling, say, or imagine that you are saying, 'Lord Jesus Christ', and, as you breathe out, 'have mercy on me.' Repeat it as often as you can; in a short while your heart will hurt you, but in a light and pleasant way: and the feeling of warmth will spread throughout your whole body. However, beware of imagination! Don't let yourself be lured by visions of any kind. Ward them off, for the Holy Fathers bid urgently that the inner prayer should remain free from visions, lest we fall into delusions."

My blind friend listened to all this carefully and started at once to do what I had told him. At night-fall, when we stopped for a rest, he devoted himself to this practice for a long time. In about five days he began to feel in his heart a delightful warmth as well as a joy beyond words and a longing for incessant prayer which stirred up in him the love for Jesus Christ. At certain times he saw light, though he could not discern objects. At other times, it seemed to him, when he entered the region of his heart, as though the flame of a burning candle flared up brightly in his bosom, and rushing outwards through his throat, filled him with light. And in this light he could see distant events, as it happened on one occasion when we were going through the forest. He was silent, wholly absorbed in the Prayer. "What a pity," he cried all of a sudden. "The church is on fire and the tower has just collapsed."

"Stop imagining things," I said to him. "This is a temptation to you — nothing but idle fancies which must be put aside. How can anyone see what is happening in the city? It is still twelve versts away." He obeyed and continued to pray in silence. When we came to the city towards evening, I actually saw there a few burnt houses and the fallen belfry which had been built on wooden piles. There were throngs of people marveling that it had not crushed any one when it fell. As I figured it out, the catastrophe had occurred at exactly the time when the blind man had told me about it.

He turned to me and said: "You told me that this vision of mine was an idle fancy, but now you see that it was not. How can I fail to love and to thank our Lord Jesus Christ who shows His grace even to sinners, the blind and the unlearned? And I thank you, too, for having taught me how to attain the inner activity of the heart."

"Surely, you must love Jesus Christ and thank Him for His mercy," I answered, "but guard yourself from believing that your visions are a direct revelation of grace. They may occur frequently in a perfectly natural order of things. For neither space nor matter can bind the human soul. It cannot only see in darkness, but also things that are a long way off, as well as those which are nearby. Only we fail to develop this spiritual power to its fullest extent. We suppress it within our crude bodies, or crush it beneath the confusion of our muddled thoughts and ideas. But when we begin to concentrate, when we retire within ourselves and become more sensitive and subtle in the mind, then the soul fulfills its purpose and unfolds its highest power. This process is a natural one. I have heard from my departed elder that even people who are not given to prayer, but who are endowed with that kind of power or acquire

it in sickness, can see in the darkest room the light flowing from
every object and can perceive things in that light. They can even
see their own doubles and enter into the thoughts of other people.
However, all that comes directly from the grace of God by the
prayer of the heart is filled with such sweetness and delight that no
tongue can describe it, nor can it be compared to anything in the
material world. For anything sensual is inferior when compared
with the sweet realization of the grace in the heart."

My blind companion listened attentively and became more humble than ever. The Prayer grew stronger and stronger in his heart
and filled him with an ineffable delight. With all my soul I rejoiced
at all this, and zealously thanked God who judged me worthy to
see such a blessed servant of His.

At last we reached Tobolsk. I took him to the almshouse and left
him there, bidding him a loving farewell. Then, once more, I set
off on my way.

For about a month I went along at leisure, thinking of the way
in which pure lives spur us on to follow their examples. I read the
Philocalia attentively and re-examined everything I had told the
devout blind man. His eagerness fired me with zeal, gratitude and
love for God, and the prayer of the heart filled me with such gladness that I could not imagine a happier person on earth. Often I
wondered whether the bliss in the Kingdom of Heaven could be
greater and fuller. Not only did I feel happy within my soul, but
the outside world, too, appeared delightful to me. Everything I
saw aroused in me love and thankfulness to God; people, trees,
plants, animals were all my kind, for I saw in all of them the reflection of the Name of Jesus Christ. At times I felt as light as if I were
bodiless and floating blissfully in the air. At other times, when I
retired within myself, I was able to see my internal organs, and mar-
veled at the wisdom with which the human body is formed. Then
again I felt a joy as if I had been made Tsar, and at such moments of
rapture I wished that God would let me die soon, so that I might
pour out my gratitude at His feet in the realm of the spirits . . .

"I was led to experience a great many other things," I said,
looking at my spiritual father, "but I should need more than

three days and nights to relate to you all that happened. Still, there is one more incident I might tell you about:

One bright summer day I noticed at the side of the road a church-yard — what is usually called a *pogost* — (that is, a cemetery) a church and clergy-houses. The bells were ringing and I went to Mass with the people who lived in the neighborhood. Some of them sat down on the ground before they reached the church. Seeing that I was hurrying along, they told me not to rush: "When the service begins, you'll have to stand about for ages. The Mass here takes a long time. Our priest is sickly and slow."

As a matter of fact, the service did last a very long time. The priest was still young but emaciated and pale; he celebrated slowly but with great devotion, and his sermon at the end of the Mass was simple and beautiful. He preached of the way of acquiring the love of God.

After the Mass he invited me to his house and had me stay for dinner. I said to him while we sat at the table: "How slowly and reverently you celebrate, Father!"

"Yes, though my parishioners do not seem to like it," he answered. "They grumble, but I can't help it. For I believe that words uttered without inward feeling and attention are useless to myself as well as to others. What really matters is the inner life and intense prayer. But only few are concerned with the inner life. The reason is that they do not care about inward enlightenment."

"And how can one attain it?" I asked. "Is is not very difficult?"

"Not in the least," was the reply. "To attain spiritual enlightenment and become a person of serene inner life, you must take one of the texts of the Holy Scripture and meditate upon it for a long time with all your power of concentration and attention. Then the light of true knowledge will be revealed to you. The same thing may be said about the prayer. If you wish it to be pure, right and sweet take up one of the short prayers of few but strong words, and repeat it often and for a long time. Then you will savor prayer."

This instruction of the priest pleased me greatly. How practical and simple it was, and yet so profound and wise! I thanked God in my mind for showing me so good a pastor of His Church.

When we finished our meal, the priest said: "Take a rest after dinner while I read my Bible and prepare my sermon for tomorrow." I therefore made my way to the kitchen. There was no one there except a very old woman who crouched in the corner, coughing. I sat down at a small window and took the *Philocalia* out of my knapsack. As I was reading it quietly to myself, I heard the old woman in the corner incessantly whispering the Jesus Prayer. Rejoicing at the most holy Name of our Lord spoken so often, I told her: "What a good thing you do, mother, by saying the Prayer constantly. It is a most Christian and most salutary one!" "Oh, yes!" she answered. "This is the only joy I have left in my life. 'Lord, have mercy on me.' "

"Have you been in the habit of saying this Prayer for very long?"

"Ever since my early youth! How could I live without it, for the Prayer of Jesus saved me from destruction and death."

"How is that? Pray, tell me about it for the glory of God and the blessed power of the Jesus Prayer." I put the *Philocalia* into my knapsack and came closer, ready to listen to her story. She told me thus:

"I was a pretty girl when I was young. My parents were about to give me away in marriage, and on the eve of the wedding my bridegroom came to see us. Suddenly, when he was about a dozen paces from our house, he collapsed and died without regaining his breath. This terrified me so that I refused to marry and made up my mind to live in virginity and prayer. Though I longed for pilgrimages to holy places, I dared not go all by myself, for I was quite young and feared that wicked people might harm me. Then, an old woman pilgrim I knew taught me to recite incessantly the Prayer of Jesus in all my wanderings. If I did so, she assured me, no misfortune could ever befall me on my journey. I trusted her and, sure enough, I walked even to far-off shrines many times, and never came to grief. My parents gave me money for my travels. As I grew old and my health failed me, the priest here out of the kindness of the heart, provided me with board and lodging."

I listened to her with joy and did not know how to thank God for this day in which I had learned so much by these edifying ex-

amples of the spiritual life. Then, asking the kindly priest for his
blessing, I started off on my way in gladness . . .

Having finished these tales, I said to my spiritual father:
"Forgive me in God's name; I have already talked too much,
and the Holy Fathers call even spiritual talk idle chatter if it is
prolonged. It is time for me to meet my fellow-traveler to Jerusalem. Pray for me, a wretched sinner, that God in His mercy
may prosper me on my journey."

"With all my soul I wish it, my beloved brother in the Lord,"
he answered. "May the all-loving grace of God overshadow your
way and guide you as the Angel Raphael guided Tobias."

JOHN OF CRONSTADT

A GENIUS OF PRAYER

JOHN During the last two decades of his life Father John Sergieff (1829-1908) acquired a wide reputation among the Orthodox population of Russia as a living saint and a great thaumaturge; even now many devout people expect that he will be canonized. The extraordinary significance of his personality is in the fact that Father John was not a monk or a hermit or even a staretz of the kind represented by St. Seraphim or the startzy of the Optina cloister, but a secular, married priest with a parish in the fortress town of Cronstadt close by the capital, St. Petersburg. No member of the secular clergy has found a place in the calendar of Russian saints and, as a matter of fact, the secular clergy as a social class has never been held in good repute by the Russian people. If a new "spiritual" type of priest has become more common during the last generation, this is partly attributable to the example and inspiration of Father John.

The life of John of Cronstadt was one of the simplest, lacking in all dramatic external events. He was the son of a poor village deacon in a remote northern province of Arkhangelsk. Although he was by no means brilliantly gifted intellectually, he nevertheless succeeded in passing through all the stages of education for the priesthood, including the highest, that of the theological academy in St. Petersburg. He was appointed to the parish of Cronstadt in 1855 and never abandoned this modest living to avail himself of a more advantageous position. His spiritual growth was gradual, marked by no crises of conversion. After three decades, his influence had spread far beyond the limits of his small town; from all parts of Russia people came to him, or sent telegrams imploring his prayers for the sick and dying. Sometimes he made journeys in order to give assistance to persons whose difficulties required his presence. Some of those who took counsel with him belonged to the social élite, and he was known and loved in the court of the last two tsars. When Alexander III was dying (1894) in Livadia (Crimea), Father John was called from Cronstadt to administer the last Sacrament.

During the long term of his priesthood Father John preached a great number of sermons, which were collected in various editions, but more important than these is the spiritual diary which was published under the title My Life in Christ. This consists of a great number of brief entries on a variety of subjects, in no particular order; the theological headings under which the excerpts of our selection are classified are those of the English editors Bickersteth and Illingworth, who abridged the first English translation, by E. E. Gulaeff.

From his diary and the reminiscences of a vast number of his contemporaries concerning him, the salient features of Father John's spirituality can be grasped. Perhaps in the present context the originality of his religious genius can best be realized by what might be called the negative approach: a statement of what he was not.

First of all, Father John was not an ascetic but was content with rejecting the world interiorly and living according to the precepts of the Church. He was not a mystic in any strict sense, nor indeed a contemplative with a taste for solitude. He was not given to the practice of any technique of mental prayer and based none of his teaching on the Philocalia. The chief source of his inspiration, apart from his own intuitions, was the Bible, both the Old Testament and the New, which he quotes abundantly. He had not even an inclination towards the kenoticism of ancient Russia: not only did he not seek humiliation, but he had an innocent weakness for rich silken cassocks given him by his admirers, and his portraits show him with his breast covered with cordons, stars, and crosses.

In all these characteristics is will be seen that he deviates sharply from the main pattern of Russian sanctity. But, to take the positive approach to his character: he was most certainly a charitable man, a great benefactor of the poor; through his hands enormous sums passed to be distributed among the needy. Yet the works of charity were not his chief claim to distinction. Although he was active and generous in both the spiritual and corporal works of mercy, he did not radiate the angelic love of a Seraphim, nor was spiritual guidance, as a prolonged, attentive, training of souls, his vocation. His specific role was that of a praying priest. He was a genius of prayer and a teacher of prayer. All his works of healing were effected by insistent, assiduous prayer, usually in union with the prayer of his patients and their friends. He was simply convinced that God cannot refuse to hear the prayer of insistent petition accompanied by the oblation of self.

The first quality of his prayer was its power. He knew, of course, the sweetness of prayer, but he did not seek it. He was not disinterested in the fashion of a mystic, but went into the presence of God to intercede for a soul, to obtain forgiveness for sin, or to pour out his troubled heart. His prayer was as intense and emotional as that of a prophet; it was miracle-working prayer. Its foundation was an extremely alert and constant awareness of the presence of God. The reality of the invisible, for Father John, was overwhelming, immediate, experimental; his faith was neither theoretical nor symbolical, but intense; he knew temptation and sin indeed, but apparently doubt was not part of his experience.

As a priest, Father John had a fruitful experience of liturgical prayer, and the influence he exerted in bringing the Eucharist to the fore was his chief legacy to the Russian Church. Whenever he celebrated Mass, he was penetrated by a vivid awareness of the transcendent drama which was being enacted. He could not keep the prescribed measure of liturgical intonation: he called out to God; he shouted; he wept in face of the visions of Golgotha and the Resurrection which presented themselves to him with such shattering immediacy. To him the liturgical mystery was a profound, living experience, and he was eager for the active participation of the congregation in it. In contradiction of the unfortunate practice still prevalent in Russia of rare, for the most part yearly, communion, he demanded that all who came to his church should communicate with him. The Russian custom prescribes confession immediately preceding each communion. Since Father John could obviously not hear the confessions in private of thousands at each Mass, he daringly established the unheard-of practice of general, vocal confession. It was an impressive, even a terrifying, spectacle: thousands of people shouting aloud their most secret sins and sobbing for forgiveness; all the barriers of ecclesiastical order and propriety were transgressed. Only a friend of the tsar could have been permitted to introduce such an innovation. No priest in Russia ventured to follow Father John's example with regard to vocal confession, but the practice of frequent communion was now initiated. Father John had set in motion the Eucharistic and liturgical revival in the Russian Church.

This was the single instance of initiative in reform on the part of John of Cronstadt; otherwise, his attitude towards the Church was that of conservative obedience. Living outside modern cultural movements, he remained untouched by the liberal thought of his time, and retained political views which were likewise highly conservative. He never separated in his mind the destiny of the Russian monarchy from that of the Church, and when the first revolution came (1905), drawing with it not only the intelligentsia but also the great masses of peasants and workers, Father John stood with the extreme reactionaries for the imperial absolutism. At that time he became the target of all the liberal papers and was hated in left-wing circles above all prominent figures of the day. It must indeed be admitted that his views on social questions were very narrow and medieval, but as a teacher of prayer, he will live in the memory of the Russian people.

MY LIFE IN CHRIST

By *JOHN SERGIEFF*

PRAYER

The Spirit of Prayer

PRAYER IS THE LIFTING UP OF THE MIND AND HEART TO GOD, THE CONTEMPLATION OF GOD, THE DARING CONVERSE OF THE creature with the Creator, the soul reverently standing before Him, as before the King and the Life Itself, giving life to all; the oblivion of everything that surrounds us, the food of the soul; its air and light, its lifegiving warmth, its cleansing from sin; the easy yoke of Christ, His light burden. Prayer is the constant feeling (the recognition) of our infirmity or spiritual poverty, the sanctification of the soul, the foretaste of future blessedness, angelic bliss, the heavenly rain, refreshing, watering, and fertilising the ground of the soul, the power and strength of the soul and body, the purifying and freshening of the mental air, the enlightenment of the countenance, the joy of the spirit, the golden link, uniting the creature to the Creator, courage and valour in all the afflictions and temptations of life, the lamp of life, success in all undertakings, dignity equal with the angels, the strengthening of faith, hope and love. Prayer is intercourse with the holy angels and saints, who pleased God since the beginning of the world. Prayer is the amendment of life, the mother of heartfelt contrition and tears; a powerful motive for works of mercy; security of life; the destruction of the fear of death; the disdain of earthly treasures; the desire for heavenly blessings; the expectation of the universal Judge, of the common resurrection and of the life of the world to come; a strenuous effort to save ourselves from eternal torments; unceasing seeking for mercy (forgiveness) of the Sovereign; walking before God; the blissful vanishing of self before the all-creating and all-filling Creator; the living water of the soul. Prayer is holding all men in our hearts through love; the descent of heaven into the soul; the abiding of the most Holy Trinity in the soul, in accordance with that which has been said: "We will come to him and will make Our abode with him."

The Lord is so near to each one, especially to the Christian who leads a holy life, that his heart and body are the temple of the Holy Ghost. "Know you not that your members are the temple of the Holy Ghost who is in you?" Therefore, how easy it is to pray in every place! The word of the prayer, or God, to Whom you pray, "is nigh thee, even in thy mouth, and in thy heart."

"It is good for me to adhere to my God," said David, who had tasted the sweetness of prayer and praising God. Other men confirm this, and I a sinner also. Observe, even here on earth, to draw near to God is a good and blessed thing (while we are yet in the sinful flesh, which has much that is agreeable and disagreeable in itself). Therefore, what blessedness it will be to be united to God there, in heaven! And the blessedness of union with God here on earth is a specimen and pledge of the blessedness of union with God after death, in eternity. You see, then, how good, merciful, and true the Creator is! In order to assure you of the future blessedness proceeding from union with Him, He allows you to experience the beginning of this blessedness here on earth when you approach Him sincerely. Yes, even here my invisible soul rests in the invisible God; therefore it will still more perfectly rest in Him when it is separated from the body.

The invisible God acts upon my soul as if He were visible, as if He were present here before me, knowing all my thoughts and feelings; every inward slothfulness, stubbornness, or other passion is always accompanied by a corresponding punishment. In general, if my inward disposition is unworthy of God, of His holiness, then I suffer punishment for it in my heart, a devouring fire; and if it is a worthy one, then I am joyful and at peace.

My heart finds its peace in the highest, in spiritual things and not in earthly and material ones. Grant, Lord, that I may ever meditate on the highest, and entirely renounce earthly wisdom. My trust is in Thy goodness! "I have lifted up my eyes to the mountains, from whence help shall come to me."

Prayer is the living water, by means of which the soul quenches its thirst. When you pray, represent to yourself as though God alone were before you, God in Three Persons, and besides Him no one else. Represent to yourself that God is in the world as the soul is in the body, though He is infinitely higher than the world, and is not limited by it. Your body is small, and it is wholly penetrated by your small soul; the world is large, but God is infinitely great, and fills everything throughout the whole of creation—"Who is everywhere present, and filleth all things."

For the soul of the pious, God-fearing man there is an invisible spiritual intercourse with God. Like a father or a stern teacher, the Lord at one time approves, at another condemns our thoughts, desires and intentions; at one time He says that this is good, and that bad. He rewards us for the good and punishes us for the evil; and all this is at once evident to the soul.

Though God knows all our needs, prayer is necessary for the cleansing and enlightenment of our soul. It is well to stand in the sunshine: it is warm and light; likewise, when standing in prayer before God, our spiritual Sun, we are warmed and enlightened.

The best moments on earth are those during which we meditate upon heavenly things in general, when we recognise or defend the truth, that heavenly dweller and denizen. Only then do we truly live. Therefore, the essential interests of the soul require that we should oftener rise above the earth, upwards to heaven, where is our true life, our true country, which shall have no end.

Why is long-continued prayer necessary? In order that by prolonged, fervent prayer we may warm our cold hearts, hardened in prolonged vanity. For it is strange to think, and still more so to require, that the heart, hardened in worldly vanity, could be speedily penetrated during prayer by the warmth of faith and the love of God. No; labour and labour, time and time are needed to attain this. "The kingdom of heaven suffereth violence and the violent bear it away." The Kingdom of heaven does not soon come into the heart when men themselves so assiduously flee from it. The Lord Himself expresses His will that our prayers should not be short, by giving us for an example the importunate widow who often came to the judge and troubled him with her requests. Our Lord, our Heavenly Father knows, even before we ask Him, what things we have need of, what we want; but we do not know Him as we ought, for we give ourselves up to worldly vanity, instead of committing ourselves into the hands of our Heavenly Father. Therefore in His wisdom and mercy He turns our needs into a pretext for our turning to Him. "Turn ye, My wandering children, even now unto Me, to your Father, with your whole hearts. If before you were far from Me, even now, at least, warm by faith and love to Me your hearts which were formerly cold."

Lord! grant me a simple, kind, open, believing, loving, and generous heart, worthy of being Thy dwelling-place, O most gracious One!

Faith in Prayer

The chief thing in prayer for which we must care above all is—lively, clear-sighted faith in the Lord: represent Him vividly before yourself and within you—then ask of Jesus Christ in the Holy Ghost whatever you desire and you will obtain it. Ask simply, without the slightest doubt—then your God will be everything to you, accomplishing in an instant great and wonderful acts, as the sign of the cross accomplishes great wonders. Ask for both spiritual and material blessings not only for yourself, but for all believers, for the whole body of the Church, not separating yourself from other believers, but in spiritual union with them, as a member of the one great body of the Church of Christ, and loving all, as your brethren or children in Christ, as the case may be. The Heavenly Father will fill you with great peace and boldness.

Prayer breathes hope, and a prayer without hope is a sinful prayer.

When you are praying, either inwardly only, or both inwardly and outwardly, be firmly convinced that the Lord is there, by you and within you, and hears every word, even if only said to yourself, even when you only pray mentally; speak from your whole heart, without in the least justifying yourself; have faith that the Lord will have mercy upon you—and you will not remain unforgiven. This is true. It is taken from experience.

Believe and trust that as it is easy for you to breathe the air and live by it, or to eat and drink, so it is easy and even still easier for your faith to receive all spiritual gifts from the Lord. Prayer is the breathing of the soul; prayer is our spiritual food and drink.

Prayer is founded upon faith. I believe that there is a God, before whom I lay my prayer, that there is an Almighty, holding all creatures in the palm of His hand, and giving various kinds of voices to His creatures, for inward intercourse amongst themselves, but not needing any voice Himself. I trust that my prayer will reach Him, or, to speak more exactly, will go direct from my heart to His ears. Similarly, the correspondence of a son with his father or mother, or between brothers and sisters, or that of a father with his children, or between friends at a distance from each other, is also founded on faith. They are sure when writing letters that the persons to whom they write are alive; they trust that their written conversation will reach them, will produce certain impressions, ideas, and feelings, corresponding to those expressed in the letter, and that they will answer the letter in accordance with its contents. As in life we are guided in many things by faith and hope, so much more in relation to the spiritual world should we "walk by faith and not by sight."

Prayer hopes to receive all things. Thrice-radiant Love, have mercy upon me!

All you who draw near to serve God in prayer learn to be like Him, meek, humble, and true of heart; do not let there be any deceitfulness or duplicity or coldness in your soul. Strive to have His Spirit, for "if any man have not the Spirit of Christ, he is none of His." The Lord seeks in us that which is like and akin to Himself, on to which His grace may be grafted. Remember that not a single word is lost during prayer, if you say it from your heart; God hears each word, and weighs it in a balance. Sometimes it seems to us that our words only strike the air in vain, and sound as the voice of one crying in the wilderness. No, no; it is not so! We must remember that God understands us when we pray, that is, our words, just as those who pray perfectly understand the words themselves, for man is God's image. The Lord responds to every desire of the heart, expressed in words or unexpressed.

Glory to the never failing power of Thy cross, O Lord! When the enemy oppresses me by sinful thoughts and feelings, and I, having no freedom in my heart, make the sign of the cross several times with faith, then my sin suddenly passes away from me, the straitness vanishes, and I obtain freedom. Glory to Thee, Lord! Lord, let nothing, nothing carnal, material, turn me away from Thee! Let me always be with Thee! How good it is to be with Thee!

Humility in Prayer

Prayer is the proof of my reasonable personality, of my likeness to God, the pledge of my future godliness and blessedness. I was created from nothing. I am nothing before God, as having nothing of my own; but, by the mercy of God, I am a being endued with reason, with a heart, with free will, and by my reason and freedom I can, by turning with my heart to Him, continually increase in myself His infinite kingdom, increase more and more His gifts in me, draw from Him, as from an everflowing inexhaustible source, every blessing, both spiritual and material, especially spiritual ones. Prayer instils in me that I am the image of God, that by the humble and thankful disposition of my soul before God, and by my free will, I infinitely increase in myself the spiritual gifts of God, that I can thus infinitely improve myself and can increase to infinity my likeness to God, my heavenly blessedness to which I am predestined. Oh! prayer is the sign of the great dignity with which the

Creator has honored me. But at the same time it reminds me of my nothingness (I am nothing, and have nothing of my own; therefore, I ask God for everything) and of my most high dignity (I am an image of God; I am made godly; I may be called the friend of God, like Abraham, the father of believers, if only I believe undoubtingly in the existence, mercy, and omnipotence of my God, and strive to become like unto Him during this life by works of love and mercy).

During prayer a sincere seeking after amendment is indispensable.

Pronounce the words of the prayer with heartfelt firmness. When praying in the evening, do not forget to confess in prayer to the Holy Ghost with all sincerity and contrition those sins into which you have fallen during the past day. A few moments of fervent repentance, and you will be cleansed by the Holy Ghost from every impurity; you will be whiter than snow, and tears, purifying the heart, will flow from your eyes; you will be covered with the garment of Christ's righteousness and united to Him, together with the Father and the Holy Ghost.

The insensibility of the heart during prayer to the truth of the words of the prayer proceeds from the heart's unbelief and insensibility, of its sinfulness; and these, in their turn, emanate from a secret feeling of pride. In accordance with the measure of his feelings during prayer a man recognises whether he is proud or humble; the more feeling, the more ardent the prayer is, the more humble he is; whilst the more unfeeling and cold it is, the prouder he is.

Lord! I am Thy vessel: fill me with the gifts of Thy Holy Spirit. Without Thee I am void of every blessing—or, rather, full of every sin. Lord! I am Thy ship: fill me with the cargo of good works. Lord! I am Thy ark: fill me, not with the allurement of love of money and pleasures, but with love for Thee and Thy living image, man.

Sincerity in Prayer

Concerning hypocritical prayer. Did the Pharisees think that they prayed hypocritically? They did not think so; they considered themselves to be right in their hypocrisy itself! It had become their habit; it had become, so to say, their nature; and they thought they were serving God by their prayer. Do the Christian hypocrites of the present day think that they pray and live hypocritically? They do not think so. They pray daily, perhaps long; they pray out of habit with their lips, but not with their hearts, without hearty contrition, without a firm desire for amendment, and only in order to fulfil the established rule, and "think" that they do "God service," whilst by their prayer they only incur the wrath of God. We all more or less sin in praying hypocritically, and shall be greatly censured for this. Humble yourself, consider yourself as the grass, which is worthless in comparison to the ancient oak-trees, or as a prickly thorn, which is nothing, which is worthless in comparison to the fragrant and delicate flowers; for you are indeed grass; you are indeed a prickly thorn, by reason of your passions.

Outward prayer is often performed at the expense of inward prayer, and inward at the expense of outward; that is, when I pray with my lips or read, if many words do not penetrate into the heart, I become double-minded and hypocritical; with my lips I say one thing, whilst in my heart I feel another. The lips speak truth, whilst the disposition of the heart does not agree with the words of the prayer. But if I pray inwardly, heartily, then, without paying attention to the pronunciation of the words, I concentrate upon their contents, their power, gradually accustoming my heart to the truth, and thus entering into the same disposition of spirit in which the words of the prayer were written. In this way I accustom myself, little by little, to pray in spirit and truth in accordance with the words of the Eternal Truth: "They that adore Him must adore Him in spirit and in truth." When a man prays outwardly aloud, then he cannot always follow all the movements of his heart, which are so rapid that he is necessarily obliged to pay attention to the pronunciation of the words, and to their outward form. Thus the prayers of many of the clergy who read rapidly become quite untrue: with their lips they seem to pray; in appearance they are pious, but their hearts are asleep, and do not know what their lips say. This proceeds from the fact that they hurry, and do not meditate in their hearts upon what they are saying. We must pray for them, as they pray for us; we must pray that their words may penetrate into their hearts and breathe warmth into them. They pray for us in the words of holy persons, and we must pray for them also.

Forced prayer develops hypocrisy, renders a man incapable of any occupation requiring meditation, and makes him slothful in everything, even in fulfilling his duties. This should persuade all who pray in this manner to correct their mode of praying. We must pray gladly, with energy, from the whole heart. Do not pray to God only when you are obliged to, either in sorrow or in need, for "God loveth a cheerful giver."

During prayer always firmly believe and remember that every thought and word of yours may, undoubtedly, become deeds. "Because no word shall be impossible with God." "But he who is joined to the Lord is one spirit." This signifies that even your words shall not be without power. "All things are possible to him that believeth." Take heed of your words; the word is precious. "Every idle word that men shall speak, they shall render an account for it in the day of judgment."

Perseverance in Prayer

It is said that we soon grow weary of praying. Wherefore? Because we do not vividly represent to ourselves the Lord, Who is at our right hand. Look upon Him unceasingly with the eyes of your heart, and then, even if you stand praying all night, you will not grow weary. What do I say—all night? You will be able to stand thus praying two and three nights without growing weary. Remember the Stylites. They stood for many years in a prayerful disposition of soul on pillars or columns, and mastered their flesh, which was the same as yours, and which was also inclined to slothfulness. And you feel oppressed by a few hours' public prayers, even by one hour's prayers.

People say that if you feel no inclination to pray, it is better not to pray; but this is crafty, carnal sophistry. If you only pray when you are inclined to, you will completely cease praying; this is what the flesh desires. "The kingdom of heaven suffereth violence." You will not be able to work out your salvation without forcing yourself.

Our heart daily dies spiritually. Only ardent, tearful prayer quickens it, and makes it begin to breathe again. If we do not daily pray with sufficient spiritual fervour, we may easily and speedily die spiritually.

Hindrances to Prayer

During prayer there sometimes occur moments of deadly darkness and spiritual anguish arising from unbelief of the heart (for unbelief is darkness). Do not let your heart fail you at such moments, but remember that if the Divine light has been cut off from you, it always shines in all its splendour and greatness in God Himself, in God's Church, in heaven and on earth, and in the material world in which "His eternal power also and divinity" are visible. Do not think that truth has failed, because truth is God Himself, and everything that exists has its foundation and reason in Him. Only your own weak, sinful and darkened heart can fail in the truth, for it cannot always bear the strength of the light of truth, and is not always capable of containing its purity, but only if it is being, or has been, purified from its sins, as the first cause of spiritual darkness.. The proof of this you may find in yourself. When the light of faith or God's truth dwells in your heart, only then is it tranquil, firm, strong, and living; but when this is cut off, then your heart becomes uneasy, weak as a reed shaken by the wind, and lifeless. Do not pay any attention to this darkness of Satan. Drive it away from your heart by making the sign of the life-giving Cross!

When praying, keep to the rule that it is better to say five words from the depth of your heart than ten thousand words with your tongue only. When you observe that your heart is cold and prays unwillingly, stop praying and warm your heart by vividly representing to yourself either your own wickedness, your spiritual poverty, misery, and blindness, or the great benefits which God bestows every moment upon you and all mankind, especially upon Christians, and then pray slowly and fervently. If you have not time to say all the prayers, it does not matter, and you will receive incomparably greater benefit from praying fervently and not hurriedly than if you had said all your prayers hurriedly and without feeling: "I had rather speak five words with my understanding . . . than ten thousand words in a tongue."

As after having unworthily communicated, so also after having prayed unworthily and coldly, our soul feels equally ill at ease. This means that God does not enter our heart, being offended at its unbelief and coldness, and allows the evil spirit to nestle in our hearts, in order to make us feel the difference between His own presence and its yoke.

Sometimes during prayer you feel a kind of estrangement from God, and despair. Do not be carried away by such a feeling; it proceeds from the Devil. Say in your heart: "I despair not of salvation, reprobate as I am; and emboldened by Thine immeasurable compassion, I come unto Thee. If there is any hope of salvation for me, if Thy loving mercy can overcome the multitude of my transgressions, be Thou my Saviour."[1]

When praying with people, we sometimes have to pierce through with our prayer as if it were the hardest wall—human souls, hardened and petrified by earthly passions—to penetrate the Egyptian darkness, the darkness of passions and worldly attachments. This is why it is sometimes difficult to pray. The simpler the people one prays with, the easier it is.

Intercession[2]

When you pray, endeavour to pray more for others than for yourself alone, and during prayer represent to yourself vividly all men as forming one body with yourself, and each separately as a member of the Body of Christ and your own member, "for we are members one of another." Pray for all as you would pray for yourself, with the same sincerity and fervour; look upon their infirmities and sicknesses as your own; their spiritual ignorance, their sins and passions, as your own; their temptations, misfortunes, and manifold afflictions as your own. Such prayer will be accepted with great favour by the Heavenly Father, that most gracious, common Father of all, with Whom "there is no respect of persons," "no shadow of alteration," that boundless Love that embraces and preserves all creatures.

When you are saying a prayer for all men, and not praying from your heart for all men, then your soul is oppressed, for God does not favour such prayer; but as soon as you begin to pray for all men from your heart, then you will immediately feel relieved, for the Lord listens mercifully to such prayers.

When you are struck by other people's suffering, and the contraction of their souls, so that you are induced to pray for them with a pitying and contrite heart, pray to God to have mercy upon them and to forgive them their sins, as you would pray for the forgiveness of your own sins—that is, implore God with tears to pardon them; likewise pray for the salvation of others as you would pray for your own salvation. If you attain to this and make it a habit, you will receive from God an abundance of spiritual gifts, the gifts of the Holy Ghost, Who loves the soul that cares for the salvation of others, because He Himself, the most Holy Spirit, wishes to save us all in every possible way, if only we do not oppose Him and do not harden our hearts. "The Spirit Himself asketh for us with unspeakable groanings."

When you are asked to pray that some one may be saved from bodily death, for instance, from drowning, from death through any sickness, from fire, or from any other disaster, com-

mend the faith of those who ask you to do so, and say in yourself: "Blessed be your faith, according to your faith may the
Lord fulfil my unworthy, feeble prayer, and may He increase
my faith."

If you wish to correct any one from his faults, do not think
of correcting him solely by your own means: you would only
do harm by your own passions, for instance, by pride and by
the irritability arising from it; "but cast thy burden upon the
Lord," and pray to God, Who "searcheth the hearts and reins,"
with all your heart, that He Himself may enlighten the mind
and heart of that man. If He sees that your prayer breathes love,
and that it really comes from the depth of your heart, He will
infallibly fulfil the desire of your heart, and you yourself will
soon tell, seeing the change that has taken place in him for
whom you have prayed, that it is the work of the right hand of
God, the most High.

Why has our sincere prayer for each other such great power
over others? Because of the fact that by cleaving to God during
prayer I become one spirit with Him, and unite with myself, by
faith and love, those for whom I pray; for the Holy Ghost acting
in me also acts at the same time in them, for He accomplishes
all things. "We, being many, are one bread, one body." "There
is one body and one Spirit."

Lord! grant that I may ever pour forth my supplications to
Thee for the whole world and for the fulfilment of the requests
of the whole Church, with all comprehensive, unfeigned love,
for by Thy grace I have to pray for the sins of all and for mine
own. Grant, O Lord, God the Father, that I may contemplate
Thine unspeakable love unto the world, manifested in giving
unto us Thy beloved Only-begotten Son. Grant, O God, Son
of God, that I may contemplate Thine exhaustion[3] in the world
and on the cross for the sake of our salvation; grant, O God, the
Holy Ghost, that I may contemplate Thy grace, abundantly
outpoured and still being outpoured upon the world, for the
sake of the merits of the Lord Jesus Christ, and so often filling
even my sinful heart; O Holy Trinity, grant that I may continually glorify Thee with my heart and mouth, and above all
by my deeds!

Thanksgiving and Spiritual Joy

As often as I prayed with faith, the Lord always heard me and fulfilled my prayers.

How easily and speedily the Lord can save us!—instantaneously, unexpectedly, imperceptibly. Often during the day I have been a great sinner, and at night, after prayer, I have gone to rest, justified and whiter than snow by the grace of the Holy Ghost, with the deepest peace and joy in my heart! How easy it will be for the Lord to save us too in the evening of our life, at the decline of our days! Oh, save, save, save me, most gracious Lord; receive me in Thy heavenly Kingdom! Everything is possible to Thee.

Concerning praise. The soul involuntarily longs to praise when we gaze upon the starry sky; but still more when, in looking upon the sky and the stars, we represent to ourselves God's providence towards men, how infinitely He loves men, cares for their eternal beatitude, not having even spared His only-begotten Son for our salvation and our repose in the Heavenly Kingdom. It is impossible not to praise God when you remember that you were predestined from the foundation of the world for eternal blessedness, quite without cause, not in accordance with your merits—when you remember what grace God has bestowed upon you for your salvation during all your lifetime, what an innumerable multitude of sins are forgiven you, and this not once or twice but an incalculable number of times, what a multitude of natural gifts are bestowed upon you, beginning with health down to the current of air, down to the drop of water. We are involuntarily incited to praise when we see with wonder the infinite variety of things created on the earth, in the animal kingdom, in the vegetable kingdom, and in the mineral kingdom. What wise order in all, both in great and small! We involuntarily praise and exclaim: "O Lord, how manifold are Thy works! in wisdom hast Thou made them all": Glory to Thee, Lord, Who hast created everything!

The sign of the Lord's mercy or of that of His most pure Mother to us, after or during prayer, is peace of heart, especially after the action of some passion, whose property is the absence of spiritual peace. By this peace of heart and a kind of holy tenderness of heart we can also easily recognise that our prayer has been heard, and that the grace asked in it has been granted to us. The success of the prayer is also recognised by the spiritual power, which we inwardly obtain for the fulfilment of the duties of our calling, and by the inward light manifestly entering into our soul.

Prayer refreshes and enlivens the soul, as outer air refreshes the body. When praying we feel braver and brighter, similarly as we feel physically and spiritually braver and fresher while walking in the fresh air.

Sometimes during a long-continued prayer only a few minutes are really pleasing to God and constitute true prayer and true service to God. The chief thing in prayer is the nearness of the heart to God, as proved by the sweetness of God's presence in the soul.

When praying fervently, either standing or sitting, or lying down or walking, and being sometimes suddenly visited by the Spirit of God and hearing His voice, we notice that He penetrates into the soul, not through the mouth, not through the nose, neither through the ears (although the Saviour bestowed the Spirit through the word and breathing, and although "faith cometh by hearing"), but straight through the body into the heart, in the same manner as the Lord passed through the walls of the house when He came to the Apostles after the Resurrection, and acts suddenly, like electricity, and more rapidly than any electric current; then we feel unusually light, because we are suddenly freed from our burden of sins, the spirit of contrition for sins, the spirit of devotion, peace, and joy visits us. Remember how the angel appeared in the shut-up prison in order to deliver the Apostle Peter; the doors were shut, the keepers standing before the doors, but the angel suddenly came upon him, and at the same moment a light shined in the prison. Thus the Spirit of God suddenly visits the chamber of our soul, the body, and the light shines in it.

"He shall cry to Me, and I will hear Him." O words most full of love! O words breathing lively trust into him who prays!

Sometimes we stand praying in church or at home, in a state of spiritual and bodily prostration; then powerless, cold, unfruitful is our soul, like some heathen, unfruitful temple; but as soon as we make an effort, and force our heart to sincere prayer to God, turn our thoughts and heart towards Him with living faith, our soul immediately becomes vivified, warm, and fruitful. What sudden tranquillity, what lightness, what emotion, what inward holy fire, what tears for our sins, what a sincere feeling of sorrow that by them we have displeased the Most Merciful Master; what light in the heart and mind, what an abundant stream of living water is diffused in the heart, flowing freely from the tongue, or from the pen and pencil, if we are writing, upon the paper! The wilderness of the soul blossoms like a lily at the coming of the Lord into the heart. Oh, why do we not turn our hearts oftener towards the Lord? How much peace and comfort ever lie concealed in Him for us! "Oh, how great is the multitude of Thy sweetness, which Thou hast hidden for them that fear Thee!"

It is sometimes well during prayer to say a few words of our own, breathing fervent faith and love to the Lord. Yes, let us not always converse with God in the words of others, not always remain children in faith and hope; we must also show our own mind, indite a good matter from our own heart also. Moreover, we grow too much accustomed to the words of others and grow cold in prayer. And how pleasing to the Lord this lisping of our own is, coming directly from a believing, loving, and thankful heart. It is impossible to explain this: it is only needful to say that when you are praying to God with your own words the soul trembles with joy, it becomes wholly inflamed, vivified, and beatified. You will utter few words, but you will experience such blessedness as you would not have obtained from saying the longest and most touching prayers of others pronounced out of habit and insincerely.

Wherever I am, as soon as I raise the eyes of my heart in my affliction to God, the Lover of men immediately answers my faith and prayer, and the sorrow immediately departs. He is at every time and every hour near me, only I do not see it, but I feel it vividly in my heart. Sorrow is the death of the heart, and it is a falling away from God. The expansion, the peace of heart through lively faith in Him, prove more clearly than the day that God is constantly present near me, and that He dwells within me. What intercessor or angel can set us free from our sins or sorows? None, but God alone. This is from experience.

I thank Thee, my Lord, my Master, and my Judge, for teaching me how to pray simply to Thee, for hearing my calling upon Thee, for saving me from my sins and sorrows, and for rightly directing my ways. I called upon Thee (in the sin of my wickedness) in the words of the Church prayer: "O Lord, our God, Who grantest forgiveness unto men through repentance . . ." And as soon as I finished this prayer, peace and lightness established themselves in my soul (June 29th, 1864).

THE TEMPLE AND ITS SERVICES

The House of God

O holy temple, how good, how sweet it is to pray in thee! For where can there be ardent prayer if not within thy walls, before the throne of God, and before the face of Him Who sitteth upon it? Truly the soul melts from prayerful emotion, and tears flow down the cheeks like water. It is sweet to pray for all.

In the Church we are freed from worldly enchantment, and from the intoxication of worldly passions and desires; we become enlightened, sanctified, cleansed in our souls; we draw near to God, we are united with God. How worthily reverenced and loved should the temple of God be! How God's saints loved it!

Truly, the temple is heaven upon earth; for where the throne of God is, where the terrible mysteries are celebrated, where the angels serve together with men, where the Almighty is unceasingly glorified, there is truly heaven, and the heaven of heavens. And thus let us enter into the temple of God, and above all, into the Holy of Holies[4], with the fear of God, with a pure heart, laying aside all passions and every worldly care, and let us stand in it with faith and reverence, with understanding attention, with love and peace in our hearts, so that we may come away renewed, as though made heavenly; so that we may live in the holiness natural to heaven, not binding ourselves by worldly desires and pleasures.

In the temple of God the simple, believing souls are as in the house of the Heavenly Father: they feel so free, so happy and light. Here true Christians have a foretaste of the future kingdom, prepared for them from the foundation of the world, of future freedom from every sin and from death, of future peace and blessedness. When do they especially have a foretaste of this? When they turn sincerely with all their soul to God, praying fervently to God, taking the firm resolution to devote their lives to God, and when doing deeds of virtue outside the temple.

The spiritual tranquillity and blessedness which we sometimes experience in God's temple during the harmonious singing and the distinct reading of the reader, or of the officiating clergy, is a foretaste of that infinite bliss which those will experience who will eternally contemplate the unspeakable beauty of God's countenance. We must be zealous about harmonious singing and distinct reading. By calling upon the names of God's saints in prayer we move them to pray for us.

Symbolism

Is it only for the adornment of your dwelling, as a beautiful piece of furniture, as an ornament, that you hang up richly painted icons in your house, without turning to them with the hearty faith, love and reverence due to holy things? Ask your heart if it is so. Icons in houses or in the temple are not intended for show, but for prayer before them, for reverence, for instruction. The images of the saints ought to be our home and church teachers. Read their lives, and engrave them upon your heart, and endeavour to bring your life into conformity with theirs.

In making the sign of the cross, believe and constantly remember that your sins are nailed to the cross. When you fall into sin, immediately judge yourself sincerely, and make the sign of the cross over yourself, saying: Lord, Thou Who nailest our sins to the cross, nail also my present sin to Thy cross, and "have mercy upon me according to Thy great mercy"; and you will be cleansed from your sin.

It is impossible to represent and to think of the cross without love. Where the cross is, there is love; in the church you see crosses everywhere and upon everything, in order that everything should remind you that you are in the temple of the God of love, in the temple of love itself, crucified for us.

The Divine Liturgy[5]

The Divine Liturgy is truly a heavenly service upon earth, during which God Himself, in a particular, immediate, and most close manner, is present and dwells with men, being Himself the invisible Celebrant of the service, offering and being offered. There is nothing upon earth holier, higher, grander, more solemn, more life-giving than the Liturgy. The temple, at this particular time, becomes an earthly heaven; those who officiate represent Christ Himself, the Angels, the Cherubim, Seraphim and Apostles. The Liturgy is the continually repeated solemnisation of God's love to mankind, and of His all-powerful mediation for the salvation of the whole world, and of every member separately: the marriage of the Lamb—the marriage of the King's Son, in which the bride of the Son of God is—every faithful soul; and the giver of the bride—the Holy Ghost.

The Liturgy is the supper, the table of God's love to mankind. Around the Lamb of God upon the holy paten all are at this time assembled—the living and the dead, saints and sinners, the Church triumphant and the Church militant.

Why should it be wonderful if God Himself, the Creator of all things visible and invisible, transforms, transubstantiates bread and wine into His own most pure Body and His own most pure Blood? In these—in the bread and wine—the Son of God does not become again incarnate, for He was already once incarnate, and this is sufficient unto endless ages; but He is incarnate in the very same flesh in which He was before incarnate, in the same manner as He multiplied the five loaves and fed with these five loaves several thousands of people. There are a great many mysteries in nature which my mind cannot grasp, although they have concrete forms, yet they exist, with their mysteries. So also, in this Sacrament of the life-giving Body and Blood, it is a mystery for me how the bread and wine are made into the Body and Blood of the Lord Himself—but the mystery of the Body and Blood really exists, although it is incomprehensible to me. My Creator (I am only His clay, for God formed me of flesh and blood and endued me with a spirit), as the most wise, the infinitely Almighty God, has innumerable mysteries: I myself am a mystery, as the work of His hands. For my soul there is the Spirit of the Lord, and for my soul and body there are His Body and Blood.

When you receive the holy life-giving Mysteries[6], steadfastly represent to yourself Christ Himself under the form of the bread and wine; make upon them the mental inscription "Jesus Christ," and with this mental inscription (whilst the sentient one already exists) send in thought into the depths of your heart, and there lay and mentally preserve the life-giving Guest. If thus, with such faith, you receive the Holy Mysteries, you will see that they will bring forth in you the deepest peace of your spiritual powers, and you will feel most wonderfully happy and light. The Lord loads us with benefits according to the measure of our faith; the Body and Blood show themselves to be life-giving, burning embers in the believer's heart, according to the measure of his heart's preparedness. The Church is heaven; the altar, the throne of life, from which God descends in the holy and most pure Mysteries to feed and give life to believers. "Great and marvellous are Thy works, Lord God Almighty!" Thou preparest us beforehand for the contemplation of the throne, and of Him Who sitteth upon it, by seeing the earthly throne in the Church, and by the contemplation, with the eyes of faith, of Him Who sitteth upon it.

"I am with you all days, even to the consummation of the world." So it is, Master: Thou art with us throughout all days;

we are not a single day without Thee, and we cannot live without Thy presence near us! Thou art with us especially in the Sacrament of Thy Body and Blood. Oh, how truly and essentially art Thou present in the Holy Mysteries! Thou our Lord in every liturgy takest upon Thyself a vile body similar to ours in every respect save that of sin, and feedest us with Thy life-giving flesh. Through the sacrament Thou art wholly with us, and Thy Flesh is united to our flesh, whilst Thy Spirit is united to our soul; and we feel this life-giving, most peaceful, most sweet union, we feel that by joining ourselves to Thee in the Holy Eucharist we become one Spirit with Thee as it is said: "He who is joined to the Lord is one spirit." We become like Thee, good, meek and lowly, as Thou hast said of Thyself: "I am meek and lowly in heart."

Preparation for Holy Communion

In receiving the Holy Sacrament be as undoubtedly sure that you communicate of the Body and Blood of Christ, as you are sure that every moment you breathe air. Say to yourself, "As surely as I constantly breathe the air, so surely do I now receive into myself, together with the air, my Lord Jesus Christ Himself, my breathing, my life, my joy, my salvation. He is my breath, before air, at every moment of my life; He is my word, before any other word; He is my thought, before any other thought; He is my light, before any other light; He is my meat and drink, before any other meat and drink; He is my raiment, before any other raiment; He is my fragrance, before any other fragrance; He is my sweetness, before any other sweetness; He is my father and mother, before any other father and mother; before the earth, He is the firmest ground, that nothing can ever shake and that bears me. As we, earthly creatures, forget that at all times we breathe, live, move, and exist in Him, and have hewed out "cisterns, broken cisterns," for ourselves, He has opened unto us, in His Holy Mysteries, in His Blood, the source of living water, flowing into life eternal, and gives Himself to us as food and drink, in order "that we may live by Him."

How long will it be before the Holy Mysteries of which we partake remind us that "we, being many, . . . are one body"; and how long will there be no mutual hearty union between us, as members of the single body of Christ? How long shall we make our own laws of life, be inimical to each other, envy each other, torment, grieve, fret, judge and abuse each other? When will the Spirit of Christ abide in us, the spirit of meekness, humility, kindness, love unfeigned, self-denial, patience, chastity, abstinence, simplicity and sincerity, contempt for earthly things and entire aspiration after heavenly ones? Lord Jesus Christ! enlighten our spiritual vision and "let Thy loving Spirit lead" us all "into the land of righteousness." Give us Thy Spirit!

He who believes in the Saviour, and feeds upon His Body and Blood, has life eternal in himself; and this is the reason why every sin occasions painful suffering and disturbance of heart. But those who have not life eternal in them drink iniquity like water, and do not suffer because life eternal is not in their hearts.

Some believe that their whole welfare and their attitude before God consists in the reading of all the appointed prayers, without paying attention to the preparedness of their hearts for prayer to God, nor to their inward amendment. Many, for instance, thus read the prayers appointed before Holy Communion; whilst at this time we should, above all, look to the amendment and preparedness of the heart to receive the Holy Sacrament. If your heart is right in your bosom; if, by God's mercy, it is ready to meet the Bridegroom, then, thank God, it is well with you, even although you have not succeeded in reading all the appointed prayers. "For the kingdom of God is not in speech, but in power." Obedience to our mother, the Church, in everything is right; and if it is possible for one "to receive" prolonged prayer, let him pray long. But "all men take not this word." If long prayer is not compatible with fervour of spirit, then it is better to say a short but fervent prayer. Remember that the one word of the publican, said from a fervent heart, justified him. God does not look at the multitude of words, but upon the disposition of the heart. The chief thing is lively faith and fervent repentance for sins.

He who comes to the Holy Cup with any passion in his heart, the same is a Judas, and comes to kiss the Son of man flatteringly.

The Fruit of a Good Communion

To the glory of the most holy name of our Master the Lord Jesus Christ and that of our Lady, the Mother of God, I have experienced a thousand times in my heart, that, after the Communion of the Holy Sacrament or after fervent prayer at home—ordinary prayer or prayer in consequence of some sin, passion, and sorrow and straitness—the Lord, at the prayers of our Lady, or our Lady herself, by the Lord's grace bestowed upon me, as though it were a new spiritual nature, pure, good, great, bright, wise, beneficent, instead of impure, despondent, languid, fainthearted, dark, dull, and evil. Many times was I thus changed, with a marvellous great change, to mine own wonder and often to that of others. Glory to Thy power, Lord! Glory to Thy mercy, Lord! Glory to Thy bounties, Lord, which Thou hast manifested upon me a sinner!

I marvel at the greatness and life-giving properties of the Holy Sacrament. An old woman who was spitting blood, and who had lost all strength, being unable to eat anything, after the Communion of the Holy Sacrament, which I administered to her, began to recover on the same day from her illness. A young girl who was almost dying, after the Communion of the Holy Sacrament began to eat, drink, and speak; whilst before this she was almost in a state of unconsciousness, violently tossed about, and could neither eat nor drink anything. Glory to Thy life-giving and terrible Mysteries, O Lord!

Men throughout all their earthly life see everything but Christ, the life-giver; this is why they have no spiritual life, this is why they are given to every passion: unbelief, want of faith, covetousness, envy, hatred, ambition, the pleasures of eating and drinking. It is only at the close of their life that they seek Christ out of crying necessity and as a custom usual amongst others. O Christ, our God, our Life and Resurrection! How low have we fallen in our vanity, how blind have we become! But how would it have been with us had we always sought Thee, had we always had Thee in our hearts? Unto them Thou art strengthening food, inexhaustible drink, shining raiment, the sun, "the peace of God which surpasseth all understanding," unutterable joy, and everything. Possessing Thee, all earthly things become dust and corruption.

As in Jesus Christ, "dwelleth all the fulness of the Godhead corporeally," so likewise in the life-giving Sacrament of His Body and Blood. In the small human body dwelleth all the fulness of the infinite, incomprehensible Godhead, and in the small "lamb,"[7] or bread, in each smallest particle, dwelleth all Divine fulness. Glory to Thy Omnipotence and Goodness, O Lord!

How many times already, O Master, Lord Jesus, hast Thou renewed my nature, heedlessly corrupted by my sins! There is no measure and number to this. How many times hast Thou saved me from the furnace burning within me, from the furnace of many and diverse passions, from the abyss of despondency and despair! How many times hast Thou renewed my depraved heart, when only I have called upon Thy Name with faith! How many times hast Thou accomplished this through the life-giving Holy Sacrament! O Lord! in truth there is no number and measure of Thy mercies unto me, a sinner. What shall I offer to Thee, or what can I render unto Thee for Thine innumerable benefits to me, Jesus, my life and my lightness? May I be prudent in my ways, according to Thy grace; for "blessed are the undefiled in the way," as Thou hast said, through the Holy Ghost, by the mouth of our forefather, David. I will endeavour to be faithful unto Thee, to be humble, meek, not irritable, gentle, forbearing, industrious, merciful, generous, not covetous, obedient.

The Word of God

As you are aware, man, in his words, does not die; he is immortal in them, and they will speak after his death. I shall die, but shall speak even after my death. How many immortal words are in use amongst the living, which were left by those who have died long ago, and which sometimes still live in the mouths of a whole people! How powerful is the word even of an ordinary man! Still more so is the Word of God: It will live throughout all ages, and will always be living and acting.

The whole Gospel is the gospel of the kingdom to which Christians are predestined, and forms as though one single promise (all the parables, all the prophecies and miracles); the epistles of the Apostles reveal in greater detail the promises of Christian hope.

Every word of Holy Writ, every word of the Divine liturgy, of the morning and evening services, every word of the Sacramental prayers and of the other prayers, has in itself the power corresponding to it and contained in it, like the sign of the honourable and life-giving cross. Such grace is present in every word of the Church, on account of the Personal Incarnate Word of God, Who is the Head of the Church, dwelling in the Church. Besides this, every truly good word has in itself the power corresponding to it, owing to the all-filling simple Word of God. With what attention and reverence, with what faith, must we therefore pronounce each word! For the Word is the Creator Himself, God, and through the Word all things were brought into existence from non-existence.

Rites and Customs of the Church

I thank my all holy, all merciful, and most wise Mother, the Church of God, for salutarily guiding me during this temporal life, and for educating me for the heavenly citizenship; I thank her for all the offices of prayers, for the Divine services, for the sacraments and rites; I thank her for the fasts so beneficial to me both in spiritual and bodily respects (for through them I am healthy both in spirit and body, calm, vigilant, and light; without the fasts I should feel extreme heaviness, which I indeed experienced when not fasting); I thank my spotless Mother the Church of God for enrapturing me with her heavenly services, transporting my spirit to heaven, enlightening my intellect with heavenly truth, showing me the way to eternal life; for delivering me from the violence and ignominy of the passions, and making my life blessed.

Our faith and Church is like a most honoured, holy, godly, firm, venerable woman, who never grows old, and in whom ever dwells a young, living spirit, giving life to her true children. As we always behave with great respect to old people, honouring their gray hair and wisdom—the fruits of experience—and highly value each of their words, and apply them to our own life, so ought we especially to honour the Church, venerate her holiness, antiquity, her unshaken firmness, her divinely enlightened wisdom and spiritual experience, her soul-saving commandments and ordinances, her Divine services, sacraments and rites. How can we do otherwise than respect her, even if only for having saved in her bosom an innumerable multitude of people, transplanting them into the abode of eternal peace and joy, not forgetting them even after their death, but remembering them until now upon earth, eternally praising and glorifying their virtues as her true children? Where will you find a more grateful friend, a more tender mother? And therefore, may Christians attach themselves wholly and with all their hearts to the Church of Christ, that they may be firmly established unto the end of their temporal life! May they all be zealous of the fulfilment of all her commandments and ordinances, and may they obtain in her eternal salvation through Christ Jesus our Lord!

Through our attachment to perishable things, by thoughts and cares about them, we lose sight of objects of the greatest importance, of the objects really natural to our souls, constituting their true and eternal element; we hew out for ourselves "cisterns, broken cisterns, that can hold no water," and forsake "the Fountain of living waters"; we do not turn spiritual, holy, heavenly and life-giving thoughts into our life, into our blood, but continue to live by worldly, earthly, passionate thoughts and aspirations, which only oppress, torment, and slay us. Oh, if we could ever reason, as the Gospel teaches us, as the holy Church teaches us in her Divine services, and prayers, at the celebration of the sacraments and other offices, as the Holy Fathers did in their writings! Then even upon earth we should all become citizens of heaven, speaking heavenly things.

Everything that the Church puts into our mouths and hearing is truth, the breathing or teaching of the Holy Ghost. Reverence every thought, every word of the Church. Remember that the domain of thought and word belongs to God as well as the whole visible and invisible world. You have nothing of your own, not even any thought or word. Everything is our Father's, everything is God's. Mingle with the common order of things, as gold melts into various forms, or as nature forms one harmonious whole. Do not lead a self-loving, separate life.

"I am the vine," says the Lord, "ye are the branches," that is the One Holy, Catholic, and Apostolic Church. Therefore, as the Lord is holy, so also the Church is holy; as the Lord "is the way, the truth, and the life," so also is the Church, because the Church is one and the same with the Lord, "His body, of His flesh, and of His bones," or His "branches," rooted in Him—the living vine, and nourished by Him and growing in Him. Never represent the Church as apart from the Lord Jesus Christ, from the Father and the Holy Ghost.

THE LIFE AND WORK OF A PRIEST

The Dignity of the Priest's Office

What a great personage a priest is! He is in constant converse with God, and God constantly replies to his speech, as whatever the ceremonies of the Church may be, whatever his prayers, he is speaking to God, and whatever the ceremonies of the Church may be and whatever his prayers, the Lord answers him. How, under these circumstances, when assaulted by passions, can the priest forget that such passions are base, impure, especially for him, and that it is impossible to let them enter into his heart, which Jesus Christ alone ought to fill entirely? A priest is an angel and not a man; everything worldly ought to be left far away behind him. O Lord, "let Thy priests be clothed with justice"; let them always remember the greatness of their calling and do not let them be entangled in the nets of the world and the Devil; let them be saved from "the cares of this world, and the deceitfulness of riches, and the lusts after other things" entering into their hearts.

As light and heat are inseparable from the sun, so holiness, instruction, love and compassion for all ought to be inseparable from the person of a priest; for Whose dignity does he bear?— Christ's. Of Whom does he so often communicate? Christ— God Himself, of His Body and Blood. Therefore a priest should be the same in the spiritual world, in the midst of his flock, as the sun is in nature: a light for all, life-giving warmth, the soul of all.

A priest ought to endeavour by every means to maintain within himself courage, boldness, daring, in spite of the bodiless enemy, who continually sows in him his illusive fear, his foolish dread; otherwise he cannot be a reprover of human vices, nor a true celebrant of the sacraments. Daring is a great gift of God and a great treasure of the soul! Courage or boldness plays an important part in earthly warfare, for it simply works wonders; but in the spiritual warfare it does far more.

The Celebration of the Divine Liturgy

The celebration of the Divine Liturgy requires an elevated soul, or a man with an elevated soul, not bound by any worldly passions, desires, and attachments to earthly delights; whose heart is wholly embraced by the flame of the Holy Ghost, by ardent love for God and mankind, for every human soul, and, above all, for the Christian soul, so that with a sincere heart he may ever rise to God in prayer: "I am come to cast fire on the earth: and what will I, but that it be kindled?" This fire was sent down from heaven upon the Apostles in the form of tongues of fire. This fire is also necessary for us, for our frozen hearts, in order to warm, soften, to melt them again and again, continually to cleanse them, in order to enlighten and renew them. Where is there to be found such a worthy priest who, like the Seraphim, would burn before the Lord with love, praise, and gratitude for His marvels of mercy and wisdom manifested unto us and within us? I am the greatest of sinners in unworthily celebrating this most heavenly Sacrament, for I have ever an impure heart, bound by desires and attachments to earthly delights. Lord, Thou seest the depths of our hearts; but "Thou shalt sprinkle me with hyssop, and I shall be made whiter than snow." "It is not wonderful if Thou hast mercy upon the pure; and it is not a great thing if Thou savest the righteous, but show the wonders of Thy mercy upon me, a sinner!"[8]

During the oblation, the whole Church, in heaven and upon earth—the Church of the first-born, inscribed in the heavens, and the Church militant, fighting against the enemies of salvation upon earth—is typically represented assembled around the Lamb, who took upon Himself the sins of the world. What a great spectacle, enrapturing and moving the-soul! Is it possible that I too am the joint-heir with the saints, if I remain faithful to the Lamb until death? Are not all my brethren too members of this heavenly holy assemblage, and joint-heirs of the future kingdom? Oh, how widely my heart should expand in order to contain all within itself, to love all, to care for all, to care for the salvation of all as for mine own! This is wisdom and the highest wisdom. Let us be simple; let us walk in simplicity of heart with all. Let us remember our high calling and election and let us continually aspire to the honour of God's heavenly calling through Christ Jesus. "We are the children of God . . . heirs of God, and joint-heirs with Christ."

Lord, how shall I glorify Thee? How shall I praise Thee for Thy power, for the miracles of healing by means of Thy Holy Mysteries, manifested upon me and many of Thy servants, to whom I, an unworthy one, have administered these Thy holy, heavenly, life-giving Mysteries after the sacrament of penitence? They confess before me Thy power, Thy goodness, loudly proclaiming to all that Thou hast stretched out Thy wonder-working hand over them and raised them up from the bed of sickness, from their death-bed, when no one expected that they would live; and then, after the communion of Thy life-giving Body and Blood they soon revived, were healed, and felt upon them at the very same hour and day Thy life-giving Hand. And I, Lord, the witness of Thy deeds, have not hitherto praised Thee in the hearing of all for the strengthening of the faith of Thy servants, and even do not know how and when to praise Thee, for every day I am occupied with some kind of work. Create Thyself a name, Lord, as Thou hast done; glorify Thyself, Thy name, Thy Mysteries.

The Priest Saying the Divine Office

I love to pray in God's temple, especially within the holy altar, before the Holy Table or the Prothesis, for by God's grace I become wonderfully changed in the temple. During the prayer of repentance and devotion, the thorns, the bonds of the passions, fall from my soul and I feel so light; all the spell, all the enticement of the passions vanish, and I seem to die to the world, and the world, with all its joys, dies for me. I live in God and for God, for God alone. I am wholly penetrated by Him, and am one spirit with Him. I become like a child soothed on its mother's knee. Then my heart is full of most heavenly, sweet peace. My soul is enlightened by the light of heaven. At such times we see everything clearly; we look upon everything rightly; we feel friendship and love towards everyone, even towards our enemies, readily excusing and forgiving everyone. Oh, how blessed is the soul when it is with God! Truly the Church is an earthly paradise.

Take me captive, Lord, in the sweet captivity of Thy Holy Ghost, so that my words may flow "as a stream in the south" to Thy glory and to the salvation of Thy people! Grant me this sweet and powerful inward impulse to set down upon parchment the fulness of spiritual visions and feelings! Let "my tongue (be) the pen of a ready writer"—of the All-Holy Spirit!

The Priest Hearing Confessions

In ministering the sacrament of penitence one feels one's own most miserable sinfulness before God, and all the misery, ignorance, and sinfulness of human nature. Confession is a cross, truly a cross! Oh, what a debtor before his spiritual children a priest feels himself to be during confession! He truly feels himself to be an insolvent debtor, a debtor guilty before the heavenly truth, and deserving of thousands of the fires of Gehenna! One sees and feels at people's deep ignorance, at their ignorance of the truths of religion, and of their sins, at their stony insensibility, that a confessor must pray for them most fervently, and teach them day and night, early and late! Oh, what ignorance! Some do not even know the Holy Trinity; they do not know Who Christ is; they do not know why they live upon earth! And what a multitude of sins! Yet meanwhile we seek enrichment, rest; we dislike labour, we become irritated when there are more of them than usual! We seek spacious abodes, rich clothing! Let us not love earthly rest, let us not become slothful, let us not be negligent in the performance of our spiritual duties, and let us not deprive ourselves of heavenly blessings and rest, for having tasted the worldly rest in abundance here, what rest can we look for there?

The Priest as Preacher, and Pastor of His Flock

What can be firmer, more unchangeable and mightier than the word? By the word the world was created and exists; "upholding all things by the word of His power"; and yet we sinners treat words so lightly, so negligently. For what do we show less respect than for the word? What is more changeable in us than the word? Oh, how accursed are we men! How inattentive we are to such precious things! We do not remember that by means of the word proceeding from a believing and loving heart, we may perform life-giving miracles for our own souls and for the souls of others; for instance, in prayer at Divine service; in sermons, at the celebration of the sacrament! Christian! value every word; be attentive to every word; be firm in the word; trust in every word of God and of the saints, as in the words of life. Remember that the word is the beginning of life.

TO MY PUPILS: You are my children, for I have begotten you through the Gospel in Jesus Christ, my spiritual blood, for my teaching flows in your veins. I have given and give you to drink of the milk of the Word, as a mother from her breast. You are my children, and therefore you are ever in my heart, and I pray for you. You are my children because you are my spiritual children. You are my children because, as a priest, I am truly a father, and you yourselves call me father. "My children!" This word is very displeasing to the Devil, who is the cause of dislike, malice, and hypocrisy; but I, God helping me, will not even for a moment obey Him, and will not call you otherwise than my children; for you are my children by faith, by the Church of God, and by the instruction and fatherly guidance you receive from me. One can only truly call others' children "my children" by the Holy Spirit, by the Spirit of truth and love.

I sometimes pray in church for God's people thus: Here, Lord, many of these who are standing in Thy temple stand before Thee with their souls idle, like empty vessels, and "know not what to pray for as they ought"; fill Thou their hearts now at this favourable time for them, in this day of salvation, by the grace of Thine All-holy Spirit, and give them to me at my prayer, to my love, filled with the knowledge of Thy goodness, and with heartfelt contrition and devotion, as full vessels; give to them Thy Holy Ghost, that "maketh intercession for us with unspeakable groanings." I myself, their pastor, am sinful and impure above all men, but do not consider my sins, Lord, despise them according to Thy great mercy, and hear my prayer at this hour, for the sake of the grace of the priesthood resting on me and dwelling in me. Grant, Lord, that this grace may not be idle in me, but that it may ever burn in me with faith, hope, love, and son-like boldness in prayer for Thy people!

When your heart is struck by the enemy nestling within you, and causing in you disturbance, straitness, and depression of spirit, do not then preach a sermon, lest, instead of profit, it should give rise to temptation; lest, instead of spiritual nourishment, it should cause spiritual dizziness and sickness. Neither administer any reproofs at such times: these would only irritate, and not correct. In general, when the enemy nestles in your soul, it is better to be more silent; we are then unworthy of the word, which is the gift of the Hypostatic Word. First drive out the enemy, bring peace to dwell in your heart, and then speak.

Priests of God! learn how to turn the bed of sorrow of the Christian sufferer into one of joy by the consolation of faith; learn how to make him, instead of—in his opinion—the most unfortunate, the happiest of men; assure him that having been "a little chastised" he "shall be greatly rewarded" afterwards, and you will be the friends of mankind, angels of consolation, instruments or ministers of the Holy Spirit, the Comforter.

The sign of the cross as a blessing from a priest or a bishop is an expression of the blessing or of the favour of God to a man in Christ and for Christ's sake. What a joyful, significative, and precious ceremony this is! Blessed are all who receive such a blessing with faith! How attentive should the priests themselves be in bestowing their blessing upon the faithful! "And they shall invoke My name upon the children of Israel, and I will bless them."

A true shepherd and father of his flock will live in their grateful memory even after his death. They will extol him; and the less he cares to be extolled here on earth on account of his zealous labours for their salvation, the more his glory shall shine after his death: even when he is dead he will make them speak of him. Such is the glory of those who labour for the common good.

My sweetest Saviour! having come down from heaven for the service of mankind, Thou didst not only preach the Word of Heavenly Truth in the temple, but Thou wentest through the towns and villages; Thou didst not shun any one; Thou visitedst the houses of all, especially of those whose fervent repentance Thou didst foresee with Thy Divine gaze. Thus Thou didst not remain sitting at home, but wert in loving intercourse with all. Grant to us, too, to be in such loving intercourse with Thy people, so that we pastors shall not shut ourselves up in our houses away from Thy sheep as if in castles or prisons, only coming out of them for services in the church or to officiate in the houses of others, only out of duty, only with prayers learned by heart. May our lips be freely opened to discourse with our parishioners in the spirit of faith and love. May our Christian love for our spiritual children be opened and strengthened by animated, free, and fatherly conversation with them. Oh what sweetness, what bliss Thou hast concealed, Lord, our boundless Love, in the spiritual converse warmed by love of a spiritual father with his spiritual children! And how is it possible not to strive upon earth with all our might after such bliss? Yet it is only a faint beginning, only a faint likeness of the heavenly bliss of love! Especially love the communion of good works, both material and spiritual. "And do not forget to do good and to impart."

The Priest in Intercession

Priest of God! believe with your whole heart, believe always in the grace given to you from God, to pray for God's people. Let not this gift of God be in vain in you, for by it you can save many souls. The Lord speedily hears your heartfelt prayer for His people, and is easily inclined to have mercy upon them, as He had at Moses', Aaron's, Samuel's, and the Apostles' prayers. Avail yourself of every opportunity for prayer—in church, when you celebrate Divine service or a sacrament, in private houses, at the ministering of the sacraments, during prayers and thanksgivings; everywhere and at all times think of the salvation of God's people, and you shall also obtain great grace of God for yourself.

When you pray with tears and love for the Lord's sheep, and your thoughts praise you to yourself, then say to them: It is not I who prayed for God's people, but the "Spirit itself" within me "maketh intercession" for them "with unspeakable groanings"; and the Spirit bound me, too, at that time, in the sweet bonds of His love and of heartfelt devotion. That this is true is evident from the fact that the sweetness of prayer and love can very soon forsake me.

A certain person who was sick unto death from inflammation of the bowels for nine days, without having obtained the slightest relief from medical aid, as soon as he had communicated of the Holy Sacrament, upon the morning of the ninth day, regained his health, and rose from his bed of sickness on the evening of the same day. He received the Holy Communion with firm faith. I prayed to the Lord to cure him. "Lord," said I, "heal Thy servant of his sickness. He is worthy, therefore grant him this. He loves Thy priests, and sends them his gifts." I also prayed for him in church before the altar of the Lord, at the Liturgy, during the prayer: "Thou Who hast given us grace at this time, with one accord to make our common supplication unto Thee," and before the most Holy Mysteries themselves, I prayed in the following words: "Lord, our life! It is as easy for Thee to cure every malady as it is for me to think of healing. It is as easy for Thee to raise every man from the dead as it is for me to think of the possibility of the resurrection from the dead. Cure, then, Thy servant Basil of his cruel malady, and do not let him die; do not let his wife and children be given up to weeping." And the Lord graciously heard, and had mercy upon him, although he was within a hair's-breadth of death. Glory to Thine omnipotence and mercy, that Thou, Lord, hast vouchsafed to hear me!

The children Paul and Olga, by the infinite mercy of the Lord, in accordance with mine unworthy prayer, have been cured of the spirit of infirmity by which they were attacked. In the case of the child Paul, his malady passed away through sleep, and the child Olga became quiet in spirit, and her little face grew bright instead of dark and troubled. Nine times I went to pray with bold trust, hoping my trust might not be shamed; that to him that knocketh it would be opened; that even on account of my importunity, God would fulfil my requests; that if the unjust judge at last satisfied the woman who troubled him, then still more the Judge of all, the most righteous Judge, would satisfy my sinful prayer for the innocent children; that He would consider my labour, my intercession, my prayerful words, my kneeling, my boldness, my trust in Him. And the Lord did so; He did not cover me, a sinner, with shame. I came for the tenth time to their home, and the children were well. I gave thanks unto the Lord and to our most speedy Mediatrix.

TEMPTATION AND VICTORY

The Tempter

The enemy daily and violently persecutes my faith, hope and love. Thou art persecuted, my faith! Thou art persecuted, my hope! Thou art persecuted, my love! Endure, faith; endure, hope; endure, love! Take courage, faith; take courage, hope; take courage, love! God is your Defender! Do not grow weak, faith; do not grow weak, hope; do not grow weak, love!

The Devil generally enters into us through one single lying imagination, or through a single false thought and sinful desire of the flesh, and afterwards he works in us and disturbs us, so incomplex is he. Cannot, therefore, the Lord of all spirits enter into us through one single thought and through true and holy love, and abide with us, and be everything to us? And therefore pray undoubtingly; that is, simply, in the simplicity of your heart, without a doubt: it ought to be as easy to pray as to think.

When you are very young, or leading the life of the sinful world, then you only know by name both Christ the Saviour and the enemy of God and mankind, the most evil Satan, and you think that Christ is very far away from you in heaven, and that there is a Devil somewhere, but not in any way near and around you, and though you hear that he is evil, you think his wickedness does not concern you; but when you grow older and enter upon the devout life, when you serve God with a pure conscience, then you will experience in your heart the difference between the easy yoke of the Saviour and the heavy burden of Satan, who pitilessly injures us.

The Perils of Ease

Our life is children's play, only not innocent, but sinful, because, with a strong mind, and with the knowledge of the purpose of our life, we neglect this purpose and occupy ourselves with frivolous, purposeless matters. And thus our life is childish, unpardonable play. We amuse ourselves with food and drink, gratifying ourselves by them, instead of only using them for the necessary nourishment of our body and the support of our bodily life. We amuse ourselves with our mental gifts, with our intellect, imagination, using them only to serve sin and the vanity of this world—that is, only to serve earthly and corruptible things—instead of using them before all and above all to serve God, to learn to know Him, the all-wise Creator of every creature, for prayer, supplication, petitions, thanksgiving and praise to Him, and to show mutual love and respect, and only partly to serve this world, which will some day entirely pass away. We amuse ourselves with our knowledge of worldly vanity, and to acquire this knowledge we waste most precious time, which was given to us for our preparation for eternity. We frequently amuse ourselves with our affairs and business, with our duties, fulfilling them heedlessly, carelessly, and wrongfully, and using them for our own covetous, earthly purposes. We amuse ourselves with beautiful human faces, or the fair, weaker sex, and often use them for the sport of our passions. We amuse ourselves with time, which ought to be wisely utilised for redeeming eternity, and not for games and various pleasures. Finally, we amuse ourselves with our own selves, making idols out of ourselves, before which we bow down, and before which we expect others to bow down. Woe to us who love the present fleeting, deceptive life, and neglect the inheritance of the life that follows after the death of our corruptible body beyond this carnal veil!

When the flesh flourishes, the soul fades; when the flesh has full liberty, the soul is straitened; when the flesh is satiated, the soul hungers; when the flesh is adorned, the soul is deformed; when the flesh overflows with laughter, the soul is surrounded by misfortune; when the flesh is in the light, the soul is in darkness—in the darkness of hell.

Sickness and Poverty

Afflictions are a great teacher; afflictions show us our weaknesses, passions, and the need of repentance; afflictions cleanse the soul, they make it sober, as from drunkenness, they bring down grace into the soul, they soften the heart, they inspire us with a loathing for sin, and strengthen us in faith, hope, and virtue.

You are ill, and your illness is very painful; you have become low-spirited and despondent; you are troubled and tossed with thoughts, each darker than the other; your heart and your lips are ready to murmur, to blaspheme God! My brother! listen to my sincere advice. Bear your illness bravely, and do not merely not despond, but on the contrary, rejoice, if you can, in your illness. You would ask me what there is for you to rejoice at when you are racked all over with pain? Rejoice that the Lord has sent you this temporary chastisement in order to cleanse your soul from sins. "For whom the Lord loveth, He chastiseth." Rejoice in the fact that now you are not gratifying those passions which you would have gratified had you been in good health; rejoice that you are bearing the cross of sickness, and that therefore you are treading the narrow and sorrowful way leading to the kingdom of heaven. Maladies in our eyes only appear painful, unpleasant, and terrible. It is seldom that any one of us during the time of sickness represents to himself the profit which his illness brings to his soul; but in God's all-wise and most merciful Providence, not a single malady remains without some profit to our soul. Sicknesses in the hands of Providence are the same as bitter medicines for our soul, curing its passions, its bad habits and inclinations. Not a single malady sent to us shall return void. Therefore, we must keep in view the utility of sicknesses, in order that we may bear them more easily and more calmly. "He that hath suffered in the flesh hath ceased from sins," says the Holy Scripture.

In sickness and, in general, during bodily infirmity, as well as in affliction, a man cannot in the beginning burn with faith and love for God, because in affliction and sickness the heart aches, whilst faith and love require a sound heart, a calm heart. This is why we must not very much grieve if during sickness and affliction we cannot believe in God, love Him, and pray to Him fervently as we ought to. Everything has its proper time. There may be an unfavourable time, even for praying.

It is never so difficult to say from the heart, "Thy will be done, Father," as when we are in sore affliction or grievous sickness, and especially when we are subjected to the injustice of men, or the assaults and wiles of the enemy. It is also difficult to say from the heart, "Thy will be done," when we ourselves were the cause of some misfortune, for then we think that it is not God's will, but our own will, that has placed us in such a position, although nothing can happen without the will of God. In general, it is difficult sincerely to believe that it is the will of God that we should suffer, when the heart knows both by faith and experience that God is our blessedness; and therefore it is difficult to say in misfortune, "Thy will be done." We think "Is it possible that this is the will of God? Why does God torment us? Why are others quiet and happy? What have we done? Will there be an end to our torments?" And so on. But when it is difficult for our corrupt nature to acknowledge the will of God over us, that will of God without which nothing happens, and humbly to submit to it, that is the very time for us humbly to submit to this will and to offer to the Lord our most precious sacrifice—that is, heartfelt devotion to Him, not only in the time of ease and happiness, but also in suffering and misfortune; it is then that we must submit our vain, erring wisdom to the perfect wisdom of God, for our thoughts are as far from the thoughts of God "as the heavens are higher than the earth."

It is impossible not to wonder at the simple-heartedness and indifference to earthly blessings of the Galilean fishermen, and at their absolute obedience to the voice of the Lord. A few words of the Saviour were enough; they left their nets, their sole wealth, their greatest treasure, and followed Him, without reasoning why and wherefore they went. What simplicity of heart! What detachment from earthly blessings! What childlike obedience! How easy is the access of the word of the Divine Messiah to simple hearts! It is spoken, and done! There are many such simple people living in labour and low estate, but there are no such men amongst the rich. What do we see in one of them when the Lord told him to sell his possessions and follow Him? He followed not the Lord, but his riches. "He went away," it is said, "sorrowful."

Desolation

Sometimes in the lives of pious Christians there are hours when God seems to have entirely abandoned them—hours of the power of darkness; and then the man from the depth of his heart cries unto God: "Why hast Thou turned Thy face from me, Thou everlasting Light? For a strange darkness has covered me, the darkness of the accursed evil Satan, and has obscured all my soul. It is very grievous for the soul to be in this torturing darkness, which gives a presentiment of the torments and darkness of hell. Turn me, O Saviour, to the light of Thy commandments, and make straight my spiritual way, I fervently pray Thee."

Unite your soul to God by means of hearty faith and you will be able to accomplish everything. Do powerful, invisible, everwatchful enemies wage war against you? You will conquer them. Are these enemies visible, outward? You will conquer them also. Do passions rend you? You will overcome them. Are you crushed with sorrows? You will get over them. Have you fallen into despondency? You will obtain courage. With faith you will be able to conquer everything, and even the Kingdom of Heaven will be yours. Faith is the greatest blessing of the earthly life; it unites the man to God, and makes him strong and victorious through Him. "He who is joined to the Lord is one spirit."

If you do not yourself experience the action of the wiles of the evil spirit, you will not know, and will not appreciate and value as you ought, the benefits bestowed upon you by the Holy Spirit: not knowing the spirit that destroys, you will not know the Spirit that gives life. Only by means of direct contrasts of good and evil, of life and death, can we clearly know the one and the other. If you are not subjected to distresses, and danger of bodily or spiritual death, you will not truly know the Saviour, the Life-giver, Who delivers us from these distresses and from spiritual death. Jesus Christ is the consolation, the joy, the life, the peace, and the breadth of our hearts! Glory to God, the most wise and most gracious, that He allows the spirit of evil and death to tempt and torment us! Otherwise we should not have sufficiently appreciated and valued the comfort of grace, the comfort of the Holy Ghost the Comforter, the Life-giver!

Never despair of God's mercy, by whatever sins you may have been bound by the temptation of the Devil, but pray with your whole heart, with the hope of forgiveness; knock at the door of God's mercy and it shall be opened unto you. I, a simple priest, am an example for you: however, I may sometimes sin by the action of the Devil, for instance, by enmity towards a brother, whatever the cause may be, even though it may be a right cause, and I myself become thoroughly disturbed and set my brother against me, and unworthily celebrate the Holy Sacrament, not from wilful neglect, but by being myself unprepared, and by the action of the Devil; yet, after repentance, the Lord forgives all and everything, especially after the worthy communion of the Holy Sacrament: I become as snow, or as a wave of the sea, by the blood of Christ; the most heavenly peace dwells in my heart; it becomes light, so light, and I feel beatified. Then, indeed, I forget all troubles, anxieties, and the oppression of the enemy, I become entirely renewed, and as though risen from the dead. Do not then despair, brethren, whatever sins you may have committed, only repent and confess them with a contrite heart and humble spirit. Glory, O Lord, to Thy mercy! Glory, O Lord, to Thy long-suffering and forbearance!

What spiritual storms, hurricanes, fearful, fiery, sudden whirlwinds, often occur in the life of man, in the life of those who endeavor to lead a Christian life, and to serve God by prayer, interceding for themselves and others before His unspeakable mercy! It is only by God's mercy that the bark in which our soul travels over life's sea towards the eternity awaiting it, is not entirely wrecked and lost!

The Spiritual Combat

Those who are trying to lead a spiritual life have to carry on a most skilful and difficult warfare, through their thoughts every moment of their life—that is, a spiritual warfare; it is necessary that our whole soul should have every moment a clear eye, able to watch and notice the thoughts entering our heart from the evil one and repel them; the hearts of such men should be always burning with faith, humility, and love; otherwise the subtlety of the Devil finds an easy access to them, followed by a diminution of faith, or entire unbelief, and then by every possible evil, which it will be difficult to wash away even by tears. Do not, therefore, allow your heart to be cold, especially during prayer, and avoid in every way cold indifference. Very often it happens that prayer is on the lips, but in the heart cunning, incredulity, or unbelief, so that by the lips the man seems near to God, whilst in his heart he is far from Him. And, during our prayers, the evil one makes use of every means to chill our hearts and fill them with deceit in a most imperceptible manner to us. Pray and fortify yourself, fortify your heart.

Do not fear the conflict, and do not flee from it: where there is no struggle, there is no virtue; where there are no temptations for faithfulness and love, it is uncertain whether there is really any faithfulness and love for the Lord. Our faith, trust, and love are proved and revealed in adversities, that is, in difficult and grievous outward and inward circumstances, during sickness, sorrow, and privations.

Do not believe your flesh when it grows weak and refuses to serve you, on the pretence of not being sufficiently strengthened by food. This is a delusion. Overcome it; pray fervently, and you will see that the weakness of your body was false, imaginary, not real: you will see in truth that "not in bread alone doth man live, but in every word that proceedeth from the mouth of God." Do not put your trust in bread.

The crucified flesh reconciles itself with the spirit and with God; whilst the flesh that is cherished, that is abundantly and daintily fed, fights hard against the spirit and against God, and becomes wholly an abomination of sin. It does not want to pray, and, in general, rebels against God by blasphemy, for instance, and estranges itself from God. This is from experience. Therefore, "they that are Christ's have crucified their flesh, with the vices and concupiscences."

Do not suffer, Lord, that even for an instant I may do the will of Thine and mine enemy—the Devil; but grant that I may continually do Thy will, alone the will of my God and my King: Thou alone, my true King by Whom all kings reign, grant that I may ever obey Thee, reverence Thee truly and firmly. "Come let us adore and fall down and kneel before the Lord Who made us"; "serve ye the Lord in fear; and rejoice unto him with trembling."

The Triumph of Grace

Wonderful is the power of faith! Only the lively thought of God—only heartfelt faith in Him—is required, and He is with me; only hearty repentance for sins, with faith in Him, is required, and He is with me; one good thought, and He is with me; a pious feeling, and He is with me. But the Devil enters into me through impure, evil, blasphemous thoughts, through doubt, fear, pride, irritability, malice, avarice, envy; therefore his power over me entirely depends upon myself; if only I keep watch over myself, and continually preserve in my mind the name of the Lord Jesus Christ, with faith and love, he will be powerless to do me any harm.

THE PURSUIT OF HOLINESS

The Ordering of the Daily Life

There is no need to ask any one whether we ought to spread or propagate the Glory of God, either by writing, or by word, or by good works. This we are obliged to do according to our power and possibility. We must make use of our talents. If you think much about such a simple matter, then, perhaps, the Devil may suggest to you such foolishness as that you need only be inwardly active.

Do not only do your work when you wish to, but do it then, especially, when you do not wish to. Understand that this applies to every ordinary worldly matter, as likewise and especially to the work of the salvation of your soul—to prayer, to reading God's word and other salutary books, to attending Divine service, to doing good works, whatever they may be, to preaching God's word. Do not obey the slothful, deceitful, and most sinful flesh; it is eternally ready to rest, and to lead us into everlasting destruction through temporal tranquillity, and enjoyment. "In the sweat of thy face," it is said, "shalt thou eat bread." O miserable soul, "carefully cultivate the talent granted unto thee," sings the Church. "The kingdom of heaven suffereth violence, and the violent bear it away," says our Lord and Saviour.

Be moderate in all religious works, for moderation, even in virtue, corresponding to your powers, according to circumstances of time, place, and preceding labour, is prudent and wise. It is well, for instance, to pray with a pure heart, but as soon as there is no correspondence between the prayer and your powers (energy), with the various circumstances of place and time, with your preceding labours, then it ceases to be a virtue. Therefore the apostle Peter says, "Add to virtue knowledge" (that is, do not be carried away by the heart only); "and to knowledge temperance; and to temperance patience."

Watch yourselves—your passions, especially in your home life, where they appear freely, like moles in a safe place. Outside

our own home, some of our passions are usually screened by
other more decorous passions, whilst at home there is no possibility of driving away these black moles that undermine the
integrity of our soul.

Speak and do everything right undoubtingly, boldly, firmly,
and decidedly. Avoid doubts, timidity, languor, and indecision.
"For God hath not given us the spirit of fear, but of power and
of love." Our Lord is the Lord of powers.

Idle talk, or amusement with trifles in the society of guests,
deprives the heart of faith, of the fear of God, and of love for
God. Guests are a scourge for a pious heart. Of course, it is
understood that I refer to guests who only occupy themselves
with trifles. Serious, religiously minded guests are very different.

The Education of the Mind

Truth is the foundation of everything that has been created.
Let truth be also the foundation of all your works (both inward
and outward), and especially the foundation of your prayers.
Let all your life, all your works, all your thoughts, and all your
desires be founded upon truth.

How must we look upon the gifts of intellect, feeling, and
freedom? With the intellect we must learn to know God in
the works of His creation, revelation, providence, and in the
destinies of men; with the heart we must feel God's love, His
most heavenly peace, the sweetness of His love, we must love
our neighbour, sympathise with him in joy and in sorrow, in
health and in sickness, in poverty or in wealth, in distinction
and in low estate (humiliation); we must use freedom, as a
means, as an instrument for doing as much good as possible,
and for perfecting ourselves in every virtue, so as to render unto
God fruits a hundredfold.

Let all knowledge relating to religion or faith be as though
always new to you—that is, having the same importance, holiness, and interest.

What does to seek distraction mean? It means to wish somehow to fill the sickly emptiness of the soul, which was created
for activity, and which cannot bear to be idle.

Remember that the intellect is the servant of the heart, which is our life; if it leads the heart to truth, peace, joy, and life, then it fulfils its destination, it is the truth; but if it leads the heart to doubt, disturbance, torment, despondency, darkness, then it does not fulfil its destination and is absolutely false ("science, falsely so called"). If the heart feels peace, joy, ease from faith in anything, this is quite sufficient; it is unnecessary, then, to require from the reason proofs of the truth of such an object; it is undoubtedly true, the heart asserts it by its life, for the purpose of all investigations is truth and life.

Do not forget yourself in looking upon the beauty of the human face, but look upon the soul; do not look upon the man's garment (the body being his temporary garment), but look upon him who is clothed in it. Do not admire the magnificence of the mansion, but look upon the dweller who lives in it and what he is; otherwise, you will offend the image of God in the man, will dishonour the King by worshipping His servant and not rendering unto Him even the least of the honour due to Him. Also, do not look upon the beauty of the printing of a book, but look upon the spirit of the book; otherwise you will depreciate the spirit and exalt the flesh; for the letters are the flesh, and the contents of the book the spirit. Do not be allured by the melodious sounds of an instrument or of a voice, but by their effect upon the soul, or by the words of the song, consider what their spirit is: if the sounds produce upon your soul tranquil, chaste, holy feelings, then listen to them and feed your soul with them; whilst, if they give rise in your soul to passions, then leave off listening to them, and throw aside both the flesh and the spirit of the music.

In educating, it is extremely dangerous to develop only the understanding and intellect, and not pay attention to the heart. We must, above all, pay attention to the heart, for the heart is life, but life corrupted by sin. It is necessary to purify this source of life, to kindle in it the pure flame of life, so that it shall burn and not be extinguished; and shall direct all the thoughts, desires, and tendencies of the man through all his life. Society is corrupted precisely through the want of Christian education.

It is time that Christians should understand the Lord, should understand what He requires of us; namely, a pure heart. "Blessed are the pure in heart." Listen to His sweetest voice in the Gospel. The true life of our heart is Christ ("Christ liveth in me"). Let all of you learn wisdom of the Apostle. This should be our common problem: to bring Christ to dwell in our hearts through faith.

In many worldly magazines and newspapers, the number of which has so greatly increased, there breathes an earthly spirit, frequently impious, whilst the Christian, in his hope, is a citizen not only of the earth, but also of heaven, and, therefore, he ought also to meditate upon heavenly things. The heathen writings of antiquity were, it would seem, often better and purer (Cicero, for instance), higher in their foundation and motive, than some writings of Christian peoples. The Personal Word of the Father, our Lord Jesus Christ, is continually and greatly offended by Christian people, who are gifted with speech, and ought to be God-like, both in their speech and writings, whilst now their words are often wasted in vain, and even tempt the Christian, who is turned aside by worldly writings from reading the Word of God and the writings of the Holy Fathers. The editors and publishers of worldly magazines and newspapers ensnare and entice the flock of Christ by the incense of flattering words. O Word of God! What answer shall we give at Thy terrible Judgment?

Here is a society of men of the world: they go on talking and talking, for the greater part amusing themselves with trifles, and there is no mention of God—the common Father of all—of His love for us, of the future life, of recompense; why is it so? Because they are ashamed to speak of God. But what is still more surprising is that even persons deeming themselves pious, themselves luminaries, seldom speak of God, of Christ the Saviour, of the preciousness of time, of abstinence, of the resurrection from the dead, of judgment, of future bliss and everlasting torments, either in their family circle or amongst men of the world, but often spend their time in futile conversations, games, and occupations! This is, again, because they are ashamed to converse upon such subjects, being afraid to weary others, or fearing that they themselves may not be able to converse heartily upon spiritual subjects. O adulterous and sinful world! Woe unto thee at the day of judgment by the universal and impartial Judge! "He came unto His own, and His own received Him not." Yes, the Lord and Creator of all is not received by us! He is not received into our houses or into our conversations; or, else, when a man reads a religious book or prays aloud, why does he sometimes do so as if against his will, reluctantly, his tongue hesitating? His mouth speaketh not out of the abundance of the heart, but out of straitness and emptiness it can scarcely speak at all. Why is this so? It proceeds from the neglect of reading books and of prayer, and from false shame sown in the heart by the Devil. What miserable creatures we men are! We are ashamed of that which ought to be regarded as the highest honour. O ungrateful and evil-natured creatures! What torments do we not deserve for such conduct!

The Education of the Spirit

"He that gathereth not with Me, scattereth." It is necessary to advance in the spiritual life, and ascend higher and higher; to increase more and more the stores of our good works. If we remain stationary at one point of mortal perfection, upon one step of the Christian ascent, it is equal to our going back; if we do not gather, it is equal to scattering.

The inner man, amidst worldly vanity, amidst the darkness of his flesh, is not so bound by the temptations of the evil one, and looks out more freely in the morning just after waking up, as a fish sometimes throws itself up playfully on the surface of the water. All the remaining time he is enveloped in almost impenetrable darkness, his eyes are covered with a bandage, which conceals from him the true state of things spiritual and physical. Take advantage of these morning hours, which are the hours of a new life, or of a life renewed by temporary sleep. They show us in part that state in which we shall be when we shall rise up renewed on that great and universal morning of the nightless day of resurrection, or when we shall rid ourselves of this mortal body.

During the night our soul is free from worldly vanities, and therefore the spiritual world can act upon it more freely, and it is free to receive spiritual impressions; so that if the man is a righteous one, his thoughts and the inclinations of his heart are the thoughts and the inclinations of the Lord Himself, or of the Angels and Saints; whilst if he is an unrepentant sinner, they are the thoughts and inclinations of the Devil himself.

In ordinary human knowledge, we learn some subject once thoroughly, and often know it well during the whole of our lifetime without our knowledge of it becoming obscured. But in the matter of religion and faith this is not so; we think that once we have learnt, felt, and touched it, the subject will always remain clear, tangible, and beloved of our soul; but it is not so: it will a thousand times become obscured to us, removed from us, and will as it were vanish from us, so that at times we feel quite indifferent to the object by which we used to live and breathe, and it will sometimes be necessary to clear the way to it for ourselves by sighs and tears, in order to see it clearly again, to grasp and embrace it with our heart. This is caused by sin.

The carnal man does not understand the spiritual blessedness that proceeds from prayer and virtue, and cannot comprehend even in a small degree what the blessedness in the next world will be. He does not know anything higher than earthly carnal happiness, and considers future blessings as imaginary visions. But the spiritual man knows by experience the blessedness of the virtuous soul, and fore-tastes future blessedness in his heart.

If any thought is life to the heart, then it is truth; if, on the contrary, it is anguish and death to the heart, then it is a lie. Our Lord is peace and life, and He dwells in our hearts by peace and life.

Peace is the integrity and health of the soul; to lose peace is to lose spiritual health.

In what does the life of a Christian consist? In having nothing in the heart but Christ, or, if possessing earthly blessings, in not in the least attaching himself to them, but in clinging with the whole heart to Christ.

I myself am all infirmity, misery. God is my strength. This conviction is my highest wisdom, making me blessed.

Humility

To be humble means to consider ourselves deserving, for our sins, of every humiliation, injury, persecution, and even blows; and to be meek means patiently to endure injustice, abuse, et cetera, and to pray for our enemies.

If you wish to be truly humble, then consider yourself lower than all, worthy of being trampled on by all; for you yourself daily, hourly trample upon the law of the Lord, and therefore upon the Lord Himself.

When any one, out of kindness, praises you to others, and they transmit these praises to you, do not consider them as a just tribute of esteem really due to you, but ascribe them solely to the kindness of heart of the person who thus spoke of you, and pray to God for him, that God may strengthen him in his kindness of heart and in every virtue; but acknowledge yourself to be the greatest of sinners, not out of humility, but truthfully, actually, knowing as you do your evil deeds.

A deep feeling of spiritual poverty, a lamentation at the existence of evil, a thirst after salvation, are to be found in every straightforward and humble soul.

Receive every one who comes to you, especially with a spiritual purpose, with a kind and cheerful aspect, although he or she may be a beggar, and humble yourself inwardly before everybody, counting yourself lower than he or she, for you are placed by Christ Himself to be the servant of all, and all are His members, although like you they bear the wounds of sin.

There is absolutely nothing for a Christian to be proud of in accomplishing works of righteousness, for he is saved, and is being constantly saved, from every evil through faith alone, in the same manner as he accomplishes works of righteousness also by the same faith. "For by grace you are saved through faith, and that (faith itself) not of yourselves, for it is the gift of God; not of works, that no man may glory." So that no one can be proud of anything.

Spiritual poverty consists in esteeming oneself as though not existing, and God alone as existing; in honouring His words above everything in the world, and in not sparing anything to fulfil them, even one's own life; in considering God's Will in everything, both for ourselves and others, entirely renouncing our own will. The man who is poor in spirit desires and says with his whole heart: "Hallowed be Thy name, Thy kingdom come, Thy will be done in earth as it is in heaven." It is as though he himself disappears; everywhere and in everything he wishes to see God—in himself and in others. "Let every thing be Thine, not mine." He wishes to contemplate God's holiness in himself and in all His kingdom, also His will; also to see Him alone entirely filling the human heart, as it should be, because He alone is all-merciful and all-perfect, all-creating; whilst the enemy—the Devil and his instruments, and those who oppose God—are thieves in the kingdom of God, and adversaries of God. To him who is poor in spirit the whole world is as nothing. Everywhere he sees God alone giving life to everything, and ruling everything; for him there is no place without God, no moment without God; everywhere and at every minute he is with God, and as though with Him alone. He who is poor in spirit does not dare and does not think of trying to comprehend the incomprehensible, to discover God's mysteries, to philosophise on the highest; he believes in the single word of the Lord, the Life-giver, knowing that every word of His is truth, spirit, and eternal life; and in the words of His Church, ever instructed in all truth by the Holy Ghost, he believes as a child believes his father or mother, not requiring proofs, but perfectly relying upon them. He who is poor in spirit considers himself the very last and the most sinful of all, reckons himself worthy of being trampled under foot by every one.

When I look more closely upon some of the poor, and talk with them, then I see how meek, lovable, humble, simple-hearted, truly kind, poor in body, but rich in spirit they are. They make me—I who am rough, proud, evil, scornful, irritable, crafty, cold towards God and men, envious and avaricious—ashamed of myself. These are the true friends of God. And the enemy, being aware of their spiritual treasures, awakens in his servants— that is, in proud, rich men—contempt and ill-feeling towards them, and would like to wipe them off the face of the earth, as if they had no right to live and walk upon it. O friends of my God, my poor brethren! It is you who are the truly rich in spirit, whilst I am the real beggar, accursed and poor! You are worthy of sincere respect from us, who possess the blessings of this world in abundance, but who are poor and needy in virtues—abstinence, meekness, humility, kindness, sincerity, fervour, and warmth towards God and our neighbour. Lord! teach me to despise outward things, to turn my mental vision inward, and to value inward, and despise outward, things. Grant that I may observe this in my relations towards the rich and powerful of this world!

Love and Forgiveness

The purer the heart is, the larger it is, and the more able it is to find room within it for a greater number of beloved ones; whilst the more sinful it is, the more contracted it becomes, and the smaller number of beloved can it find room for, because it is limited by self-love, and that love is a false one. We love ourselves in objects unworthy of the immortal soul—in silver and gold, in adultery, in drunkenness, and such like.

Love does not reflect. Love is simple. Love never mistakes. Likewise believe and trust without reflection, for faith and trust are also simple; or better: God, in Whom we believe and in Whom we trust, is an incomplex Being, as He is also simply love.

Our life is love—yes, love. And where there is love, there is God; and where God is, there is every good. "Seek ye first the kingdom of God and His righteousness, and all these things shall be added unto you." And therefore joyfully feed and delight all, joyfully gratify all and trust in the Heavenly Father for everything, in the Father of bounties, and the God of every consolation. Offer that which is dear to you as a sacrifice of love for your neighbour. Bring your Isaac, your heart, with its many passions, as a sacrifice to God, stab it of your own free will, crucify the flesh with its passions and lusts. As you have received everything from God, be ready to give back everything to God, so that having been faithful in small things you may afterwards be made ruler over many things. Look upon all passions as upon illusions, as I have found out a thousand times.

When your brother sins against you in any way—for instance, if he speaks ill of you, or transmits with an evil intention your words in a perverted form to another, or calumniates you—do not be angered against him, but seek to find in him those good qualities which undoubtedly exist in every man, and dwell lovingly on them, despising his evil calumnies concerning you as dross, not worth attention, as an illusion of the Devil. The gold-diggers do not pay attention to the quantity of sand and dirt in the gold-dust, but only look for the grains of gold; and though they are but few, they value this small quantity, and wash it out of heaps of useless sand. God acts in a like manner with us, cleansing us with great and long forbearance.

Every person that does any evil, that gratifies any passion, is sufficiently punished by the evil he has committed, by the passions he serves, but chiefly by the fact that he withdraws himself from God, and God withdraws Himself from him: it would therefore be insane and most inhuman to nourish anger against such a man; it would be the same as to drown a sinking man, or push into the fire a person who is already being devoured by the flame. To such a man, as to one in danger of perishing, we must show double love, and pray fervently to God for him; not judging him, not rejoicing at his misfortune.

Do not pay attention to the words of an arrogant man, but rather to their power. It often happens that words that appear harsh at first sight, do not proceed from any harshness of the heart, but only from habit. How would it be if every one paid strict critical attention to our words, without Christian love, indulgent, sheltering, kindly, and patient? We must have died long ago.

How good Thou art, Lord, and how near art Thou to us—so near that we may always converse with Thee, be comforted by Thee, breathe through Thee, be enlightened by Thee, find peace in Thee, obtain spiritual breadth in Thee. Lord! teach me simplicity of love for Thee and my neighbour, so that I may ever be with Thee, that I may ever find peace in Thee. Lord! grant that I may not for a single moment have fellowship with the most abominable, most evil enemy the Devil, neither by malice, nor pride, nor envy, nor avarice, nor by love of gain, nor gluttony, nor impure thoughts, nor blasphemy, nor despondency, nor falsehood, nor by anything sinful. Grant that I may ever be wholly Thine!

Almsgiving

"Thou shalt love Thy neighbour as thyself." We ought to have all things in common. As the sun, the air, fire, water, and earth are common to us all, so ought also (in part) food and drink, money, books, and (in general) all the Lord's gifts to be shared in common; for they are given in common to all, and yet are easily divisible for distribution amongst many. For we have nothing of our own, but everything belongs to God. And it is not just for the rich to keep their superfluity in their treasuries when there are so many poor people in need of the means of existence, of necessary clothing and dwellings. However, it is just that the laborious should enjoy abundance, and that the idle should endure poverty and misery. Therefore, if we know that some are poor only through their own idleness and laziness, with such we are not obliged to share the abundance earned by our labour. "If any man will not work," says the Apostle Paul, "neither let him eat." But the crying poverty arising from old age, exhaustion, from sickness, from fruitless and badly paid labour, from really difficult conditions of life, from a numerous family, from bad harvests, we must always hasten to help, especially those of us who are rich. We must be guided by the history of the times of the Apostles, by the example of the early Church.

Concerning modern works of charity. If you enjoy earthly blessings in full measure, and if you give to the needy, but indulge yourself still more, it means that you do good works without the least self-denial. Your works of charity are not great. But what else do we find? What are so-called works of charity? People arrange different entertainments with a charitable object—that is, they intentionally wish before all to serve their sinful flesh, and the Devil, and only afterwards their neighbour and God. But this is no charity at all! Such works only bear the name of charity. "Let us do evil, that there may come good." "Woe to you that are filled, for you shall hunger! Woe to you that laugh, for you shall mourn and weep!"

That man is of a noble and elevated spirit who mercifully and generously scatters his gifts upon all, and rejoices when he has an opportunity of doing good and giving pleasure to everybody without thinking of being rewarded for it. That man is of noble and elevated spirit who never grows conceited and haughty towards those who frequent him and avail themselves of his bounties, does not neglect them in any respect, does not underrate them in any degree in his thoughts, but esteems them as he esteemed them at their first meeting with him, or much higher than at that time. As it is, it often happens that we grow conceited and proud towards those who have become ours, and, having become accustomed to them, speedily grow tired of them, and reckon them as nothing: we often place a man lower than a beloved animal or a beloved object.

Bear in your heart continually the words, "Christ is Love," and endeavour to love all, sacrificing for the sake of love, not only your possessions, but even yourself.

Lord! teach me to bestow charity willingly, kindly, joyfully, and to believe that by bestowing it I do not lose, but gain, infinitely more than that which I give. Turn my eyes away from hard-hearted people who do not sympathise with the poor, who meet poverty with indifference, who judge, reproach, brand it with shameful names, and weaken my heart, so that I may not do good, so that I, too, may harden my heart against poverty. O my Lord, how many such people we meet with! Lord, amend works of charity! Lord, grant that every charity I bestow may be profitable, and may not do harm! Lord, accept Thyself charity in the person of Thy poor. Lord, deign to help me to build a house for the poor in this town, concerning which I have already many times prayed to Thee, the all-merciful, almighty, most wise, wonderful![9]

Trust in God

Let that which tranquillises my thoughts and my heart be committed to writing as a memorial to me of the constant peace of my heart amidst the cares and vanities of life. What is it? It is the Christian saying, full of living trust and wonderful soothing power: "The Lord is everything to me." This is the priceless treasure! This is the precious jewel, possessing which we can be calm in every condition, rich in poverty, generous and kind to other people in the time of our wealth, and not losing hope even after having sinned. "The Lord is everything to me." He is my faith, my trust, my love, my strength, my power, my peace, my joy, my riches, my food, my drink, my raiment, my life—in a word, mine all. Thus, man, the Lord is everything to you; and you must be everything to the Lord. And, as all your treasure is contained in your heart and in your will, and God requires from you your heart, having said: "My son, give Me thy heart," therefore, in order to fulfil God's gracious and perfect will, renounce your own corrupt, passionate, seductive will; do not know your own will, know only God's will. "Not my will, but Thy will be done."

There is nothing impossible unto those who believe; lively and unshaken faith can accomplish great miracles in the twinkling of an eye. Besides, even without our sincere and firm faith, miracles are accomplished, such as the miracles of the sacraments; for God's mystery is always accomplished, even though we were incredulous or unbelieving at the time of its celebration. "Shall their unbelief make the faith of God without effect?" Our wickedness shall not overpower the unspeakable goodness and mercy of God; our dullness shall not overpower God's wisdom, nor our infirmity God's omnipotence.

Faith gives rest and joy; unbelief, troubles and wounds.

The means for confirming and strengthening Christian hope in us are—prayer, especially frequent sincere prayer, the confession of our sins, the frequent reading of the Word of God, and, above all, the frequent communion of the holy, life-giving mysteries of the Body and Blood of Christ.

THE COMMUNION OF SAINTS, AND THE LIFE EVERLASTING

Fellow-citizens with the Saints

"Hail, Thou that art full of grace, the Lord is with Thee!" Thus does the holy Church invoke the most holy Virgin, the mother of God. But the Lord is also with every pious soul that believes in Him. The Lord's abiding with the Virgin Mary before she conceived the Saviour is not a particularity proper to the most pure Virgin alone. The Lord is with every believing soul: "The Lord is with thee." These words may be said to every one who keeps the Lord's commandments. And the Lord is near unto all, only men themselves are far from Him by their hearts, by their thoughts, their intentions, and the inclinations of their hearts, as well as by their words and deeds, which are contrary to the law of God. "Behold, I am with you all days," says our Lord, Who was born of the most holy Virgin, "even to the consummation of the world"; that is, with every one of us, at every time, throughout all generations, all ages, upon the whole space of the earth, unto the end of the world.

You constantly notice that God does not tolerate the slightest momentary impurity in you, and that peace and God Himself leave you immediately after the admittance of any impure thought into your heart. And you become the abode of the Devil if you do not immediately renounce the sin. So that at every sinful thought, and still more at every sinful word and deed, we must say, "This is the Devil." Whilst at every holy and good thought, word, and deed, we should say, "This is God"; or, "This comes from God." Imagine, therefore, now what a resplendently adorned, pure, and immovable palace of the Almighty must have been the most holy soul and the most pure body of the mother of God, in whose womb God the Word came to dwell, and abode in her by His Godhead with His most pure soul and body! Imagine what eternal, infinite, unchangeable holiness she is! Imagine of what reverence and glorification she is worthy! Imagine what we are: "A reed shaken with (the Devil's) wind." The Devil breathes his blasphemy into our hearts, and we are immediately shaken with it. We are disturbed, depressed, when we ought to despise all his blasphemies, or not pay any attention to them, looking upon them as an illusion.

We have icons in our houses, and venerate them, in order to show amongst other things, that the eyes of God and of all the heavenly dwellers are constantly fixed upon us, and see not only all our acts, but also our words, thoughts, and desires.

There is a spiritual world; there is a communion of souls with those at a distance, and with the departed; they see and hear us, and here is an evident proof of this:—A woman, whose husband was ill and was lying in a room—at a distance of some four hundred miles from her, and who afterwards died—saw one evening the people who came to him, what he was doing, and heard the words that he spoke. Do not the saints see us in the same manner? Do not they hear our prayers in the same manner?

You do not understand how the saints in Heaven can hear us when we pray to them. But how do the rays of the sun bend down from Heaven to us, lighting everything throughout the earth? The saints in the spiritual world are like the rays of the sun in the material world. God is the eternal, life-giving Sun, and the saints are the rays of this wise Sun. As the eyes of the Lord are constantly looking upon the earth and upon terrestrial beings, so also the eyes of the saints cannot but turn towards the same direction as the provident gaze of the Lord of all creatures towards where their treasures (their bodies, their works, the holy places, and the persons devoted to them) are to be found.

"For where thy treasure is, there is thy heart also." You know how quickly, how far, and how clearly the heart can see (especially the objects of the spiritual world); you notice this in all the sciences, especially in the spiritual ones, where a great deal is adopted by faith only (the vision of the heart). The heart is the eye of the human being. The purer it is, the quicker, farther and clearer it can see. But with God's Saints this spiritual eye is refined, even during their lifetime, to the highest degree of purity possible for man, and after their death, when they have become united to God, through God's grace it becomes still clearer and wider in the limits of its vision. Therefore the saints see very clearly, widely, and far: they see our spiritual wants; they see and hear all those who call upon them with their whole hearts—that is, those whose mental eyes are fixed straight upon them, and are not darkened or dimmed when so fixed by unbelief and doubt; in other words, when the eyes of the heart of those who pray, so to say, meet the eyes of those they call upon. This is a mysterious vision. He who is experienced will understand what is meant. Therefore, how easy it is to communicate with the saints! It is only necessary to purify the eye of the heart, to fix it firmly upon a saint known to you, to pray to him for what you want, and you will obtain it. And what is God in reference to sight? He is all sight, all light, and all knowledge. He everlastingly fills both Heaven and earth, and sees everything in every place. "The eyes of the Lord in every place behold the good and the evil."

We have within us a spiritual eye, with which we see a million times more than we are able to by means of our bodily sight, which is merely an instrument of our spiritual eye; a conductor through which the soul either thinks or recognises all things visible. What are the objects of contemplation for this spiritual world? Besides the visible world, there is God, an infinite Spirit, an infinite Mind, Who has created and creates all things in the material world, which is the realisation of His thoughts (ideas), and there is a spiritual world, angelic, innumerable, living in constant contemplation of the Godhead, and of all the works of His omnipotence and great wisdom. Our spiritual eye relates above all to the Lord, and in this case its functions are called contemplation and meditation on God: this contemplation and meditation on God can extend unto infinity, as God Himself is infinite, and have the property of cleansing the soul from sin, of perfecting it, and bringing it nearer and nearer to God, the source of our light, or of our thought and life. After this we contemplate the angelic orders according to the measure of God's revelation and their spiritual, light-bearing nature, their spiritual goodness, their love for God, for each other, and for mankind, their guarding actions in relation to our earth, to its elements, to human communities, to holy and other places, and especially to every Christian. Besides this, the spiritual eye turns within to the man himself, and then its function is called self-examination, self-knowledge, self-introspection, spiritual watchfulness over our own thoughts and desires.

Imitation of the Saints

How vividly God's saints represented God to themselves!— the saints who through the Holy Ghost compiled prayers for their own and our guidance. In what fear and trembling they stood before God in prayer but also with what love and hope! Every word of their prayers says: "God is with us; and God within us hears each of our words, sees every thought, every wish, every tear."

The Lord is so holy, so simple in His holiness, that one single evil or impure thought deprives us of Him, of the sweet and most sweet, of the pure and most pure, peace and light of our souls. Hence it follows that the saints are all light; they are all one fragrance, like the light of the sun, like the purest air. Lord, grant this simple holiness to me also!

The holy angels and other heavenly powers are full of pure, holy life, of unbroken peace, of unchangeable vigour, of eternal courage and strength, of indescribable beauty, light, and wisdom, of the purest love for God and men, of mutual friendship, of Divine light and enlightenment: such are also our holy guardian angels. What a wonderful nature the angels have! But

Christians who become worthy of attaining to the future life and to the resurrection from the dead will be equal to the angels, according to the word of the Lord Himself. Let us, then, zealously strive after that endless, unchangeable, undisturbed life.

When your faith in the Lord, either during your life and prosperity, or in the time of sickness and at the moment of quitting this life, grows weak, grows dim from worldly vanity or through illness, and from the terrors and darkness of death, then look with the mental eyes of your heart upon the companies of our forefathers, the patriarchs, prophets, and righteous ones— St. Simeon, who took the Lord up in his arms, Job, Anna the prophetess, and others; the apostles, prelates, venerable fathers, martyrs, the disinterested, the righteous,[10] and all the saints. See how, both during their earthly life and at the time of their departure from this life, they unceasingly looked to God and died in the hope of the resurrection and of the life eternal, and strive to imitate them. These living examples, which are so numerous, are capable of strengthening the wavering faith of every Christian in the Lord and in the future life. Those Christian communities who do not venerate the saints and do not call upon them in prayer lose much in piety and in Christian hope. They deprive themselves of the great strengthening of their faith by the examples of men like unto themselves.

Thou alone knowest the cares, labours, and sweat of Thy saints, in order to purify themselves to please Thee, the Father of all. Thou alone knowest Thy saints. Teach us to imitate them in our lives so that we too may be in union with all, through love.

Death and Eternity

A terrible truth. Impenitent sinners after their death lose every possibility of changing for good, and therefore remain unalterably given up to everlasting torments (for sin cannot but torment). How is this proved? It is plainly proved by the actual state of some sinners and by the nature of sin itself—to keep the man its prisoner and to close every outlet to him. Who does not know how difficult it is, without God's special grace, for a sinner to turn from the way of sin, that is so dear to him, into the path of virtue? How deeply sin takes root in the heart of the sinner, and in all his being; how it gives the sinner its own way of looking at things, by means of which he sees them quite differently to what they are in reality, and shows him everything in a kind of alluring light. It is for this reason that we see that sinners very often do not even think of their conversion, and do not consider themselves to be great sinners, because their eyes are blinded by their self-love and pride. And if they consider themselves sinners, then they give themselves up to the most terrible despair, which overwhelms their minds with thick darkness and greatly hardens their heart. But for the grace of God, what sinner would have returned to God? For it is the nature of sin to darken our souls, to bind us hand and foot. But the time and place for the action of grace is here alone: after death there remain only the prayers of the Church, and these prayers can be efficacious for penitent sinners alone—that is, only for those who have developed in their souls the capability of receiving God's mercy or of benefiting by the prayers of the Church— that is, the light of the good works which they have taken with them out of this life. Impenitent sinners are undoubtedly sons of perdition. What does my experience tell me when I am the prisoner of sin? I am tormented sometimes the whole day, and cannot turn to God with my whole heart, because sin hardens my heart, making God's mercy inaccessible to me. I burn in the fire, and willingly remain in it, because sin has bound my powers, and I—like one inwardly chained—am unable to turn to God until He, seeing my helplessness, my humility, and my tears, takes pity on me and bestows His grace upon me. It is not without reason that a man given over to sin is spoken of as "delivered into chains of darkness."

What is most terrible to man? Death? Yes, death. None of us can imagine, without terror, how he will have to die and breathe his last sigh. And how parents grieve when their beloved children die, when they lie breathless before their eyes! But, brethren, do not fear, and do not grieve beyond measure. By His death Jesus Christ our Saviour has conquered our death, and by His resurrection He has laid the foundation for our resurrection, and every week, every Sunday, we solemnise in the risen Christ our common future resurrection from the dead, and begin beforehand the life eternal, to which our present temporal life is but a short, narrow, and most sorrowful way. For a true Christian death is merely like a sleep until the day of resurrection, or like birth into a new life. And thus in solemnising every week the resurrection of Christ and our own resurrection from the dead, let us learn to die continually to sin, and to rise with our souls from dead works, to enrich ourselves with virtues, and not sorrow inconsolably for the dead. Let us learn to meet death without dread, as the decree of the Heavenly Father, which, through the resurrection of Christ from the dead, has lost its terror.

God grant that, even after death, our brotherly union with our departed relatives, and those whom we knew in this life, may not be broken off, that our love may not be extinguished, but may burn with a bright flame, and that constant true remembrance of those at rest may ever remain with us until our death. "With what measure you mete, it shall be measured to you again."

Ought not the Christian, who looks for eternal peace and joy in heaven, to courageously and joyfully bear all sorrows, labours, sicknesses, and injustices, all sufferings, all unpleasantnesses? In truth he ought. Otherwise, what would be the meaning of future rest and peace? What peace and rest shall there be for him who has already had peace and rest here, without enduring anything? Where would God's justice be? "We must through much tribulation enter into the kingdom of God."

All present things are but a shadow of the future. The present light is a shadow of the future ineffable light. Earthly bliss is a faint shadow of future unspeakable, eternal bliss; fire a faint shadow of the fire of Gehenna, which will burn sinners unto ages of ages; pure earthly joy a shadow of unspeakable future joys; the magnificent royal palaces a faint shadow of the resplendent mansions of Paradise prepared for those who love God and fulfil his commandments. The glorious attire of the sons and daughters of men cannot be compared with that glorious garment with which the elect shall be clothed, for they will put on Christ. "Then shall the just shine as the sun, in the kingdom of their Father," according to the Saviour's sure promise.

What blessings Thy chosen ones will enjoy in heaven with Thee, O Lord! How wearisome to the heart are all earthly delights! How destructive to the heart is even a momentary attachment to anything earthly! And what peace, what freedom, what width, what light, what joy is to be found in Thee!

Union with God

The problem of our life is union with God, and sin completely prevents this; therefore flee from sin as from a terrible enemy, as from the destroyer of the soul, because to be without God is death and not life. Let us therefore understand our destination; let us always remember that our common Master calls us to union with Himself.

Be so sure of the Lord's nearness to you that you may feel when praying to God that you touch Him, not only with your thought and heart, but also with your mouth and tongue. "The Word is nigh thee, even in thy mouth, and in thy heart"; that is, God.

That our union with God in the future world will come to pass, and that it will be for us the source of light, peace, joy, and beatitude, this we partly recognise by experience even in the present life. During prayer, when our soul is wholly turned towards God, and is united to Him, we feel happy, calm, easy, and joyful, like children resting on their mother's breast; or, I would rather say, we experience a sensation of inexpressible well-being. "It is good for us to be here." Therefore struggle unremittingly to obtain future everlasting bliss, the beginning of which you know by experience even in the present life; but bear in mind that these beginnings are only earthly, imperfect, which we see now only in part, as "through a glass darkly." How will it be with us then, when we shall indeed be most truly united to God, when the images and shadows shall pass away, and the

kingdom of truth and vision will come? Oh! we must labour
unceasingly all our life, until death, for future blessedness, for
our future union with God.

Remember that you are always walking in the presence of
of the sweetest Lord Jesus. Say to yourself oftener: "I wish so
to live that my life may gladden my Beloved, crucified for my
sake on the Cross. Above all, I will take for the companion and
friend of my life my Holy Beloved, Who instils everything into
my heart, making me thirst for the salvation of all, "rejoicing
with those who rejoice, and weeping with those who weep."
This will especially comfort my Comforter, Christ.

In order that you should have steadfast assurance during
prayer, of receiving every spiritual blessing from the Lord, believe that by uniting yourself unto the Lord during your prayer
you become one spirit with Him, and that God is most gracious,
almighty, and most wise. He is all-perfect perfection, therefore
you, too, according to your receptivity, according to your faith
and love, will become a partaker of His Divine perfections. In
the union of your soul with God, do not consider anything impossible or difficult of fulfilment, "for with God all things are
possible"—not only the things which you can think of, or are
thinking of, but also those which you cannot think of, or which
you think of as impossible, for God is an infinite Being, and all
His perfections are infinite.

The invisible, all-pervading God often and sensibly touches
my invisible soul, which, from this touch, enjoys wonderful rest
and heavenly joy. It is not the eyes which give me tidings of my
God (ordinary feelings are destined for the lower objects of
creation), not the hearing by means of words or sounds of the
voice that carries to me the message of the Incomprehensible,
but the soul itself becomes, so to say, dissolved in God.

You have felt in your heart during prayer, or during the reading of the Word of God and other holy books (and sometimes
even during the reading of worldly ones of well-intentioned
contents, in which, for instance, some event representing the
action of God's Providence upon men is described), or during
edifying conversation, "a still small voice," as though a current

of electricity was passing through your body. It is the Lord visiting you. "A still small voice"—and the Lord is in it.

As your thought is near to you, as your faith is near to you, so near is God to you, and the more lively and steadfast is your thought about God, the more lively your faith, and the recognition of your infirmity and nothingness, and the feeling of your need of God, the nearer will God be to you. Or, as air is near to your body, so near is God to you. For God is, so to say, the mental air, by means of which breathe all the angels, the souls of the saints and of living men, especially of pious ones. You cannot live for a single moment without God, and you actually live each moment in Him: "For in Him we live, and move, and are."

If you have Christian love for your neighbour, then all heaven will love you; if you have union of spirit with your fellow-creatures, then you shall have union with God and all the dwellers of heaven; if you are merciful to your neighbour, then God and all the angels and saints will be merciful to you; if you pray for others, then all heaven will intercede for you. The Lord our God is holy; be so yourself also.

Nothing is nearer to us than God. He is the God of hearts, of the very hearts, and the heart, in its turn, is nearer than anything to us. It is the whole man, "the hidden man of the heart," as the Apostle says.

My God! how the love and sincere sympathy of our neighbour towards us rejoices our hearts! Who shall describe this blessedness of the heart, penetrated with the feeling of others' love towards me, and my love to others? It is indescribable! If here on earth mutual love so rejoices us, then with what sweetness of love shall we be filled in heaven, when we shall dwell with God, with the mother of God, with the heavenly powers, with God's saints? Who can imagine and describe such bliss, and what earthly temporal things should we not sacrifice in order to obtain the unutterable bliss of heavenly love? God, Thy name is Love!—Teach me true love, strong as death. I have most plenteously tasted its sweetness from my communion in the spirit of faith, in Thee, with Thy faithful servants, and have obtained plenteousness of peace and life through it. Strengthen, O God, that which Thou hast created in me. Oh, had it ever been thus all the days of my life! Grant that I may oftener be in the communion of faith and love with Thy faithful servants, with Thy temples, with Thy Church, with Thy members!

FATHER YELCHANINOV

THE TEACHER OF SELF-EXAMINATION

YELCHANINOV The mainstream of monastic spirituality in modern Russia has its source in the revival of the ancient ascetic tradition of the Greek Fathers (contained in the Philocalia, translated by Païsius Velichkovsky) and remains true to this fountainhead. The outstanding feature of this spiritual current is its complete detachment from modern culture. At the same time, it severs all connections with the social and active-ethical spirit of medieval Russian monasticism. To the extent that its exponents are obliged to take a stand upon social and political issues, their attitude is that of extreme reaction against all liberal reforms in Russian life. In theology they take pride in being merely followers and expositors of the Patristic tradition. Indeed the reader acquainted with this tradition will find nothing original in the numerous writings of Bishop Theophanes (surnamed Govorov, "The Recluse"), who was the compiler of the second, greatly enlarged, edition of the Philocalia. Theophanes represents the ascetical tradition, Bishop Ignatius Brianchaninov the mystical. Of more practical interest are the published letters of some of the startzy, especially those of the Optina monks Macarius and Ambrosius. It is extremely difficult to find copies of these books in the United States, but we can take comfort in the consideration that the writings of St. Nilus Sorsky, who is a true disciple of this school, can serve to represent it as well as could those of the majority of its modern disciples.

From among the moderns we choose instead of Theophanes and Ignatius a man whose name is little known but whose book (the only one on the spiritual life that he has written) is of greater interest than all the volumes of Theophanes and

Ignatius for the reason that this representative of the Patristic ascetical doctrine is a true 'modern of broad and refined culture, who has passed through the fiery revolutionary atmosphere of the Russian symbolist movement.

Father Alexander Yelchaninov was our contemporary. He died an exile in Paris in 1934. Born in 1881, the son of a traditionally military family, he was graduated from the University of St. Petersburg as a student in history and philology. He gave up the offer of a career of scholarly research and for some years lived in the centers of religious-philosophical activity, which during that decade (1900-10) was at its zenith in the circles of the progressive and artistic intelligentsia. Yelchaninov was associated with the writers S. Merezhkovsky, V. Rozanov and V. Ivanov, the poet. Having moved to Moscow, where he encountered Bulgakov and Berdiaev, he became associated in particular with two remarkable men, his friends and schoolmates from boyhood days. One was Vladimir Ern, the philosopher, the other, Paul Florensky, a mathematician and later a theologian, undoubtedly a man of genius. Both placed a heavy impress upon modern Orthodox thought. At the time of the first revolution in Russian (1905-6), these friends, together with Yelchaninov and a very few others, tried to enter politics as an underground group called the "Christian Brotherhood of Struggle," with revolutionary and anarchical tendencies.

Soon after the repression of the revolutionary movement, the members of this group became conservative or national spirited, as did most of the religious intelligentsia at that time. Yelchaninov spent the last years of the old regime as a teacher and headmaster in a progressive high school in Tiflis (now Tfilisi), the capital of Georgia in the Caucasus. Education was his true calling, and when he left Russia after the Communist Revolution and established residence in Nice (France) in 1922, he returned to the teaching profession. Even after his ordination as a parish priest (he was a married man), Father Alexander was, first of all, a spiritual guide to boys and girls, one of the leaders of the Russian Christian Student Movement in Exile. His gifts as a spiritual guide were remarkable. Even as a boy he was the intellectual leader of his younger schoolmates. For him it was both a need and a joy to assist in the discovery of the dormant powers of souls. He had somewhat the Socratic method, applied to nature in such a way that he might be described as a "spiritual midwife." Far from the spirit of proselytism, and with a distaste for the use of any force whatsoever, he simply opened to those under his guidance the way to self-examination. And he himself was a master of the technique of self-examination. Perhaps this is his real vocation in the spiritual life: he is not a struggler or a mystic but a serene and kind counselor, meek but interiorly austere, a stranger to any kind of opportunism.

The harrowing experience of the Revolution and the destruction of all hope for the peaceful cultural development of Russia produced in Yelchaninov, as in so many others, a profound reaction. People who kept free of political counter-revolutionary activities and were sufficiently thoughtful to develop their spiritual lives, turned their backs upon their social and historical environment. Theirs was the apocalyptic attitude of mind which characterized the early Church and the Fathers of the Desert. Yelchaninov discovered in the Patristic writings a correspondence with his personal experience, and it is this that makes his diary of such great interest. It is an intimate disclosure of his life. Father Alexander did not publish it himself, nor is it known whether he had considered its publication, but his wife had it printed after his death.

There is no attempt made at systematization in the diary, nor is it free of the contradictions naturally contained in unstudied writing of this kind. For the attentive reader there is one special attraction: from time to time, in the course of an austere ascetic world-denial, another trend of thought reveals itself: the humanistic appreciation of freedom, the hope of Christian culture, the positive evaluation of beauty, love, and friendship. This is the residue of the great spiritual movement of the early twentieth century. Its generous dreams are dissipated; yet certain positive elements are alive under the ground of ascetic reaction, awaiting their resurrection, when they will be incorporated with the traditional ascetic-mystical doctrine of the Church.

FRAGMENTS OF A DIARY

By ALEXANDER YELCHANINOV

BEFORE PRIESTHOOD THERE WAS SO MUCH I HAD TO BE SILENT ABOUT—TO RESTRAIN MYSELF. PRIESTHOOD, FOR ME, MEANS the possibility of speaking in a full voice.

There is no consolation in suffering other than to consider it in relation to the background of the "other world." Moreover, this is essentially the only correct point of view. If this world alone exists, then everything in it is absolute nonsense: separation, sickness, the suffering of the innocent, death. But all these acquire a meaning in that ocean of life invisibly washing the small island of our earthly being. Which of us has not experienced the breath of other worlds in dreams, in prayer? When a man finds in himself the power to acquiesce in the ordeal sent by God, he accomplishes great progress in his spiritual life.

What is that continual feeling of dissatisfaction, of anxiety— our ordinary disposition—but the stifled voice of conscience speaking within us beneath the level of consciousness and often contrary to our will and declaring the untruth that our life is? As long as we live in conflict with the radiant law which has been granted us, this voice will not be silent, for it is the voice of God Himself in our soul. On the other hand, that rare feeling of keen satisfaction, of plenitude and joy, is the happiness caused by the union of the divine principle of our soul with the universal harmony and the divine essence of the world.

I am continually pondering the text: "If you had been of the world, the world would love its own." Our sufferings are the sign that we belong to Christ; and the greater they are, the more evident it is that we are not "of the world." Why did all the saints, after Christ Himself, suffer so much? Contact with the world, plunging into the midst of things, gives pain to the followers of Christ; only the children of this world suffer no pain. This is in the nature of an unerring chemical reaction.

What augments our spiritual forces?—a temptation which has been overcome.

The presence of the Infinite—of Love—in us, who are finite beings, leads to the desire of death as of an entrance into the Infinite.

Life is a precious and unique gift, and we squander it foolishly and lightly, forgetful of its brevity.

Either we look back sadly on the past or live in the expectation of a future in which, it seems to us, real life will begin. But the present—that is, what actually is our life—is spent in these fruitless dreams and regrets.

The opinion of others concerning us—that is the mirror before which we all, almost without exception, pose. A man tries to be such as he wishes to appear to others. The real man, as he actually is, remains unknown to all, often himself included, while a figure projected and embellished by the imagination conducts his life. This tendency to deceive is so great that, distorting his very nature, a man will sacrifice his own self, the unique and inimitable essence of his human personality. But how great the attraction we feel whenever we meet a person free of this cancer, and how much we love the complete simplicity and directness of children, who have not as yet entered the zone of self-consciousness. Yet we have the alternative of struggling consciously to revert from this evil complexity to simplicity. In any case, when we become aware of the presence of this evil in us, the task is already half-accomplished.

Our Lord has infinite pity for us, and yet He sends us suffering: it is only when we are stricken by calamity that we are able to yield certain sparks, a certain sacred fire. This is the meaning of wars, revolutions, sickness.

The proud man is deaf and blind to the world; he does not see the world, but only himself reflected in all things.

Sickness—what a school of humility! It makes us see that we are poor, naked and blind. [Written a short while before his death.]

How shall we comfort those who weep? By weeping with them.

What joy to be a priest! Yesterday I confessed a whole family. The children especially were lovable—two boys of about seven. All evening I was almost rapt in ecstasy. Priesthood—the only profession in which men reveal to you the most earnest side of their nature, in which you also are "in earnest" all the time.

All that is sinful in us is so inveterate, so full-blooded, that our usual languid contrition is completely disproportionate to this sinful element possessing us.

It often seems to me that the thorns and thistles of our life's condition are ordained by God in view of curing precisely our soul. I see this with absolute clearness in my personal life.

If you are seized with anger towards someone, try to imagine that both you and he must die; how insignificant his fault will then appear, and how unjust your anger, even if formally justified.

Sickness is the most favorable time for us to return to our own heart, to God. As soon as our health has improved, the possibility of this drifts once more to an infinite distance.

Faith has nothing to fear from negative polemics, the ordeal by the mind; faith is able to withstand such an ordeal. But what it has to fear in us is the terrible weakness of the spirit, "the apostasy of the heart" (Kireievsky's expression).[1]

Those who seek proof to justify their faith are on a false track. Faith is a free choice; wherever there is a desire of proof, even a desire hidden from ourselves, there is no faith. The evidences of divine manifestation must not be taken as "proofs"—this would lower, cancel, the great virtue of faith.

To free ourselves from inner chaos, we must recognize objective order.

This is the kind of man we most often encounter; he presents a combination of three traits: (1) pride—faith in his own strength, delight in his own creations; (2) a passionate love of earthly life; and (3) freedom from any sense of sin. How can such men approach God? What is their path? Can they be transformed? As they now are, they are hopelessly isolated from God; they do not even feel the need of Him. And it is this kind of personality that is cultivated by modern life, by education, literature, et cetera. The idea of God is erased from the soul. In order that such a man should be reborn, what catastrophes are required!

There is a spirituality closely enmeshed with emotions—esthetic, sentimental, passionate—which is easily combined with selfishness, vanity, sensuality. Men of this type seek the praise and the good opinion of the priest who confesses them; their confession is very difficult for him, for they come in order to complain of others, to whimper; they are full of themselves, readily accuse others. The poor quality of their religious exaltation is best demonstrated by the facility with which they pass to a state of anger, irritation. They are further from genuine contrition than the most inveterate sinners.

The man who does not order his life according to logic and common sense but proceeds from the supreme law—the law of love—is always right. All other laws are naught in face of love, which not only directs hearts, but "moveth the sun and other stars."[2] He who keeps this law within him lives. He who lets himself be governed by philosophy, politics, reason alone, dies.

Faith originates in love; love, in contemplation. It is impossible not to love Christ. If we saw Him now, we should not be able to take our eyes off Him, we should "listen to Him in rapture"; we should flock around Him as did the multitudes in the Gospels. All that is required of us is not to resist. We must yield to Him, to the contemplation of His image—in the Gospels, in the saints, in the Church—and He will capture our hearts.

What is the necessity for reading the Lives of the Saints? In the infinite spectrum of the paths leading to God, which are revealed in the lives of the various saints, we can discover our own; we can obtain guidance that will help us to emerge from the jungle in which our human sinfulness has entangled us to gain access to the path leading towards Light.

Answer to the dying woman who does not suspect the approach of death; answer to her perplexity—"I am prepared neither for life nor for death": We cannot lead a genuine and dignified life here without preparing ourselves for death, without continually meditating upon the thought of eternal life.

My rule of life: to change our residence only when circumstances become pressing; to undertake nothing in the practical sphere on our own initiative, but to mine to the depths into which God has directed us.

How pathetic the complacency of our outlook on this present life is! The insubstantial little island of our "normal" existence will be washed away in the worlds beyond the tomb.

Here is the source of sin and folly—an aimless self-will instead of voluntary and spontaneous submission to Law.

There is a certain "constricted" condition of the soul in which we find it difficult to smile; we feel neither softness nor tenderness towards anyone—in one word, a petrified insensibility. Only prayer, especially the prayer of the Church, will dispel this condition. Such a mood is habitual to the proud, the melancholy, the vain, the debauched, the miserly; but to a certain degree, it is inherent to men in general: it is the condition of sin, of the absence of grace—man's common condition. So far as the soul is concerned, this is already a hell on earth, death despite the life of the body; and it is the natural consequence of sin, which literally is death to the soul.

The normal order within our soul: (1) A mysterious life of the spirit of which we are unaware, the genuine pledge of our salvation—that which comes to us from holy baptism, from the sacraments, from the inspiration of the Holy Ghost; (2) the vaporous cloud of our psuedo-virtues, disfigured, corroded, by the acid of vainglory: our so-called good deeds, our so-called prayer, truthfulness, straightforwardness; these mists obscure the true image of our wretched soul and hinder contrition; (3) the dense clouds of the actual sins we easily forgive ourselves: our continual judgment of other men, mockery, contempt, coldness, anger; (4) lastly, interior to all this, the deep, ancient strata of hereditary corruption which we share with the whole of humanity—the fundamental sinfulness from which arise, like poisonous vapors, blasphemous thoughts and impulses, all kinds of impurities, monstrous perversions.

I think of the meaning of sweat, tears, and blood for our purification and sanctification — of work, penance, martyrdom. Through them the body is freed of its psychic-animal elements, and the spiritual impulse, meeting no obstacle, pervades the whole man; this is why the Church elevates its martyrs, emphasizing precisely the shedding of blood; and this is why people honor the dead killed in war.

We must relinquish the notion that humanity is divided into two hostile camps, two different breeds of men, the just and the sinners—the first predestined for beatitude, the second, for perdition. Nothing of the sort is true. We are all sinful, all tainted, and our Lord suffered for all of us. All are equally dear to Him, and it is to Him that the final judgment belongs. That is why Christ's words about love are directly followed by the words about judgment: "Judge not, that you may not be judged."

Often we are saddened by the faded appearance of a friend or relative who has grown old. Yet this decline is a purely physical one that opens the way for beneficent spiritual forces arising from the depths of our interior. That blossoming, the wane of which we observe with dismay in ourselves and in others—bright eyes, ruddy complexions, deep, melodious voices—all that is but the flowering of our psychic-animal nature, and is without value. The more a man loses outwardly, the more profound is the rebirth in his interior. Yet it is well if this is so, and if the passing years do not lead instead to melancholy, to the fear of old age and death, to spiritual degeneration.

How far false ideals lead us! In this manner have many revolutionists lost their souls; proceeding from a righteous (but narrow) concept of the good of the people, they have attained only to satanic hatred, lies, murder. A similar fate awaits the adherents of the ideal of nationalism unless they subordinate this ideal to a higher one.

Our whole interior life is energized by the love of God. But whence shall we derive this love? All our loves are fed by sensible impressions of the beloved object (the world, our friends and loved ones). How shall our love, our faith, endure the ordeal if they are not nourished by evidences? Yet what sensible impression can we receive of God, Whom "no man hath ever seen"? We have Christ. Thoughts of Him, prayer, the reading of the Gospels—such is the food by which the love of Him is nourished. But it may be (and such is often the case) that our hearts are too unformed, too unreceptive. In this case, we must return to the lives of the Saints, to the writings of the Fathers. They hold the same light of Christ, but with a softer quality, mellowed in passing through the prism of a saintly human soul.

Only men who have no experience in such things can speak of the uselessness of making an effort in prayer, in the love of God. All striving towards God—even the weakest, even if forced—yields a vivid and irrefutable experience of His love. A man who has had this experience will never forget it. The same can be said of love towards other men. All love carries with it its own satisfaction and recompense. Here we find the *experimental* confirmation of the words "God is Love."

The indifference of believers is something far more dreadful than the fact that unbelievers exist.

The practice of theosophy, occultism, spiritualism is not only harmful in its effect on spiritual health, but has as its basis an illegitimate desire to peep through a closed door. We are humbly to admit the existence of a Mystery, and not try to slip round by the baskstairs to listen. Moreover, we have been given a supreme law of life which leads us straight to God — love, a difficult, thorny path; we must follow it, bearing our cross, with no excursions into byways.

The death of our friends and relations provides experimental confirmation of our faith in the infinite. Our love of the departed is the affirmation of the existence of another world. In the company of the dying, we reach the frontier dividing two worlds—the world of illusions and the real world: death proves to us the reality of that which we held to be an illusion, and the insubstantiality of that which we considered real.

The man who denies his relationship to God, who refuses to be His son, is not a real man but a man diminished, the unfinished plan of a man. For to be sons of God is not only granted us as a gift but is also *entrusted* to us as a task, and the accomplishment of this task alone, through the conscious putting on of Christ and God, can lead to a full disclosure, a full blossoming, of human personality.

Sin is a destructive force—and first of all destructive of the one who is burdened with it; sin distorts, darkens, the face of man, even in the physical sense.

What is it that terrifies us most in ourselves?—the state of insensibility, of spiritual sloth, blindness. What great pain, what remorse, should be occasioned by sin, what a thirst for contrition and forgiveness should be experienced by the soul! But usually we feel nothing of the sort. And life goes on around us as if all were right with the world. Perhaps this indifference is the precise result of the spiritual deterioration consequent to sin.

There is the monastic life and the state of marriage. The third condition, that of virginity in the world, is extremely precarious and fraught with temptation; and not all are strong enough to adapt themselves to it successfully. Moreover, those who adhere to this condition are dangerous even to the persons surrounding them: the aura and beauty of virginity, which in a sense are "nuptial feathers" (when deprived of direct religious significance), exercise their powerful attraction and awaken unseemly emotions.

Our modern individualism creates special difficulties in married life. To overcome them a conscious effort on both sides is necessary, so that a marriage may be built which will be a "walking in the presence of God." (The Church alone provides a full and genuine solution for all problems.) And there is something more, something which may appear to be the simplest matter of all but is nevertheless the most difficult to achieve—the firm intention of letting each partner keep the proper place in marriage: for the wife, to be humbly content with second place; for the husband, to assume the burden and the responsibility of being the head. If this firm intention and desire are present, God

will always help us to follow this difficult path, the path of
martyrdom (the chant of the "Holy Martyrs" is sung in the
course of the bridal procession), but also a way of life that yields
the most intense joy. Marriage is a mysterious revelation. We
see in it the complete transformation of a man, the expansion
of his personality—fresh vision, a new vitality—and through it
the birth of a new plenitude.

Woman has been called a "vessel of infirmity." This "infirmity" consists especially in her enslavement to the natural, elementary forces within and outside herself. Result: inadequate
self-control, irresponsibility, passion, blind judgments. Scarcely
any woman is free of the latter; she is always the slave of her
passions, of her dislikes, of her desires. In Christianity alone
does woman become man's equal, for then she submits her temperament to higher principles and develops sound judgment,
patience, logic, wisdom. Only then does friendship with the
husband become possible.

What sources of temptation and perversion does the life of
the theater contain—for the spectator, and especially for the
actor? The habit of living, and of living vividly and eagerly, a
life of the imagination which frequently offers an experience of
far greater intensity than that of our ordinary, everyday existence; the fact of creating in ourselves "parasitical personalities"
(from that of Yepikhodov to that of Tsar Fedor Ioannovitch
in the case of Moskvine[3]): vainglory. It is for this reason that
the theater is so dangerous for weak personalities; it corrodes
them until nothing is left. However, all human activity contains
these (or other) poisons, and strong personalities alone can
resist infection and remain themselves.

The attention given to our interior life which is recommended
by religion is no less fruitful from the purely psychological standpoint—the development of the power of attention, the concentration of our conscious life, the manifestation of new powers.

If we peruse the writings of the saints and Fathers of the Church, what depths of psychological analysis we discover in them, what fine distinctions between pyschical states, what great precision in definition, and what a true classification of all the subtleties of feeling!

One of the Fathers—I do not remember which—draws an analogy between recollection during prayer and the wick of an oil-lamp. If we develop this analogy further, we shall be able to say that a continual state of contrition, humility, purity of heart, meekness, is the "holy oil" of prayer, the express condition of the lamp's burning.

"The Kingdom of God cometh not with observation . . . for behold, the Kingdom of God is within you." Could not the same be said of the eternal fire? Is not hell already here for many a human being?

We must not live superficially, but with the greatest possible tension of all our forces, both physical and spiritual. When we expend the maximum of our powers, we do not exhaust ourselves, but increase the sources of our strength.

The woman who had a spirit of infirmity had been bound by Satan. Here we are shown another source of sickness—the devil. This is the objection which can be made to those who declare (for instance, myself) that one must rejoice in sickness as in all other misfortunes, and not ask to be healed.

I seem to discover a secret fear of death in the way men seek to escape loneliness.

I realize more and more clearly that Orthodoxy is the principle of absolute freedom. It entails the fear of rules and regulations, the fear of limiting ourselves in one way or another, of placing the word, the thought, the ornamentation above the fact, or without the fact; a repugnance towards propaganda, constraint—even of a purely ideological or psychological kind—the fear of indoctrination, faith in the actual reality of the spiritual life alone. All the rest will come of itself.

Types of Christianity: (1) mentally contemplative; (2) volitional active (Catholicism); (3) intellectually ethical (Protestantism); and (4) Christianity understood as the cult of the Supreme Beauty—Orthodoxy. All the powers of the faithful are given up to this vision. All other aspects of Christianity are submitted to this conception. The opinion expressed by certain people ("Old-Believers"), that Orthodoxy is liturgical worship: this is partly true—to live theurgically ("without leaving the Temple"). But at the same time this presents certain dangers—in the event that this ideal fails, a man is left without a trained will, without ethic and mental discipline. This is why the disintegration of Orthodoxy (as, for instance, in present-day Russia) leads to dissoluteness, immorality, ignorance. The human element is not sufficiently cultivated in the Orthodox, especially in the member of the "Old-Believer" branch. Therefore, when deprived of faith, he becomes the slave of the world. And yet we refuse to consent to any religion of an inferior type: rational, volitional, ethical. We must educate the will in our religion, raise the cultural and moral level, become worthy of the precious gift which has been bestowed upon us.

Typical of the errors leading to rash judgment, to melancholy, to wrong evaluations, is "Rousseauism" in religion—the idea that here on earth, before the general judgment, there can be flawless achievements on our part, on that of other men, or of human associations.

Consequently we expect of ourselves the perfection of sanctity and are disheartened when, in our holiest moments, we discover in our hearts impurity, vainglory, duplicity; we are irritated because men whom we had considered flawless prove to be cowardly, cunning, untruthful; we despair when we see in God's own Church various schisms, disputes, and jealousies—the unleashed storm of human passions.

And yet this must be; the entire world is infected with sin; the terrible fissure runs from top to bottom of it—the cancer of decay and death—and no one and nothing can be free of corruption. If, in the most perfect of all communities, among Christ's disciples, there was a Judas, why be shocked by a Vvedensky[4] in the Russian Church? Every parish has its lesser Judas, but it also has its meek, "spirit-bearing" John, its faithful, active Peter.

The joy afforded by the veneration of icons is caused by the fact, that God, "the Word Incomprehensible," came down from heaven, was made flesh, took human form, and dwelt among us, "full of Grace and Truth," so that we have heard Him with our ears, seen Him with our eyes, touched Him with our hands.

The basic factor in our spiritual life is an eager striving to apprehend the holy in concrete, palpable form; we love to touch it, to kiss it, to wear it on our breast, to bless our houses with it. The iconoclasts tried to deprive us of these sacred objects, and when we regained them there was great rejoicing. See how cold and abstract the faith is in denominations which reject the worship of icons. While visibly rejecting the icons, they invisibly reject the Incarnation. How degenerate their entire Christianity becomes; and the Eucharist Itself, which is the centre of Christian life, becomes an abstraction of no real significance. Indeed, if among us the Word becomes Flesh, among them the Flesh has become word; the Divine Flesh, communion in which gives eternal life, is reduced by them to mere formulism.

Why is *faith* difficult? Before the fall man *knew*. Sin has hidden God from him, and faith is the piercing of this veil of sin which separates us from God.

Purification from sin leads from faith to knowledge.

Our lack of compassion, our ruthlessness towards other men, is an impenetrable curtain between ourselves and God. It is as if we had covered a plant with a black hood, and then complained that it died from deprivation of sunlight.

Several days have elapsed, and I can hardly recall (and not at all from within but only in an exterior fashion) that extraordinary feeling which came over me as we laid N. in his coffin.

Ordinarily it is the most awful moment, even hideous: the undertakers, to whom the last attendance upon the dead is but a tiresome duty, drag the body from the bed; it hangs helplessly, the head dangling—and they shove it into the coffin. The members of the family are usually sent out of the room—and so much the better.

But this time it was altogether different: there were no strangers; the priest, with a lighted candle, prayed in a low voice, and the members of the family lifted the dead man and put him gently into the coffin.

For a few seconds the most extraordinary mood came over me; it seemed to me that I had literally emerged from myself, that I was not only an onlooker, but a participant; I felt that everything was exactly as it should be, that the scene was like a painting on an icon, and that I was also part of it. I am now afraid to say anything for sure: it was something like a holy vision of the world. Thus do saints and children conceive the Church, the temple and the divine service, as something taking place at the same time in two worlds (a boy's words: "It is as if God embraced and held in His hands the whole temple").

On a lower plane, it is an aesthetic perception of the world, which one sees transfigured in a heavenly way.

The certainty that all the prophecies have been accomplished, that the times are fulfilled, and that humanity has reached a point of development in the world which will issue in terrible catastrophe for some and immeasurable joy for others—such a certainty, it seems, is inevitably discovered in all intense religious life; it is the sense of a suddenly disclosed and achieved infinity; a certainty inherent, perhaps, to all strong emotion—

be it despair, love, the impulse of faith, or prophetic ecstasy.

Birth is mystical—we are visited by a messenger from another world. This mystic sense in us is even more deeply awakened by the death of those we love—when they leave us, they draw a long cable from the tissues of our soul, so that we can no longer be content with this world alone; a telephone communicating with the infinite is thus installed in our warm, comfortable home.

Evil is not a bad habit, an incorrect attitude of the soul—it is actually an inspiration of the devil's power. This is especially obvious in the feeling of anger.

"*Mania grandiosa*" inevitably grows out of our being wrapped in ourselves. All proportions are effaced, and the ego develops and grows till it reaches the domain of madness.

Nervousness is in a certain sense the psycho-physical condition of holiness; a refined body—transformed by tears, fasting, sickness, work—becomes more susceptible to the influence of beneficent spiritual forces. But at the same time it grows morbidly sensitive to the world of gross material objects, and its reaction towards this world is nervousness.

A saint, minus his saintliness, is a neurotic. (Striking words of a doctor who had visited Mount Athos: "Well, they are all neurasthenic in there.")

The saint who has fallen and lost his sanctity becomes an easy prey to demons; this is why the Fathers of the Church assert that the condition of one who has drifted from spiritual discipline is more dangerous than that of an unspiritual person. Here is the danger of fasting, asceticism, when not regulated by an experienced director and when emptied of the content of prayer.

"Black grace." An influx of extraordinary powers, an almost infinite growth of energy, can be observed in angry men. If it is true that "if a man be kind, none will be able to resist him," it is also true, that if a man is angry, it is no less difficult to resist his strength. When a man abandons himself to irritable moods, he has opened his soul to demonic forces.

There are men of a wonderful, paradisaic character, with souls born before Adam's fall—childlike, simple, and direct, unacquainted with anger and untruth. And this is not the result of a struggle within themselves, of an effort; they are born that way—without sin. And, curiously enough, these men very often stand outside the Church, and sometimes live entirely without religion. They are too simple, too much of one piece, to be able to live by principles drawn from theology; they are too modest and chaste to express their feelings in words or signs (rites). In religion the most important thing is not faith but the love of God, and they love God, because they love Beauty, Goodness, Truth—and all these are elements of Divinity. There are many who assert that they believe in God yet lack this sense of Beauty and Goodness; they harbor sin and anger in their souls and are entirely indifferent to Truth; for them, the place of the absolute is held by a dozen particular truths to which they cling proudly. But those others, the true and simple souls who live in joy even on earth—they will surely enter after death into the kingdom of Light and Joy; by the attraction of affinity, they are in their element when in the company of simple and holy people. We, the so-called "believers," say "we shall be on our way," and we do not go; they make no statement in the matter, but simply fulfill the Father's will.

The true lover considers as traitorous and sinful in relation to the beloved all delight, any strong response, which has been experienced independently, as well as all association with other people—even the partaking of food prepared by strange hands.

There is a real sense in which the lovers merge into one; hence the pain caused by all division, by the fact of not being one.

Youthful entanglements and complexes—Hamletism—usually spring from the following sources: take a talented young man (more rarely, a girl) endowed with intelligence, imagination, a vividly impressionable nature. Under the influence of books, examples, persons, and with the aid of that very intelligence and imagination, he creates parallel personalities in himself; a whole wardrobe of masks and costumes; these are like larvae; they stifle the original kernel of personality and multiply, covering it with a parasitic growth. Hence the complexity, the entanglements, the inevitable falsifications and the loss of personality. Only as the result of strenuous effort will true personality rediscover itself among these parasites and make its way among the noisy, motley crowd of them. One may destroy these parasites by despising and ignoring them and by limiting the sphere of one's interests. But it is almost impossible to achieve this without the aid of a friend or a priest, for real personality can be so stifled and suppressed that its rediscovery offers the greatest difficulties; the inexperienced prefer the risk of giving new strength to their own larvae. Hence, usually an entangled life, a wrongly chosen profession; in the worst cases, insanity.

Abrupt, faulty speech, with pauses and searchings for words, is often the characteristic of a very sincere person, who is unable to use *clichés,* and gropes painfully for words and exact expressions. This is why I am always sympathetic towards a certain tongue-tied speech—provided, of course, that it is not a sign of sheer incapacity.

To the usual demand of the unbelievers, that "proof" should be given immediately, on the spot: you do not try to demonstrate a scientific, mathematical truth to a drunkard. Here, the same can be said: First sober yourself of your intoxication with the world—its bustle, worries, vanity—than we shall enter into conversation, and you will be able to understand. "Wisdom shall not enter the cunning soul."

Self-denial, which is so often mentioned in connection with the practice of Christianity, is conceived by certain persons as an end in itself; they look upon it as the essential implication of the Christian life.

But it is only a way and a means for achieving the end—the putting on of Christ.

Neither must we think, as do others—(falling into the opposite error) that self-denial is a renunciation of our personality, a repression of our personal inclinations, a sort of spiritual suicide. Exactly the contrary: self-denial is liberation from the slavery of sin (or else we are prisoners), and the free revelation of the true essence originally designed for us by God.

The sight of death is always edifying. However it occurs, it is always a miracle and a mystery. Our thoughts—and if death has stolen from us someone whom we cherish, our love—accompany the dying; our spirit seems to cross the threshold, to glimpse another world and be convinced of its reality. I experienced this for the first time when I saw someone tread on an earwig and "bring it to naught." Then I realized for the first time that nothing can be destroyed, that this would be nonsense which neither our mind nor our spirit could support, that even the earwig had passed into another world—vanished indeed from the realm of being as we know it, but not destroyed.

All pleasures, enjoyments, diminish and weaken the life of the soul.

The tension of effort, of work, always causes the growth of spiritual forces.

When we pray for our beloved dead, we exercise our sense of the unreality of the present world (a precious part of this world has left us) and of the reality of that other, supernatural world, whose actual existence is confirmed by our love of the dead.

Civilization was produced by the creative effort of humanity, not only independent of, but often contrary to, the law of God. It acquired solid, godless forms; it has been inspired with an alien spirit which is hostile to us.

How shall we solve this problem, we who want to live in accordance with God's law, yet do not wish to leave the world? An individual decision is easier to take—to go into the world without losing oneself, keeping one's soul dedicated to Christ, to live to the maximum the life of the Church, without being overindulgent of our selves. For society this solution is much more difficult. . . .

We often mistake for religion a vague mixture of the reminiscences of childhood, the sentimental emotions sometimes experienced in church, colored eggs, and cakes at Easter. How shall we succeed in so much as awakening a sense of the way of the Cross along which our sinful soul will be led to God? . . .

When the times are fulfilled and the end is at hand, when the world's autumn comes and God sends his angels for the harvest: what will they find in the barren fields of our hearts? And yet, the time is nearly accomplished and the end close by for each of us, even before the common harvest.

But let us not be downhearted. See how the sower goes on sowing among the rocks and thorns and by the roadside. This means that he places some hope even in such fields as these. And we know from the lives of the saints how often a soul which had seemed irreclaimably stifled by sin, blinded by passion, hardened in evil, became good earth, instinct with power for growth, purified of noxious mixtures and alien seeds.

We must not think that there is only one kind of wealth—money. One can be rich in youth, possess the assets of talent, of gifts, the capital of health. These riches too are obstacles to salvation.

Material wealth enslaves us, sharpening self-interest, corroding the heart, overwhelming us with anxiety and fear; like an insatiable demon, it demands sacrifice. Instead of serving us, it makes us serve it. Cannot the same be said of the treasures of health, strength, youth, beauty, talent? Do not they likewise confirm us in our pride and constrain the heart, leading it away from God?

Yes, truly: "Blessed are the poor" in the world's goods. How easily they gain evangelical lightness of spirit and freedom of earthly fetters; but blessed also are those who are without health and youth (for "he who suffers in the flesh ceases to sin"). Blessed the ugly, the ungifted, the unlucky—they are free of the chief enemy, pride—for they have nothing to be proud of.

But what are we to do if God has granted us this or that earthly gift? Is it possible that we shall not be saved until we are divested of it? We may keep (but not for ourselves) our riches and still be saved, but we must be interiorly free of them; we must tear our heart from them, hold our treasures as if we did not hold them; possess them, but not let them possess us; lay them at Christ's feet and serve Him through them.

If we observe sin, it means that we participate in it, and in that particular kind of sin. Does a child condemn profligacy? He cannot see it. That which we observe, we have some share in.

Sometimes it seems as if the souls of old people died gradually, along with their bodies. This impression that the soul is growing barren is derived from the fact that the body, stricken with old age, gradually ceases to be a sufficient medium of expression for the soul. The process is similar to the one we observe in decalcomania: the damp paper gives a faint outline of a picture (life); then we gradually draw this paper away (sickness, old age). The picture begins to disappear, then fades entirely (death). All that remains in our hands is a blank sheet (the dead body), but if we look at the underside, we see a bright picture (the life of the world to come).

"Thou hast effaced thy enemies by the abundance of Glory." This is the method of the spiritual struggle, the only possible one—to destroy, to "efface," the enemy, by the abundance, the power of the divine radiation.

Our continual self-justification: "this is yet but a venial sin," and our self-assurance: "I will not allow myself to commit a greater one." But bitter experience has shown us all more than once, that if we have yielded to the first impulse of a sinful act—and especially if we have indulged in it—it takes possession of us, and scarcely anyone is able to turn back.

Living corpses walk in our midst; their souls have died before the death of the body, and they have no hope of resurrection; for it is here that we prepare for ourselves the life of the world to come. And there are souls which have already, so to speak, risen from the dead before the death of the body—souls which, through acts, experience, love, have gained access to the highest life of the spirit.

In this gloomy world, even the radiance of each virtue casts its own shadow: humility, pusillanimity and cunning; kindness, injustice; the love of truth, harshness and exigence. And since we are always inclined to see the worst, it is these shadows that claim our attention, and sometimes are all that we see. To our sinful gaze the meek appear lacking in force and integration; those who are drawn to prayer, arid and selfish; the generous and disinterested, impractical and extravagant; the contemplative, lazy. The faculty of seeing the dark side of everything—even of good things—is not so much a proof of the presence of these shadows where we seem to discover them as it is damning evidence of the hidden distortions in our own nature, the sinfulness of us all.

We must not only bear misfortunes but see in them the hand of the Master of destinies.

... I will tell you the conclusion that I have long since reached from reading the Holy Fathers: periods of aridity are entirely normal, and we must bear them patiently and with equanimity. These periods secure us in the humble realization of our helplessness and compel us to place in God alone our hope for the renewal of our hearts.

Good and evil are not the sum total of good or evil deeds; men are possessed by good or evil forces. This pressure of evil, the force of this evil principle, is immense. Acts in themselves have little (religious) significance. Those which are good, so far as their results are concerned (to give food and other assistance), can be essentially bad if they come from a man who is in the possession of evil; while actions which are unavailing, foolish or even harmful, can be good if they come from a good source, if they are well-intentioned.

Often we refrain from sin, not because we have conquered the temptation or overcome it interiorly, but thanks to exterior circumstances: out of the sense of propriety, because of the fear of punishment, et cetera. But even a disposition towards sin is already a sin in itself.

However, an interior, latent sin is less serious than one which has been committed; there is no inveteration in sin, no temptation caused, no harm done, to others. There is often a desire of sin, but no acquiescence—there is struggle.

The following are the stages through which sin enters into us: the image, attention, interest, attraction, passion.

We do good, purify our heart and draw nearer to God, not in order to obtain a reward, but out of our love of God. One day I asked myself: would I remain with Christ if I knew for certain that the devil would defeat God? And I answered without hesitation: of course I would remain with Him. What has selfishness to do with it?

The inferiority-complex is nothing but pride, the concentration of attention on one's self, egotism under a different form. Neither self-exaltation nor the sense of nonentity would ever trouble the minds of the humble and simple.

The flux of time is terrifying as long as one remains motionless. We must plunge into the depths, where time is a matter of indifference.

To expect, to demand, miracles is not only wrong, inasmuch as it shows a lack of trust in God; it is also senseless, for we count millions of accomplished miracles, and if none of them has convinced us, why should we be convinced by this one miracle?

We can live—and many do—our entire life as the pale reflection of someone else, as a copy of someone else. The first, original meaning of living is to be oneself, rising to the transformation of oneself into the image and likeness of God.

On the destiny of non-Christians after death: "For whosoever have sinned without the law shall perish without the law" (Rom. 2, 12). Does this mean that those who *have not sinned* without the law will be justified? For they (verse 15) "show the work of the law written in their hearts" and in their conscience.

A vow contains a partial acceptance of the suffering which has been sent us, and our acquiescence in regard to it: Lord, Thou sendest suffering in order to enlighten us; I pray Thee, replace this suffering by some other—may my child be cured, and I promise to bear the pain under another form: fasting, pilgrimage, or other spiritual or physical sacrifices.

Sweat, tears, blood. . . . If sweat is produced by inner rebellion, anger, vindictiveness; if tears are caused by pain, offense, rage; if blood is shed without faith, the soul will not obtain any benefit.
But if all this is accomplished in the disposition of obedience, contrition, faith, it purifies and elevates us.

Happiness is not something to be aimed for; it is the result of right living. If a life is correctly built, happiness will follow: and a correct life is a just life. . . .

Why must we offer alms to every passing beggar, without inquiring into his merits, and even when we know that he is undeserving? Aside from the fact that the man who gives is spiritually enriched, while the one who closes his purse plunders himself—aside from this, if we refuse alms, especially near the church doors, we do great damage to the beggar, inciting him to anger, killing his faith, stirring up his hatred of the rich, the satiated, the pious.

Many are shocked by what they think is the worldly custom of collecting money in church.

Woe to us, if we consider this from a worldly, commonplace point of view. Generally speaking, there are no commonplace, no tiresome or non-religious matters: The "Christian outlook" is one whole. And within it, all matters are seen in their spiritual dimensions and significance. It is not so much the subject that counts as our attitude towards it. Does it not often happen that a noble, holy subject is treated in a blasphemous or hypocritical way?

St. Paul, collecting alms for the Church, transporting gifts, writes about these things without the slightest doubt that he is accomplishing a good work: those who receive are moved by this very act to praise God and to be grateful to such as not only teach the Gospel with their tongues, but also fulfill its precepts in their hearts. If we are one body bound to one Head—to Christ —then how shall we tolerate the presence amongst us of poor, hungry brothers? You must accept the collections in church as a test of your faith, your love, your patriotism. These collections are a statement, not so much of the financial obligations you have met as of the fund of charity in your heart. Take note of the sort of emotion that appeals for help arouse in your heart. With the hands of thousands of orphans and invalids Christ in person knocks at your door, and you shall open the door and let Him in; and you shall know that it is He because of the joy experienced by all merciful hearts. God is able to help through a miracle that is His own, but this miracle must be accomplished through men. Blessed are those who are the "servants of miracle."

Morality is not exactly a secondary affair in Christianity, but it is a derivative one. A morality which does not issue naturally from the plenitude of our religion is of a different order; it is either mere respectability or a matter of instinct—or, very often, an insufferable hypocrisy.

The more a man gives up his heart to God, to his vocation and to men, forgetful of himself and of that which belongs to him—the greater poise he will acquire, until he reaches peace, quiet, joy—the apanage of simple and humble souls.

There are people who, without believing in God, "live morally, doing good." This is for the most part a false morality and a false good, inwardly poisoned by vanity and pride. And if it is pure Good, these men touch God's garments without knowing it and without being able to call Him by name.

Holiness and knowledge are given by the catholic spirit.[5] Ignorance and sin are the apanage of isolated individuals. Only in the unity of the Church do we find both the latter overcome. Man finds his true self in the Church alone; not in the helplessness of spiritual isolation but in the strength of his communion with his brothers and with his Savior. The Church is a living organism, integrated by the common love, forming an absolute unity of the living and the dead in Christ.

Turning our eyes from the radiant scenes of the Gospel to ourselves, we are thrown into confusion. Not only do we not move mountains, we lack even the tranquillity, the stability, the joy, afforded by faith; melancholy, fear, a troubled heart are our common condition. In our despair we often pray for some sort of proof, some trifling sign of God's presence near us—for the slightest hint of His solicitude for us.

But the expectation of a proof of God's existence is a refusal to accomplish the heroic feat of Faith.

God does not exercise constraint, does not seek to violate us. Faith is an act of love that chooses freely.

Yet, we may object, our Lord gave Thomas a tangible evidence of His reality. But this would not help a sinful soul: we may see and not believe, as did the Pharisees. We too know of miracles which happen in our days (miraculous cures, miracles in our family, incidents in our own life which cannot be explained otherwise than by a miracle). So let God help us to remember the innumerable manifestations of His love, that we may attain to that confirmation in our faith which gives strength, joy and peace.

In marriage the festive joy of the first day should be extended to the whole of life; every day should be a feast day; every day husband and wife should appear to each other as new, extraordinary beings. The only way of achieving this: let each become more deeply spiritual, exert strong efforts in the work of self-development.

How sad and incomplete maidenhood is, and what a plenitude of life is found in womanhood. No romance is capable of replacing marriage. In romance people are seen in their richest blossoming; yet they are not themselves; romance projects an insubstantial, enhanced image of reality, and the life of both lovers is inevitably a pose, though an excusable and innocent one.

Only in marriage can human beings fully know one another— the miracle of feeling, touching, seeing another's personality— and this is as wonderful and as unique as the mystic's knowledge of God. It is for this reason that before marriage man hovers above life, observes it from without; only in marriage does he plunge into it, entering it through the personality of another. This joy of real knowledge and real life gives us that feeling of achieved plenitude and satisfaction for which we are richer and wiser.

For the education of children: the most important thing is that they should see their parents leading a deep interior life.

Why are quarrels between closely related people sometimes even useful? Because it thus comes about that the long-accumulated debris of offenses and misunderstandings is burnt away in the fire of dispute. A mutual explanation and confession is followed by a feeling of entire calm and serenity—everything has been elucidated, nothing weighs on our mind. Then the highest gifts of the soul are freed; entering into communion with one another, we come to talk over the most wonderful things, we reach a full unity of soul and mind.

The difficulty of intercourse between blood-relations, and in general in the family, derives from the fact that in the family (husband and wife, mother and children) there are usually relations of an instinctive, animal character, and if one of the members of the family leads a spiritual life, he fares badly. It has been said of this circumstance that a man's enemies are of his own household.

When, because of the merits of one being, Christ says that "now salvation hath come to this house"—these words mean that the eternal character of our earthly ties, the ties of blood, is recognized in the next world. The merits, the sufferings, of one being save his relations—how consoling and significant are these words, what an eternal value they give to our earthly life!

Why is the Church silent about the world beyond death? Man lives, thinks, and feels in the conditional forms of time and space. Outside these, we cannot think or speak.

The life beyond death is conditioned by different forms. If we try to speak of it, we shall speak in the language of earth. Hence the chaste silence of the Church.

Human limitation in itself is not stupidity. The most intelligent men are inevitably limited to a certain degree. Stupidity begins when obstinacy and self-assurance become manifest— that is, manifestations of pride.

Pride = solitude = hell's darkness. Pride, hence ambition, hence partiality, incapacity for self-estimation; hence stupidity.

The proud man is stupid in his judgments, even if he is by nature born with the mind of a genius. And vice versa: the humble man is wise, even if he is "not clever"; the essence of wisdom—the sense of Truth and humility concerning it—is accessible to him.

Concerning nonresistance to evil—Tolstoy understood it externally; and through this commandment of love, he brought about much disturbance and great evil: denial of the State institutions and of State justice, an atmosphere of revolt. The ascetic conception is the accomplishment of this commandment in individual morality.

The distrust of the intellect, of philosophy and theology, that is common in our day cannot be justified by the Gospels, or by the Fathers of the Church, who themselves analyzed and reasoned a great deal—for instance, Gregory of Nyssa, Maxim the Confessor, the Cappadocians in general. I cannot recall a single Father who feared the human intellect, reasoning, differences of opinion. That our intellectual activity must be inspired by the love of God, by the thirst for truth, is obvious enough.

What a tragedy is presented by men's relations with God. We seek Him, suffer in estrangement from Him—though we know that He dwells within our soul—and at the same time, we experience a sort of deadened feeling, a sort of inexorable petrifaction, by which we are hopelessly divided from Him.

"We have defiled Thy image, and are enslaved by lust."[6] The delights of the world present a peril to the spiritual life; the loss of cool sobriety of the spirit, of clarity of thought, of self-control; attention is diverted, the will is weakened, personality debilitated, scattered, disordered.

The force of virginity—the radiance of unsquandered sex— is sublimated into the highest spiritual values. Purity—the condition and source of genuine creation.

The entire modern world says: "You have to sin." Those who want to live by the Radiant Law are always opposed; they must not expect an easy, "agreeable" life.

Everything that environs us—our education from our very childhood, "the struggle for survival," teaches us our dignity. But if one of us can put himself in the place of the publican— and may God help us all to feel this way—let him rejoice, for he is that stray sheep, that lost drachma, for the sake of which Christ came; his salvation causes more joy in heaven than that of hundreds of just souls.

All do not realize with equal seriousness the great significance for our spiritual life of meditation on the lives of the saints. Some go so far as to say: "I have the Gospels; I have Christ; I need no intermediaries." Some do not actually utter these self-assured words, yet neither do they appeal to the saints during periods of spiritual downfall (and who has not had such experiences?). For what is a saint?—a man like ourselves, but one who, having followed the right path, has found that which we all seek: God. Why, then, should we not study them and seek what they have to teach us? Why should we not imitate them? Properly speaking, holiness is our common aim, in proportion to our powers.

It is a mistake simply to stifle or to put to sleep all that is sinful; sin will remain and will furnish a new growth, even if we pluck away the shoots.

The evil plant must be grafted onto good—that is, we must sublimate our sinfulness, transfigure it in higher spiritual states, of which this sinfulness was but a distortion. Example: St. Paul and all those who actively and consciously "build up" their souls.

The present-day attitude of proud men—to be indignant over the lies of others, to protest against injustice, to crusade for the reestablishment of truth. In their blindness, they do not notice that they themselves are entangled in lies, that they cannot stand the truth even in a one-half percent solution, that the right to truth must be merited. They cannot bear to hear the truth concerning themselves, and how can truth be told to one who is insane? What does truth matter to him? All truth concerning himself will only pour more water on the mill of his insanity.

In the presence of a rich intellectual life, the powers of the sexual sphere are to a considerable degree converted into aesthetic, moral and other energies. But if this does not occur—as with the majority of European youth—what remains is sheer bestiality, which of itself, absorbs, on the contrary, every spark of the higher manifestations.

Absolution, the remission of sins, is given by God according to the measure of our repentance and Faith.

How to distinguish genuine repentance from the formal kind, which often deceives the penitent himself? It is only necessary to disagree with him, and if his contrition does not arise from the depths of his heart, it is immediately converted into self-justification, discontent, even the feeling of offense.

Each Lent, God grants [me] during the confessions, one directing thought. This year it is the love of Christ and the essential means of struggle against sin—prayer addressed to Him.

We have no basis whatever for the expectation that God will reveal Himself to us—such as we now are—in a full and indubitable manner. But the words of the Apostle: "Every one that loveth knoweth God . . . for God is Love" (St. John) give us our direction.

Childlikeness is lost in life and recovered in holiness.

Orthodoxy in particular is sensitive to the contrast between the "intelligible beauty of the celestial world" and the beauty of "this world." We suffer from a sense of the darkness and sin which are of the texture of the world. When we become Orthodox, we all become in a way ascetics.

Only the first steps of the approach toward God are easy; the feeling that we have wings, the enthusiasm caused by the certainty of approaching God, is followed by a gradual cooling-down, by doubt; in order to sustain one's faith, it is necessary to make an effort, to struggle, to defend it.

The beginning of the spiritual life is to emerge from subjectivism, from oneself, to outgrow oneself in communion with the highest principle—with God.

Death is occurring around us with such frequency that it has almost ceased to be awful; at times it seems more real than life to me. And the greater the number of friends that have passed on to the other side, the easier this passage becomes.

Multiloquence in prayer is beneficial, were it only because our consciousness is thus for a longer time attached to the holy words. Even if we are not completely absorbed in the meaning of the words uttered, but only diverted from trifles, from vain agitation, worry, impure thoughts—even that is a great gain. And if we add to this a vivid sense of only one-hundredth of what we read, the soul acquires countless treasures.

The mysterious sphere of art—so attractive, so enchanting—affords its servants but little assistance in drawing nearer to what we call truth; their usual characteristics are selfishness, pride, the thirst for fame, often extreme sensuality. In any case—the sphere of art is not spiritual, but is merely psychological.

I read of the cases of healing by Father John of Cronstadt, and I feel puzzled; I am often inclined to consider sickness as the visitation of God, and I do not always find the courage to pray for the healing of the sick, so deeply do I acknowledge the hand and will of God in sickness. Is not the prayer for healing an intrusion into the destiny which is from God? But then, what is healing? Perhaps the liberation from sin, through the prayers of the just, with healing as a result.

The youngest children of the family and the children of old age are usually the chosen ones: the Holy Virgin, John the Baptist, Isaac, Joseph; St. Theresa was the youngest of nine children. In fairy-tales, the youngest is marked out from the others, precisely in the spiritual sense. No doubt this arises from the fact that the physical, the selfish, the passionate element has weakened in the parents, and the spiritual element has grown.

What we call actual reality is only half-real and not very actual. It is our attitude towards them which turns phenomena into this or that, gives them finishing touches, converts them into good or evil. The same can be said of human beings. No one except God knows what they are; more correctly speaking, human personality is fluid, plastic; we paint for ourselves an imaginary, schematic figure—often around some accidental feature—and then admire or condemn it. How much wiser are the simple folk; they do not invent a man, they take him as he is, often accepting without protest the most dissonant qualities.

The swiftly flowing, irresistible, dancing current of the hours, days, years often throws us into despair. We have scarcely time to live, to see our family. It is difficult to express my feeling— to be painfully aware of the poignancy and the strength of one's love, and at the same time of its vanity, its torturing ephemeralness.

. . . Has there been in my life, as in so many others, a clear, indubitable encounter with the Objective? Frankly, I must answer: no. But there have been many partial contacts: in certain rare instances of love expressed in entire self-denial; sometimes in prayer, especially during holy service, you feel that you emerge from yourself, that something "which is not yours" has entered into you; in many cases, when God's manifest help cannot be explained otherwise; this is faith no longer—it is knowledge—precise and comprehensible signals from the other world. All the rest is faith, "assisted by the love of God."

Sometimes I observe a state of the soul which, so far as outward signs are concerned, is absolutely wholesome—the person in question practises frequent and prolonged prayer, enjoys being in church; all his interests are placed in the latter. And at the same time, he is stiff, unkind, loves no one. I can hardly understand it: I know of a kind of prayer after which the entire man is changed; but I think that a prayer isolated from all else is not a right, salutary condition, for it presents only one element —the least important—form; but it lacks real, tangible results.

The cult of the cross, the infamous instrument of execution, has recruited for Christianity men with the uttermost interior freedom.

Solitude is an excellent experience and a valuable practice. An experience: has your soul anything in reserve? Can you live interiorly when that which is exterior is reduced to a minimum? For we live chiefly on outward impressions—people, business, worries. What would happen if we put all this aside? What if the doors of our exterior perception should be closed? The doors of the inner chamber of our soul would then grate open painfully, laboriously.

Concerning an accident near Paris:
Every accident is a threat and a reminder: "If you are not converted, you shall all likewise perish." Each accident is the ordeal to which our fidelity to God is submitted, an attempt on the part of the devil to shake our faith. Our terror is largely the result of the imprisonment of our mind in the flesh. The world is full of blood and tears, and we, like small children, are terrified by the sight of two hundred dead. A train gone off its

tracks, broken legs, arms and skulls are for us a reality; whereas all this is but illusion, a temporary state of being half-alive, for the fashion of this world passeth away. If we saw this accident in its spiritual aspect, the souls of the children, et cetera, we should not be afraid. If this were revealed to the mothers!

Man emerges from the Infinite and returns to the Infinite. How is it then, that during his life's brief instant, nearly every man has such great dread of everything that links him to the Infinite, all that projects beyond the common, narrow framework of everyday life? Why does he build his existence as if with the purpose of excluding all that is spiritual?

The majority of the problems of life—sorrows, interior difficulties—of which one hears during Confession, are made insoluble by the fact that men live outside the Church, yet appeal to the Church for the settlement of their difficulties. No determination to change one's life, not even a thought given to it; this is why the Church is helpless in such cases. Enter the Church, accept the entire order of Church life, and then the difficulties will be naturally resolved.

The feeling of extreme sinfulness is often, especially in youth, but another form of the passion of pride: "I am extraordinary in everything, even my sins are deeper, more dazzling, than those of other men."

"Defraud not one another, except, perhaps, by consent, for a time, that you may give yourselves to prayer". . . this is a recognition of the necessity of rhythm in the Christian life, the alternation of fasting and prayer with ordinary life. This instruction is full of the deepest wisdom: the attempt to dwell on the heights of prayer without relaxation leads to melancholy and despair.

It is not the definition of sin that is important, nor its precise psychological description, nor even correct arguments concerning the sources and consequences of sin; but the sense of the very *stuff* that sin is made of, of the nature of sin—the pain and sorrow caused by it, the thirst for liberation from it—that is important.

We must not put our vices to sleep—we must uproot them. Here lies the advantage of life in the world: through conflict with people and circumstances offering temptation, it discovers our own heart to us.

In Confession what is most important is the state of the soul which confesses itself, no matter who receives the confession. It is your confession that is important, not *he* who speaks to you. However, we often attribute the first place to the personality of the priest who confesses.

Prayer is an art; a wrongly constructed prayer augments inner chaos, especially where persons with unstable nerves are concerned.

There are two kinds of men, in so far as their capacities for spiritual understanding, if not for experience, are concerned.

The first: when conversing with them, the tongue sticks to the palate, there is no echo, no resonance—deafness and blindness. And these are nearly always people who are happy, well-fed, whose lives are well-organized. They have a sense of humour, are witty, good-natured.

And the others, who drink in every word concerning spiritual things, who understand the slightest hint, who are hard on themselves, capable of repentance and feeling, who are morbidly sensitive concerning the sorrows of others—they are the sick, the unfortunate, the dying. I used to fear them, but now I am glad of every opportunity to be in precisely such company and always learn a lesson from it.

We can already ascertain that the power exercised over humanity by Christian ideas is without precedent. This is acknowledged by the enemies of Christianity themselves. Nietzsche declares that the whole of humanity is "corrupted" by Christianity, that human psychology and morality are entirely permeated by Christian "decadence." Rozanov affirms with awe and melancholy that men are incurably infected by that "sweet poison," himself among them. We cannot say that after Christ all history became Christian; we know how far we are from it, today in particular; but we can assert that under the influence of Christian ideas, history became qualitatively different. Dough rises under the influence of yeast, yet does not become identical to yeast; wood burns under the action of fire, but the residue of ashes and cinders has nothing in common with fire. The same can be said of ideas, of their action on humanity. And such, too, was the transfiguring action of the Christian religion on humanity.

The approach of light is terrifying, torturing for untruth and sin. The fear of God is the beginning of wisdom, the beginning of repentance, the beginning of salvation.

The feeble control which we exercise over our emotions, the defective organization of the body of knowledge which we possess, result from our lack of religious culture. Hence the inner chaos of modern European minds and the disciplined character of the minds of the East, where everything is based on religion. Without this, all the effort expended in self-cultivation is fruitless.

From the beginning of Lent I read Isaac the Syrian. I am filled with admiration, moved, spiritually fed by him. I am filled with admiration by the force of his arguments, by his bold, aerial flight into the most secret spheres; I am moved by the mercifulness, by the sacred love, with which his very style is infused; I am sustained by his wise advice, always precise and concrete, always expressed in terms of love. Yet, at the same time, I am awed; he writes for monks, and he asks so much of them that he throws the lay reader into despair. What are we to hope for, we whose beings are steeped in vain agitation, untruth, anger and other passions? From monks he asks for solitude; from hermits, silence; from those who observe silence, an entire abandonment to prayer, so that even the concern entailed by the fetching of water and the collecting of alms is a betrayal of God's task. Truly, our only hope is in God's mercy, and not in our works and merits, whatever they may be.

It is always better to overcome doubt and misfortunes, not by evading them or brushing them aside, but by passing through them.

... Let us try to live in such a way that all our actions, our whole life may be, not a dreamlike vegetation, but a development as strong and deep as possible of all our capacities; and that this may take place, not some time in the future, but now, immediately, at every moment. Otherwise irresolute, disorderly living will inevitably breed impotence, flabbiness of soul, an incapacity for faith and for intense feeling; life will be spent in vain, and we shall scarcely be able to remove the cold scum— the fire of genuine heroism alone will then be able to consume it.

Laughter (not smiling) weakens man spiritually.

In answer to the question whether those who approach the Sacraments without sufficient contrition and faith are absolved of their sins, Bishop Innocent of Cherson[7] says: "Without them (faith and contrition), you will not receive absolution from God, no matter how often the priests repeats: forgiven, absolved."

An argument for materialists and atheists: religion is useful for the soul and even for the body. Spirituality is the best remedy for every kind of sickness, and it is made accessible only by religion.

Our tolerance towards those who belong to other religions, and in general tolerance towards differences in theological opinion, should first of all be nourished by the Gospels and the Church: for the Christianity of St. John is not at all identical with the Christianity of St. Peter, and that of St. Francis of Assisi is not that of Paul the Apostle. And this applies to different lands and peoples. The fulness of Truth is something absolute, and therefore incompatible with the world; the world and individual men are essentially limited, and therefore accept the truth of Christianity within a limited sphere. And because of the differing capacities of peoples and individual men, Christianity becomes peculiar in the conception of each; and yet it remains fundamentally one thing. The gifts of the Spirit also vary among individual men and peoples.

The conditions with which our Lord has surrounded us are the first stage leading to the Kingdom of Heaven; and this is the only way of salvation possible for us. These conditions will change as soon as we have profited by them; when we have converted the bitterness of offenses, insults, sickness, labors, into the gold of patience, meekness, gentleness.

Our very qualities are often turned into defects. For instance, indifference to money, to our position in the world, is sometimes not so much the result of our confidence in Divine Providence as of laziness and irresponsibility.

The affairs of our interior are always in bad condition; God forbid that one fine day we should perceive that all fares well in our soul's economy. Its condition will remain bad until God, in His infinite mercy, receives us all—the weak and the strong, the sick with sin and the righteous—were it only because of our love of Him.

Pia fraus of the Orthodox: the story of the monk-servant who reconciled through a lie two elders who had quarreled. The advice of Father John of Cronstadt: not only to abstain from repeating evil judgments, but even from communicating imaginary good ones. In general, the indifference of Orthodoxy to some kinds of untruth. In my opinion, this is the result of a certain contempt for the realities of life. Our scandals, quarrels, anger—all these are "non-existent" (though they have a certain reality), while the imaginary good (though imagined) is more real.

"Neurasthenia," "nervousness," et cetera, appear to be simply forms of sin; to wit—the sin of pride. The greatest neurasthenic of all is the devil. Can a humble, kind, patient individual be imagined as a neurasthenic? And on the contrary: why does neurasthenia inevitably express itself in anger, irritability, criticism of everyone except ourself, intolerance, hatred of other men, extreme sensibility with regard to all that concerns us personally?

The easy way in which we abandon our positions—often attained with difficulty—is truly frightful. It is only necessary for us to become aware of the slightest feeling of hostility towards us, of the faintest reproach or ridicule, and all our sympathy towards the person in question vanishes, leaving no trace. We are pleasant as long as people are pleasant to us. Yet this has nothing in common with what a genuine, brotherly attitude towards men should be.

Nature, or more correctly speaking, the Providence of God, dictates to each time of life its own spiritual regimen. With the approach of old age, the bodily capacities decrease and the conditions favorable to a concentrated interior life increase: there is less activity and more time for prayer; the organs of our exterior senses are blunted; there is less distraction, and more attention given to our inner world; a diminished ability to digest heavy, fattening food—hence, a natural disposition to fasting; enforced chastity. Blessed is he who understands these signs and goes out to meet God's solicitude for us; blessed is he who, in the construction of his life, gradually replaces corruptible building materials by fire-proof and indestructible ones.

"While we are in the body, we are absent from the Lord—for we walk by faith and not by sight"— *per fidem . . . et non per speciem* (2 Cor. 5, 7). How "absent"— is it possible for us to be entirely absent? Do we sit in the shadow of death, in the infernal regions? This is my habitual feeling, my constant grief. The escape is in the sacraments, prayer.

My constant thought—God's inaccessibility to us. His infinite distance from us; even when we approach the Holy Eucharist, when we receive the divine Body and Blood, God continues to dwell in other worlds, hopelessly far from us. The Holy Virgin alone—"one of us," of "our own race" so easily rose above the Seraphim; and this was before the incarnation of Christ; this means that there is a possibility of nearness. It is probable that only children, the most childlike alone, are close to God. But what of the others? Why are such superhuman efforts necessary (the ascetics), in order that one out of a million should behold the angels, converse with God, pray and obtain an answer? Whence this cast-iron opacity, impenetrable to God, to the Holy Eucharist, to Christ's sacrifice, to His Love?

Concentration on self—auto-eroticism—is the beginning of all sin.

Is there in me—however bad I am—anything that will consciously oppose itself to Christ when He comes in all His Glory? Will not every human soul precipitate itself towards Him, as towards something long-expected and desired?

The rule of James Lange for the spiritual life:
We must have recourse to certain words, gestures, signs (the sign of the cross, bows, genuflections) in order to maintain a religious disposition in ourselves.

But—it might be objected—what is this disposition worth, if it is the result of artificial and exterior methods?

But bodily and psychic processes are closely linked and mutually influence each other. There is nothing humiliating in the realization that the spiritual life is influenced, not by *any kind* of signs, but by pious and symbolical attitudes and gestures: our entire body—its form and outline are not accidental: "I am the image of Thy Ineffable Glory"; and sacred and symbolical gestures create the highest spiritual dispositions in the soul.

The smallest atom of good realized and applied to life, a single vivid experience of love, will advance us much farther, will far more surely protect our souls from evil, than the most arduous *struggle* against sin, than the resistance to sin by the severest ascetic methods of chaining the dark passions within us.

"And if one member suffer any thing, all the members suffer with it," is said of the Church (I Cor. 12, 26). And if we do not feel this, we are not within the Church.

"I seek for truth." Happy is he who places the accent on the last word: "Truth." It is far worse with those who proudly emphasize the word "seek," and are full of vanity because of their position among those continually tending towards truth—"Ever learning and never attaining to the knowledge of the truth" (2 Tim. 3, 7). But what is really bad, and occurs most often, is when the accent is placed on the word "I."

The effort expended in securing control over ourselves and our anarchic, autonomous nervous systems, is greatly facilitated, made quite easy, by the correct poise of attention and imagination. We shall inevitably stumble over every trifling obstacle until that which is not a trifle becomes sharply defined and convincing in our mind; until we strive with all our spiritual, emotional, and intellectual powers towards the essential, and thus remove to their proper place the trifles that poison our everyday life.

There are three stages in the struggle against "nerves"—medical treatment, self-control—and, especially—the building up of the highest values in the soul.

The cult of the dead—the most primitive form of religion— is the most striking of all that remains in godless Europe. The celebration of All-Saints' Day—the minimum spiritual life of the average European.

The ancient style of icon-painting corresponds to ancient piety (prayer, the perception of God, et cetera). Hence, as it may seem, the failure of our attempts at mastering the ancient style, for the form of our piety does not coincide with that of the eleventh to the sixteenth centuries. New ventures must spring from the fulness of a new spiritual life; otherwise, we shall obtain nothing genuine. Nevertheless our life of prayer itself follows the eternal pattern and is thus essentially the same as that of St. Paul, of Simeon the New Theologian. Therefore an icon painted according to the ancient rules, even a modest copy, serves the same purpose as the reading of the ancient ascetics— it helps us to fortify our spiritual weakness.

Realistic painting is representative of a sinful perception of the world. Therefore the decoration of churches in the realistic "Italian" style wounds our religious feeling. An icon painted according to the "rules" is at the opposite pole to this sinful perception; here we have a world transfigured, all is according to fixed conditions—harmonious.

One must be careful to avoid nervous sensibility and declamation when reading in church. The prescribed style—its monotony, its modulations which do not emphasize any special point, which place the listeners face to face with the sacred words—is a manifestation of that very freedom of Orthodoxy: the reader, the priest, does not seek to draw anyone after him, does not give his own interpretation—of these, perhaps, there are an infinite variety.

Often the words of psalms and prayers do not touch us, the

feelings to which they give utterance seem to us strange, incomprehensible. And this is quite natural, for all the conditions, the structure of our life—externally well-organized and interiorly empty—are so little in harmony with the deserts and monasteries in which the prayers were composed, with the spirit which permeated these places. At rare moments—in great affliction in solitude, if we escape for a time from the prison of our life— there arise from our heart, as our very own, the words of lamentation: "Oh Lord, come to my assistance!" Then we understand the experience of the man of silence and the recluse.

A work correctly, religiously organized cannot lead to fatigue, neurasthenia or heart disease. If these symptoms exist, it is proof that a man works "in his own name"—trusting *his own* strength, his own charm, eloquence, kindness, and not the grace of God.

Just as there are correctly poised voices, even so, there are correctly poised souls. Caruso sang without fatigue, Pushkin would never have said that the writing of poetry was fatiguing; the nightingale sings all night, and when day breaks, its voice is untired.

If we are fatigued by our work, by our relations with other people, by conversation or prayer, this means only that our soul is incorrectly poised. There are voices naturally "poised"; others are forced to seek the same results through prolonged effort and artificial exercises. The same can be said of the soul.

N's letter about the beautiful, new, empty church, the erection of which has just been completed. "There is scarcely a faithful soul in it." It seems increasingly evident to me that our decorative, pompous rites must end, have already ended, are now artificial and dispensable; they have ceased to nourish the thirsting soul and must be replaced by different, more active and more congenial types of religious communion.

How little our rites—with the priest separated from the faithful by the wall of the *iconostase*, with the freezing space of inlaid floor between the faithful and the altar, with the coolness of the "visitors" towards each other, the chalice presented in vain with the stubborn refusal to approach it—how little all this resembles the religious meetings of the age of the Apostles and the martyrs! The religious element fails, while the decorative develops; the flame in the soul diminishes, while the gilded electric lamps grow brighter.

The pattern of our relations towards our fellowmen often appears to be the following: a person pleases us, we sincerely idealize him, we see nothing bad in him; and then, suddenly, the person in question fails us in this or that, lies or brags, or proves to be cowardly, or betrays us. So we start to re-estimate his value, we erase all that we saw in him before (and which nevertheless really was there), and throw him out of our heart. I have long understood that this is a false and sinful method of human relationship. At the basis of such an attitude towards our fellowmen lie two ideas of which we are not ourselves conscious: (1) I am above sin and (2) the person on whom I have bestowed my love is also sinless. How should we otherwise explain our severe condemnation of others and our surprise if a good, kind, pious person commits a sin? Such are my conclusions drawn from sad reflections concerning our own heart, and my conviction that we ourselves are capable of all kinds of sins.

And yet, the norm of our attitude towards our fellows is to forgive endlessly, for we are ourselves in infinite need of forgiveness. And what is essential is not to forget that the good which we valued remains; as for the sin, it was always there, but we did not notice it.

In dreams we sometimes experience high and intense states of prayer, emotion, joy, such as we are almost incapable of in our waking hours. Cannot this be explained by the passive condition of our body in sleep? It presents no obstacle.

The world is crooked and God straightens it. That is why Christ suffered (and suffers) as well as all the martyrs, confessors and saints—and we who love Christ cannot but suffer.

I think that the Church must rid itself of the burden of unbelievers and of those of little faith (as has taken place in Russia); it must gather itself together, cleanse itself of its alien elements; and this will augment its lustre.

Here on earth, we have already both hell and heaven—in our passions and in our experience of God.

Very often misfortune seems to us immense because we magnify it through a certain element which is absolutely unnecessary; the expectation of disaster, its resonance in the hearts of our kin, intervals between moments of real suffering, during which we suffer in inertia, the memory of recently experienced pain. If we live in an Orthodox way, in the fulness of every moment of life, misfortune will be considerably disarmed, if not entirely overcome.

Socrates is Orthodox in the structure of his soul: one of the essential traits of Orthodoxy—the hearts in "earthen vessels" (2 Cor. 4, 7) illuminated by Grace. Precisely this attracts us in Socrates also.

How can bodily states act on the spirit? How can religious gestures, the sign of the cross, the repeating of sacred words, move our soul to action? It is normal that a motor should put wheels into action; yet it happens that a weak, defective motor cannot start working unless we push the car and set the wheels turning.

Standing in church, even when we are lazy and absent-minded, is not fruitless; if we concentrate on ourselves while standing thus, we shall perceive that at that moment we are capable of much good, and can more easily refrain from evil; it is easier to forgive and to keep one's heart at peace.

Despite the thousand obstacles arising from the agitation and vanity of our way of life, having overcome the languidness and sloth of our soul, we manage to approach the Holy Chalice, and our Lord receives us as "communicants," participants in the

Holy Supper. This participation, communion, is a great joy and a great source of strength. But we must not deceive ourselves. After the Last Supper the severest temptations awaited Christ's disciples: before their very eyes the Divine Master Whom they had recognized to be the Christ, the Messiah, the future king of Israel and of the world, the Son of God, was seized, submitted to a humiliating trial, tortured and publicly executed as a criminal in the company of thieves, thus demonstrating His helplessness before the wicked. And only after having passed through this temptation did the disciples become worthy of the dazzling light of Holy Easter.

We too shall go to meet temptation when we emerge from the church warmed by our prayers and by the prayers of those who prayed there before us, into the darkness and cold of the world outside. The temptations of that world and the greatest temptations of all, those within our own soul—await us.

May Christ help us, Christ with Whom we are bound by the closest ties, to overcome and to continue overcoming these temptations, and to preserve our joy until next Easter, and even until that Easter when we shall taste the new wine in the eternal day of the Kingdom of heaven.

Tears are so efficacious because our whole being is pervaded by the movement which they awaken. In tears, sufferings, the icy constriction of the flesh is broken and the angelic creature of the spirit is born.

The creature of the spirit is produced through tears, fasting, vigils.

Neither our natural attachment to life nor our courage in bearing our suffering, neither earthly wisdom nor even faith—however great—none of these can preserve us from sorrow for the dead. Death is a twofold phenomenon: there is the death of the departed, and the suffering and death in our own soul, occasioned by this painful process of separation. But the path of hopeless sorrow, gloom and melancholy is forbidden to the

Christian. He must not recoil before suffering or remain impotently passive in it. He must employ the full tension of his powers in order to pass *through* suffering, and to emerge from it, stronger, deeper, wiser.

No matter if we are weak in our faith and unstable in our spiritual life—the love we bear towards the departed is not weak; and our sorrow is so deep, precisely because our love is so strong. Through the tension of our love, we too shall cross the fatal threshold which *they* have crossed. Through the effort of our imagination, let us enter into the world which *they* have entered; let us give in our life more place to that which has now become their life; and slowly, imperceptibly, our sorrow will be turned into joy, which no one will take from us.

Every sort of prayer is valuable, even the inattentive one. The power and action of the word are independent of the psychological state of the one who utters it. If an injurious or obscene word pollutes and wounds the soul of the man who has spoken it, and even of the one who has heard it, the sacred words of prayer, even if they are repeated absent-mindedly, cover our mind and heart with a delicate network, and effect in us a beneficent action of which we ourselves are unaware.

A subject of my constant reflections and observation: the psychology in sin—or, to be more correct—the psychic mechanism of fallen man: instead of intuition, rational processes; instead of a fusion with objects, five blind senses (truly "external"); instead of the grasping of a whole, analysis. Primitive men with powerful instincts, although incapable of analysis and logic, are much closer to the image of Eden. How sinful an operation we perform upon children, developing in them all the traits of the fallen soul!

People are capable of a deep understanding of life; they can distinguish with great finesse many a trait in the souls of others —but how rarely (hardly ever) does a man see himself! Here the keenest sight is dimmed and becomes partial. We are overindulgent towards all the evil, and immensely exaggerate every glimpse of the good, in ourselves. I do not even mean being stricter towards oneself than towards others (which is, as a matter of fact, required); but if we simply applied to ourselves the measures we use for others—even this would open our eyes in more ways than one. But we hopelessly refuse to do so; we have become incapable of seeing ourselves and live in a state of blind security; our spiritual life has not even begun to develop, and cannot develop before we have abandoned this false attitude.

How to love our enemies? We are invulnerable to evil when we wear the armor of the Spirit, when the wickedness of men cannot reach us, when we gaze with love and pity on those who do us wrong. It is like being exposed to frost when the body is inwardly warm—for instance, after skiing.

This meekness must not be confused with a conceited shutting out of oneself from the world.

Nothing in life is accidental. He who believes in accident does not believe in God.

To take a purely ethical attitude towards our sins and strive to perfect ourselves is a superficial and absolutely fruitless occupation. If we look without God into the abyss of evil which is in us, our situation will appear hopeless. And if we hope to attain perfect virtue without God—this will make us fall into another trap; self-idolization.

In both cases a solution is possible: the recognition of God's hand over our heads.

For all of us the way to Christ is that of the renunciation of our human idiosyncrasies: humility. "He must increase; but I must decrease"—to rejoice, hearing the voice of the bridegroom. In our approach to Christ, we cannot avoid the Precursor's action.

If we take the resolution of always obeying the voice of conscience—for this is God's voice in us—such a resolution will develop in us the lost organ of communion with God.

Illness and wisdom. While demonstrating to Eudocius the Rhetorician his predisposition to philosophical studies, Plato presents as convincing qualifications: nobleness of soul, a gentle spirit, delicate health and physical debility; and this latter appears to Plato a quite important factor in the practice of wisdom.

Our *love* of God is already for us, in our own experience, the affirmation of His existence. Our love of God is God Himself within us; experiencing this love subjectively, we have already recognized God through it.

This *experience of God* is the only path which is certain and self-evident. Before his heart has been moved in this manner, a man is deaf and blind towards everything, even towards miracles. But once this interior sense of God has come to him, he needs no other miracle than that which has been accomplished within his own soul.

What a joy it is, sometimes to behold the obvious fruits of the action of faith, of the love of Christ, on the soul.

Today, for instance: N's admission that after having experienced sorrow and turned to the Church for help, he feels entirely transfigured: what was habitual, tedious, nearly dead, has been renewed with a real, vivid content; the entire world looks different. Yes, experience, personal experience alone, can lead one to this grasp of the vitality and truth of the Church and of Christ's teaching. And however bitter it may seem, suffering is the usual path leading to it.

Earthly happiness—love, family, youth, health, enjoyment of life and nature—all this "is good," and we must not think that the Higher Law severely rules it out.

What is bad is *enslavement* to our happiness, when the latter possesses a man and he is immersed in it, forgetting that which is essential.

And from the point of view of spiritual growth, sufferings are to be valued, not in themselves, but in accordance with their results. Depriving man of earthly happiness, they place him face to face with the highest values, force him to open his eyes to himself and the world, turn Him towards God.

Hence, an earthly happiness linked to the constant thought of God, from which the tension of spiritual life is not excluded, is an indubitable good. Even so, if suffering irritates and humiliates a man without transfiguring him, without producing a salutary reaction, it is a twofold evil.

This is an answer to the very common objection that the Church and the Gospels condemn *all* earthly happiness and invite us to suffer for the sake of suffering.

Our life upon earth is a semblance, the real reflection of life invisible, and we must lead here, not that simplified, unconsecrated life of the senses that is usual with us, but a full, genuine life, indissolubly linked to the Divine life and sharing its nature. This embraces not only all the essential things, but likewise all those things which are of secondary importance— from our attitude to God to our slightest word or deed.

Particularly in the instance of marriage: that which men have reduced to a mere physiological act invested with custom and ritual is the highest disclosure of human personality, the achievement of plenitude in the mysterious union of two beings which the Apostle describes when he compares this union to that of Christ with the Church.

Today, I had a delightful walk.[8] At first the ascent was rather dull—along an almost invisible path winding amidst chalk-embankments through a forest of low, rare pines. However, there were incidents offering compensation: a hare sprang almost from under my feet; I wandered across barberry-bushes and sweet-briar, shedding their blossoms. I walked slowly, reading, as I went, the Matins service and the Hours, sitting down to rest from time to time. I mounted the hill for about two hours and then reached the summit: immediately the whole landscape underwent a change: to the left, a small village scattered round a church; to the right, lovely meadows; and, directly beyond the summit, the infinite vision opening on the mountains, streaked and spotted with snow. Around me and quite near to me—torn, craggy rocks. Below—green slopes of forest; and above all, an extraordinary, snow-saturated atmosphere and absolute silence. Only from below came the sound of the brook, and a hidden spring was babbling somewhere under a rock. I sat for a long time, enjoying the stillness, the mountains, the fragrance. At my side some immortelles were blooming, the like of which I had never seen, blue with hearts of deep violet. In the valley below there were no flowers at all, but here on the hillside they were as abundant as if they had sprung, not from the earth, but from the air and sun. And I thought: this is why mountains are so beautiful; through them, as through an association with some wise human being, one drinks in freshness, clarity, calm—the qualities born of high altitudes.

"The sun is an eternal window opening on the gold of dazzling light." It is thus that I look upon this hot day: sun, *solntse* (in Russian)—salt,[9] *sol, sal.* In ancient rituals the sun is symbolized by salt; the salt purified the victims of sacrifice. The taste of the sun is bitter-salt, like that of the sea, and its odor reminds us of bitter herbs growing on dry rocks. Wormwood is much more a sun-plant than are dewy roses. These were my thoughts as, sitting on a tombstone, I rubbed a spray of wormwood between my fingers and smelled it.

I have taken in advance the resolution never, except in extreme necessity, to live in a hotel. A hotel room, even in a good establishment, is full of alien emanations, wounds my being. Alien smells, the bed on which thousands of other people have slept, the washstand, with its inevitable wisp of someone else's hair—all this is disquieting, dubious, false. How can one live and rest normally in such an environment? A private house is something entirely different, even if it is uncomfortable and without conveniences; everything in it is natural, human, of good quality.

I enjoy the quiet here, the freedom, and especially the complete leisure. This latter is decidedly necessary at times to the normal life of the soul. Our ordinary living, entirely absorbed as it is in business, and granting us scarcely a minute to breathe and collect ourselves, is seriously damaging to that subconscious life which must ripen in stillness and a certain apparent idleness.

I have a fixed dream of my hearth—even, literally, of my open fireplace with its wood-fire, of my books and my garden. Of course these are vain dreams; our whole way of life, all the social currents, are opposed to this, pointing as they do to the destruction of hearths, to the disintegration of family life, to the anthill and the beehive.

A fountain, and above it a crowned statue of the Virgin. The same image adorns my tiny room. The peasant waters his horse by the fountain; other peasants and peasant women rake hay. A silent, slow life; even the local train is in no hurry and carries only materials of good quality: logs, wood, pressed straw and hay; and the diabolical forces which rule the world cross this tiny, quiet human world only in the shape of motor-cars, flashing like lightning along the narrow strip of high-road covered with evil-smelling tar (as if to divide the world of devils from the world of God).

We live in a farm between 250 and 300 years old; low ceilings, with heavy beams, a chimney, fortress-like walls. In place of the early hearth, there is an iron stove, but even this—especially on a wet day—gives a real sense of home, of cosiness, of something long-desired. I think a real feeling of home can be had only by people who have lived in such nests as these in their own houses, with the real, living fire of a hearth and a smoky ceiling. What special attraction can be offered by our modern "home"—a flat, one of a thousand other flats which are all alike, with central heating, electric light, water-pipes instead of a well or a fountain, a lodging devoid of all special characteristics, which can be easily exchanged for another. Thus modern civilization kills the sense of home, of family life, and opens the road to socialism, communism, anarchism in souls as well as in the social order.

Good taste helps us to appreciate life, its harmony or discord, the relations between men; it assists us in ordering our life, our family, our home. Yet it sometimes makes us uncomfortable: we are offended by people's bad taste, where others would not have noticed anything. And these errors of taste are often committed by good and kind people, and we are prevented from befriending them, we are made unkind.

If we could deepen this perception, learn to see harmony and beauty (where they are to be found) beneath ugliness and disorder, we should be closer to wisdom.

Our continual mistake is that we do not concentrate upon the present day, the actual hour, of our life; we live in the past or in the future; we are continually expecting the coming of some special hour when our life shall unfold itself in its full significance. And we do not observe that life is flowing like water through our fingers, sifting like precious grain from a loosely fastened bag.

Constantly, each day, each hour, God is sending us people, circumstances, affairs, which should mark the beginning of our renewal; yet we give them no attention, and thus continually we resist God's will concerning us. Indeed, how can God help us? Only by sending us in our daily life certain people, and certain coincidences of circumstance. If we accepted every hour of our life as the hour of God's will concerning us, as the decisive, most important, hour of our life—what sources of joy, love, strength, as yet hidden from us, would spring from the depths of our soul!

Profound error concerning the so-called baseness of our flesh, of its inherent sinfulness. It is sinful in so far as the soul is sinful —it is tainted with sin, but it is sacred and is, in its essence, the image of God.

According to God's original plan, the body was sacred, and the soul within it sacred. The fall of man and the punishment incurred by sin, concerned at once the soul and the body. And we must purify our body as well as our soul. "I am the image of Thy unspeakable glory, and yet I bear the ulcers of sin."—We must treat these ulcers, recalling our beauty made after the image and likeness of God, which will arise from the dead and commune in the glory of God.

All virtues are nothing without humility. Take, for example, the Pharisees. The sum of all virtues, minus humility, equals "shipwreck in port." The characteristics of humility: not to believe in one's own qualities, not to be so much as aware of them (humble-mindedness), not to judge, to rejoice at being humiliated. And for the humble—beatitude from the very first step.

Here is a problem: having renounced ourself, to remain ourself, to realize God's plan concerning us.

The approach of light is terrifying, torturing, to the condition of darkness and sin. I constantly observe that people stubbornly avoid Holy Communion. They go to Church as if carried by an inner impulse, then stand outside in the courtyard. Many have admitted as much to me.

Between spiritual growth and vain eloquence there is an inverse ratio. The substitution of loquacity for spiritual tension is easy and attractive. Here is the temptation to which all who are under spiritual direction are subject.

"I have great faith" is a platitude on the lips of all conceited, limited people who are weak in faith. The apostles, looking upon Christ, touching Him, prayed: "Increase our faith." The Gospels state with precision the signs by which we shall know those who are of profound faith: "And these signs shall follow them that believe: In my name they shall cast out devils . . . they shall lay their hands upon the sick, and they shall recover." "Nothing shall be impossible to you." (Matt. 17) "That which you ask with faith, will be granted unto you." Does this sound like us? We, the cold, the impotent, the spiritually weak?

In this life we know for certain one thing only: that we shall die. This is the only fixed, inevitable incident common to all men. Everything else is changing, unstable, corruptible; and if we love the world, its joy and beauty, we must make room in our life for this last, final moment—our death; which, if we will it, can be beautiful too.

It is not sin alone that is terrifying, but also the despair and melancholy bred by sin. Isaac the Syrian has this to say concerning such a condition: "Have no fear, even though you fall daily; do not abandon prayer; stand firm, and the angel who watches over you will honor your patience." Let us recall the words of Christ referring to such cases: "Go and sin no more." And that is all: no curses, no excommunications. We must not submit to the evil spirit that seeks to draw us into deeper sin—melancholy. Again and again, we must fall at Christ's feet, again and again He will receive us.

The reading of Isaac the Syrian gives me a great deal of satisfaction. Especially the spirit diffused throughout his writings is excellent—tender wisdom and love, the deepest compassion for sinful humanity; his remarkable style, the terseness and force of his sayings. How convincing he is when he says, that since we have been driven out of paradise with thorns and thistles as our portion, we must not be surprised if we have to sow among thorns, and if we are severely bruised by them, even when our intentions are of the best and we are acting righteously. All this must continue until we find in our heart the paradise of divine love; then, even here upon earth, everything will become joyous and radiant for us. Let God send us but the presentiment of this joy, and meanwhile we shall live and work without murmuring, even if we have to work among "thorns."

All resistance to God has a base origin. Genuine spiritual distinction is in submission to the Supreme Will.

It is the part of wisdom—and this is true of the Christian life as well as in general—not to be over-exacting of human nature.

Neither the man, nor (even less) the woman possesses absolute power over the partner in marriage. Force exercised over the will of another—even in the name of love—kills love itself. Then the question arises: must one submit to this force when it threatens that which is most precious? The countless numbers of unhappy marriages result from precisely this—that each partner looks upon the loved one as an object for possession. Hence nearly all the difficulties of married life. The expression of the highest wisdom in marriage is the counterpart of marriage in heaven (Christ and the Church), where there is absolute freedom.

Here is something else I observe in young people: nearly all young men are melancholy, gloomy, clumsy; young girls are ethereal, simple, luminous. Everything seems easier to the latter; when they are converted to Christianity, they attain more readily the fervor born of this conversion. A young man has much more to overcome; first of all, dry reasoning, self-love, et cetera. Therefore, in the future revival of the Russian Church, woman will undoubtedly have a considerable part to play.

I observe in human beings a certain peculiarity from which I infer what seems to me an important psychological law. Often people who enjoy a leisure that is quite sufficient are nevertheless always tardy in their words and actions. There is in them a certain resistance of which they are hardly conscious, a resistance to *any sort* of action, whether agreeable or disagreeable or indifferent. When it comes to saying, undertaking, doing something, they unconsciously put on the brakes, performing a number of small, unnecessary acts, so as to defer the task which stands before them; and therefore they are always late. I think this mechanism can be discovered in every soul; in some cases it amounts to a psychotic condition; in sanctity it is effaced. Here we have a certain, elementary type of sin, of pure sin, "disinterested" and without any object.

Since the beginning of the world men have died; since the beginning of the world it has been well enough known that all earthly things are unstable, fleeting, corruptible. And yet, with a sort of blind greed, men stake all they possess, all the forces of their souls, upon this card which is bound to be trumped. They take their wealth to a bank which will certainly become insolvent.

There is one solid asset to the credit of our times: the conviction that there is no happiness to be found in the way of the world, in the path of personal gain. Until now, the whole life of this world was directed towards the goal of personal earthly happiness. Now this goal has been taken away from humanity. We all know that in these uncertain, treacherous times, no efforts will suffice to build this house of cards which constitutes our personal happiness. This represents one of the deepest sources of instability in our times. The world's values fluctuate; we dare to recognize neither the power of the Beast, nor the light yoke of Christ.

What is the task of the Christian in these critical days? Our choice is made. We have willingly accepted the "light yoke of Christ." In this struggle between light and darkness, we must

surrender all our energies, capacities, talents and material resources to the powers of Good, and we shall inherit the beati-
tudes which Christ promised to those who follow in His path,
and not the treacherous ways of early happiness.

The world is a system of symbols *a realibus ad realiora*,[10] the
reflection of the spiritual world in the corporeal forms of this
world—"the example and shadow of heavenly things" (Hebr.
8, 5). The value of symbols is the joy caused by the knowledge
that our world is a likeness of that other world. Hence—the
icons, candles, the smoke of incense.

Is the whole universe corrupted by the fall of man? Do we
not contemplate paradisial worlds when looking at the stars?

Despite all, the soul seeks happiness. Sorrow, suffering, are
of themselves not proper to man. Is not this instinctive turning
to joy and light the soul's memory of paradise lost and its striving towards it?

Why is our love of God so weak? Because our faith is weak.
And faith is weak because we are indifferent to the things of
God. Through the study and knowledge of these things faith
will arise, and from faith—love.

One hears continually: "Life is hard!" And when one cites
the examples of the saints, the usual reply is: "Well, they are
not saints for nothing: it is easy for them!" A common error.
For *them* precisely it is hard. They have overcome not only
worldly difficulties but the very essence of their humanity. The
usual path of the saint—from the abyss of sin to the summit of
holiness—is narrow and arduous. Whereas our course is always
an easy one, along the lines of least resistance; but the *fruits* of
our course are bitter and burdensome, whereas the hard way
yields the reward of true beatitude.

It is impossible to remain forever in a state of spiritual elevation. God allows certain intermissions in our fervor because He would neither supplant the courage by which we mount, nor feed the pride by which we fail. Let our heart advance in the way along which God leads us.

True, these alternations are a painful trial; but it is good for us to know through our own experience that our moments of spiritual elevation do not depend upon us, but are the gift of God, which He takes away when He deems it necessary.

In this state of dryness of the heart and of staleness, in the absence of fervent prayer, we must be careful not to give up our spiritual exercises, our daily prayer. If we abandoned them, we should do ourselves the greatest damage.

We are inclined to think that if we do not feel definite satisfaction in prayer, it is not worthwhile to pray.

We may feel deprived of beneficent consolations and yet preserve a firm will, consenting to all the difficulties which God sends us, and humbly accepting everything, even to that state of spiritual depression which we experience.

If we succeed in enduring our periods of dryness of the heart in such a manner, they will become for us a salutary spiritual exercise.

To pray fervently is given by God. To pray as well as we can is within our own power. So let us offer to God this weak, insufficient, dry prayer, as the only one we are capable of, like the mite of the widow in the Gospel. And "God's strength will flood thy impotence; and the prayer that is dry and distracted but frequent and resolute, having become a habit, having grown to be thy second nature, will turn into a prayer meritorious, luminous, full of flame." (Mark the Ascetic)

How great is the force of humility. If we sense the faintest shade of conceit in the preacher or the orator, this not only effaces all his actual merits, but even arouses our antagonism. On the other hand, the humble man, even if he possesses neither great intelligence nor talent, conquers all hearts." (Curé d'Ars)[11]

There are three degrees of óbedience: to ask advice when we feel entirely perplexed; to follow a counsel which is conformable with our own thoughts and inclinations, with our point of view; and to obey, even in contradiction of our views and desires—this last alone is true obedience.

If we may not judge, how shall we help our erring brother? By turning our attention to the beam in our own eye; only then, after we have struggled to remove it, shall we understand how deep-seated are the causes of sin, how hard it is to fight, through what means it can be cured, how great the pity and sympathy deserved by the sinner; and these feelings of yours and your experience of the struggle with sin, will help to remove the mote from your brother's eye—through sympathy, example, love. Judgment will fall away of itself.

An ambitious man is like a common bit of glass, glistening and gay in rays of light; and the stronger the light, the more the glass sparkles; but in the absence of light it is dull and colorless.

The common view of fasting is a radical misapprehension. The important element in fasting is not the fact of not eating this or that, or of depriving oneself of something by way of punishment. Fasting is but a tested method for attaining the necessary results, through the weakening of physical desire to achieve the refinement of the spiritual, mystical capacities which were obstructed by the flesh, and thus facilitating our approach to God.

In the human order, death is something unexpected, an absurdity; it neither harmonizes nor combines with any of the events that preceded it. And in view of the fact that death is a phenomenon of the higher, the divine, order, this incongruity points to the essential incongruity between the whole order of our life and the divine order.

Death is always evil and terrifying, whether it be the death of an old man or that of a child, of a just man or of a sinner. Death is always the victory of the devil, a temporary victory, yet a victory. Our body which was created for immortality, submits to the evil law of death, is separated from the soul, disrupted, stricken with decay, turned into nothing.

Through sin, death has entered the world; it enters into us from our very childhood, traces the lines of sin on our faces, extinguishes the living fire in our eyes, disables our body. But Christ is the conqueror of sin and hell, and Christ's task is chiefly the victory over death through His resurrection: "if Christ be not risen again, your faith is also vain." (I Cor. 15, 14)

Hysteria is a disintegration of personality; and it liberates tremendous energies with a power for destruction as fatal as those of the split atom.

In what does the shame (and the shamelessness) of nakedness consist, and for what reason is there an injunction against it in the Bible and in the religious consciousness of peoples? I think that "naked man" is the equivalent of "sinful man," one fallen away from God's glory. The bodies of our fathers and of the saints are vested "in light, as in a garment"; for us who have fallen, the light is replaced by clothes until the times shall be fulfilled. The "state of nakedness" represents our defiance of God, our self-affirmation in sin.

How shall we distinguish good from evil in actions and in men? The only measure is the feeling of joy, peace, love; and, vice versa, the feeling of doubt and confusion. Here we find a means of almost unerring judgment.

Contact with children teaches us sincerity, simplicity, the habit of living in the present hour, the present action—the essential element in Orthodoxy.

Children are, as it were, reborn daily: hence their spontaneity, the lack of complexity in their souls, the simplicity of their judgments and actions.

Moreover, their intuitive distinctions between good and evil are unemcumbered, their souls are free of the bonds of sin, they are not under the necessity of weighing and analyzing.

We possess all this as a birthright which we wantonly scatter on our way, so that we must afterwards painfully gather up the fragments of our lost fortune.

Be in no haste to fill an empty space of time with words and scenes, before it has been filled with a deep interior content.

In fasting—as in narcosis, intoxication, sleep—man reveals himself; some manifest the highest talents of the spirit, others only become irritable and bad-tempered. Fasting reveals the true nature of a man.

There are various forms of spiritual blindness; one is that of people who err sincerely, through lack of knowledge: (Saul, the heathens); another, that of men steeped in sin, stupefied by passion; another still, the blindness of those who have lost the criteria of truth, of the proud (my opinion is the truth, that which is not mine is error). In order that some of these souls should regain their sight, it is only necessary that they should be presented with the truth; for others, the remedy is repentance. "My spiritual sight being blinded, I come to Thee, O Christ, and even as one born blind, I call to Thee, so that Thou mayst illumine with the light of repentance those who are in darkness."

Very often sufferings do not draw the soul towards God but rather depress it in a sterile manner and become meaningless. Why were the sufferings of the prodigal son a means of salvation? Why "having retired into himself," did he discover the path of salvation? Because he remembered "the house of his father," because he was firmly convinced of its reality, because he loved it, because—and let us here discard the language of symbolism—that sinner *believed in* God. This is the saving power of suffering. This is what opens the gates of God's house —the only gates at which it is worthwhile to knock.

One must not "measure" oneself.

Coercion, even for a good end, invariably provokes resistance and irritation. The only way of convincing a man is to furnish him with an example that will inspire him with the desire of imitation; then, and then alone, will conversion be complete and fertile, inasmuch as it will be a free and independent act.

Obedience does not kill, it strengthens the will.

Why are childhood impressions so important? Why is it essential to fill a child's mind and soul with knowledge and good example, beginning with the very earliest stages of its life? In children we find undiminished the capacity for faith, simplicity, gentleness, pliability, compassion, imagination, and meekness. Now this is precisely the soil which yields a harvest many thousand times greater than the seed that has been sown. When, later in life, the soul has become as hard as flint, a man can be purified, saved, by the residue of his childhood experience. This is why it is so important to keep children close to the Church— it will give them food for their entire lifetime.

How can men have failed to observe that practically nothing has been achieved through enmity and anger, and that meekness and gentleness accomplish all things? I refer, of course, to achievements in the moral and spiritual sphere, but I am convinced that such means can be used with equal success in ordinary life.

We are fortunate if we detach ourselves interiorly and of our own initiative from the broad way of wordliness, if neither the joys of this life, nor riches, nor success, fill our hearts and lead us away from that which is essential. Otherwise God in His

wrath shatters our idols—our comfort, our career, our family
unity—in order that we may understand at last that there is one
God to whom we must bow in worship.

Our self-knowledge is astonishingly slight. By self-knowledge
I do not, of course, mean a gnawing self-analysis, nor self-
flagellation, nor that concentration on ourselves which has its
source in pride. I mean an attentive, calm survey of the soul,
a gaze turned inward, effort expended upon ourselves to the
end that our lives may be consciously built, that we may not be
carried off by passing emotions and ideas. Least of all are we
our own masters. We need practice, a discipline of attentive and
determined work upon ourselves.

My dislike and distrust of verbal methods of persuasion—
and eloquence in general—is constantly increasing. "The hidden
man of the heart, in the incorruptibility of a quiet and meek
spirit, which is rich in the sight of God." (I Peter 3, 4)

*From a letter of Father Alexander written not long before his
death:* "I have thought many things over and re-experienced
many things during this illness. Our life is a frightening, inse-
cure and uncertain thing, separated, as it is, by the thinnest
tissue from pain, suffering, death. And a man is so helpless in
face of all this darkness, so weak is the whole life of his spirit,
which is unable to resist a temperature of 40°,[12] and breaks
down when pain is acute. In general, illness humbles one considerably; God does not leave us without His comfort, but we
realize so clearly our own impotence. The only defense against
the terrors surrounding us: a faithful love of Christ, a constant
holding on to Him.

From another letter: Illness has taught me a great deal. It
has confirmed me even more deeply in the conviction that if
one is with Christ, then one is with suffering, and that there is
no other way for the Christian than through pain, interior and
exterior. And as I thought of the infinite suffering in the world,

I said to myself that through such undeserved, innocent suffering the Body—the Church of Christ—is being created and built-up.

NOTES

ST. THEODOSIUS

[1]See general Preface, p. XI.

[2]The name Caves (in Russian, Pechersk) Cloister in Kiev was given to this first-organized and most famous of Russian monasteries because of its origin in the caves where the holy founders led their ascetical life; the early caves (catacombs) were preserved as places of burial for the monks.

[3]The Russian verst is equal to about two-thirds of a mile.

[4]Theodosius, i.e., God-given.

[5]The name of this prince, as well as the date of birth of Theodosius, is unknown.

[6]Prosphora, i.e., holy bread shaped like a round loaf and imprinted with a cross; in the Eastern Mass the priest cuts small particles from this for use as hosts.

[7]The wearing of chains about the breast and waist was a Syrian ascetical invention widely imitated in ancient, and even in modern, Russia.

[8]These first Kievan "monasteries" which preceded the Caves Cloister were probably small communities without a strictly regular life.

[9]St. Anthony had spent some years as a monk at Mount Athos in Greece before settling in a cave at Kiev (about 1050).

[10]Staretz is the Russian word for elder (old man), used in the sense of spiritual father, or, in general, of a venerable monk.

[11]A monastery in Constantinople.

[12]Tmutarakan; an ancient city on the Taman Peninsula between the Black and the Azov seas. It vanished in the course of history, but in the eleventh century it was a Russian principality belonging to the Kievan dynasty.

[13]The same practice is ascribed to St. Macarius in the Egyptian *Patericon* of Palladius.

[14]These words of John Chrysostom were applied to many of the Greek and Russian saints.

[15]The schema (*i.e.*, form) is the robe of the last degree of the Eastern monastic initiation, from which the degree itself takes its name. The degrees are marked by different vestments in the following sequence: novice, rasophorus (cassock-bearing), mantle monk, schema monk.

[16]Reference is made here not to the Russian, but to the Egyptian Anthony, the founder of monasticism (fourth century). The demoniacal visions of Theodosius, like those of the Egyptian saint, have the character of menaces rather than temptations. St. Hilarion of Palestine had similar experiences.

[17]This practice on the part of the abbot is in conformity with the Studite Rule. See also the life of St. Sergius, pp. 65-6.

[18]Isiaslav, son of Yaroslav, sat on the Kievan throne from 1054 to 1079.

[19]Sviatoslav, Isiaslav's brother, was at that time prince of Chernigov, to which Tmutarakan was a dependency.

[20]A similar story is told of the patriarch Eulogius of Alexandria (seventh century).

[21]In 1073.

[22]Throughout the period from the eleventh to the seventeenth centuries, the Russian Church condemned secular music and popular songs.

[23]Stephen was an ecclesiarch; *i.e.*, the monk elected to supervise the liturgical order of the services, which is very complicated in the Eastern Church.

[24]In the eighteenth century this daring promise of Theodosius concerning the salvation of all inmates of his monastery aroused, not unnaturally, the misgivings of the Holy Synod of Russia, and the passage was eliminated from the published editions of the Kievan *Patericon*.

ST. SERGIUS

[1]Epiphanius became a monk at the Holy Trinity monastery during Sergius' lifetime. His biography of the saint was abridged by Pachomius; the present text is a further abridgement of the very prolix original.

[2]Bartholomew (Sergius is the name he took in religion) was born some time about or within the period from 1314 to 1323 in the

principality of Rostov, north of Moscow (and now part of the province of Ivanovo).

[3]Prostrations were the customary form of greeting afforded revered or powerful persons in ancient Russia, after the Byzantine example.

[4]The miracle supposed to have been wrought before Sergius' birth is described at length in one of the omitted passages of the Life.

[5]Voyevode. Originally the designation of a military chief, this came to be used as the title of a provincial governor.

[6]Radonezh, a village (for a time a small town) after which St. Sergius is called, nine miles from the monastery of St. Sergius (the town of Sergiev Posad; since the Revolution, Zagorsk, of the province of Moscow).

[7]1343-1353.

[8]Metrophan was probably one of those monks, numerous in ancient Russia, who performed the duties of a parish priest without attachment to a monastery.

[9]Kutia (or, kutya) is meal of boiled grain (wheat, nowadays rice) with honey or some other sweetening, used in the Russian Church at the commemoration of the dead: a sacred part of the funeral banquet.

[10]This custom, attributed also to St. Theodosius, is derived from the Greek Studite Rule and was probably adopted by Sergius after the introduction of this rule for the cenobitical life at about 1354.

[11]At that time the word Christians had already begun to be used in a class sense, with reference to the peasantry (Russian, krestyane).

[12]The bilo is an iron or wooden board which was used as a gong in Russian churches before the bells were introduced from the West.

[13]Lavra (laura) was an honorary name in Russia of the four prominent monasteries, among which was that of St. Sergius.

[14]The paramand is a square of cloth bearing the representation of the instruments of the Passion, which is worn by the Eastern monks under their cassocks.

[15]The most likely cause of this dissension was the introduction of a strictly ordered community life which was contrary to Russian monastic customs. Stephen, Sergius' elder brother, was the founder together with Sergius of the monastery, and a person of importance in Moscow.

[16]Twenty miles from the Holy Trinity of St. Sergius.

[17]St. Stephen of Perm, a great missionary among the Zyrians, a Finnish tribe.

[18]Theodore was a nephew of St. Sergius and the abbot of the Simonov monastery in Moscow; later, archbishop of Rostov.

[19]Here are mentioned only a few of the various monasteries founded by St. Sergius or headed by his disciples.

[20]Until the year 1448 the head of the Russian Church, the Metropolitan of Kiev (later, Moscow) was appointed by the Patriarch of Constantinople.

ST. NILUS

[1]The "Tradition to the Disciples" was probably composed at the time that the community by the Sora River was formed, but it would be more properly titled the "Rule" than is the second and larger portion of St. Nilus' work.

[2]John Climacus, an abbot in Sinai during the seventh century and the author of the *Ladder of Paradise*, a classical treatise of Eastern asceticism divided into thirty chapters or "degrees."

[3]Under the name of Holy, or Divine, Scriptures, Nilus comprehends the sacred or religious literature of the Church in its entirety, especially that of the ascetical fathers. This does not mean, however, that for him the writings of the saints and ascetics have the same authority as the Gospels.

[4]This is a covert polemic against the defenders of monastic property (St. Joseph of Volotsk), who put forth the argument of the monk's duty of alms-giving.

[5]Barsanuphius, a recluse who lived near Gaza (Palestine) in the seventh century. Together with John the "Prophet," he gave a series of answers to questions concerning the spiritual life. His teaching advocates unlimited obedience to spiritual direction.

[6]St. Isaac the Syrian, for a short time the Nestorian bishop of Nineveh (seventh century), an ascetical writer of mystical tendencies and a high poetical style.

[7]Abba Dorotheus, the disciple of Barsanuphius, who wrote down the answers of his teacher and published his own "Doctrine" and "Ascetical Sermons," which are of a more popular and ordinary character (recommended for novices).

[8]The famous founder of monastic communities in Egypt (†348) and the author of the first monastic rule.

⁹This is a feature of the Studite Rule, which was observed in some Russian monasteries (e.g., Solovki).

¹⁰Mental (or spiritual) "doing" (or "working") is a technical term referring both to ascetical self-examination and mystical prayer as it is described in section 2, p. 100.

¹¹An Egyptian monk of the fourth century, some of whose sayings are collected in the *Patericons*.

¹²An ascetical writer of the ninth century.

¹³The exegete of Scripture, author of two hundred chapters on "Continence and Virtue" (†after 450).

¹⁴The Byzantine saint of the fourteenth century; one of the exponents of Hesychast mysticism.

¹⁵In this chapter Nilus gives the psychological definitions of the different stages of sin. The Greek definitions, taken from John Climacus, are first given in literal Slavonic translation and then explained in simpler words. These are the Greek terms and the Latin equivalents: prosbole (impetus), syndyasmos (conjunctio), syncatathesis (consensus), aichmalosia (captivitas) and pathos (passio).

¹⁶The words "thought" and "imagining" are English equivalents of the Greek logismos (Latin, cogitatio). Of itself the term is, of course, without moral connotation, but since every image or thought except those concerning God distracts the monk from prayer, in ascetical writing, it is generally understood in a pejorative sense.

¹⁷Cf. Sections 3, 8, pp. 107, 125.

¹⁸Apathia (Latin, impassibilitas), a term of Stoic philosophy. This was accepted by Egyptian ascetics as an ideal of Christian perfection, despite many protests — even by several councils.

¹⁹Nilus of Sinai (†450), an ascetical writer of philosophical and liberal mind; a disciple of St. John Chrysostom.

²⁰This and analogous expressions, such as "putting" (or "holding") the mind in the heart, must here be understood in a direct, physiological sense: that is, as referring to the concentration of the interior imagination in the tract of the heart.

²¹This is the Prayer of Jesus, which has tremendous importance in the practice of all Eastern Christians. For mystics it is a starting-point and an instrument of mental prayer.

²²For a more detailed description of this Hesychast practice, see below, "The Way of a Pilgrim," pp. 280-345.

²³Accidie, the medieval technical term for the sin of despondency. See below, p. 116.

²⁴Certain hymns in the Eastern Church are called *Troparia*.

²⁵Marc the Eremite, a monk of Galatia and Palestine; an ascetical writer of the fifth century.

²⁶Here mystical and liturgical prayer are put into sharp opposition: the school of St. Nilus versus that of St. Joseph.

²⁷Probably the reference should be to Pachomius, whose rule, according to the legend, was given to him by an angel.

²⁸Sobering (Greek, nepsis) is a favorite Russian term for the ascetical spiritual life.

²⁹The system of eight principal vices, which are also referred to as "passions," or "spirits," appears first in Egyptian monastic usage as represented by Evagrins (fourth century), Nilus of Sinai, and John Cassian (fifth century). This is to be distinguished from the system of seven deadly sins accepted by the Western Church, which originated with Gregory the Great (circa 600).

³⁰In the Greco-Roman system of time calculation, preserved by the medieval Church, the day from sunrise to sunset was divided into twelve hours (a period longer in summer, shorter in winter). The ninth hour corresponds approximately to our 3 p.m.

³¹The "angelic form" (or "image") is a term current in the Eastern Church, to describe the character of the monastic order.

³²The irony in the following passage is directed against the condition of Russian monasticism in the contemporary school of St. Joseph of Volotsk.

³³Canon, i.e., a suite of hymns or prayers arranged around one theme; e.g., liturgical canons of Matins, canons of repentance, for private devotion, etc.

³⁴See Note 24.

³⁵This Will of St. Nilus was not executed by his disciples. It had a precedent in a similar Will of the Greek Metropolitan Constantine of Kiev (†1159).

³⁶A liturgical book containing hymns and prayers intended for singing and not for reading.

ARCHPRIEST AVVAKUM

¹There are three versions of Avvakum's life, known in Russian scholarly research as A., B., and C. One manuscript of the first version is in Avvakum's own hand; the others are obviously copies done by Old Believers. In 1927 the three texts were simultaneously pub-

lished (after a number of earlier editions) by the Leningrad Academy of Science in the series: "The Russian Historical Library" as Volume XXXIX, devoted to the history of the Old Believers in the seventeenth century. The three texts offer several variations, but as I. L. Barskov writes in his introduction, all three present indubitably Avvakum's own story, and he himself may have introduced the variations while the Life was being copied. Avvakum sent this story to a number of his spiritual children and to groups of Old Believers — wherefor, the copying. But, as Barskov points out, none of his contemporaries would have dared or would have been able to invent new episodes or to add new facts to the Life. It is Avvakum's own voice we hear in each one of these documents. The translator has mainly used the version A (Avvakum's autographed text), but has also borrowed from the other texts, episodes and variations which are either particularly characteristic and colorful or which help to clarify the sequence of the events narrated.

[2]The city of Nizhny-Novgorod, situated at the middle of the Volga River's course, is now called Gorky. The date of Avvakum's birth is probably 1620.

[3]They were imprisoned in a subterranean dugout.

[4]Acts viii: 26-39.

[5]Some objects of Avvakum's zeal for reform: the trained bears, like all kinds of theatrical or musical or jugglers' entertainments, were prohibited by the Church; the shaving was condemned by the "Stoglav" Council of 1551, yet began to be practised in the seventeenth century under Western influence.

[6]St. Philip was deposed and strangled by the order of John IV (called "The Terrible").

[7]St. Stephen, a missionary bishop among the heathen Finnish tribe of Zyrians in Northern Russia (fourteenth century).

[8]The patriarchate had just become vacant with the death of Joseph (1652).

[9]In 1653.

[10]Our Lady of Kazan, now St. Basil's Cathedral, the famous church on the Red Square in Moscow.

[11]The main point of difference between the old and the new rites is the number of fingers used in making the sign of the cross: two for the Old Believers, three for the Established Church.

[12]This is part of the rite of the degradation of a priest.

[13]With his usual realism regarding ritualistic symbolism, Avvakum

sees the sundering of Christ's body in the obviously new ritual gesture of the Patriarch, who took the paten and the chalice separately from the deacon.

[14]Since Avvakum had not been degraded (shorn) like his colleagues, he was accepted in Tobolsk as a parish priest.

[15]The Tsarina Mary Miloslavsky, the first wife of Alexis, was in sympathy with the Old Believers.

[16]Dauria was the name given in the seventeenth century to the country on the left bank of the Amur River. The Russians had recently undertaken the conquest of this country, and Pashkov was the captain of the expedition.

[17]It was considered indecent for a married woman to go bareheaded.

[18]Pope means priest in ancient and popular Russian.

[19]November 15, in 1656.

[20]Hostages from the native tribes (in Bratsky it was the Buriats) were kept in Siberian forts to secure the payment of tribute.

[21]The eating of "unclean" food was considered a great sin.

[22]Rtishchev was an influential boyar and one of the most cultivated and tolerant statesmen of the seventeenth century.

[23]The preparation of bread and wine for the Eucharist which constitutes the first part of the Eastern Mass.

[24]An influential boyar and a personal friend of Tsar Alexis.

[25]September 1, 1662, the day of New Year in old Russia.

[26]The Mezen is a river discharging itself into the White Sea eastward from Arkhangelsk. There, on the sea coast, was a small Russian settlement (now the town of Mezen).

[27]St. Paphnutius Monastery at Borovsk, about one hundred miles from Moscow.

[28]About ten miles from Moscow, on the Moskva River.

[29]In this letter to the Tsar, Avvakum tells that while reading the Gospel, he had a vision of his guardian angel and Christ the Lord, Who said to him: "Have no fear; I am with thee."

[30]The companions of Avvakum had their tongues cut off before they were sent into their place of deportation.

[31]Tobacco was prohibited in Muscovy in the seventeenth century and is abhorred by the Old Believers up to the present time. The Metropolitan of Gaza (in Palestine) Païsius Ligarides, came to Russia as a theological expert in 1662.

[32]Sham madness or folly was the essence of the ascetical form of

life called, in Russian, "foolishness for Christ's sake." Such sham fools were very popular in Russia, particularly in the sixteenth and seventeenth century, and many of them were canonized, although the Church in the seventeenth century began to prohibit such an ostentatious and disorderly way of life.

[33]The famous council of 1666-7, in which two Greek patriarchs participated. The council condemned the schism of the Old Believers and deposed the Patriarch Nicon himself.

[34]Deacon Theodore was banished to Pustozersk in 1668, some months later than Avvakum and his group (1667).

[35]This name is given by Avvakum to the officer who executed his sons and friends in Mezen. He gives, besides, his proper name, Ivan Yelagin.

[36]This is the end of the autobiography proper; what follows is the account of miracles wrought through Avvakum's prayers during his life.

[37]This is the delirium of the possessed, failing to recognize the place where he is.

[38]All these miraculous events and many others here omitted are, indeed, related in the autobiography of Epiphanius.

ST. TYCHON

[1]St. Tychon's first biographer was Eugene Bolkhovitinov, the well-known historian who was later the Metropolitan of Kiev; he published his Life in 1796.

[2]St. Tychon was born in 1724, the son of a country cleric ("reader") in the province of Novgorod.

[3]The poverty and coarseness of life in the church school of the eighteenth century is depicted by Gogol in his Viy.

[4]In Russia large brick stoves are used as sleeping places.

[5]A parody of the ritual of incensing a bishop in church.

[6]An archimandrite is the abbot of a large and privileged monastery.

[7]The consistory is the administrative office of the diocese.

[8]In the Eastern Orthodox churches, behind the icon wall, in addition to the altar (which is in Greek *trapeza*, table), there is a second table in the lefthand corner called in Greek *thysiasterion* (altar), where the holy bread and wine for the Eucharist are prepared. This preparation (*proscomedia*) is the first part of the liturgy

of St. John Chrysostom (and that of St. Basil); from the liturgical loaves (*prosphora*) small particles are cut for the consecration, in the name of Christ, Our Lady, the saints, the living and the dead. The congregation bring their own sacred loaves with the list of names of their living and dead in remembrance of whom particles are taken for the Holy Eucharist.

⁹Bishops were appointed by the Emperor in Russia; candidates were nominated by the Holy Synod. The use of lots at the elections indicates the reliance upon God's choice.

¹⁰The Laura of the Holy Trinity, founded by St. Sergius near Moscow.

¹¹St. Tychon speaks of the times before the great secularization of 1764, when the ecclesiastical serfs were brought under the jurisdiction of the State.

¹²At the theological seminary in Novgorod, when Tychon was still a layman and was named Timothy Sokolov.

¹³Kvas is a Russian national beverage, the product of the fermentation of rye bread; it is sour and non-alcoholic.

¹⁴The two successors of Tychon in the See of Voronezh bore the same name.

¹⁵As a bishop in retreat Tychon received a small allowance from the State (five hundred rubles).

¹⁶In the eighteenth century the government tried to diminish the number of the clergy and monks by enlisting superfluous or unlearned men in the army.

¹⁷The *omophorium* is a bishop's vestment corresponding to the Latin *pallium* but broader, and knotted about the neck.

¹⁸This was the inundation of 1777.

¹⁹Freely composed sermons were rare and even disapproved of in the Russian Church at that time; the priests were obliged to read sermons from one of the books approved by the Holy Synod.

²⁰The Russian word means "see-saw," a popular means of amusement. One of the famous sermons of St. Tychon was directed against a semi-pagan folk feast in Voronezh called the Yarilo.

²¹The seven-year war of 1756-63.

²²The Russian-Turkish war of 1768-74.

²³No doubt St. Tychon speaks in this letter of his own experience.

²⁴This is a saying of St. Arsenius of Egypt.

ST. SERAPHIM

[1]The monastery of Sarov was situated in the province of Tambov in the midst of the dense virgin forests which, even now, cover an area of many hundred miles surrounding the contiguous portions of the provinces of Nizhny-Novgorod (Gorky) and Tambov.

[2]"The Slavonic word Umileniye was used for the Greek κατάνυξις, compunction. Its verb, however, means to touch, move affect, and the Russians use the word in a very full sense but with little that is specific to compunction. It is, in fact, not specific at all but a general emotion, particularly the wholehearted receptive response of the mind in prayer. 'Tenderness' is the nearest literal equivalent." "The Way of a Pilgrim." (Dobbie-Bateman)

[3]See below, pp. 280-385.

[4]The Eastern form of the Ave Maria is: "Hail, Virgin Mother of God, Mary full of grace, the Lord is with thee! Blessed are thou amongst women, blessed is the fruit of thy womb, for thou hast borne the Savior of our souls."

[5]This phenomenon of Elevation is observed in mystics of both East and West.

[6]The so-called "icon not made with hands" of Our Lord, the original of which legend ascribes to Jesus Himself; Abgar, King of Edessa, of the Eastern legend, corresponds to Veronica of the West.

[7]From the Eastern prayer to the Holy Spirit, "O King of Heaven."

[8]"Apophatic" in Greek means negative, or, defined by negation. The term "apophatic," or negative, theology (theologia negativa) was coined by Pseudo-Dionysius Areopagitas.

[9]N. F. Fedorov (1828-1903) was a Christian thinker of originality whose main preoccupations were with the peaceful organization of labor and the doctrine of the resurrection of the dead.

[10]Philaret, Metropolitan of Moscow (1782-1868), a famous theologian and preacher; the most authoritative of the princes of the Church in the nineteenth century.

[11]"Great John" is the name of the largest church tower in the Kremlin. In this instance the name of the tower is applied to its largest bell.

[12]N. A. Motovilov was a noble squire whom Seraphim had healed. He was the most devoted of the saint's sons and left memoirs concerning him.

[13]St. Seraphim quotes from a hymn of Matins in the Orthodox Church.

[14]This is the end of the prayer to the Holy Spirit quoted above (note 7).

[15]The sacramental words used at the Orthodox "Chrismation," which corresponds to the sacrament of Confirmation in the Western Church and is performed, in the East, immediately after Baptism. Thus Seraphim might speak of them as part of the Baptismal rite.

THE PILGRIM

[1]Saint Demetrius, Metropolitan of Rostov (1651-1709) was a well-known religious writer, who composed a classical collection of the Lives of Saints in twelve volumes and a tract on the refutation of the Old-Believers. He was the representative of the Kievan (i.e., the Latin scholastic) school in the Russia of Peter I.

[2]These are Byzantine mystical theologians of the fourteenth century. The first Slavonic translation of the *Philocalia*, by Paisius Velichkovsky, contained the works of about thirty Greek fathers.

[3]Saint Innocent, a missionary and the first Bishop of Irkutsk (1680-1731), canonized in 1805.

[4]Callistus, confused in the *Philocalia* with a Patriarch of Constantinople, is probably an ascetic contemporary with the Patriarch (fourteenth century).

[5]In these reasonings of the schoolmaster one sees the blending of the Orthodox doctrine on the holiness of matter with some ideas contained in Schelling's philosophy of nature, which was very popular among Russian romanticists.

[6]The Poles are Roman-Catholic.

[7]The *Acathist* is a cycle of hymns or prayers of praise in honor of Christ, Our Lady or the Saints: from the Greek word meaning "non-sitting," i.e., "standing" prayers.

[8]The simple advice of Peter the Damascene on prayer seems to be very remote from mental prayer as advocated by the Pilgrim.

JOHN OF CRONSTADT

[1]This quotation is from the prayers before Holy Communion.

[2]In this section Father John speaks particularly of his own experience as an intercessor in prayer for his fellow-men.

[3]"Exhaustion" here has the meaning of "kenosis."

[4]The sanctuary behind the icon-wall, where the altar stands: the sanctuary itself is called the altar in the Russian Church.

[5]"Liturgy" in the Greek and Russian Churches refers to a particular service, the Mass. It is used in this sense here.

[6]"Holy Mysteries" is the usual Orthodox designation of the Eucharist.

[7]A particle of the liturgical bread, broken from the Prosphora in the name of Christ and used in the Eucharist, is called the "Lamb."

[8]The quotation is from an evening prayer attributed to St. John Damascene.

[9]Father John speaks here of the almshouse which he built in Cronstadt.

[10]These are the orders of the saints officially established in the Orthodox Church. "Disinterested physicians" has reference to some of the martyrs, for the most part named in pairs, who, according to the legends concerning them, practised medicine during their lives, e.g., Cosmas and Damianus. "The righteous" is the official designation of lay saints who were not martyrs.

FATHER YELCHANINOV

[1]Ivan Kireievsky (1806-56), a philosopher and writer. One of two brothers who were founders of the ideological Slavophile movement in Russia.

[2]From Dante's *Divine Comedy*: "L'amor che muove il sol e l'altre stelle."

[3]The roles of Yepikhodov (from Chekhov's *The Cherry Orchard*) and Tsar Fedor (from the tragedy of Alexis Tolstoy) were the most popular in the repertoire of Moskvin, the actor of the Moscow Artistic Theatre.

[4]The priest Alexander Vvedensky, later Metropolitan, was one of the leaders of the so-called Living Church, a group of schismatics within the Russian Church (since 1922) aiming at the creation of a reformed Orthodoxy, communist in its social aspects.

[5]The Russian word here is "sobornost." In the Russian conception of catholicity, the emphasis is placed on the corporate, common life and spirit.

[6]The quotation is from one of the prayers before Holy Communion.

Notes 499

[7]Innocent Borisov, Archbishop of Cherson (1800-57), the most famous among the Russian preachers of the nineteenth century. He is representative of humanistic and even liberal tendencies connected with Western (German) philosophy and theology.

[8]This and the following scenes of nature depict Provence, in the neighborhood of Nice.

[9]"Sol" means "salt" in Russian.

[10]"A realibus ad realiora" — from reality to a higher reality — was a formula of religious symbolism as defined by the Russian poet Viacheslav Ivanov.

[11]Jean-Baptist Vianney (1786-1859); a parish priest near Lyons, France, canonized in 1905.

[12]40° Celsius equals 104° Fahrenheit.

A SHORT BIBLIOGRAPHY

OF RUSSIAN SPIRITUALITY

GENERAL

ANONYMOUS: *Orthodox Spirituality*, by A Monk of the Eastern Church. London: The Society for Promoting Christian Knowledge, 1945; New York, 1945.

ARSENIEV, N.: *Mysticism and the Eastern Church*. London, 1926.

BULGAKOV, S.: *The Orthodox Church*. London, 1933.

FEDOTOV, G.P.: *Sviatye drevnei Rusi*. Paris, 1931. (In Russian.)

FEDOTOV, G.P.: *Russian Religious Mind*. Cambridge: Harvard University Press, 1946; Harper Torchbook edition, 1960.

FLOROVSKY, G.V.: *Puti russkago bogosloviia*. Paris, 1937. (In Russian.)

GORODETSKY, N.: *The Humiliated Christ in Modern Russian Thought*. London, 1938.

LEV HIEROMOINE: "Une forme d'ascèse russe: la folie pour le Christ," *Irénikon*, April, 1927.

SMOLITCH, J.: *Leben und Lehre der Starzen*. Vienna, 1936.

TRUBETSKOI, E.: *Die religiöse Weltanschauung der altrussischen Ikonenmalerei*. Paderborn, 1927.

ST. THEODOSIUS:
THE FIRST REPRESENTATIVE OF KENOTICISM

NESTOR: "Zhitie prep. Feodosia" in *Chtenia v Obshchestve Istorii i Drevnostei*. Moscow, 1858, 1879, 1899 (3 editions). (In Russian.)

ST. SERGIUS:
THE FIRST HERMIT AND MYSTIC

ZERNOV, N.: *St. Sergius, Builder of Russia*. London; The Society for Promoting Christian Knowledge, 1937; New York, Macmillan, 1939.

ST. NILUS SORSKY:
THE TEACHER OF SPIRITUAL PRAYER

NIL SORSKY: *Predanie uchenikam i ustav*, ed. Borovkova-Maikova. St. Petersburg. (In Slavonic.)

HAUSHERR, I.: "Un grand mystique byzantin: Introduction à la vie de Syméon le Nouveau Théologien" in *Orientalia Christiana*, V, XII. Rome, 1928.

———————— "La méthode de l'oraison hésychaste" in *Orientalia Christiana*, V, IX. Rome, 1927.

HOLL, K.: *Enthusiasmus und Bussgewalt beim griechischen Mönchtum*. Leipzig, 1898.

AVVAKUM: THE CONSERVATIVE REBEL

ARCHPRIEST AVVAKUM: *The Life of Archpriest Avvakum by Himself*, trs. J. Harrison and H. Mirrlees. London, 1924.

PASCAL, PIERRE: *La vie de l'archiprêtre Avvakum, écrite par lui-même, avec introduction et commentaire*. Paris, 1938.

PASCAL, PIERRE: *Avvakum et les débuts du raskol*. Paris, 1938.

ST. TYCHON: A WESTERNIZING KENOTIC

TYCHON ZADONSKY: *Tvorenia* (5 vols.). Moscow, 1898-9. (In Russian.)

ST. SERAPHIM: MYSTIC AND PROPHET

CHICHAGOV, LEONID: *Letopis' Serafimo-Diveievskago monastyria*. Moscow, 1896.

DOBBIE-BATEMAN, A.F.: *St. Seraphim of Sarov: Concerning the Aim of the Christian Life*. London: The Society for Promoting Christian knowledge, 1936.

"THE PILGRIM" ON MENTAL PRAYER

ANONYMOUS: *The Way of a Pilgrim*, trs. R. M. French (2 vols.). London, 1931, 1943.

JOHN OF CRONSTADT: A GENIUS OF PRAYER

SERGIEFF, JOHN ILIYTCH: *My Life in Christ*, trs. E. E. Goulaeff. London, 1897.

FATHER JOHN: *Thoughts and Counsels: Selected by C. Bickersteth and A. Illingworth*. London, 1899.

FATHER YELCHANINOV: THE TEACHER OF SELF-EXAMINATION

YELCHANINOV, ALEXANDER: *Zapisi*. Paris, 1935, 1937 (2 editions). (In Russian.)

A CATALOG OF SELECTED DOVER BOOKS IN ALL FIELDS OF INTEREST

CONCERNING THE SPIRITUAL IN ART, Wassily Kandinsky. Pioneering work by father of abstract art. Thoughts on color theory, nature of art. Analysis of earlier masters. 12 illustrations. 80pp. of text. 5⅜ x 8½. 23411-8

ANIMALS: 1,419 Copyright-Free Illustrations of Mammals, Birds, Fish, Insects, etc., Jim Harter (ed.). Clear wood engravings present, in extremely lifelike poses, over 1,000 species of animals. One of the most extensive pictorial sourcebooks of its kind. Captions. Index. 284pp. 9 x 12. 23766-4

CELTIC ART: The Methods of Construction, George Bain. Simple geometric techniques for making Celtic interlacements, spirals, Kells-type initials, animals, humans, etc. Over 500 illustrations. 160pp. 9 x 12. (Available in U.S. only.) 22923-8

AN ATLAS OF ANATOMY FOR ARTISTS, Fritz Schider. Most thorough reference work on art anatomy in the world. Hundreds of illustrations, including selections from works by Vesalius, Leonardo, Goya, Ingres, Michelangelo, others. 593 illustrations. 192pp. 7⅛ x 10¼. 20241-0

CELTIC HAND STROKE-BY-STROKE (Irish Half-Uncial from "The Book of Kells"): An Arthur Baker Calligraphy Manual, Arthur Baker. Complete guide to creating each letter of the alphabet in distinctive Celtic manner. Covers hand position, strokes, pens, inks, paper, more. Illustrated. 48pp. 8¼ x 11. 24336-2

EASY ORIGAMI, John Montroll. Charming collection of 32 projects (hat, cup, pelican, piano, swan, many more) specially designed for the novice origami hobbyist. Clearly illustrated easy-to-follow instructions insure that even beginning papercrafters will achieve successful results. 48pp. 8¼ x 11. 27298-2

THE COMPLETE BOOK OF BIRDHOUSE CONSTRUCTION FOR WOODWORKERS, Scott D. Campbell. Detailed instructions, illustrations, tables. Also data on bird habitat and instinct patterns. Bibliography. 3 tables. 63 illustrations in 15 figures. 48pp. 5¼ x 8½. 24407-5

BLOOMINGDALE'S ILLUSTRATED 1886 CATALOG: Fashions, Dry Goods and Housewares, Bloomingdale Brothers. Famed merchants' extremely rare catalog depicting about 1,700 products: clothing, housewares, firearms, dry goods, jewelry, more. Invaluable for dating, identifying vintage items. Also, copyright-free graphics for artists, designers. Co-published with Henry Ford Museum & Greenfield Village. 160pp. 8¼ x 11. 25780-0

HISTORIC COSTUME IN PICTURES, Braun & Schneider. Over 1,450 costumed figures in clearly detailed engravings–from dawn of civilization to end of 19th century. Captions. Many folk costumes. 256pp. 8⅜ x 11¾. 23150-X

FRANK LLOYD WRIGHT'S DANA HOUSE, Donald Hoffmann. Pictorial essay of residential masterpiece with over 160 interior and exterior photos, plans, elevations, sketches and studies. 128pp. 9¼ x 10¾. 29120-0

THE MALE AND FEMALE FIGURE IN MOTION: 60 Classic Photographic Sequences, Eadweard Muybridge. 60 true-action photographs of men and women walking, running, climbing, bending, turning, etc., reproduced from rare 19th-century masterpiece. vi + 121pp. 9 x 12. 24745-7

1001 QUESTIONS ANSWERED ABOUT THE SEASHORE, N. J. Berrill and Jacquelyn Berrill. Queries answered about dolphins, sea snails, sponges, starfish, fishes, shore birds, many others. Covers appearance, breeding, growth, feeding, much more. 305pp. 5¼ x 8¼. 23366-9

ATTRACTING BIRDS TO YOUR YARD, William J. Weber. Easy-to-follow guide offers advice on how to attract the greatest diversity of birds: birdhouses, feeders, water and waterers, much more. 96pp. 5³⁄₁₆ x 8¼. 28927-3

MEDICINAL AND OTHER USES OF NORTH AMERICAN PLANTS: A Historical Survey with Special Reference to the Eastern Indian Tribes, Charlotte Erichsen-Brown. Chronological historical citations document 500 years of usage of plants, trees, shrubs native to eastern Canada, northeastern U.S. Also complete identifying information. 343 illustrations. 544pp. 6½ x 9¼. 25951-X

STORYBOOK MAZES, Dave Phillips. 23 stories and mazes on two-page spreads: Wizard of Oz, Treasure Island, Robin Hood, etc. Solutions. 64pp. 8¼ x 11. 23628-5

AMERICAN NEGRO SONGS: 230 Folk Songs and Spirituals, Religious and Secular, John W. Work. This authoritative study traces the African influences of songs sung and played by black Americans at work, in church, and as entertainment. The author discusses the lyric significance of such songs as "Swing Low, Sweet Chariot," "John Henry," and others and offers the words and music for 230 songs. Bibliography. Index of Song Titles. 272pp. 6½ x 9¼. 40271-1

MOVIE-STAR PORTRAITS OF THE FORTIES, John Kobal (ed.). 163 glamor, studio photos of 106 stars of the 1940s: Rita Hayworth, Ava Gardner, Marlon Brando, Clark Gable, many more. 176pp. 8⅜ x 11¼. 23546-7

BENCHLEY LOST AND FOUND, Robert Benchley. Finest humor from early 30s, about pet peeves, child psychologists, post office and others. Mostly unavailable elsewhere. 73 illustrations by Peter Arno and others. 183pp. 5⅜ x 8½. 22410-4

YEKL and THE IMPORTED BRIDEGROOM AND OTHER STORIES OF YIDDISH NEW YORK, Abraham Cahan. Film Hester Street based on *Yekl* (1896). Novel, other stories among first about Jewish immigrants on N.Y.'s East Side. 240pp. 5⅜ x 8½. 22427-9

SELECTED POEMS, Walt Whitman. Generous sampling from *Leaves of Grass*. Twenty-four poems include "I Hear America Singing," "Song of the Open Road," "I Sing the Body Electric," "When Lilacs Last in the Dooryard Bloom'd," "O Captain! My Captain!"–all reprinted from an authoritative edition. Lists of titles and first lines. 128pp. 5³⁄₁₆ x 8¼. 26878-0

PERSPECTIVE FOR ARTISTS, Rex Vicat Cole. Depth, perspective of sky and sea, shadows, much more, not usually covered. 391 diagrams, 81 reproductions of drawings and paintings. 279pp. 5⅜ x 8½. 22487-2

DRAWING THE LIVING FIGURE, Joseph Sheppard. Innovative approach to artistic anatomy focuses on specifics of surface anatomy, rather than muscles and bones. Over 170 drawings of live models in front, back and side views, and in widely varying poses. Accompanying diagrams. 177 illustrations. Introduction. Index. 144pp. 8⅜ x11¼. 26723-7

GOTHIC AND OLD ENGLISH ALPHABETS: 100 Complete Fonts, Dan X. Solo. Add power, elegance to posters, signs, other graphics with 100 stunning copyright-free alphabets: Blackstone, Dolbey, Germania, 97 more–including many lower-case, numerals, punctuation marks. 104pp. 8⅛ x 11. 24695-7

HOW TO DO BEADWORK, Mary White. Fundamental book on craft from simple projects to five-bead chains and woven works. 106 illustrations. 142pp. 5⅜ x 8. 20697-1

THE BOOK OF WOOD CARVING, Charles Marshall Sayers. Finest book for beginners discusses fundamentals and offers 34 designs. "Absolutely first rate . . . well thought out and well executed."–E. J. Tangerman. 118pp. 7¾ x 10⅝. 23654-4

ILLUSTRATED CATALOG OF CIVIL WAR MILITARY GOODS: Union Army Weapons, Insignia, Uniform Accessories, and Other Equipment, Schuyler, Hartley, and Graham. Rare, profusely illustrated 1846 catalog includes Union Army uniform and dress regulations, arms and ammunition, coats, insignia, flags, swords, rifles, etc. 226 illustrations. 160pp. 9 x 12. 24939-5

WOMEN'S FASHIONS OF THE EARLY 1900s: An Unabridged Republication of "New York Fashions, 1909," National Cloak & Suit Co. Rare catalog of mail-order fashions documents women's and children's clothing styles shortly after the turn of the century. Captions offer full descriptions, prices. Invaluable resource for fashion, costume historians. Approximately 725 illustrations. 128pp. 8⅜ x 11¼. 27276-1

THE 1912 AND 1915 GUSTAV STICKLEY FURNITURE CATALOGS, Gustav Stickley. With over 200 detailed illustrations and descriptions, these two catalogs are essential reading and reference materials and identification guides for Stickley furniture. Captions cite materials, dimensions and prices. 112pp. 6½ x 9¼. 26676-1

EARLY AMERICAN LOCOMOTIVES, John H. White, Jr. Finest locomotive engravings from early 19th century: historical (1804–74), main-line (after 1870), special, foreign, etc. 147 plates. 142pp. 11⅜ x 8¼. 22772-3

THE TALL SHIPS OF TODAY IN PHOTOGRAPHS, Frank O. Braynard. Lavishly illustrated tribute to nearly 100 majestic contemporary sailing vessels: Amerigo Vespucci, Clearwater, Constitution, Eagle, Mayflower, Sea Cloud, Victory, many more. Authoritative captions provide statistics, background on each ship. 190 black-and-white photographs and illustrations. Introduction. 128pp. 8⅞ x 11¾. 27163-3

CATALOG OF DOVER BOOKS

ANATOMY: A Complete Guide for Artists, Joseph Sheppard. A master of figure drawing shows artists how to render human anatomy convincingly. Over 460 illustrations. 224pp. 8⅜ x 11¼. 27279-6

MEDIEVAL CALLIGRAPHY: Its History and Technique, Marc Drogin. Spirited history, comprehensive instruction manual covers 13 styles (ca. 4th century through 15th). Excellent photographs; directions for duplicating medieval techniques with modern tools. 224pp. 8⅜ x 11¼. 26142-5

DRIED FLOWERS: How to Prepare Them, Sarah Whitlock and Martha Rankin. Complete instructions on how to use silica gel, meal and borax, perlite aggregate, sand and borax, glycerine and water to create attractive permanent flower arrangements. 12 illustrations. 32pp. 5⅜ x 8½. 21802-3

EASY-TO-MAKE BIRD FEEDERS FOR WOODWORKERS, Scott D. Campbell. Detailed, simple-to-use guide for designing, constructing, caring for and using feeders. Text, illustrations for 12 classic and contemporary designs. 96pp. 5⅜ x 8½.
25847-5

SCOTTISH WONDER TALES FROM MYTH AND LEGEND, Donald A. Mackenzie. 16 lively tales tell of giants rumbling down mountainsides, of a magic wand that turns stone pillars into warriors, of gods and goddesses, evil hags, powerful forces and more. 240pp. 5⅜ x 8½. 29677-6

THE HISTORY OF UNDERCLOTHES, C. Willett Cunnington and Phyllis Cunnington. Fascinating, well-documented survey covering six centuries of English undergarments, enhanced with over 100 illustrations: 12th-century laced-up bodice, footed long drawers (1795), 19th-century bustles, 19th-century corsets for men, Victorian "bust improvers," much more. 272pp. 5⅜ x 8¼. 27124-2

ARTS AND CRAFTS FURNITURE: The Complete Brooks Catalog of 1912, Brooks Manufacturing Co. Photos and detailed descriptions of more than 150 now very collectible furniture designs from the Arts and Crafts movement depict davenports, settees, buffets, desks, tables, chairs, bedsteads, dressers and more, all built of solid, quarter-sawed oak. Invaluable for students and enthusiasts of antiques, Americana and the decorative arts. 80pp. 6½ x 9¼. 27471-3

WILBUR AND ORVILLE: A Biography of the Wright Brothers, Fred Howard. Definitive, crisply written study tells the full story of the brothers' lives and work. A vividly written biography, unparalleled in scope and color, that also captures the spirit of an extraordinary era. 560pp. 6⅛ x 9¼. 40297-5

THE ARTS OF THE SAILOR: Knotting, Splicing and Ropework, Hervey Garrett Smith. Indispensable shipboard reference covers tools, basic knots and useful hitches; handsewing and canvas work, more. Over 100 illustrations. Delightful reading for sea lovers. 256pp. 5⅜ x 8½. 26440-8

FRANK LLOYD WRIGHT'S FALLINGWATER: The House and Its History, Second, Revised Edition, Donald Hoffmann. A total revision—both in text and illustrations—of the standard document on Fallingwater, the boldest, most personal architectural statement of Wright's mature years, updated with valuable new material from the recently opened Frank Lloyd Wright Archives. "Fascinating"—*The New York Times*. 116 illustrations. 128pp. 9¼ x 10¾. 27430-6

THE WIT AND HUMOR OF OSCAR WILDE, Alvin Redman (ed.). More than 1,000 ripostes, paradoxes, wisecracks: Work is the curse of the drinking classes; I can resist everything except temptation; etc. 258pp. 5⅜ x 8½. 20602-5

SHAKESPEARE LEXICON AND QUOTATION DICTIONARY, Alexander Schmidt. Full definitions, locations, shades of meaning in every word in plays and poems. More than 50,000 exact quotations. 1,485pp. 6½ x 9¼. 2-vol. set.
Vol. 1: 22726-X
Vol. 2: 22727-8

SELECTED POEMS, Emily Dickinson. Over 100 best-known, best-loved poems by one of America's foremost poets, reprinted from authoritative early editions. No comparable edition at this price. Index of first lines. 64pp. 5$\frac{3}{16}$ x 8¼. 26466-1

THE INSIDIOUS DR. FU-MANCHU, Sax Rohmer. The first of the popular mystery series introduces a pair of English detectives to their archnemesis, the diabolical Dr. Fu-Manchu. Flavorful atmosphere, fast-paced action, and colorful characters enliven this classic of the genre. 208pp. 5$\frac{3}{16}$ x 8¼. 29898-1

THE MALLEUS MALEFICARUM OF KRAMER AND SPRENGER, translated by Montague Summers. Full text of most important witchhunter's "bible," used by both Catholics and Protestants. 278pp. 6⅝ x 10. 22802-9

SPANISH STORIES/CUENTOS ESPAÑOLES: A Dual-Language Book, Angel Flores (ed.). Unique format offers 13 great stories in Spanish by Cervantes, Borges, others. Faithful English translations on facing pages. 352pp. 5⅜ x 8½. 25399-6

GARDEN CITY, LONG ISLAND, IN EARLY PHOTOGRAPHS, 1869–1919, Mildred H. Smith. Handsome treasury of 118 vintage pictures, accompanied by carefully researched captions, document the Garden City Hotel fire (1899), the Vanderbilt Cup Race (1908), the first airmail flight departing from the Nassau Boulevard Aerodrome (1911), and much more. 96pp. 8⅞ x 11¾. 40669-5

OLD QUEENS, N.Y., IN EARLY PHOTOGRAPHS, Vincent F. Seyfried and William Asadorian. Over 160 rare photographs of Maspeth, Jamaica, Jackson Heights, and other areas. Vintage views of DeWitt Clinton mansion, 1939 World's Fair and more. Captions. 192pp. 8⅞ x 11. 26358-4

CAPTURED BY THE INDIANS: 15 Firsthand Accounts, 1750-1870, Frederick Drimmer. Astounding true historical accounts of grisly torture, bloody conflicts, relentless pursuits, miraculous escapes and more, by people who lived to tell the tale. 384pp. 5⅜ x 8½. 24901-8

THE WORLD'S GREAT SPEECHES (Fourth Enlarged Edition), Lewis Copeland, Lawrence W. Lamm, and Stephen J. McKenna. Nearly 300 speeches provide public speakers with a wealth of updated quotes and inspiration–from Pericles' funeral oration and William Jennings Bryan's "Cross of Gold Speech" to Malcolm X's powerful words on the Black Revolution and Earl of Spenser's tribute to his sister, Diana, Princess of Wales. 944pp. 5⅜ x 8⅜. 40903-1

THE BOOK OF THE SWORD, Sir Richard F. Burton. Great Victorian scholar/adventurer's eloquent, erudite history of the "queen of weapons"–from prehistory to early Roman Empire. Evolution and development of early swords, variations (sabre, broadsword, cutlass, scimitar, etc.), much more. 336pp. 6⅛ x 9¼.
25434-8

CATALOG OF DOVER BOOKS

THE STORY OF THE TITANIC AS TOLD BY ITS SURVIVORS, Jack Winocour (ed.). What it was really like. Panic, despair, shocking inefficiency, and a little heroism. More thrilling than any fictional account. 26 illustrations. 320pp. 5⅜ x 8½. 20610-6

FAIRY AND FOLK TALES OF THE IRISH PEASANTRY, William Butler Yeats (ed.). Treasury of 64 tales from the twilight world of Celtic myth and legend: "The Soul Cages," "The Kildare Pooka," "King O'Toole and his Goose," many more. Introduction and Notes by W. B. Yeats. 352pp. 5⅜ x 8½. 26941-8

BUDDHIST MAHAYANA TEXTS, E. B. Cowell and others (eds.). Superb, accurate translations of basic documents in Mahayana Buddhism, highly important in history of religions. The Buddha-karita of Asvaghosha, Larger Sukhavativyuha, more. 448pp. 5⅜ x 8½. 25552-2

ONE TWO THREE . . . INFINITY: Facts and Speculations of Science, George Gamow. Great physicist's fascinating, readable overview of contemporary science: number theory, relativity, fourth dimension, entropy, genes, atomic structure, much more. 128 illustrations. Index. 352pp. 5⅜ x 8½. 25664-2

EXPERIMENTATION AND MEASUREMENT, W. J. Youden. Introductory manual explains laws of measurement in simple terms and offers tips for achieving accuracy and minimizing errors. Mathematics of measurement, use of instruments, experimenting with machines. 1994 edition. Foreword. Preface. Introduction. Epilogue. Selected Readings. Glossary. Index. Tables and figures. 128pp. 5⅜ x 8½. 40451-X

DALÍ ON MODERN ART: The Cuckolds of Antiquated Modern Art, Salvador Dalí. Influential painter skewers modern art and its practitioners. Outrageous evaluations of Picasso, Cézanne, Turner, more. 15 renderings of paintings discussed. 44 calligraphic decorations by Dalí. 96pp. 5⅜ x 8½. (Available in U.S. only.) 29220-7

ANTIQUE PLAYING CARDS: A Pictorial History, Henry René D'Allemagne. Over 900 elaborate, decorative images from rare playing cards (14th–20th centuries): Bacchus, death, dancing dogs, hunting scenes, royal coats of arms, players cheating, much more. 96pp. 9¼ x 12¼. 29265-7

MAKING FURNITURE MASTERPIECES: 30 Projects with Measured Drawings, Franklin H. Gottshall. Step-by-step instructions, illustrations for constructing handsome, useful pieces, among them a Sheraton desk, Chippendale chair, Spanish desk, Queen Anne table and a William and Mary dressing mirror. 224pp. 8⅛ x 11¼. 29338-6

THE FOSSIL BOOK: A Record of Prehistoric Life, Patricia V. Rich et al. Profusely illustrated definitive guide covers everything from single-celled organisms and dinosaurs to birds and mammals and the interplay between climate and man. Over 1,500 illustrations. 760pp. 7½ x 10⅛. 29371-8

Paperbound unless otherwise indicated. Available at your book dealer, online at **www.doverpublications.com**, or by writing to Dept. GI, Dover Publications, Inc., 31 East 2nd Street, Mineola, NY 11501. For current price information or for free catalogues (please indicate field of interest), write to Dover Publications or log on to **www.doverpublications.com** and see every Dover book in print. Dover publishes more than 500 books each year on science, elementary and advanced mathematics, biology, music, art, literary history, social sciences, and other areas.